REF
345.7305
tINT

D0859045

The
Criminal Records Manual

Criminal Records in America:
A Complete Guide to Legal, Ethical, and
Public Policy Issues and Restrictions

by
Derek D. Hinton
And
Larry D. Henry, Esq.

©2008 By Facts on Demand Press
PO Box 27869
Tempe, AZ 85285
800-929-3811
www.brbpub.com

The Criminal Records Manual

Criminal Records in America:
  A Complete Guide to Legal, Ethical, and Public Policy Issues and Restrictions

Third Edition, First Printing

©2008 by Facts on Demand Press
PO Box 27869
Tempe, AZ 85285
800 929-3811

Written by: Derek D. Hinton and Larry D. Henry, Esq.
Edited by: Michael L. Sankey and Kim Ensenberger
Cover Design by: Robin Fox & Associates

Publisher's Cataloging-in-Publication
(Provided by Quality Books, Inc.)
Hinton, Derek.
  The criminal records manual : the complete national
reference for the legal access and use of criminal
records / by Derek D. Hinton and Larry D. Henry ;
[edited by Michael L. Sankey, Kim Ensenberger]. -- 3rd
ed.
  p. cm.
  Includes index.
  ISBN-13: 978-1-889150-54-3
  ISBN-10: 1-889150-54-1

  1. Criminal registers--United States. 2. Police--
Records and correspondence--Access control--United
States. 3. Criminal registers--United States--States--
Directories.   I. Henry, Larry D. II. Sankey, Michael
L., 1949- III. Ensenberger, Kim. IV. Title.

KF9751.H56 2008   345.73'052
                  QBI08-600190

The material in this book is presented for educational and informational purposes only and is not offered or intended as legal advice in any manner whatsoever. The materials should not be treated as a substitute for independent advice of counsel. All policies and actions with legal consequences should be reviewed by your legal counsel. Specific factual situations should also be discussed with your legal counsel. Where sample language is offered, it is only intended to illustrate a potential issue. A sample policy cannot address all specific concerns of a particular company and should not be relied on as legal advice.

Table of Contents

Introduction

Experience is a good teacher, but she sends in terrific bills.
                                                    - Minna Antrim

This book is written to benefit the public, employers, pre-employment screening companies, and criminal record vendors.

We especially hope this book helps the small employer who cannot change the world, but is tending his own garden, who is using criminal records in the hiring process because he believes in his gut that it is the right thing to do, and is ordering criminal records in an effort to insure that other employees and the general public are not exposed to someone who would do them harm.

At the same time, most of us believe that any criminal record should not inevitably disqualify an individual from all future employment. We hope this book gives guidance to the employer who knowingly hires the individual with a criminal record, and who does not automatically reject everyone with any past transgression, regardless of severity and passage of time.

For the individual who has committed a crime in which there was no victim and is trying to find a job - keep looking. Employers are out there who will hire you. Regarding those employers who will not, consider this: do you really want to devote whatever you have to offer to them anyway?

Finally, to the felon who committed a crime — who hurt, stole from or defrauded another — we will work up all the sympathy we can for you with what sympathy is left over for your victims. We do hope that you can turn your life around. You will have to earn an employer's trust. Depending upon the crime, that may be a long journey but as the Chinese proverb says, "a trip of thousand miles begins with one step." Take your steps and if you stay on the right path you will complete your journey. You will return to the workforce.

The purpose of this book is to help all of the above parties understand the various types and degrees of criminal records, how they can be legally used, and the public policy issues associated with their use.

—Derek Hinton

—Larry D. Henry

Chapter 1

Privacy Issues and Criminal Records

Memories are the key not to the past, but to the future.
—Corrie Ten Boom

I believe that men, at heart, are good.
—Anne Frank

The quotes above are amazing statements considering the sources.

Corrie ten Boom, a Dutch woman, was born in 1892 and put into a concentration camp for sheltering individuals — Jewish individuals who had done nothing wrong — from certain death. Hiding Jews brought hideous reprisals. Yet, Corrie and her family hid Jews on principle. Her most noble, selfless, and courageous deeds were rewarded with a stint in Ravensbruck Concentration camp. There she watched her sister die. Her father also died, and Corrie's brother died of a disease contracted at the camp.

The story of Anne Frank is well known. Anne died in a World War II concentration camp, and yet, her amazing statement, "I believe that men, at heart, are good," lives on. She was a better person than we.

Yet, we can agree with Anne Frank. The problem is, the quote is not speaking in absolutes, but rather in "averages." The average person is good. The heck of it is, averages are averages. An old mentor was fond of saying "a man can drown in a river that, on average, is an inch deep." While on average, man is good, there are some deep, deep holes out there that will drown you.

Why All This Attention to the Use of Criminal Records?

Consider the following quote from Al Capone—

You can get much farther with a kind word
and a gun than you can with a kind word alone.

We hate to admit it, but we think Chicago gang leader Al Capone was right.

Certainly everyone would wish all individuals were created to at least behave in a responsible manner, and that given the same stimuli, individuals would exhibit enlightened behavior. But the problem is that there are some people who, to quote a Southern friend of ours, "just ain't right." All the wishing in the world will not change that fact. The vast majority of us behave as responsible members of society — but lock our doors at night. We avoid going to certain areas at certain times. We spend huge sums on everything from police protection, jails, prisons, court systems, and security systems to airport metal detectors, department store surveillance equipment and gated communities. We also order criminal records before hiring individuals who will spend half their waking lives among us.

In fact, our federal and state governments have identified certain occupations and positions and determined that employers should be required to check their criminal record history prior to hiring these employees. At the same time, our federal and state governments have enacted complex laws and regulations that restrict employers from seeing or using certain criminal records that do exist.

Comedian W. C. Fields once said there is not an adult alive who, at one time or another, has not wanted to boot a child in the rear. There is probably not a working adult who at one time or another has not wanted to wring a co-worker's neck. Of course we don't do it. Frustration goes hand-in-hand with work. Nearly 98.7 percent of us never go past daydreams in which we have a co-worker in a headlock and are giving him a good and true Dutch rub or worse.

Yet, there are those who "ain't right." They have a history. So, the need to check criminal records exists.

And so, to paraphrase Corrie Ten Boom's quote, are "memories — perhaps court-recorded criminal record memories — the key not to the past, but to the future?" Or, is Anne Frank's sentiment correct, that "men, at heart, are good" — good and perhaps undeserving of having past transgressions interfere with their unfettered pursuit of life?

This discussion is ongoing in American society and legal systems: "given that most individuals are good, even those who have previously done bad, should we not let bygones be bygones and suppress previous records of criminal behavior?"

Why shouldn't we? We have a system that is pretty decent at catching wrongdoers. Crime usually does not pay. Thus, wrongdoers are usually caught. They are put before a jury of their peers and guilt or innocence is — correctly or incorrectly — adjudicated. Provided the individual is deemed guilty of the offense with which he has been accused, a penalty — too harsh, just right, or too lenient — is rendered. The individual serves whatever penalty is meted out (if any) and is judged to have "paid his debt to society." Justice has been served. The victims have received retribution in relation to the offense. The slate has been wiped clean. While law enforcement, in case of a repeat offense, might need to have record of this information, why in the world should this information be "public information?"

As will be seen in a later chapter, not all states have come down on the same side of the fence on the issue of public access to criminal records.

Criminal Records Are Public

One of the first issues that has been decided regarding criminal records is the most basic: are criminal records, as a rule, public?

Criminal records are a matter of public record. The accusation, trial and sentencing are public record. The Supreme Court, in a 1976 decision (Paul v. Davis, 424 U.S. 693), effectively ended debate on whether the records were public or private. Interestingly, this case revolved around a criminal charge that was dismissed. In the Paul v. Davis case, a flyer identifying "active shoplifters" was distributed to local merchants. The flyer included a photograph of Edward C. Davis III, who had been arrested on a shoplifting charge. When the charge was dismissed, Davis brought an action against Edgar Paul, the local chief of police. Davis alleged that the distribution of the flyer had stigmatized him and deprived him of his constitutional rights.

In a 5-to-3 decision, the Court held that Davis had not been deprived of any constitutional rights under the *Due Process Clause.* The Court also emphasized that constitutional privacy interests did not cover Davis' claims. The Court stated that the constitutional right to privacy was limited to matters relating to "marriage, procreation, contraception, family relationships, and child rearing and education." The publication of records of official acts, such as arrests, did not fall under the rubric of privacy rights.

So criminal records are, as a rule, accessible. Some may find this lack of privacy disturbing, almost "Orwellian." After all, government agencies have collected all this sensitive information and it is available to the general public. We believe the public debate on this aspect of privacy has become somewhat convoluted.

Originally, the information was public to protect citizens. The thought was that the government could not secretly charge a person, convict him, and put him away. The charges, court decision, and penalties were public.

Consider the former Soviet Union. Now there was a society with a lot of privacy. A person could be accused, sentenced, shipped to prison, and worked to death in privacy.

And the crime that the person was accused? Private information. The verdict? The sentence? Private.

The point is, privacy is not an automatic good. If you are considering in-home care for an elderly parent, a business venture with a neighbor, or thinking about hiring a nanny for your child, you may well appreciate the fact that these records are public rather than private.

This does not mean you can use the records for any purpose once you obtain them. If you use them or attempt to use them for an illegal purpose such as blackmail, you may join the ranks of potential blackmailees. Generally speaking, criminal records are accessible by private citizens on other private citizens. These records may be used for any legal purpose.

Identity Theft is an Ongoing Concern

While criminal information is public, the issue seems to be re-addressed on a yearly basis in various states due to identity theft. Some state, county, and federal agencies are not only concerned with making offense data private, but also they want the identifying information private too – primarily the date of birth and to a lesser extent Social Security Numbers (these are less frequently found on criminal records than the DOB). In effect, they agree that the criminal record itself is public, but the identifying information should be private. This is reminiscent of Chevy Chase giving baseball scores (but no team names) in the old *Saturday Night Live* skit: "3-2, 4-1, 2-0..." Those were the scores. Criminal records without personal identifiers are similarly enlightening.

Some agencies have established review boards or committees to look at this problem. The Social Security Number is almost always non-existent and the trend is for the date of birth to be redacted from the records.

The lack of these identifiers on the free Internet sites makes sense; the lack of these identifiers when the government agency is presented with a signed release does not seem to make sense. Again, the main concern is identity theft — which is a growing problem in our society — but identity thieves are typically attempting to find better false identities than can be obtained from criminal records. Add to that, few identity thieves will go to the trouble of completing a release. Without identifiers to distinguish them, "Computer twins" (two people with same first name, middle initial, last name, or with a similar name and the same date of birth) cause problems for employers — how do you match a record to an applicant? There is now a need to be cautious not to disqualify a job applicant simply because the applicant's name matches that on a criminal record.

Employers and Job Applicants

The workplace — this is where the real debate rages. Is it moral, ethical, or just *right* for employers to order criminal records on job applicants?

Getting down to brass tacks, no one objects to an employer *ordering* a criminal record on a job applicant. The objection is that the employer may *use* the information, e.g., refuse to hire the applicant based on information on the criminal record.

So, why do some people believe employers should never use information obtained on a criminal record to discriminate against an applicant? The reasoning is this: if the person is applying for a job, then that must mean he has completed his punishment. Of course, this assumes the person has not fled prosecution, escaped from incarceration, or is seeking a job that would be barred from holding. That person has paid the price for his offense and his debt to society is over. Furthermore, to deny him a job is to nudge him into obtaining needed money from one of two undesirable alternatives:

- Depend on the state or the kindness of family, friends or charity for the rest of his life.

- Steal or otherwise unlawfully obtain what is needed to live.

So, in other words, the argument is that after someone has paid his debt to society, it would be immoral, wrong or, at a minimum, vindictive to continue to punish an individual for something already paid for.

And, not only is it wrong from a moral standpoint, but also it is wrong from a public policy standpoint because the continued punishment for past undesirable behavior will not only fail to deter but may also *cause* future undesirable behavior.

It is a compelling, logical argument. Do you buy it? What would your reaction be in the following scenario? Assume you had your children in a daycare that — in a spirit of progressive rehabilitative fervor — hired a convicted pedophile who had done his time. Remember, the pedophile has paid his debt to society. Would your kids be at the daycare come Monday morning? Humph. Societal Neanderthal.

While most states have enacted laws to prevent convicted pedophiles from working with children, the example is instructive. This is not a cut-and-dried issue — and job-relatedness is a key consideration. Job-relatedness is discussed at length in Chapter 10.

Consider another angle to the debate: the nature of the offense.

Ann Frank and Corrie ten Boom were not just ushered off to prison camps. They were arrested, found guilty, and shipped off. Their "crimes" were documented — and their crimes were "on the books." So, the fact that something is on the books and the person has been found guilty is something for the beholder to consider. If you think this is something that could never happen here, think again, maybe about Rosa Parks — or another person writing a letter from a Birmingham jail — and the "crimes" for which they were "guilty."

Not all of us are fighting for universal justice. Consider this fellow. He was ticketed after he went to help a person who had been knocked down by a police horse. The police use the horses to control the crowd, but when the horse reared up, the police started writing fines under the presumption of protecting their officers and the four-legged city property from getting hurt. We might laugh at a criminal record for "failure to yield to a police horse." An employer, however, might not laugh when reading a criminal record of "obstruction of police duty."

In Chapters 8 and 10, federal hiring guidelines are examined. These guidelines emphasize that employers have some responsibility to ascertain that the individuals actually committed the crimes for which they were arrested.

The point here is that once it has been determined that the individual actually committed the action of which he was accused, the nature of the crime itself should be considered. "Obstruction of police duties" sounds pretty bad, but not determining the facts of the situation could cause an employer to reject the best candidate or deny a promotion to a deserving employee.

This issue is subjective. It is not a matter of law so much as it is judgment, common sense, and fairness. Subjective as it may be, there are several cut-and-dried circumstances relating to the record that can be used as a factor in your decision-making process, either as an employer or as an individual thinking about where you stand on the issue.

There are also several other criteria that, perhaps while they are not so clear cut, can be used, again, either to evaluate an applicant if you are an employer or to think about where you stand on the issue the next time this aspect of privacy comes front and center as a political issue. Several schools of thought advocate considering the criteria of whether there was a *victim* of the crime and, if so, was he the victim of a *violent* crime?

Employer Use of Criminal Records—The "Big 4" Considerations

Later chapters will discuss employer use of criminal records extensively, but the Big 4 considerations for employers are:

- **Severity** - How bad was the crime? Was it a felony or misdemeanor?

- **Job-Relatedness** - Regardless of severity, is the crime related to the job? For example, a serious, felony embezzlement charge might be less pertinent to a driving job than a "minor" driving while impaired misdemeanor.

- **Timing** - How long ago was the incident? The more recent, the more pertinent.

- **Certainty** - There are arrests and there are convictions—the law distinguishes between an accusation and a conviction.

Where to start?

Prior to discussing the use of criminal records, criminal records need to be understood. "Criminal Record" means different things to different people and in fact, laws distinguish between various types and degrees of criminal records. There are arrests—and there are convictions. There are felonies—and there are misdemeanors. There are federal crimes—and there are state crimes. The trouble is, in all of these areas, the distinction between the two can be blurry. In the chapters to follow, these differences will be defined.

Chapter 2

Essential Criminal Record Terminology

*"They say the best men are molded out of faults, and,
for the most, become much more the better for being a
little bad."*

-- William Shakespeare

Criminal record terms are important to understand because important decisions are made based on knowledge of their meaning. For example, while used interchangeably by the media at times, there is a huge legal difference between someone arrested and someone convicted. Yet you will often read the "criminal history" of someone who was arrested years ago for a misdemeanor (but not convicted) equated with a convicted felon.

> A *Criminal Record* is a paper or computerized accounting that includes individual identifiers and describes an individual's arrests and subsequent dispositions.

Keep in mind that this "accounting" may be complete or incomplete. Also, not all parts may be available to the public, depending on the administering jurisdiction's rules. Criminal history records do not include intelligence or investigative data or sociological data such as drug use history.

In most states, the available public criminal records will only include information on juveniles if they are tried as adults in criminal courts. Even then, a juvenile criminal record does not usually include all the data describing that subject's involvement in the juvenile justice system. There are a multitude of rules among the various states that exclude certain records on the basis of youthful offender [not juvenile], first offender for certain offences expunged records, sealed records and the like.

Two important record types are associated with, and sometimes even confused as, criminal records:

- *Incarceration Records* are histories of time spent in jail/prison.

- *Sexual Offender Records* indicate if a person is registered on a state sexual offender registry.

Refer to Chapter 3 for more about these two important record categories.

Felonies and Misdemeanors

There are two broad categories of criminal severity — felonies and misdemeanors. In the United States the distinction between the two has been blurred. Here are the common definitions:

- A *Felony* is the more serious class of offense and punishment ranges from imprisonment for more than one year up to the death penalty.

- A *Misdemeanor* is an offense of a minor degree and is anything less than a felony.

There are degrees of severity within both definitions. For example, "gross misdemeanors" are more serious misdemeanors. Incidentally, the use of misdemeanors records by employers varies by state, as explained in Chapter 11.

Some people believe that misdemeanor records should be ignored, that misdemeanors really do not mean anything, and to base any kind of decision on a misdemeanor is wrong. They have a good point, but nothing a good barber could not disguise.

Seriously, there are several scenarios in which misdemeanor records might prove critical: Do I like the moral character of this job applicant? Is my daughter's boyfriend really okay? Has this potential babysitter committed an offense I should worry about? Having knowledge from a misdemeanor record might help to clear the muddy waters.

Whatever the scenario, there are two cogent reasons why misdemeanors should be considered:

- A misdemeanor record may be as pertinent as a felony, or more. From a human resource viewpoint, this is especially true if the misdemeanor is job-related.

- Many recorded misdemeanors are originally the result of plea-bargaining to a felony charge.

Even so, it is important — sometimes legally necessary — to understand the difference between felonies and misdemeanors. The distinctions between felonies and misdemeanors, and the reasons that felonies are not necessarily more important or significant than a misdemeanor, are discussed in later chapters.

Felonies, Misdemeanors ... and Woopsies (Infractions)

Several private companies have collected criminal data from multiple city, county and state sources and created "criminal record" databases. These databases are increasingly used by employers despite their limitations discussed in Chapter 6. These databases have, in the practical world, created another, lower level of offense. These offenses are often traffic offenses—but may not even involve a moving violation and don't appear on the Department of Motor Vehicles Driving Abstract. Parking violations and "overweight on one axle" are some of the more common. Perhaps the most common is "unspecified by state."

If you are an employer and use these database products, don't assume that everything that appears below the "Criminal Record Database Search" heading is a "criminal" record.

With or Without a Disposition?

The terms "arrest" and "disposition" were used in the definition of a criminal record.

- An *Arrest* is the taking of an individual into custody by law enforcement personnel and a record is made of that act; e.g., the person's behavior is arrested in order to charge the person with an illegal act.

- An arrest differs from a conviction. A *Conviction* is a finding of guilt after a judicial trial. In some states, a conviction includes deferred sentences and in other states it does not.

- A *Disposition* is the final outcome. This may or may not be a conviction. A dismissal or a finding-of-not-guilty is a disposition or the "conclusion" for the charge.

It is important to note that many criminal records may not contain a disposition. Some states will purge a record (at least from the public file) if there is no disposition after a specified time frame. About half of all state criminal record repositories 1) do not release records without dispositions after a period of time, usually one year; or 2) will not release records without dispositions at all. On the other hand, there are times when a case is dropped, but the record without disposition remained on the books because the court failed to notify the record center. As a practical matter, if someone is not charged with a crime within a year or two of an arrest, then a decision has been made by the prosecutor not to prosecute. No criminal proceedings are commenced in that circumstance. However, a charge could be kept open because the accused has left the jurisdiction, but ordinarily a charge will be filed and a warrant issued. After reviewing criminal records for years one truth exists: there are always exceptions.

There are some state and federal laws that regulate the use and reporting of criminal records without dispositions, as you will see in Chapters 8, 9 and 11. However, there are also *common practices* that will affect the reporting of dispositions.

How a Criminal Record Moves Through the Courts

Lynn Peterson, a very highly regarded professional public record searcher, has been gracious to provide this book with her **Criminal Case Flowchart**. This chart, shown on the following page, maps the events during a "criminal proceeding" at a court.

While the flowchart may be simplified, it does point out the four key situations when a criminal record is created or modified.

1. At a Booking (arrest record). Notice that the record is reported to the state central repository of records and then, in turn, to the Federal Bureau of Investigation (FBI. Because the defendant is not booked, misdemeanor citations frequently are not reported to the state repository. If the case is from a federal court, the information is not reported to a state agency.

2. At Filing of Charges with Court. Misdemeanor citation records may get picked up here. The court docket index begins.

3. At the Disposition and Sentencing connection. Notice that at the sentencing the case is again reported to the state and forwarded to the FBI. Also notice on the chart the dotted line there is no connection from the Dismissed box to May Go to State and the State or FBI box, or just FBI if a federal case. A dismissal is not always automatically reported to the state (and FBI). Courts sometimes neglect to forward information regarding convictions to the state repository. More about this later.

4. At the Incarceration and Jail/Prison connection. The Jail and Prison boxes reflect secondary criminal records. The state prison records are readily available. While some sheriff departments provide online inmate locators, most do not.

CRIMINAL CASE FLOWCHART

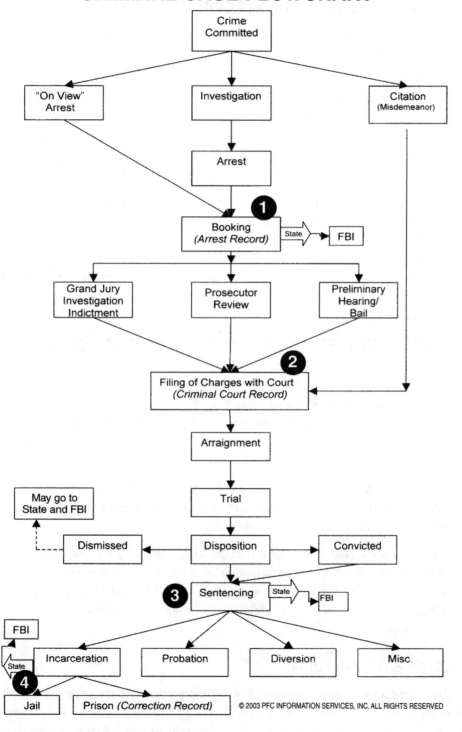

© 2003 PFC INFORMATION SERVICES, INC. ALL RIGHTS RESERVED

The Flowchart's Record Creation Points

Each one of the four record-creation points is very significant to searchers and to the end-users of criminal records. We will reference the significance of these record-creation points throughout this chapter and also in chapters to follow.

The chart distinctly illustrates the three different kinds of records that are often generically referred to as "criminal records" – arrest records, criminal court records, and correction records. They come into the flow at different points in the process and include different information. But to a record searcher, these criminal records will vary widely in substance, accuracy, and purpose, as you will learn throughout this book.

Fingerprints, usually taken at the time of a booking, also can become part of a criminal record. The flow chart also indicates when major misdemeanors and felony arrest records and convictions are submitted to a central state repository. In turn, these state repositories submit criminal record activity to the FBI's National Crime Information Center (NCIC). When these transfers take place, the fingerprints are normally submitted as well.

Distinction Between Public & Non-Public Criminal Records

One of the most significant keys to understanding the U.S. criminal record system is to know the differences between *public record* and *non-public record* criminal records. Thus, the police and prosecutors can obtain juvenile, sealed, and expunged records, so they are not secret records.

- *Non-Public criminal records* are available only to law enforcement or criminal justice agencies, or other groups that have been granted statutory authority to access the records.

- *Public criminal records* are those that can be obtained by a private citizen without some form of government authorization. The vast majority of criminal records found at the county level are public records. Public access to state criminal record depositories is somewhat more complicated.

FBI Records are Non-Public

Perhaps the most famous of the non-public criminal records are those at the FBI. The FBI makes its records available to law enforcement agencies nationwide and to certain approved entities and a few employers who have been granted access via legislation.

Even so, these entities' access to these records is not carte blanche. For example, gun dealers have access to FBI records in order to screen potential gun purchasers. Over the telephone (via modem going through the FBI state gateway), dealers can usually obtain an answer within minutes. However, they are only allowed to use the system for potential gun purchasers. A gun dealer may not use the system to open up a pre-employment screening business on the side.

A valuable component of the FBI's records is that they are nationwide. While the FBI does not have record of all crimes — let alone dispositions — it does have records from across the country. The data is incomplete. This may be a shock to moviegoers who see an infallible database that has every detail of every record from every court in the country. A search of the FBI's system — even when it is conducted through a local state repository — is a linked search that encompasses much of the other state and federal law enforcement records. For more about the FBI system, turn to Chapter 5.

Non-Public State Repository Criminal Records

While central criminal record repository data is available to the general public in most states, other states have classified their repository criminal records or portions thereof as non-public information.

Louisiana is good example of a state whose central repository considers *criminal records* non-public. Record access from the Bureau of Criminal Identification in Baton Rouge is limited only to agencies that have specific authorization by law. California, New York, and North Carolina have similar restrictions. That does not mean that felony and misdemeanor records are not available in these states. For example, in Mississippi, New York, and North Carolina an agency that over sees the state's court system offers access to a statewide database of *court records*, which contains the criminal information! Another factor to consider is that most states cloak or mask certain portions of their records to the public, but do provide full information to those with statutory access.

Public Criminal Records

Nearly all county courts and most state record repositories classify their records as public.

As a counter-example to Louisiana with its restrictions, Florida is "open." Florida's state agency records are available to search without restriction to anyone by mail, in-person, or by computer. Florida offers record going back to the 1930's. The agency's search fee at press time is $23 per name.

Hybrids: States with Release Requirements

Anyone who has conducted nationwide criminal record searches knows that there are states where the repository records are not strictly public or non-public. While these states do not have statutory prohibitions at the state level as Louisiana does, neither do these "hybrid" states follow Florida's example of open records for all.

The most common requirement is a signed release by the subject of the request. As with many aspects of criminal records, there may be no other consistency between the states that require a release. Some states, Indiana for example, require that a release request be on a specific, state-approved form if the record is requested by mail or in person. Ohio has no state specific form, but requires the release to be signed and a witness signature if the record is accessed by mail or in person. Virginia has a special form that must contain the notarized signature of the subject as well as the notarized signature of the requester. All these searches are at the state's repository; in Virginia, almost all counties' court docket records are available *free* on the Internet *without* restriction.

The second most common type of hybrid access requires the subject's fingerprints. A record request from an employer *must* include a set of the subject's fingerprints at nine state repositories, or merely a thumbprint, as they do in West Virginia. In 23 states, submission of fingerprints is optional. In essence, the supplying of fingerprints means that the subject has given approval for the record search. Nearly all states that process fingerprints as part of a record request also will submit the prints to the FBI to determine if the subject may be "wanted" in another state or by the feds. The submission of fingerprints is "an option" in 19 states. In 10 states, fingerprints are not asked for.

To find the individual search requirements and options for each state, turn to Chapter 12.

Significant Criminal Record Phrases

"Crime, like virtue, has its degrees."

-- Jean Rucine

Criminal records often contain a myriad of unfamiliar terms or meanings. Each state has a veritable dictionary of crimes and penalties. While it is true that the definitions of most common crimes and penalties are fairly uniform from state to state, arcane state-unique terms are frequently found. In one state, a pyramid scheme is a fraud; in another, that same crime might be known as a Ponzi scheme.

Unfortunately, these and other inconsistencies have led to the development of great gray areas in the use of criminal records. In one state, a family-related court matter may result in a publicly accessible criminal record, but in a neighboring state, a family court record is not public. These gray areas are why individuals, particularly employers, now have a much more difficult time understanding what they are and are not getting, and may affect their decision.

Quasi-Dispositions

Adding to the mix, states have developed modified convictions, also known as "quasi-dispositions." These phrases include:

- **"Prayer for Judgment"** A request of the court to give leniency in which no finding of guilt by the court is found.

- **"1ˢᵗ Offender Act"** After fulfilling the terms of probation, and release by the court prior to the termination of the period thereof, upon release from confinement, the defendant is discharged without court adjudication of guilt. The discharge completely exonerates the defendant of any criminal purpose and does not affect any of his civil rights or liberties. The defendant is not considered to have a criminal conviction.

- **"Diversion Programs"** A court direction that calls a defendant, who has been found guilty, to attend a work or educational program as part of probation. Usually, a "diversion" will "set aside" the criminal record.

- **"Deferred Adjudication of Guilt"** The final judgment, usually after the defendant admits his guilt, is delayed for a period of time, usually years. This can be likened to probation before a final verdict. If probation is completed without incident, the charges are usually dropped and the case dismissed. During the "probationary period," the disposition is not necessarily considered a conviction, and may or may not wind up on the record of the subject's criminal history.

- **"Deferred Sentence"** This is similar to a Deferred Adjudication of Guilt but a guilty plea has been entered and accepted by the court. The sentence is deferred, delayed, for a probation-like period and, if successfully completed, the guilty plea is withdrawn and the charge(s) is dismissed. States adopt one of these procedures.

Other Key Phrases

Listed below are certain words and phrases used frequently in the criminal record process.

Arraignment	A court hearing in a criminal case where a defendant is advised of the charges and asked to plead guilty or not guilty.
Bench Warrant	A process initiated by the court or "from the bench" for the arrest or the attachment of a person.
Class	Within government jurisdictions, the severity of a felony or misdemeanor is ranked by classification, moving from most serious to least serious.
Consecutive Sentence	Two or more sentences which run one after another.
Concurrent Sentence	Two or more sentences which run at the same time.
Docket	A docket is index of a court's records. A docket can be a list of cases on a court's calendar *or* a log containing the schedule and all the actions involved within a court case.
General Jurisdiction Courts	These courts hear felony cases. Some also hear misdemeanor cases. General jurisdiction trial courts have the authority to oversee a full range of civil and criminal litigation, usually handling felonies and higher dollar civil cases. The general jurisdiction court will often serve as the appellate court for cases appealed from limited jurisdiction courts and even from the local courts. Many court researchers refer to general jurisdiction courts as **upper courts.**
Limited Jurisdiction Courts	These courts are limited in the types or classes of criminal cases they may hear. Limited jurisdiction trial courts handle smaller civil claims (usually $10,000 or less), misdemeanors, and pretrial hearings for felonies. Localized municipal courts also are referred to as courts of limited jurisdiction. Many court researchers refer to limited jurisdiction courts as **lower courts.**
Non-Biometric Identifiers	Non-physical (e.g. non-fingerprints, non-photographic) criteria used to determine the correct identity of a person when doing a criminal record check. In addition to name, may include aliases, date of birth, address, Social Security Number, etc.

Preliminary Hearing   At this hearing the prosecution presents evidence that a crime has been committed and that the defendant committed the crime. The proof of "guilt" is quite low.

While there is no overall translation list of every code, term, phrase, or descriptive nuance used by every state and county court, and criminal record agency, we have compiled some of the common terms and abbreviations. In Appendix 4 are two Glossaries:

- Common Criminal Records Offense Terms
- Common Criminal Records Offense Abbreviations

Victimless and Non-Violent Crime

"A man who has never gone to school may steal
from a freight car, but if he has a university
education he may steal the whole railroad."
--Franklin D. Roosevelt

Outside of strictly legal definitions, two other terms are frequently used to describe a crime: "Victimless" and "Non-Violent." The terms try to describe the seriousness of the crime by considering who was injured and what type harm was done. Was there a victim? Was the victim injured by violence or "merely" inconvenienced?

Victimless Crime

Some dispute there is such a thing as victimless crime. Others insist that an illegal transaction between two consenting adults is, by definition, victimless.

Drug possession, prostitution, public drunkenness, and sexual mores offenses are the most common crimes described by some as victimless. Proponents argue that there are no victims of this "crime," arguing that these alleged victims were victimized by bad law, and not by the lawbreaker. Others insist that there are indeed victims such as the Drug Enforcement Agent killed in the line of duty or that society as a whole is damaged through the degradation of morals, whatever the morals might be.

Violent Crime

More and more, a distinction is being made today regarding whether a crime was "violent." For example, some "three strikes and you're in prison" laws take into consideration whether one or all of the strikes were violent. There is some credence to classifying a crime as violent or non-violent. However, the distinction has its limitations. Consider the following true story.

You tell her the non-violent crime wasn't as serious...

I have a co-worker friend who brought her two-year old to daycare before coming to work. She parked her car, ran her daughter into the room right inside the door, and came back to her car within four minutes to find her purse had been stolen. Inside her purse was the typical stuff: driver's license, credit cards, cell phone and checkbook — as well as an undeveloped roll of film taken over the course of a month of her daughter and family. Also, on this day, she had a ring that had belonged to her husband's grandmother. The diamond ring was not worth a fortune, but it was the only thing of the grandmother's they had.

Within an hour, the thief was caught on video purchasing more than $500 of merchandise using one of the stolen credit cards, and in the following days and weeks, wrote $4,000 in bad checks.

Everyday at lunch, my co-worker drove across town to her credit union to sign affidavits as the bad checks rolled in. She worked with all her credit card issuers and spent some pleasant time in the State Department of Health making sure her birth certificate was notarized in all the right places so she could move on to the lines and waiting rooms of the friendly, helpful, and courteous Department of Motor Vehicles to replace her driver's license. She also spent some quality time at the local office of the Social Security Administration getting her Social Security card replaced. While without identification, she needed lots of cash for purchases — from a bank account soaked by bad checks.

Meanwhile, she visited the businesses that had accepted the bad checks and asked for video and witnesses to identify the thief. The police were bemused by these efforts — it happens all the time and the thief is rarely caught. In this case, thanks to my co-worker's prodding, cajoling, and investigative work, the thief was arrested and later received a $200 fine and a suspended sentence for writing a bad check. There were no charges filed for the actual theft, and the film, ring, purse and its contents were never found.

If you suggest that non-violent crimes are less serious that violent crimes to my friend, choose your words with care. I didn't and came close to being a violent-crime victim.

Chapter 3

Other Important Criminal Offender Records

"One of the difficulties in the language is that all our words, from loose usage, have lost their edge."
-- Ernest Hemmingway

There are several other types of public records that, while not strictly "criminal records," will disclose past criminal activity. While the information may not be particularly germane or useful for employment screening in all cases, the careful researcher may choose to search these various sources to complement his criminal record check.

Following is a short overview of some "non-criminal criminal records." Please note that additional information on sexual offenders and incarcerations records is provided in Chapter 12.

Incarceration Records

Federal Incarceration Records

These are records of offenders who have been incarcerated in a federal facility after commission of a federal offense. The information is public record, and the value of this search is that you do not have to know the particular federal court that convicted the individual. The federal incarceration search is nationwide in scope.

The downside of this search is that it will not disclose minor offenses or, at least, those that did not result in incarceration.

The Federal Bureau of Prisons offers an inmate locator on its website, www.bop.gov. At the website, click "Inmate Info" at left. This Inmate Locator database also contains information about former inmates, dating back to 1982.

The following article, written by Lawrence C. Lopez, is an interesting overview of this website. Thank you to Mr. Lopez for allowing us to include the article.

About the Federal Bureau of Prisons Website

by Lawrence C. Lopez

While this can be a very useful tool, a few words of warning are in order: it is not search-friendly.

I tested it on a couple of names and found the following:

While it provides name, race and age to the nearest year, it does not have middle initials, Jrs., exact DOBs or other details that can help you determine if the inmate Joe Blow is the same Joe Blow that you are researching.

There does not appear to be any standardized data input provisions. For example, I searched for an inmate whose first name is Natel but could not find him that way -- he was only listed as "N." And testing for the last name "Johnson" I found 66 "Joseph Johnson" entries, and 12 "Joe Johnson" entries as well as three "J. Johnson" entries on inmates whose first names may or may not have been Joe.

Do not use "Senior" or "Jr." or the like when you search. In my tests, the database located two "Charles Keating" entries of ages that seem to correspond to the former Arizona S&L chief and his son. But when I searched for "Charles Keating Junior" or "Jr." or "III", the database told me there were no entries.

Overall, this is a great database, but it takes a fair amount of patience to search properly. For those who have serious searching needs, I would recommend cross-searching the names in PACER, which should show the conviction that put the subject into prison in the first place. Of course, many PACER courts do not go back to 1982. PACER is so good and cheap that you might as well run it too, unless all you are looking for is where a current inmate is presently imprisoned.

==================

Lawrence C. Lopez is the chairman of Strategic Research and head of its Northeast operations. Strategic Research specializes in complex civil litigation, due diligence and criminal cases, along with research for news organizations. Mr. Lopez has worked previously with the Associated Press as an investigative reporter and has spent four years as a senior investigator at the Investigative Group International. Mr. Lopez can be reached at www.srresearch.com.

State Incarceration Records

Most states allow access to incarceration records. As with federal incarceration records, state incarceration records may offer current and past information regarding an individual's incarceration history. In most states, inmates on probation are considered as current inmates. Nearly every state permits access to current inmate records via their website. Most state websites also provide past inmate records.

You will read how to access incarceration records from every state as you read Chapter 12. Many states offer free access to limited records is available via the Internet.

Here are recommended websites that have multiple links to state inmate locators:

- http://www.corrections.com/links/show/30
- http://www.blackbookonline.info/
- http://www.brbpub.com/pubrecsites.asp

Parole Records

"Parole" means to release from confinement after serving part of a sentence, usually with terms and conditions provided in the parole order.

Federal Records

After serving all or part of their sentence, most federal offenders are paroled. These records are a matter of public record and may prove useful in detecting a previous offense. The United States Parole Commission is responsible for the supervision of parolees and mandatory releasees. The FOIA Unit may be reached at 301-492-5821.

State Records

There is usually a central state repository for verification of historical parole information. To track or verify current parolees, you must contact the appropriate State Parole Board.

Probation Records

"Probation" means relief of all or part of a sentence on the promise of proper conduct.

Federal Probation Records

Some federal offenders are not sentenced to prison, but instead are fined and sentenced to probation. Probation means that all or part of the sentence has been reduced in return for a promise of proper conduct. These records are public, but must be obtained by contacting the Federal Chief Probation Officer in the judicial district where the individual was sentenced.

State Probation Records

Most states do not have a central state repository for the records of individuals currently serving probation. However, these records do not have the utility of other records. Depending on the state, a number of the incarceration agency websites permit online searches of current inmates and some have limited searching for former inmates, including those on probation.

State Registries of Sexual Offender Records

In 1994, the Jacob Wetterling Crimes Against Children and Sexually Violent Offender Registration Act was enacted. This Act required all states to establish stringent registration programs for sex offenders by September 1997, including the identification and lifetime registration of "sexual predators." The Jacob Wetterling Act is a National law that is designed to protect children and was named after Jacob Wetterling, an eleven year-old boy who was kidnapped in October 1989. Jacob is still missing.

Megan's Law, the first amendment to the Jacob Wetterling Crimes Against Children and Sexually Violent Offenders Act, was passed in 1996. Megan's Law goals include—

Sex Offender Registration - Each state and the federal government are compelled to register individuals who have been convicted of sex crimes against children.

Community Notification - Each state and the federal government are compelled to make private and personal information on convicted sex offenders available to the public. Community notification is based on the presumption that it will:

- Assist law enforcement in investigations;
- Establish legal grounds to hold known offenders;
- Deter sex offenders from committing new offenses, and;
- Offer citizens information to protect children from victimization.

More About Megan's Law

Megan's Law is named for 7-year-old Megan Kanka who was brutally raped and murdered in Monmouth County, NJ.

Megan's Law, which went into effect on October 31, 1994, requires law enforcement agencies to provide information about convicted sex offenders to community organizations and the public. The law provides that sex offenders are required to register with the police, including offenders who were on parole or probation as of October 31, 1994. Also, repeat offenders, regardless of date, are required to register.

Under Megan's Law, sex offenders are classified in one of three levels or "tiers" based on the severity of their crime as follows: high (Tier 3); moderate (Tier 2); or low (Tier 1).

When a registered sex offender moves into a community, there is a notification process. Neighbors are notified of Tier 3 offenders. Registered community organizations involved with children such as schools, daycare centers, and camps are notified of Tier 3 and Tier 2 offenders. Local law enforcement agencies are notified of the presence of all sex offenders.

Residents may visit local law enforcement and review all registered sexual offenders in the community or county. The information provided includes the offender's name, description of offense, personal description, photograph, address, place of employment or school, and a description of the offender's vehicle and license plate number.

Typical offenses include aggravated sexual assault, sexual assault, aggravated criminal sexual contact, endangering the welfare of a child by engaging in sexual conduct, kidnapping, and false imprisonment.

The criteria for implementing Megan's Law are left up to the states, with the understanding that the state is to follow certain specific guidelines. Despite the guidelines, disparities have resulted among the states' rules and access. For instance, many states make information on registered offenders available on the Internet or by mail; some states, for only the severe offenders, either one or by access methods; and some states barely make the information available at all.

For a links to each state's searchable site, see Chapter 12. Below are several recommended websites with overall links lists —

- www.nsopr.gov
- www.paokayrentsformeganslaw.com/html/links.lasso
- www.brbpub.com

Federal Fugitives

Through the U.S. Marshal's Service, the federal government maintains files on individuals who are wanted fugitives. These wanted individuals — assuming their guilt — have not yet "paid their debt to society" and, needless to say, are probably not a good bet as an employee, business partner, or as a prospect for a position requiring responsibility.

There is not a readily available database of federal fugitives open to the private sector. However, when asked about a criminal record search some state agencies will check with the FBI for outstanding federal warrants.

Most Wanted Lists

Many federal agencies (and some international agencies) have a web- page of a Most Wanted List with name-searching capabilities. A web- page with links to lists maintained by the FBI, U.S. Marshal, the Bureau of Alcohol, Tobacco, and Firearms (ATF), the Drug Enforcement Administration (DEA), and even the U.S. Postal Service is found at www.usa.gov/Citizen/Topics/MostWanted.shtml.

A quick way to find each state's Most Wanted Lists is at www.ancestorhunt.com/most-wanted-criminals-and-fugitives.htm.

Where found, county sheriff websites often provide data on County Most Wanted individuals. These same sheriff websites may include missing persons, sexual predators, warrants, arrests, DUIs, and other types of local pages as a public service. For those interested in these sites, www.searchsystems.net does a good job of collecting these URLs.

Military Criminal Records

Some individuals are convicted of crimes while in uniform. Courts-martial information and military incarceration information are available, and they may prove useful to evaluate an applicant if the individual in question was in the armed forces. These courts-martial offenses are not limited to military crimes such as disobeying orders or AWOLs, but include the counterpart of the usual civilian crimes of robbery, rape, assault, etc. Often employers do not think of military records because of the small percentage of our population that now has had military service. As a result, criminal records may not be discovered. One applicant tried to use this lack of knowledge to use his military record as part of his qualifications for employment. His records showed his last "assignment" to be: Disciplinary Barracks, Fort Leavenworth, Kansas, i.e., he was in the military prison, but to someone unfamiliar with the military, it may look like any other duty assignment.

Per Les Rosen, author of the *Safe Hiring Manual*...

> "In order to avoid potential Equal Employment Opportunity Commission (EEOC) claims, an employer should treat a dishonorable discharge in the same fashion as a criminal conviction. A general discharge or undesirable discharge may or may not have any bearing on employment and generally should not be the basis of an employment decision."

We believe this is good advice. The next section provides further details on how to obtain military records.

National Personnel Records Center (NPRC)

The National Personnel Records Center (NPRC) keeps military service records, and is under the jurisdiction of the National Archives and Records Administration. The address is The National Personnel Records Center, Military Personnel Records, 9700 Page Avenue, St. Louis, Missouri 63132, fax: 314-801-9195, www.archives.gov/veterans/military-service-records/.

The type of information released to the general public is dependent upon the veteran's authorization. Also, the key to searching military records is form SF-180 (or a signed release). The key military record is the DD-214. Federal law [5 USC 552a(b)] requires that all requests for records and information be submitted in writing. Each request must be signed and dated. The NPRC categorizes two types of requesters:

With the Veteran's Authorization

The veteran (or next-of-kin if the veteran is deceased) must authorize release of information. The authorization must 1) be in writing; 2) specify what additional information or copies are requested that NPRC may release; and 3) include the signature of the veteran or next-of-kin.

Without the Veteran's Authorization

This request for information by the general public, including someone who is not next-of-kin, is treated as a Freedom of Information Act (FOIA) request. A limited amount of data can be released from a record to a member of the general public.

Using Form SF-180

The SF-180 is a form specifically used to request military records. If you wish to search the records of an individual and the subject does not provide you with the DD-214, then you must use the SF-180 to request a copy of the DD-214. This form can be requested in writing from the NPRC or can be downloaded as a PDF file. The form and instructions are found at www.archives.gov/st-louis/military-personnel/standard-form-180.html. The SF-180 form also may be obtained from the Department of Defense, Federal Information Centers, local Veterans Administration offices, and from veterans' service organizations.

A veteran or the veteran's next-of-kin may use the eVetRecs system at www.archives.gov/veterans/evetrecs/ to create the request for a copy of the DD214, or may mail or fax the SF-180.

Use of the SF-180 is not mandatory; however, a request must be in writing and signed by the requester. Include as much of the following information as possible: the veteran's complete name used while in service, the service number or Social Security Number (SSN), branch of service, and dates of services if known. The date of birth (DOB) is helpful. If the records were part of the 1973 fire, then including the place of entry, discharge, and last unit of assignment is quite helpful.

The turnaround time for most requests takes about 10 days plus mail time. However, requests that involve reconstruction efforts due to the 1973 fire, or older records that require extensive search efforts may take 6 months or more to complete. Reconstruction requests are taking on average 4 1/2 weeks to complete.

About the DD-214

DD-214 is the name of the document that military personnel receive when discharged from the U.S. Navy, Army, Air Force, Marine Corp, or Coast Guard. There are actually a number of different copies of the DD-214 with different sets information. A discharged service person receives Copy 1, which has the least information. Copy 4 gives the nature of the discharge – General, Honorable, Dishonorable, Bad Conduct, Undesirable – and details of service. There are codes that characterize the service record including SPD (Separation Program Designator), SPN (Separation Program Number), and RE (Re-Entry). For a discharged service person to get Copy 4, the person must actually ask for it.

Military Branches - Internet Sources

The official sites include—

www.army.mil	The U.S. Army
www.af.mil	The U.S. Air Force
www.navy.mil	The U.S. Navy
www.usmc.mil	The U.S. Marine Corps
www.arng.army.mil	The Army National Guard
www.ang.af.mil	The Air National Guard
www.uscg.mil/default.asp	The U.S. Coast Guard

There are other sources of information, while not truly "criminal records," may indicate behavior that could be an important factor when considering an individual for employment or other legitimate purpose.

The rest of this chapter is devoted to a review of various federal resources, many of which are often searched by pre-employment screening companies.

Federal Agency Sanctions and Watch Lists

This section examines public record databases of individuals and companies that have sanctions, violations, enforcement actions, or warnings initiated against them by one of these federal government departments—

- Commerce Department
- Food & Drug Administration
- GSA – Government Services
- Human Health Care Services Department
- Justice Department
- Labor Department
- State Department
- Treasury Department

Commerce Department

The Bureau of Industry and Security (BIS), part of the U.S. Department of Commerce provides lists relevant to import/export transactions. www.bis.doc.gov

Denied Persons List

The purpose of the Denied Persons List is to prevent the illegal export of dual-use items before they occur and to investigate and assist in the prosecution of violators of the Export Administration Regulations. www.bis.doc.gov/dpl/default.shtm

Unverified List

This is a list of parties whom BIS has been unable to verify the end use in prior transactions. The Unverified List includes names and countries of foreign persons who in the past were parties to a transaction with respect to which BIS could not conduct a pre-license check (PLC) or a post-shipment verification (PSV) for reasons outside of the U.S. Government's control. If you would like to be informed when changes occur to the Unverified List, consider subscribing to the BIS Email Notification Service.

See www.bis.doc.gov/enforcement/unverifiedlist/unverified_parties.html.

Entity List

The Entity List, available in PDF or ASCII text format, is a list of parties whose presence in a transaction can trigger a license requirement under the Export Administration Regulations. The list specifies the license requirements that apply to each listed party. These license requirements are in addition to any license requirements imposed on the transaction by other provisions of the Export Administration Regulations. www.bis.doc.gov/entities/default.htm

FDA – Food & Drug Administration

FDA regulates scientific studies that are designed to develop evidence to support the safety and effectiveness of **investigational drugs (human and animal), biological products, and medical devices**. Physicians and other qualified experts (clinical investigators) who conduct these studies are required to comply with applicable statutes and regulations intended to ensure the integrity of clinical data on which product approvals are based and, for investigations involving human subjects, to help protect the rights, safety, and welfare of these subjects.

For further information about the lists below, contact the Food and Drug Administration, Office of Enforcement, 5600 Fishers Lane, HFC-230, Rockville, MD 20857; 240-632-6853, fax: 240-632-6861.

FDA Enforcement Report Index – Recalls, Market Withdrawals, and Safety Alerts

The FDA Enforcement Report, published weekly, contains information on actions taken in connection with agency regulatory activities. Activities include Recall and Field Correction, Injunctions, Seizures, Indictments, Prosecutions, and Dispositions. A record of all recalls (Class I, II, and III), including pre-1995, can be found at www.fda.gov/opacom/Enforce.html.

Visit www.fda.gov/opacom/7alerts.html for the most significant product actions of the last 60 days, based on the extent of distribution and the degree of health risk. These recalls on the list are mainly Class I, the most serious category.

Information regarding individuals sanctioned by the FDA may be accessed through the FDA bulletin boards. For more information, contact the PHS Alert System Manager, Office of Research Integrity, 1101 Wootton Parkway, Rm 750, Rockville, MD 20852, 301-443-5330.

Debarment List

The FDA maintains a list of individuals and entities that are prohibited from introducing any type of food, drug, cosmetics or associated devices into interstate commerce. The list is at www.fda.gov/ora/compliance_ref/debar/

GSA – Government Services

Excluded Party List

The Excluded Parties List System (EPLS) contains information on individuals and firms excluded by various federal government agencies from receiving federal contracts or federally approved subcontracts and from certain types of federal financial and non-financial assistance and benefits. Note that individual agencies are responsible for the timely reporting, maintenance, and accuracy of their data which feeds into this single comprehensive list. Information shown may include names, addresses, DUNS numbers, SSNs, Employer Identification Numbers or other Taxpayer Identification Numbers, if available and deemed appropriate and permissible to publish by the agency taking the action. www.epls.gov

Human Health Services, Department of

Excluded Individuals/Entities (LEIE)

The LEIE maintained by the Office of Inspector General (OIG) for the HHS is a list of currently excluded parties for convictions of program-related fraud and patient abuse, licensing board actions and default on Health Education Assistance Loans. The purpose is to prevent certain individuals and businesses from participating in federally funded health-care programs. The database may be searched or downloaded from a webpage. The searchable database is found at http://exclusions.oig.hhs.gov/. The downloadable database is at http://oig.hhs.gov/fraud/exclusions/database.html.

Health Education Assistance Loan (HEAL)

Between 1978 and 1998, the Health Education Assistance Loan (HEAL) program provided federal insurance for educational loans made by private lenders to more than 156,000 graduate health professions students. Students included were in schools of medicine, osteopathy, dentistry, veterinary medicine, optometry, podiatry, pharmacy, chiropractic, health administration, or clinical psychology. New HEAL loans were discontinued September 30, 1998.

By law, HEAL borrowers in default on their loans are published quarterly. They can be searched by name, discipline, state, amount due and school. For details, visit http://defaulteddocs.dhhs.gov/search.asp.

Justice Department

There are a number of divisions within the Justice Department that maintain news articles, stories, and most wanted lists that can be very useful for research and investigation purposes. Listed below are searchable sites for these most wanted lists and other searchable sites.

Bureau of Alcohol, Tobacco, Firearms and Explosives

Below are four resources:

- Federal Firearms License Validator - https://www.atfonline.gov/fflezcheck
- Most Wanted List - www.atf.gov/wanted/index.htm
- Out of Business Records - 800-788-7133, ext. 1590
- Federal Firearms Licensees list local or nationwide - 202-927-8866

Bureau of Investigation (FBI)

The FBI's Most Wanted site at www.fbi.gov/wanted.htm contains numerous lists to search, including kidnappings, missing persons, unknown bank robbers, and others. Department FOIA instruction are found at http://foia.fbi.gov/foia_instruc.htm. You can request online.

Drug Enforcement Administration (DEA)

Search DEA fugitives at www.usdoj.gov/dea/fugitives/fuglist.htm by Field Division, from a map showing the states within each division. Major international fugitives and captured fugitives also are found here.

State Department

ITAR Debarred List

A list compiled by the State Department of parties that are barred the International Traffic in Arms Regulations (ITAR) (22 CFR §127.7) from participating directly or indirectly in the export of defense articles, including technical data or in the furnishing of defense services for which a license or approval is required. www.pmddtc.state.gov/debar059.htm

Nonproliferation Sanctions Lists

The State Department maintains lists of parties that have been sanctioned under various statutes and legal authority. Seven separate lists are found at the webpage including Sanctions for the Transfer of Lethal Military Equipment and under Missile Sanctions laws. www.state.gov/t/isn/c15231.htm

Treasury Department

Specifically Designated Nationals (SDN) List

The U.S. Department of the Treasury, Office of Foreign Assets Control (OFAC) publishes a list of individuals and companies owned or controlled by, or acting for or on behalf of, targeted foreign countries, terrorists, international narcotics traffickers, and those engaged in activities related to the proliferation of weapons of mass destruction. The site also indicates individuals and entities that are not country-specific. Collectively, these individuals and companies are called "Specially Designated Nationals" or "SDN." Their assets are blocked and U.S. persons generally prohibited from dealing with them.

In addition, the Export Administration Regulations require a license for exports or re-exports to any party in any entry on this list that contains any of the suffixes "SDGT," "SDT," "FTO," or "IRAQ2." OFAC's "Hotline" is 1-800-540-6322. www.treas.gov/offices/enforcement/ofac/sdn/

Chapter 4

Why Employers Use Criminal Records

Somebody once said that in looking for people to hire, you look for three qualities: integrity, intelligence, and energy. And if they don't have the first, the other two will kill you. Think about it; it is true. If you hire somebody without the first, you really want them to be dumb and lazy.

—Warren Buffet

You can dream, create, design and build the most wonderful place in the world, but it requires people to make the dream a reality.

—Walt Disney

Some employers order criminal records on applicants because the law requires it. Others order criminal records because they fear the harm that may come to them, their business, or other employees if they hire someone they shouldn't. A growing reason why businesses order criminal records is the fear of being sued for negligent hiring.

Watching an employer who does a lot of hiring, but neglects to order criminal records is like watching a train wreck in slow motion. You can see the disaster coming from a long way away and the wreck is inevitable, but you can't do anything to stop it.

In this chapter are the main reasons why the larger and progressive employers decide to order criminal records, how they go about it and the laws and regulations that affect their use of the records. While criminal records are legal to use, there are issues to watch.

The Negligent Hiring Doctrine

Created through case law, negligent hiring is a legal doctrine that imposes a duty upon employers to "assess the nature of the employment, its degree of risk to third parties, and then perform a reasonable background investigation to insure that the applicant is competent and fit for duty." A closely associated theory is negligent retention. Negligent retention is when the employee, already hired, is retained when the employer knows, or should have known, that the employee was unfit to be retained.

The primary difference between the two is timing. Negligent hiring is a matter of "should have known" before hiring. Negligent retention is a matter of "should have become aware of" after hiring. Employers are most often faulted for failing to order a criminal record check before someone is hired. The fact that the employer has conducted a criminal background check negates the claim. A review of negligent hiring cases establishes that the search of criminal records does not have to be perfect—only reasonable and customary.

Although there is no consistent, *de facto* requirement that demands an employer check applicants for a criminal record, as discussed earlier, there may be state and federal industry-specific requirements that require a criminal record be obtained. Different courts have come to different conclusions, but the trend is clearly moving in the direction that employers have more obligations to perform checks, depending on the nature of the job.

The "Nature of the Position"

There is a difference in the degree and nature of care that must be used between hiring a daycare worker and a construction worker. Clearly, a daycare worker working unsupervised in close proximity to young children probably presents more of a risk than does someone stomping on a shovel. On the issue of "job relatedness," courts have been extremely liberal in their opinions, a trend that says it is the employer's responsibility not to put the wrong person on the job.

Protections Afforded

It is important to note that ordering criminal records can offer protection to the employer, even if no information is found. In court, the employer is portrayed as an uncaring entity that was too cheap to spend even a nominal amount to insure that someone was not injured — and it is time to punish the employer for his greediness.

What if the employer does order a criminal record and, through no fault of his own, the crime committed in Tupelo, Mississippi by the applicant does not appear in the Dallas County, Texas search performed by the employer? The point is the employer tried. The employer assessed the nature of the job, its degree of risk and then conducted a background investigation perhaps above that required by law. The fact that this search effort did not reveal information is another matter.

Florida House Bill H0775 — An Example of a Law Creating a Presumption *Against* Negligent Hiring

A statute, approved by Florida Governor J. Bush on May 26, 1999, which became effective on October 1, 1999, created a presumption against negligent hiring when employers take certain pre-employment screening steps. Employers who follow the steps will be presumed not to have been negligent if the background investigation fails to reveal any information that reasonably demonstrates the unsuitability of the applicant for the particular work to be performed, or for employment in general. One of these steps is ordering a criminal record.

Among the prescribed steps are:

- Ordering a Florida state criminal record check.

- Taking reasonable efforts to contact the applicant's past employers.

- Having the applicant complete an employment application that elicits the following information:

  o Convictions of crimes including type, date, and penalty imposed;

  o Whether the applicant was a defendant in a civil action for an intentional tort, including the nature and disposition of the action.

- A driving record must be ordered if it is relevant to the work to be performed.

- The employer must interview the applicant.

Notice that the law does not require that employers find criminal record information if there is any to be obtained. The law only requires that employers make a state inquiry.

Nothing in this legislation requires employers to adopt new procedures. It does afford some protection to those employers who attempt to hire safe, responsible employees.

...And for the Rest of the Country?

Do you have a similar law in your state? Even if not, the steps prescribed by this Florida law make good sense. While your state may not have codified the protection, a plaintiff would have a tough time proving hiring negligence against you if you had taken the "Florida steps."

In other words, even if you are not in Florida, following the Florida guidelines may provide your company *de facto* protection, if not codified protection. Further there may be "common law" in your state, i.e. court decisions, outlining a reasonable background check.

Workplace Violence

Workplace violence can be related to negligent hiring/retention in that employers have been sued for hiring/retaining someone with a propensity for violence, and that employee subsequently harms another employee or third party. A negligent hiring suit does not always follow an act of workplace violence, but when a lawsuit results, courts have increasingly found that employers have at least some duty to provide a safe workplace. The risk to employers is that the negligent hiring/retention is the employer's separate act apart from the violent act of the employee. An employer can obtain insurance for his vicarious liability for the wrongs (torts) of his employees. However, if a jury were to find the failure to do a background check was a willful act by an uncaring and greedy employer, it may be liable for punitive damages to punish the employer and serve as an example to other uncaring employers. The catch is that public policy may prohibit an employer from obtaining insurance to cover his willful acts.

Reports from Ronet Bachman, a statistician with the Bureau of Justice Statistics, say "each year, nearly one million individuals become victims of violent crime while working or on duty. The victimizations account for 15 percent of the more than 6½ million acts of violence experienced by U.S. residents age 12 or older."

Unfortunately, these statistics do not show the percentage of these victimizations committed by co-workers, but unempirical surveys have shown that co-workers do commit a significant percentage of these victimizations.

Even if an employer is not sued for an act of workplace violence committed by an employee, workplace violence is, to put it mildly, not conducive to productivity. Among those persons injured by crime victimizations at work, an estimated 876,800 workdays were lost annually, costing employees more than $16 million in wages[1]. This

---

[1] Per a study by the Department of Justice, see www.ojp.usdoj.gov/bjs/pub/ascii/thefwork.txt

does not include the "sick days" and the "annual leave" that the victim might not otherwise take.

The fact is the hiring process is one of the areas where the employer is most able to control the qualities of who they employ. More and more employers are ordering criminal records as a measure that helps thwart workplace violence.

Workplace Theft

It is tough for a business to make a profit when some of its best customers are employees who are not paying for the goods. John Locke, known as the Philosopher of Freedom, felt men entered into society to preserve their property. Many employers are ordering criminal records for the same reason.

Retailers attribute 42.7 percent of their inventory shrinkage — $12 *billion* lost annually in missing merchandise, cash, and fraud — to employee theft. As a rule, retailers spend approximately $3,500 to recruit, screen, and hire one employee. The length of time worked by a dishonest employee is 9.4 months. The average cost of hiring and releasing a dishonest employee averages $15,000. In order to thwart the onslaught of shrinkage, large retailers hire 10 loss prevention employees per $100 million in annual sales, with an average of 1.12 employees per store specifically dedicated to loss prevention.

Considering that 42 percent of inventory losses come from employees — and that the total recruiting and screening cost is around $3,500 — a $20 criminal record check makes good sense.

What if Your Employees Must Enter Canada?

Some businesses require their employees go into Canada. Under sections 19(1)(c) and 19(2)(a) of the Canada Immigration Act of 1976, individuals who have been convicted of a "crime or offense" are considered "inadmissible" and precluded from entering in Canada.

Therefore, prior to being permitted to enter into Canada, U.S. workers are subject to random criminal history checks by the Canadian authorities who use information obtained from the NCIC. Using the NCIC database, Canadian authorities are able to determine whether an individual has a "criminal record" and therefore, cannot be admitted without first obtaining a "Minister's Permit." According to the Canadian Consulate General, a "Minister's Permit" can be issued in a limited number of instances to overcome the inadmissibility rules. This decision to issue or deny a permit is entirely discretionary with the Canadian office before which the request is pending and will be based on such factors as:

- The seriousness of the past offense.

- The number of past offenses committed.

- The perceived likelihood that the individual will commit another offense.

A Minister's Permit can only be obtained from a Canadian Consulate, are expensive to obtain, and are good for only a limited period of time.

As discussed earlier, the vast majority of US employers do not have access to NCIC, and so many employers who require their employees to travel into Canada order a criminal record from public record sources in the U.S. This decreases problems at the border.

When Obtaining Records is Required by Law

There are many smart reasons to order criminal records on employees, a few dumb ones, and several cases in which the federal or state government has given one of our fathers' all-time favorite reasons: "Because I said so."

A number of industries have federal or state mandates. These mandates are laws that generally require a criminal record to be performed prior to hiring. The law may include penalties against a firm for hiring someone who does not pass the criminal record check.

Although this book cannot list every state and federal requirement, we have selected several useful examples. The first three are federally related.

Motor Carrier Hazardous Material Regulations

The events surrounding the war on terrorism in 2001 started a trend toward more criminal record checking requirements on employers. In particular, Section 1012 of the Patriot Act includes a requirement that state department of motor vehicles is not be allowed to issue or renew hazardous material endorsements on commercial driver licenses until the individual was approved by the Department of Transportation, which checks for criminal information from the Department of Justice. Implementation of this requirement has not been finalized. While employers will not have access to the actual criminal record, it does involve a check for certain crimes. You would dare not let a person without DOT endorsement drive for your company. A copy of Section 1012 follows: More information on this section and its effect on driver license issues can be found on the American Association of Motor Vehicle Administrators website: www.aamva.org/KnowledgeCenter/Driver/Licensing/PatriotAct.htm.

SEC. 1012. LIMITATION ON ISSUANCE OF HAZMAT LICENSES.

(a) LIMITATION-

(1) IN GENERAL- Chapter 51 of title 49, United States Code, is amended by inserting after section 5103 the following new section:

Sec. 5103a. Limitation on issuance of hazmat licenses

(a) LIMITATION-

(1) ISSUANCE OF LICENSES- A State may not issue to any individual a license to operate a motor vehicle transporting in commerce a hazardous material unless the Secretary of Transportation has first determined, upon receipt of a notification under subsection (c)(1)(B), that the individual does not pose a security risk warranting denial of the license.

(2) RENEWALS INCLUDED- For the purposes of this section, the term "issue", with respect to a license, includes renewal of the license.

(b) HAZARDOUS MATERIALS DESCRIBED- The limitation in subsection (a) shall apply with respect to--

(1) any material defined as a hazardous material by the Secretary of Transportation; and

(2) any chemical or biological material or agent determined by the Secretary of Health and Human Services or the Attorney General as being a threat to the national security of the United States.

(c) BACKGROUND RECORDS CHECK-

(1) IN GENERAL- Upon the request of a State regarding issuance of a license described in subsection (a)(1) to an individual, the Attorney General--

(A) shall carry out a background records check regarding the individual; and

(B) upon completing the background records check, shall notify the Secretary of Transportation of the completion and results of the background records check.

(2) SCOPE- A background records check regarding an individual under this subsection shall consist of the following:

(A) A check of the relevant criminal history databases.

(B) In the case of an alien, a check of the relevant databases to determine the status of the alien under the immigration laws of the United States.

(C) As appropriate, a check of the relevant international databases through Interpol-U.S. National Central Bureau or other appropriate means.

(d) REPORTING REQUIREMENT- Each State shall submit to the Secretary of Transportation, at such time and in such manner as the Secretary may prescribe, the name, address, and such other information as the Secretary may require, concerning--

(1) each alien to whom the State issues a license described in subsection (a); and

(2) each other individual to whom such a license is issued, as the Secretary may require.

(e) ALIEN DEFINED- In this section, the term "alien" has the meaning given the term in section 101(a)(3) of the Immigration and Nationality Act.

(2) CLERICAL AMENDMENT- The table of sections at the beginning of such chapter is amended by inserting after the item relating to section 5103 the following new item:

5103a. LIMITATION ON ISSUANCE OF HAZMAT LICENSES.

(b) REGULATION OF DRIVER FITNESS- Section 31305(a)(5) of title 49, United States Code, is amended--

(1) by striking "and" at the end of subparagraph (A);

(2) by inserting "and" at the end of subparagraph (B); and

(3) by adding at the end the following new subparagraph:

(C) is licensed by a State to operate the vehicle after having first been determined under section 5103a of this title as not posing a security risk warranting license denial.

(c) AUTHORIZATION OF APPROPRIATIONS- There is authorized to be appropriated for the Department of Transportation and the Department of Justice such amounts as may be necessary to carry out section 5103a of title 49, United States Code, as added by subsection (a).

Commercial Drivers and HAZMAT Endorsements

Exactly what crimes prevent a covered commercial driver from obtaining a hazmat endorsement on his commercial driver's license and what crimes will cause the endorsement to be rescinded?

The following information answers this question and is taken direct from the Transportation Security Agency.

Please note: Any hazmat truck driver who has a disqualifying offense that prohibits holding a Hazardous Materials Endorsement (HME) must immediately surrender the HME to the state Department of Motor Vehicles.

The following list was specifically designed to identify disqualifying crimes that pose a potential threat to the nation's transportation network. The list is comparable to assessment standards applied to millions of airport and airline employees.

These crimes are only disqualifying if they are considered felonies in the appropriate jurisdiction, civilian or military. An applicant is disqualified from holding an HME if he or she was convicted* or found not guilty by reason of insanity within the past seven years, was released from prison within the past five years, or is wanted or under indictment, for any of the following crimes:

- Assault with intent to murder

- Kidnapping or hostage taking

- Rape or aggravated sexual abuse

- Extortion

- Robbery

- Arson

- Bribery

- Smuggling

- Immigration violations

- RICO[2]

Distribution of, possession with intent to distribute, or importation of a controlled substance ("simple possession" of a controlled substance without an intent to distribute is not considered disqualifying)

Dishonesty, fraud, or misrepresentation, including identity fraud (e.g., felony-level embezzlement, tax evasion, perjury, and false statements to the Federal government)

Unlawful possession, use, sale, manufacture, purchase, distribution, receipt, transfer, shipping, transporting, delivery, import, export of, or dealing in firearms or other weapons

Conspiracy or attempt to commit any of these crimes

---

[2] Racketeer Influenced and Corrupt Organizations Act

An applicant will be permanently disqualified from holding a HME if he or she was ever convicted* or found not guilty by reason of insanity of any of the following crimes:

Murder   Sedition

Terrorism   Espionage

Treason

Unlawful possession, use, sale, distribution, manufacture, purchase, receipt, transfer, shipping, transporting, import, export, storage of, or dealing in an explosive or explosive device

RICO violations (if the crime underlying the RICO conviction is on the list of permanently disqualifying crimes)

A crime involving a transportation security incident (i.e., security incident involving a significant loss of life, environmental damage, transportation system disruption, or economic disruption in a particular area)

Improper transportation of a hazardous material (minor infractions involving transportation of hazardous materials will not disqualify a driver; for instance, no driver will be disqualified for minor roadside infractions or placarding violations)

Conspiracy or attempt to commit any of these crimes

* Convicted means any plea of guilty or *nolo contendere* or any finding of guilt.

Federal Aviation Regulations

This example outlines certain Federal Aviation Administration requirements.

TITLE 14--AERONAUTICS AND SPACE

CHAPTER I--FEDERAL AVIATION ADMINISTRATION, DEPARTMENT OF TRANSPORTATION (Continued)

PART 107--AIRPORT SECURITY--Table of Contents

Sec. 107.31 Employment history, verification and criminal history records checks.

(a) Scope. On or after January 31, 1996, this section applies to all airport operators; airport users; individuals currently having unescorted access to a security identification display area (SIDA) that is identified by Sec. 107.25; all individuals seeking authorization for, or seeking the authority to authorize others to have, unescorted access to the SIDA; and each airport user and air carrier making a certification to an airport operator pursuant to paragraph (n) of this section. An airport user, for the purposes of Sec. 107.31 only, is any person making a certification under this section other than an air carrier subject to Sec. 108.33.

(b) Employment history investigations required. Except as provided in paragraph (m) of this section, each airport operator must ensure that no individual is granted authorization for, or is granted authority to authorize others to have, unescorted access to the SIDA unless the following requirements are met:

(1) The individual has satisfactorily undergone Part 1 of an employment history investigation. Part 1 consists of a review of the previous 10 years of employment history and verification of the 5 employment years preceding the date the appropriate investigation is initiated as provided in paragraph (c) of this section; and

(2) If required by paragraph (c)(5) of this section, the individual has satisfied Part 2 of the employment history investigation. Part 2 is the process to determine if the individual has a criminal record. To satisfy Part 2 of the investigation the criminal record check must not disclose that the individual has been convicted or found not guilty by reason of insanity, in any jurisdiction, during the 10 years ending on the date of such investigation, of any of the crimes listed below:

(i) Forgery of certificates, false marking of aircraft, and other aircraft registration violation, 49 U.S.C. 46306;

(ii) Interference with air navigation, 49 U.S.C. 46308;

(iii) Improper transportation of a hazardous material, 49 U.S.C. 46312;

(iv) Aircraft piracy, 49 U.S.C. 46502;

(v) Interference with flightcrew members or flight attendants, 49 U.S.C. 46504;

(vi) Commission of certain crimes aboard aircraft in flight, 49 U.S.C. 46506;

(vii) Carrying a weapon or explosive aboard aircraft, 49 U.S.C. 46505;

(viii) Conveying false information and threats, 49 U.S.C. 46507;

(ix) Aircraft piracy outside the special aircraft jurisdiction of the United States, 49 U.S.C. 46502(b);

(x) Lighting violations involving transporting controlled substances, 49 U.S.C. 46315;

(xi) Unlawful entry into an aircraft or airport area that serves air carriers or foreign air carriers contrary to established security requirements, 49 U.S.C. 46314;

(xii) Destruction of an aircraft or aircraft facility, 18 U.S.C. 32;

(xiii) Murder;

(xiv) Assault with intent to murder;

(xv) Espionage;

(xvi) Sedition;

(xvii) Kidnapping or hostage taking;

(xviii) Treason;

(xix) Rape or aggravated sexual abuse;

(xx) Unlawful possession, use, sale, distribution, or manufacture of an explosive or weapon;

(xxi) Extortion;

(xxii) Armed robbery;

(xxiii) Distribution of, or intent to distribute, a controlled substance;

(xxiv) Felony arson; or

(xxv) Conspiracy or attempt to commit any of the aforementioned criminal acts.

Banking Industry Regulations

Here are excerpts from regulations concerning the banking industry. (www.fdic.gov/regulations/laws/rules/1000-2100.html)

Federal Deposit Insurance Act

SEC. 19. PENALTY FOR UNAUTHORIZED PARTICIPATION BY CONVICTED INDIVIDUAL.

(a) PROHIBITION.--

(1) IN GENERAL.--Except with the prior written consent of the Corporation--

(A) any person who has been convicted of any criminal offense involving dishonesty or a breach of trust or money laundering, or has agreed to enter into a pretrial diversion or similar program in connection with a prosecution for such offense, may not--

(i) become, or continue as, an institution-affiliated party with respect to any insured depository institution;

(ii) own or control, directly or indirectly, any insured depository institution; or

(iii) otherwise participate, directly or indirectly, in the conduct of the affairs of any insured depository institution; and

(B) any insured depository institution may not permit any person referred to in subparagraph (A) to engage in any conduct or continue any relationship prohibited.

(2) Minimum 10-year prohibition period for certain offenses.--

(A) IN GENERAL.--If the offense referred to in paragraph (1)(A) in connection with any person referred to in such paragraph is--

(i) an offense under--

(I) section 215, 656, 657, 1005, 1006, 1007, 1008, 1014, 1032, 1344, 1517, 1956, or 1957 of title 18, United States Code; or

(II) section 1341 or 1343 of such title which affects any financial institution (as defined in section 20 of such title); or

(ii) the offense of conspiring to commit any such offense, the Corporation may not consent to any exception to the application of paragraph (1) to such person during the 10-year period beginning on the date the conviction or the agreement becomes final.

More About State Mandated Regulations

Every state has a myriad of laws that mandate criminal record checks for certain occupations. Usually these occupations are regulated by state licensing boards. Examples of typical industries involved include:

- Public School Teachers, Bus Drivers
- Child Care
- Elderly Care
- Heath Care
- Insurance
- Gaming
- Security and Investigation
- Service workers performing work in customers' homes
- Service workers performing work in schools

Within each broad industry within each state are differing requirements. For example, within the health-care category, the requirements for nurse aides might be completely different from radiologists. In the next state, an occupation's requirements may be the same but requirements can vary, or licensing of that profession may be altogether non-existent.

In later chapters, you will learn that certain state criminal justice agencies restrict the general public from access to their criminal record databases. However, ALL state agencies do permit access by employers who are mandated by state law to do criminal record checks.

Summary

Some employers order criminal records because they believe it will lower their liability or improve their bottom line. Other employers do so because they are required by law. Some do it for both reasons. The real question for most employers is not whether they will screen their applicants, but what can they afford to do. The law does not require a perfect background screening; rather only a reasonable one. Factors include the risk associated with the position, the total cost for all applicants and how far back is it reasonable to check.

The chapters to follow provide information for those employers who choose to obtain and use criminal record information.

Chapter 5

Advice When Obtaining Criminal Records Yourself

The closest to perfection a person comes is when he fills out a job application form

- Stanley J. Randall

There are several ways you can obtain a criminal record on an individual. First you have to choose between doing it yourself or hiring someone to do it for you.

If you plan to do it yourself, and you will be requesting criminal records from various locales, you will need source materials to tell you where to look and what procedures are there. What county courts will you need to search? What records will the state repository be able to supply you? Which federal court has jurisdiction?

If you need criminal records from multiple locales, or have more than an occasional need for criminal records, you probably will decide to hire someone else with expertise in the field — a criminal record vendor, classified as a consumer reporting agency under the Fair Credit Reporting Act (FCRA), 15 U.S.C. §1681 et seq. These record experts offer advantages — they know the territory and have knowledge about such things as costs, turnaround times, and what doors to open. Some have specialized search tools that you are not likely to have. When using a vendor, however, you are getting into an area where there are laws and provisions of which you should be aware. The next chapter evaluates the use of criminal record vendors.

You may not need a vendor. If you are in need of only a single record, or if you have a low *volume* of requests — and the *nature* of the request is simple — it will be easy enough to do it yourself.

Your decision to do it yourself or hire a retriever will, in large part, depend on whether you are doing local searches, e.g., searches in your immediate vicinity, or remote searches, e.g., searches from those locales too distant to conveniently do yourself. Let us look at some of the things you will need to know.

Know Thy Repositories

The first step in searching criminal records is to know where to look. This chapter will make you aware of the possible record locations — the county, the state repository, the state court administration, and even the federal courts. Deciding which locations to search requires a basic understanding of the differences.

Criminal Records at the County Level

The county courts that oversee felony cases are actually part of the state court systems. Misdemeanor cases are held at local courts that can be either part of the state court system, or a local court many be a municipal or town court.

The secret to determining where a criminal court case may be located is to understand how the court system is structured in that particular state. There are over 7,000 significant courts in the U.S. that maintain a database of criminal records. Note that these courts generally submit records of major misdemeanors, felony arrest records, and convictions to a central state repository. The states, in turn, submit criminal record activity to the FBI's National Crime Information Center, which is not open to the public.

The general structure of all state court systems has four parts:

- Appellate courts
- Intermediate appellate courts
- General jurisdiction trial courts
- Limited jurisdiction trial courts

The two highest levels — appellate and intermediate appellate courts — only hear cases on appeal from the trial courts. Opinions of these appellate courts are of interest primarily to attorneys seeking legal precedents for new cases.

How Courts Maintain Records

When a case is filed or a warrant is issued, it is assigned a case number. This is the primary indexing method in every court. In searching for case records, you will need to know — or find — the applicable case number. If you have the number in good form already, your search for records connected to this case should be fast and reasonably inexpensive.

Case numbering procedures may not be consistent throughout a state's court system. One district may assign numbers by district while another may assign numbers by location (division) within the district, or by judge. Keep in mind, case numbers appearing in legal text citations may not be adequate for searching unless they appear in the proper form for the particular court where you are searching.

Docket Sheet

All basic case information from cover sheets and from documents filed as a case goes forward is recorded on the docket sheet. Thus, the docket sheet contains an outline of the case history from initial filing to its current status.

While docket sheets differ somewhat in format, the basic information contained on a docket sheet is consistent from court to court. All docket sheets contain:

- Name of court, including location (division) and the judge assigned;
- Case number and case name;
- Names of all plaintiffs and defendants/debtors;
- Names and addresses of attorneys for the plaintiff or debtor;
- Nature and cause (e.g., statute) of action.

Court Record Searching Tips

Search procedures will literally vary all over the map. In some locales, a computer terminal in the lobby lets you do an initial search of the docket index by using name, DOB or other identifying information such as a partial SSN. From this computer, you only will be able to determine if that jurisdiction has criminal files of some type on the individual—or an individual with the same or similar name. The attending clerk should be able to tell you if the records from other courts, or other jurisdictions, are also on that computer database. That is helpful. If your search finds there are no files — no hits — that match the subject's name, you can be on your way. However, if you do find a match or potential match, the computer terminal will point you to the actual files, which are usually on paper. From here, turn to the clerk who may allow you to search the actual files; but most likely, the clerk will locate and search the files for you. There may be a fee, and there may be a wait. In other jurisdictions, the clerk may have control of the computer and will do all the searching while you wait.

Below are some useful tips for searching court records.

- **Learn the index and record systems.** Most courts are computerized, which means that docket sheet data is entered into a computer system. Within a state or judicial district, the courts *may* be linked together via a single computer system. Access to this system may or may not be open to the public, depending on the state.

Docket sheets from cases closed before the advent of computerization may not be in the computer system. For pre-computer era cases, most courts keep summary case information on microfilm, microfiche, or index cards.

Often, the images of actual case documents are not available on computer and are found in paper files only available to be photocopied. You may inquire about where you must go for photocopies by contacting the court where the case records are located.

- **Be aware of restricted records.** Most courts have a number of types of case records, such as sealed, mental, or juvenile, which are not released without a court order.

- **Watch for name variations from state to state.** Do not assume that the structure of the court system in another state is anything like your own. In one state, the Circuit Court may be the highest trial court whereas in another it is a limited jurisdiction court. Examples are: (1) New York, where the Supreme Court is not very "supreme," and the downstate court structure varies from upstate; and (2) Tennessee, where circuit courts are in districts.

- **Watch for combined courts.** In many instances the two types of courts within a county, e.g., a circuit court and a district court, are combined. When phoning or writing these courts, we recommend that your specifically state in your request that you want both courts included in the search.

- **Use a SASE.** If you send requests by mail, include a self-addressed, stamped envelope (SASE). This may very well insure quicker service.

Administrative Office of the Court Records

In some states there is an alternative to searching the central state repository. Every state has a court administration that oversees the state's trial and appellate court system. In a surprising number of states – 28 – some or all of the state trial courts at the county (or parish) forward court records to the administrative office of the courts, often referred to as the AOC. The AOC then offers a searchable database to the public, usually online.

A Valuable Resource

A search from one of these court systems can be a particularly useful tool in those states that do not permit a state repository search – such as New York, North Carolina, or Utah.

Another value to using these record systems is there may be a higher likelihood that the disposition records are forwarded in a timely manner. Thus, the database may be very current.

State-by-State Variations

But there are many nuances to these searches. The value of an AOC court search varies by state. All counties may not be included. There may be no uniformity with respect to the length of time criminal activity is archived. For example, one county may have cases dating back for seven years, while another county may have only two years of history. The use or lack of identifiers as part of the search varies widely from state-to-state, but searches do not involve fingerprints.

When an AOC system is available, you need to know (1) the court structure in that state, (2) which particular courts are included in their online system, and (3) what types of cases are included.

Chapter 12 provides details on how to search records from the state AOCs.

The State Central Repository

As mentioned, all states have a central repository of criminal records of those individuals who have been subject to that state's criminal justice system. A state's record repository will not include records of crimes its citizens committed in other states. The information at the state repository is submitted by state, county, parish, and municipal courts as well as from local law enforcement. Information forwarded to the state includes notations of arrests and charges, sometimes the disposition, and a set of fingerprints.

The Non-Uniformity of State Systems

As you might expect, state statutes governing dissemination of public criminal history records are as varied as those statutes dealing with non-public information. A few states have no statutory provisions setting statewide policies on access by non-criminal justice agencies; in these states, the Federal Department of Justice regulations control access and use. In a few other states, the statute simply delegates to a designated official the authority to issue rules and regulations on dissemination. In states that do have laws dealing with the subject, the statutory approaches vary. In Florida and other "open record" states, anyone can obtain access to criminal history records for any purpose. In states which prohibit access and use except for limited purposes specifically authorized by statute, it is a criminal offense to release criminal history records for unauthorized purposes. The other states fall somewhere in between, and as pointed out earlier, those states with release requirements are hard to categorize.

The text below on Searching State Repositories is an excerpt from *The Public Record Research TIPS Book* by Michael Sankey, published by Facts on Demand Press. This text details some of the non-uniformity issues and other concerns about limiting a search to only a state repository.

Searching State Repositories

There are two factors that must be taken into account when searching criminal records at the state law enforcement repositories:

1. Access Restrictions

2. Accuracy of Record Content

Record searchers and record vendors need to be aware of these factors. Often this means educating the end-users of the records.

Restrictions to Access Factor

You do not waltz into a state police headquarters and demand to view the record index like you would at a courthouse. A key point for a criminal record searcher is once a record from the court reaches the law enforcement agency in more than half the states the record is no longer public. Most law enforcement agencies impose a set of requirements for access and do not offer on-site searching. Often a set of fingerprints must be submitted to do a record search.

Consider the following statistics from BRB Publications[3] about restrictions on criminal record requests from the public —

*   23 states release criminal records (name search) to the general public without consent of the subject.

*   18 states require a signed release from the subject.

*   9 state require submission of fingerprints

*   6 states have closed their records.

Several states, Minnesota for example, offer access to limited and to full records, depending if the requester presents a signed release.

---

[3] Taken from the *Public Record Research System*, BRB Publications, Inc. www.brbpub.com

[**Editor's note:** Chapter 12 specifies the states in each of the categories mentioned above.]

All states will process record requests from requesters who have legislative authority to obtain records. These requesters include criminal justice-related agencies (courts), occupational licensing boards, and often industries dealing with the healthcare, or with the care of the young or aged.

The Accuracy of the Records

As noted, many employers and state licensing boards depend on state criminal record repositories as their primary resource when performing a criminal record background check. But in some states this can be a questionable practice if this is the only resource used, even if fingerprints are submitted.

There are four reasons why the completeness, consistency, and accuracy of state criminal record repositories are open to accuracy concerns—

- Level of Automation
- Level of Quality Control
- Timeliness of Receiving Arrest and Disposition Data
- Timeliness of Entering Arrest and Disposition Data into the Repository

The Disposition Reporting Factor

Remember the Criminal Case Flowchart on page 15? One of the key record creation points is when a case receives a disposition. The problem is that in many states, there is no automated system that insures the disposition is reported by the courts to the state. This includes a guilty or a not-guilty verdict. Thus a record search may indicate an open case when in fact the case was dismissed or the subject may have already served time or probation.

The lack of dispositions can complicate things. State and federal laws are very strict about what records employers can and cannot use when making hiring decisions. There can be strict compliance rules in place. Many states have enacted laws that prohibit the disclosure of criminal information if a disposition is missing. The following is a case example from public record searching expert Lynn Peterson:

> "For example, in Pennsylvania, if you conduct a criminal check using the State Police Index (EPATCH) and the subject has a criminal record but the disposition is missing, you will receive a message that the request is pending. If the State Police do not come up with the disposition, they will eventually mail

you a report that indicates "no record." This means that the State Police may very well report someone as being clear, when, in fact, the person has a record."

So how widespread is the disposition problem? Consider these examples—

- Only 30 states generate lists of arrests with no dispositions in order to give notice to criminal justice agencies and courts about obtaining missing dispositions.

- 12 states report they each have from 7,000 to 148,500 final court dispositions that cannot be linked to an arrest record.

- Only 21 states report they receive final felony trial court dispositions for 70% or more arrests within last five5 years.

The Data Entry Factor

Recording dispositions is not the only problem state repositories are facing. Many states have funding concerns and non-automated systems that may lead to delays in data input—

- 27 states report they have a significant backlog (from 160 man-hours to 30,400 man-hours needed) for entering court data into the criminal history database.

- Only 25 states have fully automated criminal history files with a master name index. The remaining 25 states are partially automated.

The statistics shown above and the statistics in the table below come from the U.S. Department of Justice, Bureau of Justice Statistic's Survey of State Criminal History Information Systems, 2003 (released in 2006) with updated content researched by BRB Publications.

The Survey can be viewed at www.ojp.usdoj.gov/bjs/abstract/sschis03.htm.

Table of State Repository Record-Keeping

State	% Arrests with Final Dispositions	Average # of Days to Receive and Process Submitted Arrest Data	Average # of Days to Receive and Process Submitted Dispositions
AL	45%	37	30+
AK	87%	30	n/a
AR	81%	37-44	60
AZ	58%	1	70
CA	75%	1	60
CO	17%	2-4	2
CT	100%	213	2-4

State	% Arrests with Final Dispositions	Average # of Days to Receive and Process Submitted Arrest Data	Average # of Days to Receive and Process Submitted Dispositions
DE	94%	2	2
DC	46%	2	2
FL	70%	12	63
GA	70%	3	197
HI	90%	1-7	57
IA	95%	2	80
ID	66%	42	17
IL	52%	10	150
IN	45%	17	1
KS	50%	11	21
KY	69%	1-90	30
LA	40%	3-15	n/a
MA	100%	1-30	2
MD	90%	1	61-63
ME	90%	1-14	1
MI	80%	15-30	1-180
MN	41%	20	4
MO	76%	114	n/a
MS	40%	105	1000
MT	85%	28	3
NC	89%	1-18	1
ND	86%	n/a	n/a
NE	62%	25-50	180
NH	80%	35-56	7-14
NJ	84%	2-12	2
NM	32%	75	3
NV	37%	2	60
NY*	85%	1	1
OH	65%	15	22
OK	32%	95-97	n/a
OR	50%	1-22	30
PA	60%	1	n/a
RI	86%	1-67	5
SC	70%	13	2-4
SD	98%	1-10	28
TN	23%	1-12	35
TX	66%	1-9	30

State	% Arrests with Final Dispositions	Average # of Days to Receive and Process Submitted Arrest Data	Average # of Days to Receive and Process Submitted Dispositions
UT	64%	48-52	31
VA	84%	2-8	3-16
VT	96%	17	24
WA	79%	4	32
WI	77%	9	6
WV	40%	10	n/a
WY	73%	9	n/a

* NY statistics refer to the record repository maintained by the Office of Court Administration.

The Common Sense Approach

Please don't misunderstand the message here – there are certainly good reasons for performing a search of a state repository record database. A statewide search covers a wider geographic range than a county search. And a state search is certainly less expensive than a separate search of each county. Many states do have strong database systems. But for proper due diligence for performing a criminal record search, using a state search AND a county search of criminal records AND even a search from a database vendor should be considered. This is extremely critical for employers making hiring decisions in states with legislative limitations on using criminal records without dispositions or using misdemeanor records.

However, a few states do make this approach somewhat difficult. Some court clerks are instructed not to honor mail requests to perform criminal record name searches. The state administration instructs the clerk to send the requester to the state police repository. Unless the requester can do an on-site search of the index or hire a researcher on-site, there is always a question of *how accurate is the state search?*

In summary, the source of the vast majority of any state's records is from county courts and law enforcement. The crime trail begins when a criminal action is first processed at the local or county level, then it is gradually forwarded to the state repository. What information is reported, when it is reported, and how it is reported will all affect the quality and completeness of state data.

Searching Several Record Locations

Obtaining a criminal record from your own county or obtaining a state criminal record from your state repository is one thing. You can become familiar with the methods and procedures in your own backyard and perhaps cobble together an efficient process. Obtaining a criminal record from a distant, out-of-state county is often a horse of a different color. Just because your local county clerk or state agency does things a certain way does not mean you can expect the same process and courtesies elsewhere.

Often, the first obstacle is simply determining what county level agencies should be searched. There are, after all, more than 3,200 U.S. counties, parishes, and cities to choose from. Let us say that you are checking for a criminal record for someone who lists a ZIP Code in Crittenden County, Arkansas. You may not know that directly across the river is a rather large place called Memphis, Tennessee. To complicate matters, a few miles south of Memphis, just past Graceland, is Mississippi. Should you check these areas that border on Crittenden County?

Once the scope of your search is determined, next is the matter of determining the address of the county courts, the identifying information needed, the prices, who to make the check payable to (if the search is being conducted through the mail), and the turnaround times that can be expected.

Do-It-Yourself Search Quandary

Here is a typical example: assume an individual applies for a position at an office in Chicago, Illinois. This individual had previously lived and worked in Mannford, Oklahoma. If the Chicago employer decides to order a county criminal record, he must first determine the county where Mannford is located. Through the use of a map, city/county cross directory or other method, the employer determines Mannford is located in Creek County. A good cross directory is *The Ultimate County Locator CD* [4].

Now, the employer must find out where the county seat or courthouse is located. Assuming the employer eventually determines that the Creek County courthouse is located in Sapulpa, Oklahoma, the employer must now determine how to get access to the records there. This problem is further compounded by the fact that there are three courthouses in Creek County, each with a separate database of records.

The area code and telephone number to call, address, cost and procedures are all questions that must be answered. At all three of the district courts in Sapulpa, the clerk will *not* do a records search for you, so our employer in Chicago will have to hire a

---

[4] *The Ultimate County Locator with Adjoining County Search CD*, © BRB Publications, www.brbpub.com

public record retriever to go in for him, as this employer obviously cannot do it personally.

Other courts may make the records available over the phone, although this is becoming rare and is not as dependable as an in-person search or even a mailed-in request. Further, most requesters like a written record of the results of their search; a phone search is not particularly reliable. Most jurisdictions, whether they are county or state level, charge a fee for a criminal record. This fee may be a set fee, or it may be based on whether a criminal record exists. The fee may depend on how extensive the record is. Many jurisdictions charge a set fee plus the cost for any copies they make. For mailed-in requests, the court may require a self-addressed, stamped envelope. The vast majority of jurisdictions do not take credit cards. They may take checks — business, cashiers, and money order are preferred over personal checks — and many will wait for the check to clear before mailing your search results. This results in a considerable turnaround time.

The complexity of obtaining records from distant sources, again whether county or state, coupled with the fact that there is usually a cost in time as well as money, is what prompts many employers to use a record retrieval service.

State Versus County Searching

The decision on whether to order a state or a county criminal record requires an understanding of the differences between the two. This is not necessarily an "either/or" decision. At its most basic, the question can be phrased: "Would you like that search to be a mile wide and an inch deep, or a mile deep and an inch wide?"

A Mile Wide and an Inch Deep

A state search is a wide search, encompassing all counties within the state. As discussed earlier however, state searches are dependant on the counties reporting the information. A state search, while broad, may not have the latest information, or the detailed information that might be contained in a county search.

A Mile Deep and an Inch Wide

A county search is a deep search, often containing the latest and most complete information available *from that particular county*. The drawback inherent in a county search is the limited scope of the search. Many U.S. cities have spilled over into several counties. A search in one county — while revealing a great level of detail in that county — may literally miss criminal information that occurred across the street. Consider places like the City of Texarkana, where the state boundary line is a main street.

What is an upstanding, conscientious, resourceful criminal record searcher to do? Well, it depends. In those states in which a state repository search is not available, your decision will be fairly easy. You take what you can get.

A strategy that many searchers use is to first order a state record, if access is available. If something comes up that is conclusive, then the process may well end there. A pharmacy that discovers multiple convictions for drug trafficking on a subject's state search probably will not go much farther in the process.

Often, a state search may prove inconclusive, i.e., not contain the disposition. In a case such as this, the results of the state search would point to the county where the latest information could be obtained. The state search might also serve to validate a locale where the searcher had intended to search.

Conversely, if you start with a county search in a locale where there are close, adjoining counties and find something inconclusive — minor arrests or minor convictions — it may be cause for concern. It may behoove you to order a statewide search to see if anything else pops up.

Using the Freedom of Information Act and Other Acts

The Federal Freedom of Information Act (FOIA) has no bearing on state, county, or local government agencies because these agencies are subject to that state's individual act. Further, the government agencies that handle criminal records generally have systems in place to release information, so the FOIA is not needed.

However, if you are trying to obtain non-criminal records from agencies, there are many useful Internet sites that give the information you need to complete such a request. A great resource for FOIA and also for finding state's open record laws is *The Open Government Guide* at www.rcfp.org/ogg. Also, we recommend these sites—

- http://spj.org/foia.asp
- http://epic.org/open_gov/rights.html

As a side note, the fact that a record is supposed to be public and obtainable does not necessarily mean that the bureaucrats will agree. As we discussed earlier in this book there are competing interests on the proving issue. There are some privacy issues. There are some privacy advocates who push to make prison/criminal records confidential. At times, lawsuits are necessary to force the release of this "public information." This points to the reality that checking criminal records is a complicated process once you leave your own backyard.

Searching Federal Court Records

Searching records at the federal court system can be one of the easiest or one of the most frustrating experiences that record searchers may encounter. Although the federal court system offers advanced electronic search capabilities, at times it is practically impossible to properly identify a subject when searching civil or criminal records.

Before reviewing searching procedures, a brief overview is in order.

United States District Courts

The United States District Courts are the courts of general jurisdiction, or trial courts. All civil and criminal cases go to the U.S. District Courts. All bankruptcy cases go to the U.S. Bankruptcy Courts.

There are 89 districts in the 50 states, which are listed with their divisions in Title 28 of the U.S. Code, Sections 81-144. District courts also exist in Puerto Rico, the U.S. Virgin Islands, the District of Columbia, Guam, and the Northern Mariana Islands. In total there are 94 U.S. district courts in 500 court locations. Some states, such as Colorado, are composed of a single judicial district. Others, such as California, are composed of multiple judicial districts – Central, Eastern, Northern, and Southern.

Author Tip

Approximately 5 percent of the criminal records in the U.S. are records of federal offenses. Lack of good identifiers — and the time, expense and legal liabilities this lack may cause — as well as the limited number of records present keep federal criminal records from being used by the vast majority of U.S. employers. As a federal court's jurisdiction can include a population of millions, the chance of a name error on a federal record is greater than at the county level. More care must be taken when connecting a name to a federal record.

United States Court of Appeals

The United States Court of Appeals consists of thirteen appellate courts that hear appeals of verdicts from the district and bankruptcy courts. Courts of Appeals are designated as follows:

- The Federal Circuit Court of Appeals hears appeals from the U.S. Claims Court and the U.S. Court of International Trade. It is located in Washington, DC.

- The District of Columbia Circuit Court of Appeals hears appeals from the district courts in Washington, DC as well as from the Tax Court.

- Eleven geographic Courts of Appeals — each of these appeal courts covers a designated number of states and territories.[5]

Supreme Court of the United States

The Supreme Court of the United States is the court of last resort in the United States. The Supreme Court is located in Washington, DC, where it hears appeals from the United States Courts of Appeals and from the highest courts of each state.

Other Federal Courts of Note

There are three significant special/separate courts created to hear cases or appeals for certain areas of litigation that demand special expertise. These courts are the U.S. Tax Court, the Court of International Trade, and the U.S. Court of Federal Claims.

How Federal Trial Court Cases are Organized

When a case is filed with a federal court, a case number is assigned. District courts index by defendant and plaintiff as well as by case number. Bankruptcy courts usually index by debtor and case number. Therefore, when you search by name you will first receive a listing of all cases where the name appears, both as plaintiff and defendant.

To view case records you will need to know or find the applicable case number. Case numbering procedures are not consistent throughout the federal court system. One judicial district may assign numbers by district while another may assign numbers by location (division) within that judicial district or by judge within the division. Remember that case numbers appearing in legal text citations may not be adequate for searching unless they appear in the proper form for the particular court.

As in state court systems, information from cover sheets and from documents filed as a case goes forward is recorded on the docket sheet, which then contains the case history from initial filing to its current status. While docket sheets differ somewhat in format, the basic information contained on a docket sheet is consistent from court to court.

At one time, cases were assigned within a district based on the county of origination. Although this is still true in most states, computerized tracking of dockets has led to a more flexible approach to case assignment. For example in Minnesota and Connecticut, rather than blindly assigning all cases from a county to one judge, their districts use random numbers and other methods to logically balance caseloads among their judges.

---

[5] The Appendix lists the circuit number and location of the Court of Appeals for each state.

This trend may appear to confuse the case search process. Actually, finding cases has become significantly easier with the wide availability of the U.S. Party/Case Index and PACER (see below). Also helpful is when on-site terminals in each court location contain the same database of district-wide information.

Access to Federal Court Criminal Records Online

Numerous programs have been developed for electronic access to federal court records. Over the years, the Administrative Office of the United States Courts in Washington, DC has developed a number of innovative public access programs—

- The U.S. Party/Case Index

- PACER

- Case Management/Electronic Case Files (CM/ECF)

The U.S. Party/Case Index

The U.S. Party/Case Index, actually part of PACER, is a national locator index for U.S. District, Bankruptcy, and Appellate courts. By using the U.S. Party/Case Index searchers may conduct nearly nationwide search to determine whether or not a party is involved in federal litigation.

If you find there is a case in existence involving a particular subject, then you need to visit the PACER or CM/ECF site for the particular jurisdiction where the case is located. The Case Number field in the output will be a direct link to the full case information on the court's computers, whether the court is running the Internet version of PACER or the newer PACER on the CM/ECF system.

You may access the U.S. Party/Case Index via the Internet at http://pacer.uspci.uscourts.gov. Subscribers to PACER automatically have access to the U.S. Party/Case Index with their existing PACER login and password.

The U.S. Party/Case Index allows searches 1) by party name or Social Security Number in the bankruptcy index, 2) party name or nature of suit in the civil index, 3) defendant name in the criminal index, and 4) party name in the appellate index. The information provided by the search result will include the party name, the court where the case is filed, the case number and the filing date.

To retrieve more information on a particular case found while searching the U.S. Party/Case Index, access the PACER system for the jurisdiction where the case resides as indicated by the court abbreviation. Usually the Case Number will be a link to the case summary information at that court's PACER site.

At press time, there were a number of courts not participating in the U.S. Party/Case Index. Non-participating Appellate Courts include the Second, Fifth, Seventh, and Eleventh Circuits. Non-participating District Courts include the Indiana Southern District, New Mexico District, and the U.S. Virgin Islands District.

PACER

PACER, the acronym for **P**ublic **A**ccess to **E**lectronic **C**ourt **R**ecords, provides docket information online for open and some closed case information at most U.S. District Courts. Cases for the U.S. Bankruptcy Courts and for U.S. Court of Federal Claims are also available.

A key point to consider is that each court maintains its own database of case data and decides what to make available on PACER. Also, several courts provide case information on Internet sites without support of the PACER Service Center.

PACER sign-up and technical support is handled at the PACER Service Center in San Antonio, Texas; phone 800-676-6856. A single sign-up is good for all courts; however, some individual courts may require further registration procedures. Many judicial districts offer to send a PACER Primer that has been customized for that district. The primer contains a summary of how to access PACER, how to select cases, how to read case numbers and docket sheets, some searching tips, who to call for problem resolution, and district specific program variations.

You may search by case number, party name, or filing date range in the U.S. District Courts. You may search by case number or party name in the U.S. Courts of Appeals.

PACER provides the following information

- A listing of all parties and participants including judges, attorneys, trustees
- A compilation of case related information such as cause of action, nature of suit, dollar demand
- A chronology of dates of case events entered in the case record
- A claims registry
- A listing of new cases each day in the bankruptcy courts
- Appellate court opinions
- Judgments or case status
- Types of case documents filed for certain districts.

PACER Problems

There are two inherent problems when searching PACER records—

1. How far back records are kept

2. Lack of identifiers

Since each court determines how records will be indexed and when records will be purged, this can leave a searcher guessing how a name is spelled or abbreviated, and how much information about closed cases a search will uncover. The bottom line is that a PACER search may not come close to matching a full seven-year search of the federal court records available by written request from the court itself or through a local document retrieval company.

Another problem is the lack of identifiers. Most federal courts do not show the full DOB on records available to the public. Some courts show no DOB at all. Thus, if the name searched for is common and the search results show two or more hits, each individual case file may need to be reviewed to determine if the case belongs to the subject in mind.

An excellent FAQ on PACER is at http://pacer.psc.uscourts.gov/faq.html.

Miscellaneous Online Systems

RACER is a comparable system to PACER. A few courts still maintain and offer access through RACER. Over the years some courts have developed their own legacy online systems. In addition to RACER, Idaho's Bankruptcy and District Courts have other searching options available on their websites. Likewise, the Southern District Court of New York offers CourtWeb, which provides information to the public on selected recent rulings of those judges who have elected to make information available in electronic form.

Case Management/Electronic Case Files (CM/ECF)

CM/ECF is the relatively new case management system for the Federal Judiciary for all bankruptcy, district, and appellate courts, replacing the aging electronic docketing and case management systems. CM/ECF allows courts to accept filings and provide access to filed documents over the Internet. Attorneys may use CM/ECF to file documents and manage official documents related to a case. Case Management/Electronic Case Files case information is available to the public. Searchers access CM/ECF via PACER.

For details, visit http://pacer.psc.uscourts.gov/cmecf/index.html.

It is important to note that when you search ECF, you may be searching ONLY cases that have been filed electronically. Since a case may not have been filed electronically through CM/ECF, you must still conduct a search using PACER to determine if a case exists.

Most individual courts offer tutorials on how to use CM/ECF for their district. Functioning as a search mechanism, CM/ECF attaches to the relevant docket entries and to PDF versions of related documents filed with or issued by the court. A user may access PDF attachments through a hyperlink that appears with the docket entry.

Because PACER and CM/ECF database systems are maintained within each court, each jurisdiction will have a different URL or modem number. Accessing and querying information from PACER and CM/ECF is comparable; however the format and content of information provided may differ slightly.

Searching Records by Mail and In Person

There are certain pre-set standards for federal courts that most all courts follow. At press time, the search fee is $26 per item. 'A search' is one party name or case number. The court copy fee is $.50 per page. Certification fee is $9 per document, double for exemplification, if available. If you request documents by mail, it is best to always enclose a stamped self-addressed envelope unless a court indicates otherwise. Most courts accept fax requests or will suggest a copying/search vendor. Before releasing records, assume that the court will require prepayment, as most do.

The article below is provided by Michael Sankey, author of the *Public Record Research TIPS Book* by Facts on Demand Press.

More Federal Courts Searching Hints

Check the assigned counties of jurisdiction for each court within a state. Usually accessible from the web, this is a good starting point for determining where case records may be found.

Searchers need to be sure that the court's case index includes all cases open or closed for that particular period, especially important if using CM/ECF. Be aware that some courts purge older, closed paper case files after a period of time, making a search there incomplete after the purge date. Purge times vary from court to court and state to state. Some courts purge within a few months of a case closing.

Often, court personnel are very knowledgeable open cases, but are sometimes fuzzy in answering questions about how far back case records go on PACER, and whether closed cases have been purged. If you are looking for cases older than a year or two, there is no substitute for paying for a real, on-site search performed by court personnel or by a local document retriever.

Most federal courts no longer provide the date of birth or the Social Security Number on search results. However, a handful will provide the last four digits of the SSN, or they may provide the birth month and year of birth, but not the day.

> ## What If the Record Search Results Do Not Include Identifiers?
>
> This is a struggle and a tough problem to solve, especially if a searcher is dealing with a common name. Here are several ideas for trying to ferret out a false-positive:
>
> **View Case Files** - If possible, review the documents found in the case files for any hints of identification. At some district courts, clerks will look at paper case file records, if any, to determine if other identification exists that can match the requester's identifiers.
>
> **Incarceration Records** - Searching prison records is sometimes an excellent alternative means for identity verification. Search the Bureau of Prisons at www.bop.gov.
>
> **News Media** - Some record searchers have been successful in confirming an identity by using news media sources such as newspapers and web news media. Even blogs may help.

The Appendix gives the locations of all the U.S. District Courts shows which districts provide personnel identifiers for record searchers..

The Criminal Justice Information Services (CJIS) Databases

The Criminal Justice Information Services (CJIS) Division, February 1992, serves as the FBI's focal point and central repository for criminal justice information services in the FBI. It is the largest division in the FBI. Programs initially consolidated under the CJIS Division include the National Crime Information Center (NCIC), Uniform Crime Reporting (UCR), and Fingerprint Identification. In addition, responsibility for several ongoing technological initiatives were also transferred to the CJIS Division, including the Integrated Automated Fingerprint Identification System (IAFIS), (NCIC 2000), and the National Incident-Based Reporting System (NIBRS).

The NCIC Database

The FBI database's formal name is the *National Crime Information Center (NCIC)* and is an automated database of criminal justice and justice-related records maintained by the FBI. The database includes the "hot files" of wanted and missing persons, stolen vehicles and identifiable stolen property, including firearms. Two important points about the NCIC are:

1. The NCIC is not nearly as complete as portrayed in the movies. Because of the chain of events that must happen in multiple jurisdictions in order for a crime to appear in NCIC, many records of crime do not make it.

2. The information the NCIC does have is predominantly solely arrest-related. The disposition of most crimes in NCIC must be obtained by going to the adjudicating jurisdiction. This can be an important issue to employers as will be detailed later in the federal and state legal chapters.

This national database is currently evolving due to the National Crime Prevention and Privacy Compact, which is discussed later in this chapter.

Source of the NCIC Data

The sources of the FBI's information are the counties and states that contribute information as well as the federal justice agencies. Public criminal records are found at federal court repositories (for federal crimes), state repositories, and county courthouses. As discussed earlier, private citizens and businesses — non-criminal justice agencies — cannot, as a general rule, obtain access to the national FBI database. However, because the FBI database is perhaps the most well known repository of criminal records, some discussion is in order.

Access to NCIC files is through central control terminal operators in each state. The operators are connected to NCIC via dedicated telecommunications lines maintained by the FBI. Local agencies and beat officers can access the state control terminal via the state law enforcement network. Inquiries are based on name and other non-fingerprint identification. Also, most criminal history inquiries of the Interstate Identification Index (usually referred to as "III" or the "Triple I") system are made via the NCIC telecommunications system.

Interstate Identification System

The *Interstate Identification Index (III)* is an "index-pointer" system for the interstate exchange of criminal history records. Under III, the FBI maintains an identification index to persons arrested for felonies or serious misdemeanors under state or federal law. The index includes identification information such as name, date of birth, race, and sex, FBI Numbers and State Identification Numbers (SID) from each state holding information about an individual. Search inquiries from criminal justice agencies nationwide are transmitted automatically via state telecommunications networks and the FBI's National Crime Information Center (NCIC) telecommunications lines. Not all states participate in the III. Those not participating include Maine, Vermont, the

District of Columbia as well as these territories; Guam, Puerto Rico, American Samoa, Northern Mariana Islands, and Guam.

Searches are made on the basis of name and other identifiers. The process is entirely automated and takes approximately five seconds to complete. If a hit is made against the Index, record requests are made using the SID or FBI Number, and data are automatically retrieved from each repository holding records on the individual and forwarded to the requesting agency.

> **NCIC data may be provided only for criminal justice and other specifically authorized purposes. For criminal history searches, this includes criminal justice employment, employment by federally chartered or insured banking institutions or securities firms, and use by state and local governments for purposes of employment and licensing pursuant to a state statute approved by the U.S. Attorney General. Inquiries regarding presale firearm checks are included as a criminal justice use.**

The bold section in the NCIC definition above is significant. Occasionally, an employer happens upon a "good deal." This good deal usually consists of a friend in law enforcement who obtains criminal records from NCIC and provides them free or sells them to the employer. The problem is that this is illegal, and the Feds have been targeting and prosecuting violators. If you want to check criminal records and have a friend in law enforcement — and want to keep the friend — you should not use the friend as a source of criminal records.

To participate in III, states need an automated criminal record system compatible with the III system and capable of responding automatically to interstate and federal/state record requests. The III held the criminal histories of more than 61.3 million individuals as of July 2007 from the forty-eight participating states. As of that date, ten also participated in the National Fingerprint File (NFF). NFF states have assumed responsibility for providing III-indexed records for criminal and noncriminal requests.

National Crime Prevention and Privacy Compact

The entire FBI record system and infrastructure is currently in a state of transition due to the National Crime Prevention and Privacy Compact. The compact became law when passed by Congress and signed by President Clinton in October 1998. It became effective in April 1999, when ratified by the second state. The compact's purpose is to authorize and require participating state criminal history repositories and the FBI to make all unsealed criminal history records available in response to *authorized* non-criminal justice requests.

This compact is changing the functions and relationship between the FBI and state systems. To understand how, it is helpful to look at past system performance and the new, evolving system.

Before the Compact

Before the compact, arrest fingerprint cards were submitted to the FBI by federal, state and local agencies on a voluntary basis. Law enforcement agencies, primarily local police and sheriff's offices, maintained a system of records specific to their state or locality and submitted duplicate prints of arrested and charged persons to the FBI. In exchange, local authorities received information on the individual's prior nationwide criminal history.

The FBI would report its findings back to the state and maintain the new fingerprint and accompanying data in its criminal history files. The FBI began maintaining this duplicate criminal history file in 1924, and by the late 1990's had over 200 million fingerprint cards on file.

After the Compact

The compact provides a decentralized national records system and is intended to facilitate efficient and effective exchange of criminal records. States must ratify their participation in the compact. Once a state has ratified the compact, they are required to forward criminal record information to the FBI. The FBI, rather than actually storing duplicate information, will instead store the "pointer" information. This information will point the inquiring party to the state holding the information. Therefore, there will be far less duplication of information.

At least twenty-seven states have formally ratified membership in the Compact. Ten other states and territories have signed a Memorandum of Understanding through which they effectively subscribe to the Privacy Compact. The rest of the states are expected to ratify the compact in two to five years. For more information, go to www.search.org/programs/policy/compact.asp.

When the system is fully operational nationwide, the III index maintained at the national level will contain personal identification data on individuals whose criminal records are maintained in state criminal record repositories (state offenders) and in the criminal files of the FBI (federal offenders), but it will not contain any charge or disposition information. The index will serve as a "pointer" to refer inquiring criminal justice agencies to the state or federal files where the requested criminal history records are maintained. The records will be exchanged directly between the states and between state and federal criminal justice agencies by means of telecommunications lines linking federal, state, and local criminal justice agencies throughout the country. The laws and policies of the receiving jurisdictions will govern dissemination and use of the records obtained by means of the system. Each state will enforce its own laws and policies within its borders; federal law will govern record dissemination and use by federal agencies.

An excellent review of National Crime Prevention and Privacy Compact can be found at www.ojp.usdoj.gov/bjs/abstract/ncppcrm.htm.

Automated Fingerprint Identification Systems

The Integrated Automated Fingerprint Identification System (IAFIS) is a national fingerprint and criminal history system maintained by the FBI's Criminal Justice Information Services (CJIS) Division. The IAFIS provides automated fingerprint search capabilities, latent searching capability, electronic image storage, and electronic exchange of fingerprints and responses to approved entities. By of submitting fingerprints electronically, agencies receive electronic responses to criminal ten-print fingerprint submissions within two hours and within 24 hours for civil fingerprint submissions.

The IAFIS maintains the largest biometric database in the world, with fingerprints and corresponding criminal history information for more than 55 million subjects. The fingerprints and corresponding criminal history information are submitted voluntarily by state, local, and federal law enforcement agencies.

Other Available Resources

There are several premier resources for obtaining the information you need to order criminal records on your own. *The Sourcebook to Public Record Information*[6] is printed annually. This same information is available by online subscription via the Internet, with weekly updates. Go to www.brbpub.com and look for the Public Record Research System. All products contain a city/county cross reference that references cities to counties. Therefore, if you know the city or ZIP Code where your subject lived, worked, or perhaps ran into trouble, these resources will point you to the county to search. These products list addresses, availability, prices, and turnaround times for state and local searches.

---

[6] *The Sourcebook to Public Record Information*, © BRB Publications, Tempe, AZ, 800-929-3811; www.brb.pub.com

Advice When Using a Criminal Record Vendor

We always admire the other fellow
more after we have tried to do his job.
— William Feather

If you plan on ordering any type of volume of criminal records from a variety of county or state sources, your best bet probably will be to hire a vendor to perform the searches for you. The service will be faster and more convenient. Many vendors provide in-depth customer services such as interpreting obscure provincial charges that court personnel are not equipped to do.

Businesses that provide criminal records may be court retrievers, private detectives, or pre-employment screening companies. For purposes of discussion here, they will be referred to as "criminal record vendors."

The Advent of Criminal Record Vendors

The criminal record retrieval business exploded in the 1990s. Sophisticated companies that had a nationwide customer base and provided other types of computerized pre-employment screening information (such as driving records or employment history reports) began setting up nationwide criminal record retrieval networks. As they grew, these national companies hired employees and contracted with multiple local companies that had courthouse retrieval services. Some purchased and absorbed local retrieval firms. Small retrievers, who heretofore serviced one or two local employers, began to branch out into new counties and market to new industries.

Part of the reason for this explosion has been the increase in negligent hiring lawsuits. In the 1970s and even the early 1980s, the negligent hiring suit was still a gleam in most plaintiff attorneys' eyes. The idea that an employer would be held responsible for an act of his employee — even when the employee was acting outside the scope of his employment — was farfetched for the times.

For whatever reasons, workplace violence also became a bigger issue, possibly due to the 24-hour news coverage by the cable news networks. Historical statistics regarding workplace violence were not tracked as they are today. Our tolerance of violence is less. One theory is that women entering the workplace in greater numbers have caused greater awareness. Years ago, if a couple of assembly-line workers working on a Ford Model T or a couple of roustabouts drilling an oil well went to fisticuffs, often the attitude was "well, boys will be boys." Today, on the other hand, a couple of men fighting in a mixed-gender office is not acceptable.

In any event, businesses have increasingly felt compelled to order criminal records on employee applicants. In doing so they have encountered the morass that is the present state of our criminal record repositories available to employers. The employer's solution is to outsource the criminal record research work, which has led to the proliferation of criminal record vendors.

Types of Vendor Services Offered

There are three broad categories of services provided by criminal record vendors. One category consists of the hands-on court record retrievers and the general search firms that employ any number of record retrievers to "cover" certain geographical areas. These companies obtain the records for other companies that, in turn, sell that information to employers. The general search firms are, in effect, the "wholesalers" of the records.

The second broad type of vendor is the all-encompassing pre-employment screening company that sells to the end-user — employers. Pre-employment screening companies are, in effect, the "retailers" of the information.

It is important to note several variations. Many private investigators offer the above-mentioned "record retrieval" or "pre-employment screening" services.

The third category includes a number of vendor companies that specialize in compiling proprietary databases of public records. These companies, sometimes known as public record provider companies, may compile federal, state and county-specific databases of criminal record activity. However, the caveat is that some of these databases require steps be taken to insure compliance with the FCRA and even state law e.g., §1786.53, California Civil Code. This issue is discussed in detail in Chapters 8 and 9.

Retrievers and Search Firms

Local document retrievers use their own personnel to search specific requested categories of public records usually in order to obtain documentation for legal compliance such as incorporations, for lending, and for litigation. They do not usually review or interpret the results or issue reports in the sense that investigators do, but rather return documents — the results of searches. While document retrievers tend to be localized, there are some who offer a national network of retrievers and/or correspondents. The retriever or personnel go directly to the agency to look up the information. A retriever may be relied upon for strong knowledge in a local area, whereas a search generalist has a breadth of knowledge and experience in a wider geographic range.

Wholesalers (companies that sell their information to consumer reporting agencies or to another vendor rather than to the end-user) frequently use local document retrievers. Whether wholesalers are "consumer reporting agencies" under the FCRA is the subject of current debate and we do not take sides on that argument in this book.

Companies That Provide Records to Employers

Those companies that provide records to end-users, e.g., employers using criminal records as a factor in establishing eligibility for employment, *are* "consumer reporting agencies." They may obtain criminal records directly from the jurisdiction or from a criminal record wholesaler. In turn, they provide these records to employers for a fee. In Chapter 8, the significance of being a Consumer Reporting Agency (CRA) is discussed at length.

Because criminal records are by no means the only type of pre-employment screening information needed by employers — these companies also provide other services. These services may include driving records, also known as motor vehicle reports or MVRs. Other services offered may be employment histories, educational verifications, SSN verifications, immigration status verification, employment credit reports, and worker's compensation history reports along with other industry-specific screening tools.

In the criminal record arena, most of these companies offer statewide records. A few only offer county records. Because of their cost, limited scope and lack of positive identifiers, federal criminal records are a distant third offering.

Benefits of Service Vendors

Professional criminal record service vendors offer (or should offer) several benefits. These benefits are knowledge and expertise, faster turnaround time, quality control,

FCRA protections, and ancillary tools that may include automated delivery, email ordering and Internet gateways.

The Knowledge Benefit

The first knowledge aspect is simply having the information on hand to obtain a criminal record from any county in the country. Service providers will have the know-how to obtain criminal records from locales nationwide. They have the databases that can quickly cross-reference the city to the county. They then should be able to immediately ask for the information required by the jurisdiction along with any necessary forms. Earlier in this book, some of the problems inherent in cross-country county searches were detailed.

The Turnaround Benefit

The faster, the better — if it is accurate. Turnaround advantages are usually directly attributable to having someone "on the ground" who can physically go into a jurisdiction, get the information, get it court-certified if need be, and get out. Counties and states are, of course, becoming more computerized, but this does not mean they are allowing outsiders to perform computerized searches of their databases. Any court that is computerized is marginally faster for retrieving records. Those jurisdictions that allow online access let the researcher get to the records from afar, so you may expect a speedier turnaround time.

The Expertise and Quality Control Benefit

Many service providers can provide valuable expertise in deciphering reports, knowing what courts will contain what types of offenses. That same service may be able to provide guidance regarding state law. Perhaps more importantly, service providers worth their salt will "salt" their requests to their field people with known records. "Salting" means that, unknown to the field agent, the provider will occasionally ask the agent to perform a search on an individual who is known to have criminal record in that jurisdiction. If the agent comes back with a "clear" report — a "no record found" — the provider knows he has a problem: the agent is not doing a thorough job. Most service providers let their court record retrievers know they are salting their records, and a retriever doing thousands of requests for a service provider will not want to gamble the entire book of business to save a few pennies once in awhile with a "lazy search." Some submit the same record request to multiple retrievers to see if they will all return the same information. In this manner, service providers can maintain a reasonable degree of quality control.

Incidentally, phone searches — especially those performed by a court deputy clerk — are among the least reliable searches. If you absolutely, positively need to know, for the record, an individual's criminal history from a jurisdiction, get it in writing some way or another.

Fair Credit Reporting Act Protections

The FCRA is discussed at length in later chapters, but it is appropriate to point out here that this law can be to the record requester's advantage if a vendor is used. While an employer may be sued over a wrongful employment practice, when a company uses a criminal record vendor to obtain criminal records, the company is afforded some legal protections.

If an employer orders a criminal record on his own and bungles the search, e.g., obtains the wrong record and fires an employee, he is going to have his hands full. If he orders the record from a "consumer-reporting agency" and takes the same action due to the vendor's mistake, the employer will be somewhat shielded from liability.

Ancillary Tools That Criminal Record Vendors Provide

Some criminal record vendors offer ancillary tools that can make the difference between a sub-par and an excellent search.

Database Assisted Searches

When a vendor says he offers a database search, three of your primary questions should be: "how far back do the records go?", "how current are they?", and "what is in the database?" As detailed in the next several chapters, the FCRA requires additional compliance procedures when public record information is used for employment purposes and the public record information is not the latest available. This fact in no way negates the value of database-assisted searches, as explained below.

There are three main factors that hamper the value of public criminal record searches, particularly for employers ordering criminal records on job applicants.

- Knowing where to look
- Turnaround time
- Cost

A database search can address all three. A database search is one in which a vendor has obtained a database of criminal records (and incidentally, as discussed previously, some of these "criminal" records are not criminal at all, but rather "infractions") from a county or state, or, the vendor has warehoused previously ordered criminal records. Because the records are database, the turnaround can be instantaneous as opposed to the hours or days a physical search of a jurisdiction can take. Because there are fewer costs per item associated with a database search, the price is usually less.

Perhaps the biggest advantage, however, is that the database search can — with the right system — *dramatically* increase the scope of the search and thereby make the difference between finding or not finding a criminal record. This search is not directed to a location, but any record associated with the subject of the search.

What is the "right" system? Well, there are variations of database searches, some limited and some global. An example of a limited database search would be one in which a vendor purchases a county's database of criminal records. Say, for example, the vendor purchases the Watadoosie County criminal record database. It should be noted that most counties do not make their entire database available, but some do. When the vendor's client wants to search Watadoosie County, he may be offered the option of searching just the vendor's Watadoosie database.

This limited database search would address two of the three issues: turnaround and cost. But, when you combine databases from multiple sources, the search value rises dramatically.

A global database search differs from a limited database search in that it searches records from various sources and databases. To illustrate, let us go back to the Watadoosie County example. An employer orders a criminal record from Watadoosie County. The vendor employing a global search would — regardless of whether Watadoosie's county data was in his database — perform a search of all the other data in his database. This might mean searching county databases from across the country or across the street, which might happen to be another county. This may disclose that the crime was committed while the subject was away on vacation, school, or at a location that the applicant did not disclose as a former residence.

The global database also might contain previously ordered criminal records. Our employer requesting a Watadoosie County record might discover a criminal record that had been ordered by a previous employer six months earlier from a different county. Warehousing previously ordered criminal records can be particularly effective if a vendor has a high concentration of clients in a particular industry.

Database Caveats

As you can see, database searches can be a powerful tool in criminal record searches. However, they are supplemental and not a substitute. The main reasons why are detailed below.

Criminal record vendors also should offer you options and inform you of the type of search they are performing. If you want a current, up-to-the-minute search of Watadoosie County, that should be what you get.

Perhaps the main caveat with database searches — if the information is to be used for employment purposes and is not the latest available — a notice must be sent to the subject of the search. This FCRA requirement is discussed at length in Chapter 8.

The following sidebar is an edited excerpt from a recent article written by Lester S. Rosen, author of *The Safe Hiring Manual.* We thank Mr. Rosen for allowing us to edit and reprint.

Shortcomings of Vendor Criminal History Databases

There are a number of public record vendors who advertise they have a "national database of criminal record information." Let's start by saying that vendors may have records from many jurisdictions and/or courts but no one, not even the FBI, has a "nationwide" database that includes all cases in every jurisdiction/court. That only exists in the movies. **The fact is there are informational shortcomings of all such databases and there is no such thing as a truly "national" criminal record database.** Perhaps the vendor has purchased some "data" from every state — be it a list of current inmates, or local police records, or unified court records — but no one has all the "data" from all the jurisdictions. Even "statewide" criminal history databases are problematic. Both database vendors and Consumer Reporting Agencies (CRAs) that use these databases must be very clear in their marketing and contracts not to mislead their customers to believe that they are receiving a service that does not exist. CRAs that make such a claim are risking legal liability in the event a criminal is hired when a search of a statewide or "national" database fails to uncover a criminal record.

Listed below are three major reasons a database search may fail to discover a criminal matter.

Completeness — The various databases that vendors purchase or collect may not be the equivalent of a true all-encompassing multi-statewide database. First, the databases purchased by the vendor for resale (or accessed as a gateway) may not contain complete records from all jurisdictions. For example, not all unified court systems contain all counties. Second, for reporting purposes, the records that are actually reported may be incomplete or lack sufficient detail about the offense or the subject. Third, some databases contain only felonies or contain only offenses where a state corrections unit was involved. Fourth, the database may not carry subsequent information such as a pardon or some other matter that could render an item not reportable under the FCRA.

Name Variations — An electronic search of a vendor's database may not be able to recognize variations in a subject name, which a person would notice if looking at the index. The applicant may have been arrested under a different first name, or some variation of first and middle name. A female applicant may have a record under her maiden name.

Timeliness — There is always the possibility that the records in a vendor database are stale to some extent. The vendor may only enter new data at intervals that may lag behind the timeliness of the available index from the corresponding state or county agency. Generally, this means that the most current offenses are the ones least likely to appear in a search of a vendor database.

Criminal record vendors should make clear what data they are providing when their customers are performing a search of that vendor's database. These searches are ancillary and can be very useful, but proceed with caution. In other words, it cannot be assumed that a search of a proprietary criminal history database solely meets the level of due diligence required to be compliant with the FCRA.

Lester S Rosen[7]

Using Credit Headers as Criminal Record Pointers

The major credit bureaus contain files on hundreds of millions of people and credit header reports can be a powerful tool to address the problem of knowing where to look for criminal records.

Credit headers are, at their most basic, credit reports without any credit information. They only contain the "headings" of credit reports, which is primarily identifying information such as name, and current and past addresses.

Some vendors have a program in which a credit header is ordered and the past addresses are used to order criminal records from the locales in which the person has resided. It can be a slick tool, particularly if the header-to-county criminal record jurisdiction is automated. For example, an employer might decide to order a criminal record from every county where his applicant had resided the past three years. The vendor would order a header report, and his system would determine if there were multiple addresses.

---

[7] Lester S. Rosen, author of *The Safe Hiring Manual*, ©, BRB Publications, www.brbpub.com

If so, the vendor would cross-reference the addresses against his county directory and automatically order the requisite criminal records.

Adjoining County Database

An up-and-coming tool offered by a few vendors is an adjoining county locator. This tool provides employers with adjoining county information, including relative population of adjoining counties. This helps employers make more informed and complete searches.

For example, assume an employer requests a count criminal record from "Podunk County." Vendors offering the adjoining county locater could find adjoining counties and provide them to the employer. If one of the counties was high population "Gotham County," the employer might well choose to order a criminal record from both Podunk and Gotham counties and compound the value of the search.

Author Tip

The *Ultimate County Locator With Adjoining County Search*[8] is a CD and database product that lists adjoining counties of every county in the U.S., and lets you cross-reference ZIP Codes or place names to counties. The database also lists those counties that adjoin Canada or Mexico.

Where to Find a Vendor

We list several good sources below. When you search for a vendor using a search engine on the Internet, you will find a myriad of screening companies. Some of the more professional websites can indicate their high level of technical expertise and ability to meet fast turnaround times. That is all well and good, but be sure to look or ask for their statements on compliance with FCRA. If they respond to your FCRA inquiry with a "of course we have Fine Criminal Record Access," you should suddenly remember you are late for a meeting.

As we have discussed however, many industries have their own specific laws and nuances regarding criminal records. If you are able, talk to others in your industry to determine what vendor they use. What you are looking for is a criminal records vendor who might "specialize" in your industry.

---

[8] *The Ultimate County Locator With Adjoining County Search*, © BRB Publications, Tempe, AZ; 800-929-3811 or visit www.brbpub.com

The first bullet below is a site that lists 250+ of the nation's leading screening firms. The second bullet refers to specialty vendors and record retrievers.

- www.brbpub.com Click on the section called *Screening firms* and you will be able to search among 250+ of the nation's leading screening companies. Also, this site is an excellent source to find specialty vendors. Click on *Sources and Search Firms*.

- www.preemploymentdirectory.com/ The National Institute for the Prevention of Workplace Violence offers an excellent list of screening firms. Firms pay to be on this list.

- *The Manual to Online Public Records*[9] has an entire section dedicated to finding specialty vendors. This book is available at many bookstores, and can be ordered through most U.S. bookstores.

How to Choose the Best Vendor for You

You will not see the consumer magazines reviewing the different criminal record services and issuing "best buys" any time soon. However, like a consumer magazine, the information here can help to point out a provider's attributes that you should evaluate before making a decision.

The business of criminal record retrieval is more of a service than a product. It probably won't always be so. Someday you may be able to choose a criminal record service by price and turnaround time. All systems will be computerized, right down to the municipal court level. Criminal records will become a commodity. Today they are not. It is a service because there are so many variables. Knowledge — operational, legal and otherwise — affects the quality of the service as much as price and turnaround. The following are some attributes you can use to compare vendors.

Consider Vendor Accuracy

Accuracy can be hard to gauge. You can ask if the vendor "salts" his requests with known criminal records on a random basis. You can do the same to the vendor if you have some known records in a given jurisdiction.

One of the biggest causes of "inaccuracy" in criminal records is actually misidentification. In fact, the criminal record is accurate, but not accurate for the individual on which it was ordered. This usually happens in instances when a record is ordered on a subject with a common name or the individual's identifying information at the jurisdiction is incomplete. This will be discussed in detail in the next chapter, but for purposes here, look at an example of the vendor's criminal record report. You

---

[9] *The Manual to Online Public Records*, © Facts on Demand Press, Tempe, AZ; 800-929-3811.

should be able to readily distinguish between the information you used to request the search and the information that was actually returned from that jurisdiction. Better is a section on the report that highlights discrepancies between the two.

Consider Vendor Knowledge

The most accurate report in the world is of limited value if you do not fully understand what it means. Most vendors will help you decipher unusual reports, and some have a glossary with common terms and charges defined. If they do not, you may start with the glossary and common abbreviations section of this book.

A report that includes coding and ambiguous abbreviations may look impressive in your file, but how meaningful is it? Can you explain what it means in court? For all reports, except those you deal with regularly, interpretation assistance can be very important. Some information vendors offer searches for information they really do not know much about through sources they only use occasionally. Protecting their credibility or their professional pride sometimes prohibits them from disclosing their limitations — until you ask the right questions.

A vendor also should be knowledgeable about laws regarding the use of criminal record information. This includes the FCRA as well as EEOC information discussed later in this book. If you are in an industry with some unique requirements, connecting up with a vendor with knowledge and experience in your industry is an excellent benefit.

Consider the Vendor's Ancillary Services

Database, adjoining county and credit header-assisted searches were discussed earlier. If you believe these services could improve your results, look for a vendor who offers them.

What is the Turnaround Time?

The faster the better as long as it is not traded for accuracy. The vendor should publish an expected turnaround schedule for each state served, and have a standard for counties.

Consider Price

Do you get what you pay for? Yeah, this little homily probably has a grain of truth, but on the other hand, there are people who go to different car dealerships and buy identical cars and the price they pay differs by thousands. Buyer beware. One of them made a "best buy," and one of them paid more than he should have. The fair price could be somewhere in between.

With that said, there are a lot of hucksters who have opened themselves a little website, bought a phone, and gone into the criminal record business. They may be less expensive — until their erroneous report causes you to hire or fire someone you should not, the turnaround is not what they said it would be, or their lack of knowledge catches up to them, or you, in other ways.

Consider the Locale

"I lost my glasses in the alley, but the light is better out here on the street corner."

This is a punch line to an old joke, but instructive when choosing a vendor. With the Internet and other computerized ordering and delivering systems, the locale of your vendor and proximity to you should not be an issue, but it might be. A vendor in the state capital might offer quicker access to state agency records. A vendor might be able to deliver a hard copy of a document overnight from the local courthouse.

Summary

All of the above factors are useful to compare vendors. Our best advice when choosing a vendor: talk to the vendor's customers. They have first-hand knowledge of that vendor's accuracy, turnaround, and overall knowledge.

If you are a user in a specialized industry, or you have unique requirements, it also may behoove you to determine how many other customers in your industry that vendor has.

Chapter 7

Evaluate Your Record Request Process

I Really Want to Know...Who Are You?

—The Who

Ever wonder if the rock band *The Who* ever ordered criminal records on their roadies? Ah, probably not. In any event, if you have decided to order criminal records on job applicants, you should look at several issues within your criminal record process.

The record request process involves a number of steps. These steps should be followed whether you plan to access the records yourself or if you plan to use a vendor.

Proper identification — and recognition of improper identification before action is taken — is of primary importance. Two other processes you should examine are the use of misdemeanor records and proper documentation.

Identification Issues

A key issue in using criminal records is evaluating whether the information you have received pertains to the person on whom you inquired. It sounds so simple. Yet, more criminal record legal trouble starts here more than anywhere else.

There are two categories of methodology used to identify individuals when ordering criminal records.

Biometric Identifiers   Demographics

It is important to understand the strengths and limitations of both.

Biometric Systems

Biometric systems measure an individual's unique physical characteristics. The most common biometric identifiers are fingerprints and retina scans. Of these, fingerprints are far more common and the only biometric identifier in use for criminal record matching. The use of other biometrics such as DNA and retina scans are found in the criminal justice field, but their use for matching an individual to past records is novel.

The problem is that existing technology for storing, copying, and matching these great biometric identifiers — fingerprints, photographs and retina scans — makes their use slow and expensive. Nevertheless, the definition of "expensive" has changed since the war on terrorism began. Fingerprinting applications have been jump-started, and prices for them are expected to decrease. Although rarely used by the general public, fingerprinting will become more common. As mentioned earlier, fingerprinting drivers who apply for new or renewed hazardous material endorsements has been proposed and the means of implementation is under study. A short discussion on the fingerprinting process is in order.

Fingerprints

Fingerprint identification is based upon the fact that individual fingerprints have unique characteristics. These characteristics are whorls, arches, loops, ridge endings, and ridge bifurcations.

Many fingerprints today are still taken the way they were decades ago: with paper and ink. The fingerprints are taken and put on a "ten-print" card. This card is then scanned and digitized for matching purposes.

Finger scan systems can be broadly categorized into two types—verification systems and identification systems. It is important to understand the distinction, and the cost between the two systems varies several hundredfold.

Verification systems capture the flat image of a finger and perform a one-to-one verification. That is, the original print is compared to the subsequent print to determine if it matches. A verification is performed in a few seconds. Applications of this technology have filtered down to the private sector, including personal computer security.

On the other hand, identification systems are used by law enforcement to match one set of fingerprints against millions of other, current prints. To be accurate, this one-to-many task requires that the original fingerprints be of a higher standard of clarity. Currently, a basic fingerprint identification system used simply to capture, digitize and transmit fingerprints costs more than $10,000.

As discussed earlier, few employers have been granted statutory authority to use fingerprints in order to the FBI's NCIC database. As a result, for criminal record searches, most employers will continue to use non-biometric identifiers—name, DOB, address, etc. In the business, the term used for this type of matching criteria is "demographics."

Demographic Identifiers

Using demographic identifiers means using items such as name, SSN, address, DOB, or other non-physical characteristics in order to identify a person.

Every person's fingerprint is unique. Every person's name is not, even when combined with a DOB. The SSN should be a unique identifier, but many criminal records do not have an SSN attached to it, and, imagine this: the criminal speaketh with forked tongue when asked for his correct SSN! (So, the number on this record winds up being the wrong one, maybe even yours.)

When using non-biometric identifiers, employers and the record retrievers need all the demographics they can get. Unfortunately there is a misconception on the part of some employers that a key demographic — the DOB — cannot be obtained from job applicants. Because of its importance, it deserves a detailed discussion. Then there is the problem of honest mistakes by intake clerks who mistype SSNs, DOBs, etc. We have seen records where there are multiple charges and, in accordance with normal procedure, the arresting authority fills out the identifiers for each charge. On the first charge, the year of birth is 1970, for the second 1971, for the third 1972, and so on. The same can and does occur with an SSN.

Asking for the Date of Birth

An area that gives many employers pause is asking applicants for their DOB. A correct DOB is very important when ordering a criminal record. Many jurisdictions ask that a DOB be included in a criminal record request. Some may not perform a name search without a DOB attached. The main reason for asking for a DOB, as discussed earlier, is to have another identifier. Criminal records frequently do not contain an SSN, and while using the name and DOB is not always conclusive, it certainly is quite rare for there to be two people with the same name and DOB, in the same jurisdiction.

The problem arises when employers are afraid to ask applicants their DOB. What's the reason for their fear? Since the EEOC prohibits age discrimination, some employers reason that they are much less likely to be accused of age discrimination if they do not know the age of the applicant.

The fact of the matter is that the EEOC does not prohibit employers from asking applicants for their DOB as long as it is asked for a legitimate, non-discriminatory reason and not used for an impermissible purpose. In practice, asking for DOB should be done uniformly, not just on select applicants. Obtaining and providing a full DOB does not violate the Age Discrimination Employment Act (ADEA) for in background screening.

In fact, the EEOC has put out an 11-page guidance document regarding job advertising, and pre-employment inquiries — such as those asked for on printed employment applications — under the ADEA. See www.eeoc.gov/policy/adea.html. You may be interested to know that the chairman of the EEOC who signed this document into law was U.S. Supreme Court Justice Clarence Thomas. Would it be a safe bet that during his confirmation hearing Justice Thomas may have later wished for a few good hardball, age-related inquiries if they would make some other questions go away?

In any event, a copy of the 1989 EEOC guidance document that addresses the subject of asking for the DOB is provided in Chapter 10.

Matching the Date of Birth with the Name

A jurisdiction may be using a name and DOB from the employer to make a match. Many employers believe that a full first and last name with a DOB is unique. It is not. As an exercise, pick a first and last name, and DOB. Assume the chances of there being another person with the same first and last name and a matching DOB are only one in one million. Calculated, there are about 300 of these combinations in the U.S. The fact is, however, that the chances are much greater than one in one million for most names. There are a lot of common first names — David, John, Debbie, and Karen — and a whole lot of Smiths, Joneses, and other ubiquitous surnames. That's not to mention the possibility of identity theft.

The lesson in all this is:

> *Look very carefully at any criminal records for identifying information that does **not match** your subject's information.*

Do not just assume that the information returned applies to your subject. For example, if you order information on John Doe, 1/1/61 and a record comes back on John Quincy Doe, 1/1/61, be sure to ascertain your subject's middle name. If you order a record on Jane Doe, DOB of 12/12/62, SSN of 123456789 and a record comes back on Jane Doe, 12/12/62, SSN of 12345678, do not automatically assume it is Jane — but do not assume it isn't. Many records contain an address. If that address was not included in the credit-header information or on the driver's license, then the record probably does not belong to your applicant.

A solution could be as simple as running a check on the SSN, or questioning Jane and speaking with the company or jurisdiction that supplied the record. The solution may come down to this: have your applicant fingerprinted and submit those prints for comparison with those taken at the time of arrest.

Again, simply not reviewing the information they have received is a common area where employers stub their toe when ordering criminal records. They order a report on one person, get back a record on another and, because they have not looked carefully at the record, they mistakenly take some adverse action against their applicant or employee. It is certainly not fair to disqualify an individual for having a name similar to one on a criminal record, or any public record. This mistake should be avoided.

The Importance of Proper Documentation

On the next page is an example of a criminal Background Check Release Form that appears in *25 Essential Lessons for Employee Management* by employment expert Dennis DeMey and published by Facts on Demand Press. You may download copies of employment related forms by going to www.brbpub.com/forms/.

This form has fields for commonly used demographic data and also includes a place for the applicant to give his permission for your search. It should be noted that the vast majority of record requests do not require a notary signature and seal.

Sample Criminal Record Release Form

Criminal Background Check – Release Form

NAME_____

          Last   First   Middle   Maiden

ADDRESS_____

          Street   City   State

ALIASES OR OTHER NAMES USED _____

DATE OF BIRTH _____ AGE ____ RACE _____ SEX ____

SOCIAL SECURITY # _____

DRIVER'S LICENSE # _____ STATE _____

I hereby authorize _____ of _____

              Name   Name of Company

_____

              Company Address/City/State/Zip

to conduct a criminal background check on myself through the

_____ .

             Name of State and Police Agency

X_____

        Applicant Signature

STATE of:_____ This Instrument was acknowledged before me this ____ day of

COUNTY of:_____ _____, 20 _____, by _____

My commission will expire: _____AS WITNESS.

_____

_____

      Notary Public   No.

Pros and Cons of Using Misdemeanor Records

Perhaps you are thinking you will not hire anyone with a felony conviction, but you will let misdemeanor records slide. Perhaps you will ignore arrest records unless there is more than one in the past year, but a felony conviction — regardless of age — will always disqualify an applicant. Whoops, it is not that easy. Here are some facts to consider before deciding how to evaluate misdemeanor and felony records, as well as convictions and arrests.

Misdemeanor records were defined earlier as "offenses of a minor degree and anything less than a felony." Misdemeanors are often discarded as a factor by some, like "college records," e.g., "if-not-for- the-grace-of-God-there-go-I" records.

Well, sometimes misdemeanors *are* minor. Let those of you without misdemeanor sin cast the first stone while we duck. Before dismissing them though, consider:

1. A misdemeanor record may be more pertinent than a felony.

How? Imagine you own a construction company and your crew needs some extra hands at an excavation project. One individual who applies for a job looks to be a good prospect, but he has a conviction for felony embezzlement. Should this automatically disqualify the applicant? After all, if while that person is on the job he wants to slyly peer around and sneak a dirt clod or two in his pocket to take home, well then, no harm is done.

On the other hand, assume you are hiring drivers to haul away the dirt fill that Mr. Sticky Fingers has not spirited away in his pockets. One prospect who applies for this position has "just" one misdemeanor on his record: a Driving While Intoxicated (DWI) conviction. If you hire this individual, and, while drinking, he has an accident that injures someone, you might as well buy a mirror and start practicing saying, "it was just a misdemeanor" without looking dumb. Good luck.

The same analysis can be applied to felonies as well. Sometimes a crime becomes a "felony" for political reasons rather than a true measure of fault or risk. For example, possession of certain eagle feathers is a felony, but how many jobs are affected by such a conviction.

The point? Consider the severity of the crime in relation to the *job-relatedness* of the crime.

2. Many recorded misdemeanors are for felony crimes.

Sad to say, but the fact that an offense was recorded as a misdemeanor does not mean that the crime committed was a misdemeanor. Plea Bargains — a plea of guilt to a lesser offense in return for a lighter sentence — are common in the legal system. Overloaded court systems, prosecutors with a challenging case to prove, and savvy defense attorneys all contribute to the fact that charges are often downgraded in return for defendant's guilty plea.

Author Tip

If you have an applicant with a few "minor" convictions, do some digging to determine what happened in the legal proceeding process. Look at an arrest record —if the law allows — and compare it to the applicant's version of the incident. If this is a key position and the record troubles you, you may wish to call the court or prosecutor to find out what you can. We have noted that prosecutors are willing to help. Sometimes they are more forthcoming to an attorney so you might consider having your lawyer call.

If you are an employer using criminal records, make sure you do not make a decision based on mistaken identity by using all the identification information at your disposal and examine criminal records received for identifiers. Making an adverse decision on an applicant based on a criminal record that does not pertain to him/her is one of the more common mistakes made. It is a mistake that can cause real upset for the subject of the search. We urge those using criminal record reports to use great care when reviewing them.

If you do obtain a criminal record on an individual and it is correct, you should determine whether the crime(s) was a felony or misdemeanor. However, this felony/misdemeanor evaluation should be done in conjunction with job-relatedness. A felony – though more "serious" – may not be as big a factor as a more "minor" misdemeanor.

Chapter 8

Compliance With the Fair Credit Reporting Act

The law is not an end in itself, nor does it provide ends. It is preeminently a means to serve what we think is right.

— Justice William J. Brennan, Jr.

As discussed earlier in this book, the vast majority of criminal records used outside of law enforcement are used for employment purposes. If you are obtaining criminal records from a vendor and using these records to make decisions (e.g., you are not merely reselling the records) a law called the Fair Credit Reporting Act (FCRA) will almost certainly regulate the vendor. As discussed earlier, if a vendor does not have a good knowledge of the FCRA, it is a good indicator to choose another vendor.

The FCRA directly affects areas as diverse as what information can be contained on a report, to what notifications to make to the subject prior to the criminal record inquiry.

FCRA and Employers

The first hurdle to understand is that the "Fair Credit Reporting Act" is really misnamed. It should be called the "Fair Credit *and Employment* Reporting Act." The lack of "employment" in the title has contributed to the lack of understanding and knowledge of this law in employment screening. If you are an employer, ordering criminal records on potential employees, you will want to be familiar with this law.

There are three main areas in which the FCRA can affect an employer ordering criminal records—

- **Releases** — What notifications must be made and permissions granted from the subject of the search?

- **Arrest vs. convictions, seven-year rule** — What information can appear on the report, and what must be suppressed?
- **Aged public record for employment purposes** — With the vendor databases records, what additional notifications to the subject must be performed?

Before detailing specifics, it is helpful to have a general overview of the act.

Overview of The Fair Credit Reporting Act (FCRA)

In general, the FCRA manages the relationship between the parties who are involved in informational transactions that fall under the Act. Usually, there are at least three affected parties:

- The provider of the information
- The subject of the information
- The user of the information

Before going further, several terms must be defined.

Consumer Reporting Agency

A *Consumer Reporting Agency (CRA)* is "any person which, for monetary fees, dues, or on a cooperative nonprofit basis, regularly engages in whole or in part in the practice of assembling or evaluating consumer credit information or other information on consumers for the purpose of furnishing consumer reports to third parties, and which uses any means or facility of interstate commerce for the purpose of furnishing consumer reports." 15 U.S.C. §1681b (f)

Consumer Report

The term consumer report was used in the definition above. A *Consumer Report* is "any written, oral, or other communication of any information by a consumer reporting agency bearing on a consumer's credit worthiness, credit standing, credit capacity, character, general reputation, personal characteristics, or mode of living which is used or expected to be used or collected in whole or in part for the purpose of serving as a factor in establishing the consumer's eligibility for:

- credit or insurance to be used primarily for personal, family, or household purposes;
- employment purposes; or
- any other purpose authorized under section 1681b, §1681a(d)(1)."

What are Employment Purposes?

Employment purposes, when used in connection with a consumer report means " a report used for the purpose of evaluating a consumer for employment, promotion, reassignment or retention as an employee." 15 U.S.C. §1681a(h)

What is the Purpose of the FCRA?

The purpose of the FCRA is to facilitate the flow of essential information concerning an individual's background, while at the same time protecting that individual's privacy rights and minimizing the risks of inaccurate reports. This is accomplished through the imposition of statutory and regulatory safeguards imposed on CRAs and the users and providers of the information. The regulations are designed to ensure the accuracy of the information being provided.

A failure to comply with the FCRA's requirements exposes the CRA as well as the CRA customer, to both civil liability, 15 U.S.C. §1681o. Unlawful obtaining of information may result in criminal penalties, 15 U.S.C. §1681q.

In addition to the federal FCRA, there are state versions of the FCRA. Often, these state versions are more restrictive than the federal FCRA. Their interrelationship will be detailed later.

The Sword and the Shield

The FCRA is both a triple-edged sword *and* a triple-sided shield. The sword imposes obligations on providers, users, and consumers. The shield protects.

The Sword Hanging over CRAs

Criminal record vendors must comply with a host of regulatory guidelines, among the most critical is to "use reasonable procedures to insure maximum possible accuracy" of the information they report. Failure to comply with these requirements can expose the CRA to civil penalties. In addition, CRAs must provide to users a notice of their responsibilities. This is shown in the Appendix. Incidentally, there is another entity regulated by the FTC. These are the *furnishers* of information. This would include creditors reporting credit transaction histories. We have not seen any attempt to enforce "furnisher obligations" on courts or state agencies that maintain criminal records. A copy of the notice to furnishers is shown in the Appendix.

The Shield Protecting CRAs

On the other hand, the FCRA recognizes the need for the free flow of essential information. It recognizes that mistakes will be made and that some information is subjective, e.g., the "truth" of an event can be viewed differently by the consumer and reporting company. The FCRA therefore offers CRAs a shield against defamation and slander lawsuits if they act without malice and a modicum of care. 15 U.S.C. §1681h(e).

The Sword Hanging over Users

The sword hanging over users is not very sharp but is does have a little edge to it. Among the more prominent requirements imposed on users is—

1. The duty to inform job applicants before the users order information from a CRA that a consumer report will be obtained and obtain the consumer consent (an employer can refuse to hire someone who will not consent to such a report).

2. Notify the consumer before the user "takes adverse action along with providing a copy of the consumer report in question to the consumer," (e.g., not hire the person based in whole or part upon the information received).

3. Provide the consumer with the Federal Trade Commission-authored "summary of their rights" notice. A copy of this notice is shown in the Appendix.

4. Provide notice to the consumer stating the adverse action and how to contact the CRA.

The Shield Protecting Users

Most of the shield afforded to users is provided by the CRA. If an employment decision is made based on erroneous information, an employer obtaining the information on his own will be defending his data retrieval practices, but the employer using a CRA is usually able to defer this liability to the CRA, provided he chooses his CRA with some due diligence.

The Sword Hanging over Consumers

The consumer's ability to successfully sue CRAs is somewhat constrained by the FCRA. Consumers will not "win the lottery" by suing a CRA even when the CRA has, in fact, reported erroneous information that harmed the individual—provided the CRA has taken reasonable precautions to report accurate information. While the FCRA mandates that CRAs must verify information if disputed by consumers, the FCRA gives them time — about 30 days — to verify and correct the information. While a consumer is not required to dispute information with the CRA, damages would be greatly reduced in some instances where the CRA would not have reason to doubt the accuracy of the information and it would not be liable at all unless the consumer made it aware of the inaccuracy. However, without the FCRA, a consumer would have no right to have the provider of the report investigate the accuracy of something in a report, let alone within 30 days. Thus, while the consumer may lose the right to sue for defamation, he gains the ability to quickly resolve an issue and to minimize any damage inaccurate information might cause.

For the most part however, the FCRA does not threaten, but instead protects consumers.

The Shield Protecting Consumers

This is probably the biggest goal of the FCRA. Most of the law deals with consumer protections, from releases that must be provided to the individual, to the information that can be reported, to the procedures in case of disputed accuracy.

Primary Effects of the FCRA on Employers Using a Vendor to Obtain Criminal Records

Criminal records obtained from a vendor and used for employment purposes are "consumer reports," as defined by the FCRA. So are other reports obtained from vendors, such as driving records, credit reports, and employment histories. The following discussion on releases and notifications is not exclusive to criminal records.

There are three primary areas where the FCRA will affect employers who obtain criminal records from criminal record vendors. As discussed above, the FCRA affects the entire relationship, and the three areas discussed below pertain to the major considerations of employers using criminal records obtained from a vendor.

Releases and Notifications

1. Written Notification Before Ordering

Before ordering a criminal record from a vendor who you intend to use as a factor in establishing an individual's eligibility for employment, the FCRA requires that:

> (i) a clear and conspicuous disclosure has been made in writing to the consumer at any time before the report is procured or caused to be procured, in a document that consists solely of the disclosure, that a consumer report may be obtained for employment purposes; 15 U.S.C. §1681b(b)(2)(A)

So, "a clear and conspicuous disclosure" must be made to the applicant. It cannot be buried in the job application, but must be a separate document. In the next paragraph, the FCRA requires the consumer to authorize the company to obtain the report.

> (ii) the consumer has authorized in writing (which authorization may be made on the document referred to in clause (i)) the procurement of the report by that person. 15 U.S.C. §1681b(b)(2)(B)

This is a detailed section of the law, in that it goes to the level of mandating what can and cannot be on the written disclosure. CRAs, for their part, must obtain certification from the employer that he has given the required notice and received written authorization from the employee or applicant to obtain the report. So, the FCRA imposes the obligation on the employer to disclose that a consumer report will be obtained and obtain releases, but it also imposes the obligation on the CRA to obtain certification from the employer that it will be done. The CRA does not receive a copy of this release. Rather the FCRA allows it to rely upon certification. Undoubtedly this is the case to avoid excessive exchange of paper in an increasingly electronic age.

2. Notices Required Before and After "Adverse Action" is Taken

The FCRA also requires that before an employer takes any "adverse action" based in whole or part on the criminal record, the employer must provide the applicant or employee a copy of the report and a written description of the consumer's rights as written by the Federal Trade Commission. The Federal Trade Commission (FTC) is the primary agency that enforces and interprets FCRA issues. The FCRA does not set forth any period of time between providing the notice that the employer take adverse action and actually taking that action. The FTC has stated that the time depends on many factors but the time should be sufficient to allow the consumer to discuss the report with the employer. FTC Opinion Letter, *Lewis June 11, 1998.* The employer is not required to take any action based on what the consumer has related. A copy of this notice can be found in the Appendix.

> *Adverse Action* is defined by the FCRA as "a denial of employment or any other decision for employment purposes that adversely affects any current or prospective employee." {15 U.S.C. §1681a}

Aside from the above requirements *before* taking adverse action, there are other, somewhat redundant, steps that must be taken *after* the adverse action.

> (1) provide oral, written, or electronic notice of the adverse action to the consumer;
>
> (2) provide to the consumer orally, in writing, or electronically the name, address, and telephone number of the consumer reporting agency (including a toll-free telephone number established by the agency if the agency compiles

and maintains files on consumers on a nationwide basis) that furnished the report to the person; and a statement that the consumer reporting agency did not make the decision to take the adverse action and is unable to provide the consumer the specific reasons why the adverse action was taken; and

(3) provide to the consumer an oral, written, or electronic notice of the consumer's right to obtain, under section 612 [§ 1681j], a free copy of a consumer report on the consumer from the consumer reporting agency referred to in paragraph (2), which notice shall include an indication of the 60-day period under that section for obtaining such a copy; and to dispute, under section 611 [§ 1681i], with a consumer reporting agency the accuracy or completeness of any information in a consumer report furnished by the agency. {615(a)} 15 U.S.C. §1681m(a), §615a

3. A FCRA Notification Exception

The prior written notice and release, as well as the adverse action requirements, have been modified for trucking companies that pre-screen commercial drivers applying for a job remotely. It should be noted here that while the FCRA may waive the prior written notice, there are some states that still require a written release be obtained before ordering certain information that will be used for employment screening. Driving record (MVR) reporting — in some states — is an example of information where written permission prior to ordering is required in all cases involving employment. The availability of driving records is also regulated by the Driver's Privacy Protection Act (DPPA), 18 U.S.C. §2721 et seq. Each state has implemented the DPPA with its own statute. The availability of information and the procedure to obtain that information vary. This is another example of why it is difficult for a non-CRA to conduct an effective and thorough background check

No doubt about it, the following information detailing the commercial driver limited exemption is dry-as-a-sawpit stuff. If you are not a trucking company hiring drivers by phone, mail, or computer, skip it. If you are a trucking company, find a vendor who knows your business.

The *government-speak* for the disclosure-and-release waiver in those instances when a trucking company is pre-screening applicants from a remote location is as follows:

(i) the consumer is applying for a position over which the Secretary of Transportation has the power to establish qualifications and maximum hours of service pursuant to the provisions of section 31502 of title 49, or a position subject to safety regulation by a state transportation agency. This provision, 15 U.S.C. §1681m(a), was added in 1998. The proposed legislation included all consumers who apply for a job remotely. Congress, in its wisdom, limited the provision to truck drivers; and

(ii) as of the time at which the person procures the report or causes the report to be procured the only interaction between the consumer and the person in connection with that employment application has been by mail, telephone, computer, or other similar means. {604(b)(2)(B) and (C)}

In addition, the adverse action requirements have been amended, as follows:

(B) Application of drivers by mail, telephone, computer, or other similar means.

(i) If a consumer described in subparagraph (C) applies for employment by mail, telephone, computer, or other similar means, and if a person who has procured a consumer report on the consumer for employment purposes takes adverse action on the employment application based in whole or in part on the report, then the person must provide to the consumer to whom the report relates, in lieu of the notices required under subparagraph (A) of this section and under section 615(a), within 3 business days of taking such action, an oral, written, or electronic notification—

a. that adverse action has been taken based in whole or in part on a consumer report received from a consumer reporting agency;

b. of the name, address, and telephone number of the consumer reporting agency that furnished the consumer report (including a toll-free telephone number established by the agency if the agency compiles and maintains files on consumers on a nationwide basis);

c. that the consumer reporting agency did not make the decision to take the adverse action and is unable to provide to the consumer the specific reasons why the adverse action was taken; and

d. that the consumer may, upon providing proper identification, request a free copy of a report and may dispute with the consumer reporting agency the accuracy or completeness of any information in a report.

(ii) If, under clause (B)(i)(IV), the consumer requests a copy of a consumer report from the person who procured the report, then, within 3 business days of receiving the consumer's request, together with proper identification, the person must send or provide to the consumer a copy of a report and a copy of the consumer's rights as prescribed by the Federal Trade Commission under section 609(c)(3)

(C) Scope. Subparagraph (B) shall apply to a person procuring a consumer report on a consumer in connection with the consumer's application for employment only if

(i) the consumer is applying for a position over which the Secretary of Transportation has the power to establish qualifications and maximum hours of service pursuant to the provisions of section 31502 of title 49, or a position subject to safety regulation by a State transportation agency; and

(ii) (ii) as of the time at which the person procures the report or causes the report to be procured the only interaction between the consumer and the person in connection with that employment application has been by mail, telephone, computer, or other similar means. {604(b)(3)(B) and (C)}

Told you it was dry stuff. Again, this is a narrow exception for trucking companies hiring commercial drivers in certain instances. These nuances are found throughout federal and state laws that impact background screening. Some of the legislation lacks apparent logic because it is the product of the political process.

FCRA Restrictions on Reporting Arrest Information

The FCRA also affects employers obtaining criminal records from criminal record vendors because it prescribes limits on what data can be provided. A criminal record contains information on a consumer's character, personal characteristics, or mode of living and thus falls within the definition of a consumer report. 15 U.S.C. §1681a(d)(1), §603(d)(1). It also limits the amount of time arrest information may be reported. This does not apply to conviction information.

An Arrest was previously defined as follows:

An *Arrest* is the taking of an individual into custody by law enforcement personnel (i.e. the person's behavior is arrested) in order to charge him with an illegal act.

A Conviction, in contrast to an arrest, was previously defined as follows:

A *Conviction* is a finding of guilt after a judicial trial. However, some states have expanded this definition to include such dispositions as a "deferred sentence, adjudication withheld." These are proceedings in which the defendant admits guilt, but if he behaves himself for a specified period of time, the charges are dismissed. With recent changes, these dismissals may still be considered convictions.

However, since the FCRA does not define the term "conviction," what a "conviction" is can vary from state to state and from statute to statute. Have we confused you yet?

The FCRA states that a CRA may not report arrest information that is older than seven years. In the fed's inimitable legal-speak, it is worded as follows:

> (a) *Information excluded from consumer reports.* Except as authorized under subsection (b) of this section, no consumer reporting agency may make any consumer report containing any of the following items of information:
>
>> (2) Civil suits, civil judgments, and records of arrest that from date of entry, antedate the report by more than seven years or until the governing statute of limitations has expired, whichever is the longer period. {605(a)(2)}

A clear distinction is made for conviction information. Conviction information may be reported without limitation. The FCRA spells it out it in subsection (5). Continuing from part (b) above, they are saying no CRA can report...

>> (5) Any other adverse item of information, other than records of convictions of crimes which antedates the report by more than seven years. {605(a)(5)}

The FCRA originally limited the reporting of "conviction" to seven years as well. This restriction was dropped in 1998.

A FCRA Arrest Information Exception

Of course, it would not be federal law without an exception would it? Above, in part (a) it says "...except as authorized under subsection (b)..."

Subsection (b) allows arrest data older than 7 years to be reported if the report will be used in connection with a job where the annual salary is (or expected to be) $75,000 or more.

> (b) *Exempted cases.* The provisions of subsection (a) of this section are not applicable in the case of any consumer credit report to be used in connection with...
>
>> (3) the employment of any individual at an annual salary which equals, or which may reasonably be expected to equal $75,000, or more. 15 U.S.C. §1681c(b)

FCRA Caveat

If the federal FCRA was the only law pertaining to the use of arrest records, we could be on our merry way. Unfortunately, some states also have laws that restrict the reporting of arrest and conviction information. Some states do not want employers to use *any* arrest information or only some arrest information. Some state laws still limit conviction information to seven years and some states prohibit the consideration of some specific convictions no matter how recent. In other words, some state laws are in direct conflict with the federal FCRA. In the next chapter, the federal and state law interrelation is discussed in detail. The point is, while the federal FCRA guidelines discussed above are the norm, they are not absolute in all states.

Using Aged Public Records for Employment Purposes

Criminal record vendors providing public record information to companies intending to use the information for employment purposes — and the information is likely to have an adverse impact on the individual — must either insure the information they are providing is up-to-date, or, they must notify the subject of the report that a report is being provided along with the name and address of the person to whom it is being reported. 15 U.S.C. §1681k, §613

When will this come into play with a criminal record vendor? When a database contains public record data that is not the most complete or up-to-date available from actual public sources, **and** the record contains derogatory information, e.g., an arrest or conviction record.

> **An Example—** A vendor has obtained Watadoosie County's entire database and the database contains less than up-to-date info. ACME Employer requests a criminal record on an individual and that vendor reports a record containing an arrest and conviction. The subject of the search must be notified by the vendor that a report has been provided to ACME, along with ACME's address.
>
> The record vendor warehouses criminal records previously ordered by other clients. ACME requests a criminal record. The vendor searches his database and informs ACME that a criminal record was ordered on the subject by another employer two months previously. ACME elects to obtain the two-month-old record instead of ordering a fresh record. If the two-month-old record is clear, e.g., it does not contain a record of arrest or conviction, the notice need not be sent by the vendor, as there is nothing on the report "likely to have an adverse effect upon the consumer."

What about these searches using aged data? A database search can be FCRA compliant, but wholly deficient for employment due diligence. If an employer searches a database that has not been updated in 60 days, recent information may be missed. For honest business practices and self-protection, the CRA should clearly state that it is accessing a database, and not "retrieving." If the vendor cuts a corner and the employer hires an individual because the retriever did not retrieve the proper record, and if the employer is sued, the retriever also could be sued. So, when a vendor states that his database searches are FCRA compliant, that is great — but it is not the only consideration.

Again, some states step into this area and prohibit some or all database records, e.g., Kentucky, KRS §367.310. See Chapters 11 and 12 for more detail. By now you should have caught on to the reality that there are multiple rules for reporting all kinds of information. Understanding this is not for the weak hearted. Are you up for this? If so, keep reading.

Using Records from Vendor Databases

In the previous chapter, database searches were discussed and it was noted that they could assist users by addressing three aspects of criminal record searching:

- Knowing where to look
- Turnaround time
- Cost

Database searches can be dynamite—but if you avail yourself of a vendor who uses them, insure that he is complying with the following FCRA requirement.

This requirement regarding aged public record for employment purposes is found at 15 U.S.C. §1681k, section 613 of the FCRA. The FCRA text is as follows:

Public record information for employment purposes

(a) *In general.* A consumer reporting agency which furnishes a consumer report for employment purposes and which for that purpose compiles and reports items of information on consumers which are matters of public record and are likely to have an adverse effect upon a consumer's ability to obtain employment shall

1. at the time such public record information is reported to the user of such consumer report, notify the consumer of the fact that public record information is being reported by the consumer reporting agency, together with the name and address of the person to whom such information is being reported; or

2. maintain strict procedures designed to insure that whenever public record information which is likely to have an adverse effect on a consumer's ability to obtain employment is reported it is complete and up to date. For

purposes of this paragraph, items of public record relating to arrests, indictments, convictions, suits, tax liens, and outstanding judgments shall be considered up to date if the current public record status of the item at the time of the report is reported.

Oh, one more thing. The feds do grant themselves an exemption:

(b) *Exemption for national security investigations*. Subsection (a) does not apply in the case of an agency or department of the United States Government that seeks to obtain and use a consumer report for employment purposes, if the head of the agency or department makes a written finding as prescribed under section 15 U.S.C. §1681k(b).

Since there are state laws in direct conflict with the federal FCRA, and you must follow the state law in some instances. The next chapter details these instances.

Chapter 9

The Federal FCRA Interrelation with State FCRAs

Laws are like sausages.
It's better not to see them being made.
—Otto von Bismarck

When the German statesman Otto von Bismarck said the public should not watch sausage or laws being made, he was making a couple of points.

Explicit in the comment was that watching either of the processes was not a pretty sight. When making "law," unwritten deals are cut between incongruous allies who are interdependent on secret deals later denied.

Implicit was the thought that after the process, the laws and sausages would not look too bad. The finished law would be a blend of the various constituencies and while not perfect, perhaps a pretty good compromise.

The federal FCRA and its relationship with the various state FCRAs is different. The laws in and of themselves are kind of pretty, but when you take the finished product, e.g., how the federal and state FCRAs interrelate, it gets ugly and unduly complicated.

By most accounts, the original federal FCRA was a thoughtful, forward-looking piece of legislation. It certainly stood the test of time well, protecting users, consumers, and providers. The original law was enacted in October 1970, and while amended several times over the years, the amendments were, until the late 1990s, minor. The September 30, 1996 "amendment" was really a rewrite of the law. It was after this rewrite that the interrelationship between the federal and state FCRAs got ugly. The ugliness is seen, in great part, in our efforts to unravel the complexity and figure out — on a state-by-state basis — which law (federal or state) we should be trying to follow.

What Do Federal and State Interrelations Have To Do with Ordering Criminal Records?

As we saw in the previous chapter, Section 605 of the federal FCRA allows criminal record *conviction* information to be reported through a CRA in perpetuity. Non-conviction information must be, ahem, arrested after seven years, i.e., suppressed or hidden. So far, so good. The rub comes when you have a state with its own version of the FCRA, or employment statutes, in conflict with the federal version. Now you find yourself in a position where an interpretation based on the interrelation of the state and federal law will dictate what information you can receive from a criminal record provider.

Why is it so complicated?

Prior to the 1996 FCRA amendment, federal and state law (when a state law was present) was consistent. Furthermore, when there was a difference, the federal FCRA pre-empted the state law.

Prior to a 1998 amendment (Consumer Reporting Employment Clarification Act of 1998) there was no distinction made between arrests and convictions. The 1998 Act was retroactive to the effective date of the 1996 amendments. §7, PL 105-347. The FCRA simply stated that there were to be no:

> "Records of arrest, indictment, or conviction of crime which, for the date of disposition, release or parole, antedate the report by more than 7 years."

Unless–

> The report was to be used in connection with

- "(1) a credit transaction involving, or which may reasonably be expected to involve, a principal amount of **$50,000** or more;
- (2) the underwriting of life insurance involving, or which may reasonably be expected to involve, a face amount of **$50,000** or more; or
- (3) the employment of any individual at an annual salary which equals, or which may reasonably be expected to equal **$20,000** or more."

That was simple enough. The 1996 FCRA amendment **changed** the exceptions to read—

> "The report was to be used in connection with

- (1) a credit transaction involving, or which may reasonably be expected to involve, a principal amount of **$150,000** or more;

- (2) the underwriting of life insurance involving, or which may reasonably be expected to involve, a face amount of **$150,000** or more; or

- (3) the employment of any individual at an annual salary which equals, or which may reasonably be expected to equal **$75,000** or more."

As noted above, exactly one year after the 1996 amendment was effective there was another amendment entitled "The Consumer Reporting Employment Clarification Act of 1998." This clarification changed the *type* of information that could be reported to today's federal standard. It also created an FCRA reporting distinction between arrest information and conviction information. In 2003, the FCRA was again subject to major revisions which amended 15 U.S.C. §1681t to provide that the FCRA limitations on arrests and convictions pre-empted state laws on this data unless those state statutes were in effect on September 30, 1996.

Today, the FCRA allows conviction information to be reported by a CRA regardless of the record's age. Non-conviction records must be suppressed if they did not happen within the past seven years and do not meet the exceptions as outlined above. However, there are eleven states that have their own version of the FCRA, nine of which were in effect on September 30, 1996 and this pre-empts the FCRA. Some states still limit the release of *records with convictions* to seven years, and no more.

In summary, there is a slew of federal law and state laws dealing with exceptions to rules for the types of information that may be reported.

When in Conflict, Which Law — Federal or State — Pre-empts the Other?

The Federal FCRA provides the answer ... if you can decipher it.

Thank heaven the federal FCRA clears all this up with section 15 USC §1681t(a), *Relation to State Laws.* It says this:

> Except as provided in subsections (b) and (c), this title does not annul, alter, affect, or exempt any person subject to the provisions of this title from complying with the laws of any State with respect to the collection, distribution, or use of any information on consumers, or for the prevention or mitigation of identity theft except to the extent that those laws are inconsistent with any provision of this title, and then only to the extent of the inconsistency.

Okay, this is saying that the federal law does not overrule a state law unless it is "inconsistent" (this is not a self-defining term and creates significant legal issues when comparing the competing state statutes), and if it does, only the conflicting parts of the state law are overruled. There was that first sentence, though, about "except as provided in subsections (b) and (c)." Section (c) we can skip. However, Subsection (b) says:

> *General exceptions.* No requirement or prohibition may be imposed under the laws of any State
>
> (1) with respect to any subject matter regulated under
>
>> (E) section 605, relating to information in consumer reports, except that this subparagraph shall not apply to any State law in effect on September 30, 1996.

We don't know about you, but our heads are starting to hurt. Once this has been read about 40 times however, it can easily be determined that this says that the federal law prevails over the state law unless the state law was in effect on or before September 30, 1996. It is bad enough that the *General Exceptions* stopped here, but it tries to get worse.

Section 1681t goes on to list about 32 different subjects within the FCRA that may or may not be subject to a state enacting a law on that issue.

Now we are looking around for Werner Von Braun's pager number. The sum of this is that there are at least 52 potential sets of rules on what can be reported, FCRA, the 50 states and the District of Columbia.

Examples—

State A has a 7-year restriction in 1992. It has not updated its law to date. State law prevails.

State B had no law in 1996, but its legislature passed one that was more restrictive than the federal law in 1998. The federal law applies.

Summary of FCRA and State Law Interrelations — Good News for Users

It is a devilishly complex task to determine what information should be reported, but if you are a user of criminal records — say, as part of your duties as an employer — *there is good news.* You don't have to understand and monitor the intricacies of compliance because you are not at risk. Why? Because, *in regard to reporting information,* the FCRA and the state equivalents do not apply to you. They apply to the CRAs. CRAs are prohibited from reporting the information. As a recipient or user of the information, you are not prohibited by the FCRA from using the information.

What you do have to concern yourself with is the **use** of criminal record information — both arrest and conviction information. For employers, there are federal EEOC guidelines and there are also several states that prohibit employers from using arrest information and even some conviction information if the arrest information does not have a resulting conviction, or if the disposition is pending.

The following chapter deals with federal considerations when using criminal records for employment purposes. Following the federal chapter, state guidelines are detailed.

Chapter 10

Title VII and Criminal Records

Justice will only exist where those not affected by injustice are filled with the same amount of indignation as those who are affected.

–Plato

Determining how you feel about the issue as a moral or political matter is one thing. However, when you are an employer, many issues have already been decided for you. It is your responsibility to be aware of what is legal and what is not. When it is your business, you are considered accountable. When considering minorities, the main federal law dealing with the legality of criminal records is Title VII of the Civil Rights Act (www.eeoc.gov/policy/vii.html).

Criminal Records and Bias Employment Practices

What is "fair?" Title VII of the Civil Rights Act prohibits apparently neutral or "color blind" employment practices if these practices have a disparate impact against minorities or other protected groups.

Why this prohibition exists requires some explaining. Consider this scenario. Assume you were to receive employment applications by mail and had an independent third party delete any references to race. In addition, names, all addresses, and any other clues that someone might use to infer an individual's race were suppressed. Now, assume that criminal records checks were ordered and those found to have a criminal record of any severity were automatically disqualified. You might think that because you did not even know the race of the person being disqualified, you could not possibly be discriminating against minorities. You would be wrong.

The Use of Statistics

The Equal Employment Opportunity Commission (EEOC) enforces Title VII. The EEOC position is that "an employer's policy or practice of excluding individuals from employment on the basis of their conviction records has an adverse impact on Blacks and Hispanics in light of statistics showing that they are convicted at a rate disproportionately greater than their representation in the population." (Policy Statement on the Issue of Conviction Records Under Title VII [February 4,1987]).

The leading Title VII case on the issue of conviction records is Green v. Missouri Pacific Railroad Company. (523 F.2d 1290, 10 EPD ¶ 10, 314 (8th Cir. 1975). In this case, the court held that the defendant's policy of refusing employment to any person convicted of a crime other than a minor traffic offense had an adverse impact on Black applicants and was not justified by business necessity. In a second appeal following remand, the court upheld the district court's injunctive order prohibiting the defendant from using an applicant's conviction record as an absolute bar to employment, but allowed it to consider a prior criminal record as long as it constituted a "business necessity." The EEOC later expanded on "business necessity," and this subject will be addressed later.

The main point here however, is that an employer's policy or practice of excluding individuals from employment on the basis of their conviction records, although neutral on the face of the policy, may have an adverse impact on Black and Hispanics in light of statistics showing that they are convicted at a rate disproportionately greater than their representation in the population.

"May have" an adverse impact? Yes, statistics also can be used by the employer for defense. The EEOC has stated that "when the employer can present more narrowly drawn statistics showing either that Blacks and Hispanics are not convicted at a disproportionately greater rate or that there is no adverse impact in its own hiring process resulting from the convictions policy, then a no-cause determination would be appropriate." By "more narrowly drawn statistics," the EEOC means that "local, regional, or applicant flow data" may be different from the national statistics, and more appropriate. So, if an employer could prove that Whites in their town were evenly convicted in relation to their population with minority groups, the "blind" exclusion policy would probably cause no EEO problems.

Granted, few employers have a statistician on staff who is monitoring local and national rates of conviction, so it would be a task to turn around the "adverse impact" position with statistics. The key point for an employer to take away from all this is that the EEOC does presume that employers using criminal records as an absolute bar to employment has a disparate impact. So, this aspect of Title VII is something for the employer to be aware of when using criminal records *even though* his employment procedures may seem neutral. A "cookie cutter" or blanket policy of exclusion based on a criminal conviction is not the intelligent way for an employer to operate.

What are the EEOC's Guidelines?

Thus far, the EEOC and *conviction* records have been discussed. The EEOC also differentiates between arrest and conviction records.

EEOC Policy on the Use of Arrest Records

In short, the EEOC summarizes its policy regarding the use of arrest records by saying that:

> "The use of arrest records as an absolute bar to employment has a disparate impact on some protected groups and arrest records cannot be used to routinely exclude persons from employment. However, conduct which indicates unsuitability for a particular position is a basis for exclusion. Where it appears that the applicant or employee engaged in the conduct for which he was arrested and that the conduct is job-related and relatively recent, exclusion is justified."

Obviously, there are some subjective factors here. First, notice that the EEOC notes that Blacks and Hispanics are not only convicted of crimes at a disparate rate than non-protected groups, but also that they are also arrested at a disparate rate.

Again, with the use of arrest records, no blanket exclusions—no matter how color blind—should be adopted.

Second (provided that you have not hired a statistician to disprove a disparate impact in your hiring area using local statistics) there must be a *business necessity* for using the arrest records as a factor in your decision-making.

There must be a business necessity for your use of arrest records.

Business necessity revolves around two issues—

1. Credibility. Did the individual actually do the act for which he was arrested?

2. After establishing that an applicant has committed a crime, the employer must connect that act to the job performance. Congress has not defined business necessity, but in the Civil Right Act of 1991, Congress made it clear that courts were to apply the EEOC standard. *El v. Southeastern Pennsylvania Transportation Authority,* 479 F.3d 232, 241 (3ʳᵈ Cir. 2007). What business necessity entails is a hiring criteria that measures the minimum qualifications for the successful performance of the job in question, but an employer need

not set the lowest possible standard for success. *Id.,* p. 242. Thus, business necessity is an indefinite concept. The bottom line is whether a five-year-old conviction for theft makes the person more likely to steal again than some one who never committed that crime in the first place.

The Job-Relatedness Issue

The EEOC has ruled that "an employer may deny employment opportunities to persons based on any prior conduct which indicates that they would be unfit for the position in question, whether that conduct is evidenced by an arrest, conviction or other information provided to the employer. It is the conduct, not the arrest or conviction per se, which the employer may consider in relation to the position sought."

So, if you believe that the individual committed the conduct, even if you know the individual committed the conduct because you watched him do it, there is another consideration: job-relatedness.

Sometimes this is easy. A convicted pedophile's prior conduct would make him unfit to work in a daycare position. The individual applying for a job digging a ditch should probably not have his past bad check charge exclude him. Sometimes job-relatedness is not easy to determine, and, the problem is, you can not just impose a strict standard, e.g., "I will hire anyone with a criminal record unless it directly relates to the position being sought" because the courts, through the negligent-hiring doctrine have sometimes been extremely liberal in what they consider job-related. Consider what an appeals court found job-related. *See El v. Southeastern Pennsylvania Transportation Authority, (SEPTA),* 479 F.3d 232 (3rd Cir. 2007)

The *El* case is the first reported decision that treated a criminal background check as any other employment-screening tool. Any screening tool should be validated to show that it accurately measures the job-related criteria. In other words, is past conviction of a particular offense an accurate predictor of future criminal activity of a similar nature? The district court rejected any common sense validation, i.e., "everyone knows" that you do not hire someone convicted of "X" to do this job. Rather, the court required empirical proof that the Plaintiff's criminal past created an elevated risk. In *El,* the employer presented expert testimony to support the employer's concerns. Without this expert testimony supporting this test the plaintiff would have prevailed. In this case, the employer had identified specific crimes that had the highest and most unpredictable rates of recidivism, and thus, presented the greatest danger to the public that rode the bus.

The Case of Malorney vs. B & L Motor Freight, Inc

In this case, a hitchhiker sued the employer of an over-the-road truck driver for sexual assault committed by the truck driver.

Here is the case summary. A man named Edward Harbour applied for a position of over-the-road driver with defendant, B & L. On the employment application, Harbour was questioned as to whether he had any vehicular offenses or other criminal convictions. His response to the vehicular question was verified by B & L, but Harbour's negative reply to the criminal conviction question was not checked by B & L. It turns out that Harbour did have a history of convictions for sex-related crimes. Harbour had been arrested just the previous year for aggravated sodomy of two teenage hitchhikers while driving an over-the-road truck for another employer. Upon being hired by B & L, Harbour was given the company's written instructions, which included a prohibition against picking up hitchhikers in a B & L truck.

Later, Harbour picked up the plaintiff, a 17-year-old hitchhiker. In the sleeping compartment of the truck, he repeatedly raped, assaulted, and viciously beat her. After being released, the plaintiff notified police and Harbour was arrested, convicted, and sentenced to 50 years with no parole. The plaintiff sued B & L for negligent hiring.

B & L contended that it could not foresee that one of its drivers would rape and assault a hitchhiker, and that sexual assault isn't job-related to driving a truck anyway. The circuit court denied B & L's motion for summary judgment. B & L appealed. The appellate court agreed with the circuit court (did not rule for B & L), and stated:

> "...it is clear that B & L has a duty to entrust its truck to a competent employee fit to drive an over-the-road truck *equipped with a sleeping compartment*. Lack of forethought may exist where one remains in voluntary ignorance of facts concerning the danger in a particular act or instrumentality, where a reasonably prudent person would become advised on the theory that such ignorance is the equivalent of negligence. B & L gave Harbour an over-the-road vehicle *with a sleeping compartment* and B & L knew, or should have known, that *truckers are prone to give rides to hitchhikers despite rules against such actions* and so the question now becomes one of fact—whether B & L breached its duty to hire a competent driver who was to be entrusted with a B & L over-the-road truck." (*Italics added*).

As talk-show host Johnny Carson would have said, "that's wild, weird, wacky stuff." Virtually all trucks, employed in interstate commerce, many in intrastate commerce, and some in intra-city commerce, are equipped with a sleeping berth for the driver. How this fact was used as a justification or business necessity to order a criminal record is instructive to the careful employer who has to consider job-relatedness.

Before you dismiss a criminal offense as unrelated to the job, give this case a quick remembrance if only in your subconscious. The courts have caused many employers grief by making some interesting determinations.

Four Important EEOC Notices

The Appendix contains copies of four important notices published by the EEOC. These notices have set the bar, so to speak, on what an employer and cannot do with criminal records.

- Evaluation of employer's policy of refusing to hire individuals with conviction records

- Commission's procedure for determining whether arrest records may be considered in employment decisions

- Job advertising and pre-employment inquiries

- A business justifying the exclusion of an individual from employment on the basis of a conviction record

For more information about the EEOC, visit its website at www.eeoc.gov.

Chapter 11

State Restrictions on Criminal Record Use by Employers

Crime, like virtue, has its degrees.
— Jean Racine

As an employer, you have learned that the EEOC guidelines restrict the use of arrest and conviction records and you now know all the legal precautions you must take, right? Not so fast, Denny Crain. Some states have their own regulations on what information is available or employers may use. These restrictions can be more restrictive than the federal EEOC guidelines.

We will do our best to guide you through these various state restrictions, but keep in mind laws are subject to change — restrictions can change in the blink of a legislator's eye on the last day of the session. Some of the information is a matter of interpretation and some laws are tucked away in obscure places to be discovered by accident. Although the following information is accurate to the best of our knowledge and research, do not treat it as gospel, it may be a good idea to first seek legal advice before applying this to a particular situation.

The following material highlights laws throughout the various states that impact the use of criminal records by employers. This is a good standing in the federal system under which we operate. Each state is free to create its own rules to implement the values of the people of that state. Such variations create a difficult patchwork for a CRA to monitor. Most CRAs will attempt not to provide, to an employer, information that the employer is prohibited from using. The restriction is usually not upon the CRA but the user.

The next chapter examines specific laws from each state.

States That Prohibit the Use of Arrest Records (i.e., non-conviction records)

Several states have made a legislative, public-policy decision that certain arrest records are irrelevant and should not be considered by employers when making employment decisions. There are one of two theories used to justify this approach. The first being that one is innocent until proven guilty and records showing less than guilt should not be used; or second, the use of this data promotes discrimination and it will not be allowed it to be used. While it is true that some people are arrested without any cause, it is equally true that some people who are arrested have committed some crime. Whether these people are prosecuted sometimes has nothing to do with their guilt. Rather, it may depend on the caseload of the prosecutor's office, or what priorities the prosecutor has regarding what crime will be perused. If correctly used, arrest records and other non-conviction information can be very helpful to track down important information. If any employer makes a decision on the simple fact of an arrest, then precluding its use is appropriate public policy in our opinion.

States that have made this decision regarding arrest records have addressed the issue by either restricting their state from releasing the information, by prohibiting employers from using the information, or a combination of both.

At the time of this writing, several states occasionally prohibit employers from reviewing arrest records without a resulting conviction unless the charge is pending, or they restrict the release of non-conviction records. So...

- If an arrest has been made and the individual is not convicted, then the information should not be reviewed by an employer.

- If an arrest has been made and there is no disposition yet, then the arrest may be reviewed, in some states, because the result is pending.

Please note that even here there are shades of prohibition. Some states' laws clearly prohibit the practice, while other states pre-employment Inquiry Guides put out by their versions of the EEOC simply note that it is "improper." This is a complex and occasionally contradictory area. The same state may have laws prohibiting the use of arrest information while in another area requiring all records of the past seven years to be reviewed.

The following attempts to generally summarize where there are arrest restrictions. The states that have some type of prohibition against employers reviewing arrest records are—

- **California:** California Labor Code §432.7(a) Employers may not inquire about arrests that did not result in a conviction unless the charge is still pending.

- **Connecticut:** CGSA 46a-80(d) Employer may not consider arrests not resulting in convictions. There is no exception for pending charges.

- **Hawaii:** HRS §378-2.5 Employer may inquire regarding <u>convictions</u> for any felony, pornography misdemeanor, sexual offense misdemeanor, controlled substance misdemeanor (only for 5 years), DUI (only for 5 years). Other convictions listed above within 10 years. By implication arrest information may not be considered.

- **Massachusetts:** MGLA 151B §4(9) Employer may not ask an applicant about an arrest, detention or disposition for which a conviction did not result. However, this does not restrict an employer from obtaining and viewing such information. *Ryan v. Chief Administrative Justice*, 779 N.E. 2d 1005 (Mass. App. 2002); *Bynes v. School Committee of Boston*, 581 N.E. 2d 1019 (Mass App. 1991)

- **Michigan:** MCLA §37.2205a Employer may not request, make or maintain a record of misdemeanor arrests.

- **New York:** NY EXEC §296(15) No employer may consider an arrest without a conviction except for pending charges. Similarly an employer cannot consider cases terminated "in favor of the individual" NY EXEC §296(16). The latter phase is not defined. Does it mean a dismissal or acquittal or is a finding of guilt on a lesser included misdemeanor when the defendant was charged with a felony also "in favor of the individual"?

- **Ohio:** OHST §2953.33b No employer may consider an arrest without a conviction except for pending charges. Further, employers are to consider convictions in the last three years, but for certain jobs and professions, convictions may be considered for ten years. 5 MRSA§5303.

- **Pennsylvania:** 18 PACSA §9125. Employer may only consider convictions. However, if an employee committed a crime while employed by the employer, the employer may consider that conduct even if the employee is not convicted. *Cisco v. UPS,* 476 A.2d 1340 (Pa. Sup. 1984).

- **Rhode Island:** RIST §28-5-7 (7) Except for law enforcement, employer may not <u>ask</u> on an application about any arrest not resulting in a conviction. However, note case law in Massachusetts regarding a similar restriction.

- **Utah:** UAC §R606-2(v) Employer may not inquire regarding arrest records.

- **Wisconsin:** Wis.St §111.335 Employer may not inquire regarding arrest records.

States That Prohibit the Release of Certain Criminal Records

The following is a list of states that restrict the release of certain criminal record information. These statutes are generally directed to the operation of certain state agencies that maintain criminal records. These are not restrictions on the use of criminal records by an employer. Further, these statutes do not restrict the release of any criminal record at a county level or with any other state agency not included within the legislation:

- **Alaska:** AK ST 12.62.160(b)(8) Non-conviction information may not be released.

- **Connecticut:** CGSA §54-142(m) Non-conviction information may be released only for research purposes or to a criminal justice agency.

- **Georgia:** Ga.Code Ann. §35-3-34(a). First-offender records of arrest, charges, and sentences may not be released.

- **Hawaii:** H.Rev. St. §846-9. Records of arrests without a conviction cannot be released. There is an exception if the accused was found not guilty due to mental or physical defect.

- **Idaho:** IS ST §67-3008(2)(b). Arrest older than 12 months without a disposition may be released only upon a signed release.

- **Illinois:** 20 ILCS 2630/5. Arrests without a conviction are not to be released.

- **Indiana:** IC 10-13-3-11. Arrests more than one year old without a conviction may not be released. This statute, if applied literally would prohibit the release of arrest information on a case being tried or actively being prosecuted or where the defendant has fled the jurisdiction.

- **Iowa:** IGA §692.2. Arrests more than 18 months old without a conviction may not be released without a signed release.

- **Kentucky:** 502 KAR 30:060. Non-conviction data may be released only to criminal justice agencies and criminal justice employers.

- **Maine:** 16 MRSA §613. Non-conviction detail may not be released except to criminal justice agencies, pursuant to statute or court order, or research activities.

- **Minnesota:** MSA §364.04. Non-conviction information may not be provided to **public** employers.

- **Missouri:** VAMS 610.105. Any case that is nolle prossed, dismissed, found not guilty, or sentence is suspended is closed. Those found not guilty by reason of mental disease are closed except to law enforcement agencies, child-care facilities, and in-house service providers. This is a very broad exclusion of public records as it closes, e.g., makes unavailable, cases where a person was actually found guilty, but his sentence was suspended.

- **New Mexico:** NMSA §28-2-3(B). Public employers cannot receive from the state criminal records where there was no conviction **except** charges involving "moral turpitude".

- **North Carolina:** 12 NCAL 03B.0502(g) Arrest data without a disposition will be disseminated if an interval of one year, from the date of the arrest, has not elapsed which would lead officials of the Identification Section to reasonably believe that the arrest in question is still in the judicial process.

- **Oregon:** ORS 181.560(2). State police shall not release non-conviction data and, if records only contain non-conviction information, the department shall state that there is no criminal record.

- **Pennsylvania:** 18 PACSA§9121. State and local law enforcement shall not release arrest information where there is no conviction or the matter is not pending that is older than two years. This statute cures the situation noted in regard to the Indiana statute infra.

- **Virginia:** VAST §19,2 -389(2). Records of arrests older than a year cannot be furnished unless a disposition has been recorded and no active prosecution is pending.

- **Washington:** WRC §43.43.815. State patrol can furnish **conviction** records to employers.

States That Prohibit the Use of Misdemeanor Convictions

Several states also restrict the use by employers of misdemeanor convictions.

If the arrest prohibition is an attempt by some states to address the credibility issue, the misdemeanor prohibition is an attempt to address the job-related issue. These states have decided that in some cases, misdemeanor infractions should not be considered by employers—that they are never job related.

States that to some degree limit employers from reviewing misdemeanor records are—

- **California**: Employers cannot consider convictions for possession of small amounts of marijuana (less than 1 oz) Labor Code §432.8.

- **Hawaii:** Employers cannot consider misdemeanor convictions for which a jail sentence cannot be imposed. (They are restrictive on felony convictions too.) Possibly those crimes classified as offenses. Convictions for an offense do not constitute a crime and do not give rise to any civil disability. *HRS §701-107(5).* The law is not clear on this issue. See Employment Discrimination Because Of One's Arrest And Court Record in *Hawaii, 22 U. Haw L. Rev. 709 (2000).*

- **Massachusetts:** Employers cannot ask an employee/applicant about or maintain records regarding any misdemeanor conviction where the date of such conviction or completion of incarceration, whichever date is later, occurred five or more years prior to the date of application for employment, unless such person has been convicted of any offense within the five years immediately preceding the date of such application for employment. MELA 151B §4(9). Also included are first-time convictions for drunkenness, simple assault, speeding, minor traffic violations, affray or disturbance of the peace. *Id.* These are very vague descriptions that do not necessarily track any existing criminal statute.

- **Minnesota:** Employers cannot consider misdemeanor convictions for which a jail sentence cannot be imposed.

Such policies paint with a broad brush and expose a naive view of criminal offenses. The old fashioned crimes: murder, armed robbery, arson, rape, and the like are long time serious crimes, i.e. felonies. This view considers misdemeanors as not serious. However, each state has hundreds of crimes on the books. Many of those statutes were enacted in response to special interest groups or to a uniquely tragic episode. The proponents tell the legislature that you must make this act a felony or you will not appreciate that this is SERIOUS. So they buckle to the pressure and a new felony is born. Some of these are appropriate and some are not. For an employer, what is important, as noted by the EEOC in its guidance letters, is what did the applicant do and is that related to the job? Assume you are hiring a bookkeeper, which is more job related: misdemeanor petty thefts or a federal felony of possessing an eagle feather? (16 U.S.C. §668) Some states would let you know about the feather but not the thefts. Further, in this time of overwhelmed criminal courts, guilty defendants enter into plea arrangement where the felony is dismissed and they plead guilty to a misdemeanor. They really are felons in misdemeanor clothing with the blessing of the state. Unfortunately, practical considerations force prosecutors to do this. The hiding of criminal conduct is an unintended (we hope) consequence of a court crisis.

Secret Criminal Records

Some convictions disappear due to the records being sealed, expunged, annulled, and the ultimate — pardoned. Convictions and sometimes simply a record of arrest can be erased from the public record. Sometimes this action is taken in response to the determination that the accused was truly innocent and the record of even the arrest adversely impacts the person's reputation. The court expunging or sealing this record can be seen by the innocent person as an official statement by the government of his innocence. An official "we are sorry" so to speak, e.g., *Delaware, 11 Del. C §4372.*

However, most of such erasures have nothing to do with police or prosecutorial mistakes. Rather many states have statutory procedures whereby a convicted person may petition the court if he/she has met certain conditions, post conviction. It is an attempt to give the person a fresh start. These erasures are sometimes not totally complete because law enforcement will still have access to the records including the conviction, e.g., *Florida, FSA §943.0585(4)(a).* The point here is that the state does not want to repeatedly provide first offenders status to someone who is a career criminal.

The impact of these statutes and practices is to deny access to the public to these records. The convicted person may say that he/she has never been convicted of a crime, e.g. *Rhode Island RI ST §12-1.3-4(b); Washington, WRC §9.94A.640(c) and 9.96.060; West Virginia, WV.ST §61-11-25(e).* Employers are not to consider such records when hiring a person, e.g. *Colorado, CRSA 24-72-308(1)(f)(1); Oklahoma, 2205 §19(F); Virginia, VA ST §19.2-39.4(A).*

Most states have laws that provide all or part of the above provisions. Thus, as a general matter a CRA should not pick up and knowingly report such an erased record to any user. The state has made a policy decision for its citizens to treat that matter as it never happened. The wisdom of specific decisions to erase certain convictions can certainly be questioned, like the case where a man in Michigan had two convictions for child molestation expunged. Obviously, Jessica's Law was not in place at the time. But, you may ask: "If these were expunged how would someone know about them?" Think of this as divine intervention. The man also had a later conviction for failure to register as a sex offender which was not expunged. That conviction could be reported and used by an employer.

States That Limit the Use of First Offense Records

Two states, as a blanket policy, give first offenders a mulligan.

- **Georgia:** Certain first offender crimes in which the offender has been discharged without court adjudication of guilt are not reportable under

Georgia law and a notification of discharge and exoneration is to be placed upon the record by the court. The discharge is not considered a conviction of a crime and may not be used to disqualify a person in any application for employment.

- **Massachusetts:** Employers may not inquire or maintain records related to a first conviction for any of the following misdemeanors: drunkenness, simple assault, speeding, minor traffic violations, affray, or disturbance of the peace. However, those categories are very vague and do not track any specific offense/crime; thus, application of this restriction might be difficult.

States That Restrict the Reporting of Records Based on Time Periods

State Reporting Restrictions

There is a big difference in a state law that restricts the *use* of a criminal record by *employers* and a state law that restricts what a *vendor,* i.e., consumer reporting agency, CRA, can *report.* Several states restrict what a vendor can report, i.e., they have different limitations than the federal FCRA based on time periods. However, there are many exceptions and many of the states are changing their laws to mirror the federal guidelines. (For more information on this complex interrelation, see Chapter 9.)

States that still **restricted vendor reporting** of criminal conviction information **to seven years are** California, Colorado, Kansas, Maryland, Massachusetts, Montana, New Hampshire, New Mexico, New York, Texas, and Washington.

However, Kansas, Maryland Massachusetts, New Hampshire, and Washington waive the time limit if the applicant is reasonably expected to make $20,000 or more annually. In New York, the exception is $25,000. In Colorado and Texas, the figure is $75,000. Further, since Colorado and Texas enacted their FCRA analog statutes after September 30, 1996, they are preempted by the FCRA 15 U.S.C. §1681t(b)(1)(E). California removed its $75,000 salary cap after September 30, 1996, and as such, at least that portion of the law is preempted. An interesting argument could be made that the entire statute is preempted since it was amended after the cut off date.

Is it any wonder that many employers and vendors concentrate on complying with the federal FCRA?

States That Limit Record Access to Employers Only Within Certain Industries

Finally, some states have tried to do your thinking for you. If you are in an industry they have deemed to be critical (or the industry had good lobbyists), you are privileged for criminal record access and use from the state repository. These states permit access, by statute, to certain industries such as schools, childcare, nurseries, etc.

If, on the other hand, you are some poor soul trying to eke out a living by running a small business in some "non-critical" industry, you may be up a river for state repository access.

However, as discussed earlier, criminal records from the counties will almost certainly be available and the fact that the state prohibits access to its repository should not prove a deterrent, in some respects, to getting the information you need. In fact, as was discussed earlier, county records can be superior to statewide records. The next chapter provides state-by-state information.

The previous information is enough to make one's head spin, but CRAs, vendors and the like must keep all this in mind when reporting records. It is a difficult task. At times it becomes nearly impossible when having to determine which state law applies to a particular report.

Legal Concerns Versus Gut Reactions

Employers will find times when their legal concerns conflict with their gut feelings.

We will not tell you what to do if you are the owner of a laundromat hiring an employee to collect the change from your equipment and you find a recent misdemeanor conviction for theft. We won't even give advice to you if you are running a daycare or hiring a nanny to watch your children, and your state prohibits your use of all available arrest information.

We will tell you to weigh your options, give it some thought, and use your common sense. Here is an example:

> **Example—**
>
> There once was an old, no-nonsense safety director at a huge trucking company. He was a "law and order" man, not given to (or accepting of) most any illegal dalliance you would care to name. He was in charge of screening and hiring the truck drivers. The company used terminals in a state that

restricted the use of misdemeanor records. We discussed the issue of finding a misdemeanor DWI on a potential driver.

The CRA educated him on the law. He educated the CRA on what he thought about the law. He ended the conversation with this thought that has stuck with us: "Son, I'd much rather be sitting there in the witness box explaining why I didn't hire that driver than be sitting there explaining to the jury why I did hire him after he's killed somebody."

Food for thought.

If You Get Into Trouble

Here in the "Land of the Free and Home of the Brave" anyone can sue most anyone for anything. It is American's national pastime.

If you are an employer and order criminal records, chances are, they will keep you out of court for more than they will bring you to court. However, there is always the chance that a prospective or current employee will sue you in relation to ordering a criminal record. If you have ordered a criminal record and taken an adverse action against the subject of the report for something you have found on the report, there is a slim chance you will get sued (or more likely, threaten to be sued). There are several reasons criminal record lawsuits are rare.

Consider first that most people do not have criminal records. The percentage of records you will find that contain a criminal record will vary greatly depending on your applicant pool. (You could expect differing percentages for nuns and pro football players for instance.) A good average to use for illustrative purposes is 13 percent.

This means that 87 percent of the time a criminal record is ordered, it will come back with no criminal record activity. We are litigious, but not yet so much so that the 87 percent will cause any trouble.

That leaves 13 percent. As we have discussed, you will not take adverse action on all 13 percent of these individuals. Some of the criminal activity will be minor, non-job-related activity. Let us say you have ordered 1000 criminal records. Of this amount, 130 will have criminal records. You may take adverse action against 100 of the 130 applicants.

Of the 100 individuals, most who are turned down for employment will apply elsewhere. Whether the applicant goes down the street or gets ticked at you depends on how many other roughly equal opportunities to yours exist, and how many similar others there are will influence the applicant's reaction. In our experience, far fewer than

1 in 100 applicants turned down by a job for a criminal record sue or threaten to sue. You can see, though, that even if it *were* 1 in 100 refused applicants, that is only 1 in 1000 criminal records ordered.

Compare this to the damage that could have been caused by even one of the 100 in 1000 applicants you turned away. Truly, the fear of being sued is far greater than the chance of being sued.

Most legal issues revolve around an applicant stating that the record does not belong to him rather than whether the law permits the employer to see/use the record. This assertion by the applicant could be true and the FCRA requires the employer to hear the applicant out. If reasonably possible, the issue should be checked out before a final decision is made. The lack of identifiers in some courts or clerical errors can cause a record to be mismatched. So the advice to the employer is to listen to the applicant's protest. If the employer listens, lawsuits can be avoided.

If You Do Get Hit by Legal Lightning

> *When you go into court you are putting*
> *your fate in the hands of twelve people who*
> *weren't smart enough to get out of jury duty.*

-- Norm Crosby

When you did *not* use a vendor

The first advice we can give if you get sued is to procure an attorney who specializes in your trouble. Due, at least in part, to the litigious society in which we live, specialties have come about in law. Just as you would not go to your family physician to perform a triple bypass on your heart, we would advise you not to hire your business attorney to handle your criminal record employment case. Find an attorney well versed in employment law and, better yet, an employment lawyer who knows criminal records and background screening. The National Association of Professional Background Screeners, napbs.com, may be able to identify such lawyers for you.

If you obtained the record from a vendor

If there is a dispute as to the accuracy of the record or a question as to whether the report you received pertains to your applicant (the two most common reasons for disputes) and you used a vendor, call your vendor. He may be able to direct you to an attorney well versed in FCRA protections.

Most attorneys, even those specializing in employment law, are not aware of the provisions of the FCRA, and you need to find one who is.

One benefit of this advice is that you are more likely to win your case if it goes to court. The huge benefit of this advice is that an attorney who knows his stuff in this area will likely short circuit the case long before it goes to trial. Even if you have an in-house employment attorney, or one on retainer, we recommend a consultation with an attorney who knows the FCRA.

Chapter 12

State Statutes, Restrictions, and Records Access Procedures

This chapter presents extensive details for each state for the following information—

- Statutes regarding use of criminal records by employers and related employer restrictions.

- Overview of state criminal record agencies, including record access.

- Overview of each state's court system and if statewide court records are accessible.

- Links to searching the states' sexual offender registries and databases of incarceration records.

Editor's Note: Some of the profiles that show online access to criminal records include fees. Please be advised that fees are always subject to change, and there is a growing trend among state agencies to increase record fees.

Alabama

Alabama Statutes & Related Employer Restrictions

General Rule: The director of the Department of Public Safety may open to any person for inspection criminal history information on any individual if the individual has given written permission. AL ST §32-2-61. Person means any individual, partnership, corporation, association, business, government, governmental agency, or any other public or private entity. AL ST §32-2-60.

Exception: Fingerprints, photographs, and other records of youthful offenders shall not be open to public inspection. A youthful offender is an individual below 21 years of age. AL ST §15-19-7.

Definitions: Criminal History Information – includes arrest, detention, or initiation of criminal proceedings. AL ST §32-2-60.

State Statutes and Codes: www.legislature.state.al.us/prefiled/prefiled.html

Legislative Bill Search: www.legislature.state.al.us

Alabama State Criminal Records Agency

Alabama Bureau of Investigation, Identification Unit - Record Checks, PO Box 1511, Montgomery, AL 36102-1511, (courier address: 301 S Ripley St, Montgomery, AL 36104.) **Phone:** 334-353-4340, 334-353-7800 **Web:** http://dps.alabama.gov/ABI/cic.aspx

Search Notes: Records are available to the general public. The request must be on state form ABI-46. The form can be obtained from the webpage or call to have copy sent. Include the following in your request-notarized release from subject, date of birth, Social Security Number, full name, race, sex. Two witnesses may attest to signature instead of a notary. Fingerprints optional. 100% of the record files have fingerprints.

What Is Released: All records or arrests are released, including those without dispositions. The following data is not released: juvenile records. 45% of arrests in database have final dispositions recorded, 65% for those arrests in last 5 years.

Access Methods: mail, in person, online.

Online Searching: This agency recommends that searchers contact www.background.alabama.gov/. This is a subscription service with a $25 search fee and an $75 annual fee. Employers using a CRA must be registered first.

Alabama Sexual Offender Registry

Department of Public Safety , Sexual Offender Registry, PO Box 1511, Montgomery, AL 36102-1511, (courier address: 301 S Ripley, Montgomery, AL 36102.) **Phone:** 334-353-1172; **Fax:** 334-353-2563 **Web:** http://community.dps.alabama.gov/

Note: Sections 15-20-21 to 37, defines criminal sex offenders and is part of the Alabama Community Notification Act.

Online Searching: Search sex offender data and a felony fugitives list at the home page. Search by name, ZIP, city or county. Missing persons and felony fugitives also shown.

Alabama Incarceration Records Agency

Alabama Department of Corrections , Central Records Office, PO Box 301501, Montgomery, AL 36130, (courier address: 301 S. Ripley Street, Montgomery, AL 36130.) **Phone:** 334-353-9500, 334-353-3883 http://doc.state.al.us

Online Searching: Information on current inmates only is available online at http://doc.state.al.us/inmatesearch.asp. Location, AIS number, physical identifiers, and projected release date are released. The database is updated weekly. Questions regarding specific inmates can be sent to pio@doc.state.al.us.

Alabama State Court System

Court Administrator: Director of Courts, 300 Dexter Ave, Montgomery, AL, 36104; 334-954-5000. www.alacourt.gov

Court Structure: Jefferson County (Birmingham), Madison (Huntsville), Marshall, and Tuscaloosa Counties have separate criminal divisions for Circuit and/or District Courts. Misdemeanors committed with felonies are tried with the felony. The Circuit Courts are appeals courts for misdemeanors. District Courts can receive guilty pleas in felony cases.

Find Felony Records: Circuit Courts

Misdemeanor Records: District Courts, Municipal Courts

Online Access: A commercial online subscription services at www.alacourt.com draws its data from the State Judicial Information System (SJIS). This system is comprehensive and user friendly, includes civil, criminal, DR, traffic, warrants, and trial court dockets statewide. A record request form is found at http://helpdesk.alacourt.gov/requestform.asp that allows you to specify case data or search on a county basis.

Also, State Supreme Court and Appellate decisions are available at www.alalinc.net and at http://www.judicial.state.al.us/..

Searching Hints: Although in most counties Circuit and District courts are combined, each index may be separate. Therefore, when you request a search of both courts, be sure to state that the search is to cover "both the Circuit and District Court records." Several courts do not perform searches. Some courts do not have public access computer terminals.

Alaska

Alaska Statutes & Related Employer Restrictions

General Rule: Criminal Justice Information may be provided for any purpose, except it may not be released if the information is non-conviction information or correctional treatment information. AK ST §12.62.160 (b)(8).

Criminal Justice Information, including information relating to a serious offense, may be provided to an interested person if the information is requested for the purpose of determining whether to grant a person supervisory or disciplinary power over a minor or dependent adult. AK ST §12.62.160 (b)(9)

The following information may not be disclosed   AK ST §40.25.120

1) records of vital statistics and adoption proceedings

2) records pertaining to juveniles

3) medical and related public health records

4) records required to be kept confidential by law

Sealed Records of an arrest, charge, conviction, or sentence may be denied by the subject of the record. AK ST §12.62.180 (d). Information that is sealed may only be provided:

a. For record management purposes

b. Criminal justice employment purposes

c. For review by the subject of the record

d. Research and statistical purposes

e. When necessary to prevent imminent harm to a person

f. For a use authorized by statute

Definitions: AK ST §12.62.900

Criminal Justice Information – includes criminal history record, nonconviction information, and correctional treatment information.

Criminal History Record – included past conviction information, current offender information, and criminal identification information.

Past Conviction Information – includes the terms of any sentence, probation, suspended imposition of sentence, discretionary or mandatory parole, and information that a criminal conviction has been reversed, vacated, or set aside.

Serious Offense – a conviction for a violation or an attempt to commit a felony or a crime involving domestic violence.

Interested Person – person that employs, appoints, or permits a person who would have supervisory or disciplinary power over a minor or dependent adult.

Agency Guidelines for Pre-Employment Inquiries: Alaska Department of Labor and Workforce Development, Alaska Employer Handbook, "Pre-Employment Questioning" available online at www.labor.state.ak.us/handbook/AERM.pdf

State Statutes and Codes: www.legis.state.ak.us/folhome.htm

Legislative Bill Search: www.legis.state.ak.us/basis/start.asp

Alaska State Criminal Records Agency

Department of Public Safety, Records and Identification, 5700 E Tudor Rd, Anchorage, AK 99507 **Phone:** 907-269-5767; **Fax:** 907-269-5091 **Web:** www.dps.state.ak.us

Search Notes: The state has three types of record searches; Full Criminal History, Interested Person, and Any Person. Searches may be name-based or fingerprint-based. A Full History is only available to the subject or to government agencies. "Interested Party" results are for those granting supervisory power over children or dependent adults and contain all records. Include the following in your request-set of fingerprints, full name. Fingerprints return state records and for "Interested person" requesters who so desire national results from FBI files.

What Is Released: "Any Person" contain past convictions and current offender information. Name searches return state records only. All records are released, including those without final dispositions, to "Interested Person" requesters. "Any Person" requesters receive criminal records and open cases. Juvenile records are not released unless adjudicated as an adult or if a serious traffic offense. It takes 5 days for arrests, 120 days for dispositions before new records are available for inquiry. 88% of arrests in database have final dispositions recorded; 85% for those arrests in last 5 years. Approximately 66% of records are fingerprint-supported.

Access Methods: mail, in person.

Alaska Sexual Offender Registry

Department of Public Safety , Statewide Services Div-SOCKR Unit, 5700 E Tudor Rd, Anchorage, AK 99507 **Phone:** 907-269-0396; **Fax:** 907-269-0394 **Web:** www.dps.state.ak.us/sorweb/Sorweb.aspx

Note: AS 18.65.087 authorizes the Department of Public Safety to maintain a central registry of sex offenders required to register under AS 12.63.010 and to make information about the offender available to the public. Only offenders convicted of the sex offenses specified under AS 12.63.100 are required to register. The following information about those offenders available to the public: name, address, photograph, place of employment, date of birth, crime for which convicted, date of conviction and place and court of conviction.

Online Searching: Name searching and geographic searching is available at the website. This is the primary search offered by the agency.

Alaska Incarceration Records Agency

Alaska Department of Corrections , DOC Classification Office, 550 W 7th Ave, #601, Anchorage, AK 99501 **Phones:** 907-269-7426, 907-269-7397; **Fax:** 907-269-7439 **Web:** www.correct.state.ak.us

Alaska State Court System

Court Administrator: Office of the Administrative Director, 820 W 4th Ave, Anchorage, AK, 99501; Telephone: 907-264-8232; Records: 907-264-0491. www.state.ak.us/courts.

Court Structure: Alaska has a unified, centrally administered, and totally state-funded judicial system with 4 Judicial Districts. Municipal governments do not maintain separate court systems. Alaska has 15 boroughs, not counties. 3 are unified home rule municipalities that are combination borough and city, and 12 boroughs. There are also 12 home rule cities which do not directly coincide with the 4 Judicial Districts. In other words, judicial boundaries cross borough boundaries.

The superior court is the trial court of general jurisdiction. There are 34 superior court judgeships located throughout the state. The district court is a trial court of limited jurisdiction and hears cases that involve state misdemeanors and violations of city and borough ordinances, first appearances and preliminary hearings in felony cases. Municipal governments do not maintain separate court systems.

Find Felony Records: Superior Courts

Misdemeanor Records: District Courts, Magistrate Courts

Online Access: You may do a name search of a partial statewide Alaska Trial Courts database index at www.courtrecords.alaska.gov/. There is an old and a new system since the Alaska Court System is migrating to a new electronic case information system called CourtView. Search results give case number, file date, disposition date, charge, and sentence. Note that the initial index gives the only the name used on the first pleading.

The home web page gives access to Appellate opinions. The site at http://government.westlaw.com/akcases/ provides access to opinions of the Alaska Supreme Court and Alaska Court of Appeals.

Searching Hints: Magistrate Courts vary widely in how records are maintained and in the hours of operation (some are open only a few hours per week)

Arizona
Arizona Statutes & Related Employer Restrictions

General Rule: The director shall authorize the exchange of criminal justice information with any non-criminal justice agency pursuant to a statute, ordinance, or executive order that specifically authorizes it for the purpose of evaluating the fitness of current or prospective licensees, employees, contract employees or volunteers. Fingerprints and appropriate fee must be submitted along with the request.

The director shall authorize the exchange of criminal justice information with any individual for any lawful purpose on submission of the subject of record's fingerprints and appropriate fee. ARS §41-1750(G)(2) and (4).

Definitions: ARS §41-1750(Y)

Criminal History Record – includes notations of arrest, detentions, indictments, and other formal criminal charges, and disposition arising from those actions, sentencing, formal correctional supervisory action, and release. It does not include information relating to juveniles unless they have been adjudicated as adults.

General Rule: Consumer Reports – A consumer reporting agency may furnish a consumer report to a person that it has reason to believe intends to use the information for employment purposes. ARS §44-1692(A)(3)(b)

Consumer Reports Definitions - ARS §44-1691(3)

Consumer Report: any written, oral, or other communications which bear on a consumer's credit worthiness, credit standing, credit capacity, character, general reputation, personal characteristics, or mode of living which is used . . . for . . . employment purposes.

Caveat – A person cannot automatically be disqualified from employment because of a prior conviction for a felony or misdemeanor within or without this state. However, if the offense has a reasonable relationship to the function of the employment or occupation, then employment may be denied. ARS §13-904(E).

State Statutes and Codes: www.azleg.state.az.us/ArizonaRevisedStatutes.asp

Legislative Bill Search: www.azleg.state.az.us/Bills.asp

Arizona State Criminal Records Agency

Department of Public Safety, Applicant Team One, PO Box 18430//Mail Code 2250, Phoenix, AZ 85005-8430, (courier address: 2320 N 20th Ave, Phoenix, AZ 85009.) **Phone:** 602-223-2223; **Fax:** 602-223-2972   **Web:** www.azdps.gov/

Search Note: Record access is limited to agencies that have specific authorization by law including employers or employment search firms located in AZ, but results are sent to the employer. Results from out-of-state requesters can only be sent to the subject. Include the following in your request-full set of fingerprints plus demographic information on the applicant. Be sure to address requests to Applicant Team One. Fingerprints are required for a search. 100% of arrest records are fingerprint supported.

What Is Released: All records are released, including those without dispositions. The following data is not released: bulk data purchase. After receiving, it takes about 14 days before new records are available for inquiry. 58% of arrests in database have final dispositions recorded, 60% within last 5 years.

Access Methods: mail.

Arizona Sexual Offender Registry

Department of Public Safety , Sex Offender Compliance, PO Box 6638//Mail Code 9999, Phoenix, AZ 85005-6638, (courier address: 2102 W Encanto, Phoenix, AZ 85009.) **Phone:** 602-255-0611; **Fax:** 602-223-2949 **Web:** http://az.gov/webapp/offender/main.do

Note: The county sheriff is responsible for registering sex offenders living within their county. Arizona has approximately 15,000 registered sex offenders.

Online Searching: Searching of Level 2 and Level 3 offenders is available online at the website above. Search for an individual by name, or search by ZIP Code or address for known offenders. The site also lists, with pictures, absconders who are individuals whose whereabouts are unknown. A download is available from the webpage for $25.00.

Arizona Incarceration Records Agency

Arizona Department of Corrections , Records Department, 1601 W. Jefferson St., Phoenix, AZ 85007 **Phone:** 602-542-5586; **Fax:** 602-542-3965 **Web:** www.adc.state.az.us

Online Searching: Search online at home page. You must provide last name, first initial or ADC number. Any add'l identifiers are welcomed. Location, ADC number, physical Identifiers and sentencing information are released. Inmates admitted and released from 1972 to 1985 may not be searchable on the web. Also available is ADC Fugitives - an alphabetical Inmate Datasearch listing of Absconders and Escapees from ADC.

Arizona State Court System

Court Administrator:	Administrative Office of the Courts, Arizona Supreme Court Bldg, 1501 W Washington, Phoenix, AZ, 85007; 602-452-3300. www.supreme.state.az.us.
Court Structure:	The Superior Court is the court of general jurisdiction. Justice and Municipal courts generally have separate jurisdiction based on case types. Most courts will search their records by plaintiff or defendant.
Find Felony Records:	Superior Courts
Misdemeanor Records:	Justice of the Peace, Municipal Courts

Online Access: The Public Access to Court Case Information is a valuable web service providing a resource for information about court cases from 153 out of 180 courts in Arizona. Courts not covered include certain parts of Pima, Yavapai, Mohave, and Maricopa counties. Information includes detailed case information (i.e., case type, charges, filing and disposition dates), the parties in the case (not including victims and witnesses), and the court mailing address and location. Go to www.supreme.state.az.us/publicaccess/notification/default.asp.

Opinions from the Supreme Court and Court of Appeals are available from the website.

Maricopa County Justice Court case histories available free at www.superiorcourt.maricopa.gov/docket/JusticeCourtCases/caseSearch .asp.

Searching Hints: Public access to all Maricopa County court case indexes is available at a central location - 1 W Madison Ave in Phoenix. Copies, however, must be obtained from the court where the case is heard.

Arkansas

Arkansas Statutes & Related Employer Restrictions

General Rule: Conviction Information shall be available to any non-governmental entity authorized by the subject of the record in writing or by state or federal law to receive such information. ACA §12-12-1009(a)(2).

Non-conviction information shall be made available for non-criminal justice purposes. ACA §12-12-1009(c). Exceptions to releasing non-conviction information:

- Any person under 16 years of age who was convicted and given a suspended sentence, subsequently received a pardon for the conviction, and has not since been convicted of another criminal offense will have the criminal record expunged ACA. §16-90-601.

- Release of criminal history information for non-criminal justice purposes shall be made only by the Identification Bureau of the Department of Arkansas State Police... and such compiled records will not be released or disclosed for non-criminal justice purpose by other agencies in the state. ACA §12-12-1011.

Definitions: ACA §12-12-1001

>Conviction Information – criminal history information disclosing that a person has pleaded guilty or nolo contendere to, or was found guilty of a criminal offense in a court of law together with sentencing information.

>Criminal History Information – includes notations of arrest, detentions, indictments, disposition of charges, formal criminal charges, as well as notations on correctional supervision and release

>Non-conviction Information – arrest without disposition, as well as all acquittals and all dismissals.

>Expunge – record or records in question shall be sealed, sequestered, and treated as confidential. ACA §16-90-90(a)(1). Sexual offenses against those under the age of 18 cannot be expunged. ACA§16-90-901(a)(3).

State Statutes and Codes:

>www.arkleg.state.ar.us/NXT/gateway.dll?f=templates&fn=default.htm&vid=blr:code

Legislative Bill Search: www.arkleg.state.ar.us

Arkansas State Criminal Records Agency

Arkansas State Police, Identification Bureau, #1 State Police Plaza Dr, Little Rock, AR 72209
Phone: 501-618-8500; **Fax:** 501-618-8404   **Web:** www.asp.arkansas.gov

Search Note: The public may obtain criminal history records, including third parties on behalf of employers. A signed, notarized release form must be on file with the requesting entity. Include the following in your request-notarized release from subject, name, date of birth, sex, SSN, driver's license number. Fingerprints are not required, but may be included. 100% of the arrest records are fingerprint supported. Is it suggested to use the Bureau's request form (ASP-122) for manual requests.

What Is Released: Manual requests will not include pending arrests or records without dispositions, unless the requester is entitled to federally disqualifying arrests. Online records will show records w/o dispositions. Felony records without dispositions are released only to employers and licensing boards, otherwise all records without disposition are not released. Records are available for the past 25 years. Older records are located in the off-site State Archives. The following data is not released: pardons and juvenile records. 81% of arrests in database have final dispositions recorded, 79% for those arrests in last 5 years.

Access Methods: mail, in person, online.

Online Searching: Online access available to only employers or their agents, and professional licensing boards. A subscriber account with the Information Network of Arkansas (INA) is required, a $75 annual fee is imposed. The search fee is $22. Searches are conducted by name. Search results includes registered sex offenders. For more info on this online service, see https://www.ark.org/criminal/index.php. Accounts must maintain the **signed release** documents in-house for three years. For an excellent overview of record **release provisions** visit https://www.ark.org/ina/sub/bgcheck_agreement.php.

Arkansas Sexual Offender Registry

Arkansas Crime Information Center , Sexual Offender Registry, One Capitol Mall, 4D200, Little Rock, AR 72201 **Phone:** 501-682-7441; **Fax:** 501-682-2269 **Web:** www.acic.org/Registration/index.htm

Online Searching: Searching is available at www.acic.org/soff/index.php. Search by name or location (county). Includes Level 3 and Level 4 offenders. Also, registered sex offenders are indicated on the criminal record online system maintained by the State Police; however, this system is only available to employers and professional licensing boards.

Arkansas Incarceration Records Agency

Arkansas Department of Corrections , Records Supervisor, PO Box 8707, Pine Bluff, AR 71611-87077500 Corrections Circle, Pine Bluff, AR 71603.) **Phone:** 870-267-6424, 870-267-6999 **Web:** www.adc.arkansas.gov/

Online Searching: The online access at www.adc.arkansas.gov/inmate_info/index.html has many search criteria capabilities. Questions may be directed to adc.inmate.info@arkansas.gov. Location, ADC number, physical Identifiers and sentencing information, release dates are released. The inmate access web page offers a download of the inmate database, fees involved.

Arkansas State Court System

Court Administrator: Administrative Office of Courts, 625 Marshall St, Ste 1100, Little Rock, AR, 72201; 501-682-9400, 501-682-6849. www.courts.state.ar.us.

Court Structure: Circuit Courts are the courts of general jurisdiction and are arranged in 28 circuits. Circuit courts consist of five subject matter divisions: criminal, civil, probate, domestic relations, and juvenile. The Circuit Clerk handles the records and recordings. District courts, formerly known as municipal courts before passage of Amendment 80 to the Arkansas Constitution, exercise county-wide jurisdiction over misdemeanor cases, and preliminary felony cases. The City Courts exercise city-wide jurisdiction and operate in smaller communities where District Courts do not exist.

Find Felony Records: Circuit Courts

Misdemeanor Records: District, City, Justice of the Peace and Police Courts

Online Access: The AOC website provides access to Supreme Court Opinions and Appellate Court dockets, or access via http://courts.state.ar.us/online/or.html where you will also find Court of Appeals dockets, corrected opinions, and parallel citations. An attorney search, court rules and administrative orders are also available. Online access to courts at the county level remains almost non-existant.

Searching Hints: Many courts that allow written search requests require an SASE. Fees vary widely across jurisdictions as do prepayment requirements.

California

California Statutes & Related Employer Restrictions

Expunged Record: Juvenile Records may be expunged. Penal Code §1203.45; misdemeanor records may be sealed after one year without further violations – may seek to have the convictions set aside and sealed. Penal Code §1203.4a. Felony convictions can also be set aside and sealed after the conditions of the probation have been fulfilled. Penal Code §1203.4.

Consumer Report: Investigative Reports – An investigative consumer reporting agency shall only furnish an investigative consumer report[not to be confused with the same term used in the FCRA, which means a consumer report including personal interviews]... to a person it has reason to believe intends to use the information for employment purposes. Cal. Civil Code §1786.12(d)(1).

If an investigative consumer report is sought for employment purposes, the person seeking the report must have provided disclosure in writing to the consumer and the consumer must authorize in writing. Cal. Civil Code §1786.16(a)(2).

An investigative consumer report may not contain 1) bankruptcies which antedate the report by more than 10 years, 2) suit and satisfied judgments, unsatisfied judgments, paid tax liens, accounts placed for collection, records of arrest indictment, information, misdemeanor complaint, or conviction of a crime which antedate the report by more than 7 years, or 3) unlawful detainer actions where the defendant was the prevailing party or where the action is resolved by settlement agreement. Records of arrest, indictment, information, misdemeanor complaint, or conviction of a crime shall no longer be reported if at any time it is learned that a full pardon has been granted or a conviction did not result, except that information may be reported pending pronouncement of a judgment on the particular subject matter of those records. Cal. Civil Code §1786.18(a)(7).

Additionally, an investigative consumer report may not contain information that is adverse to the consumer if it was obtained through a personal interview with a neighbor, friend, or associate of the consumer or with another person with whom the consumer is acquainted, unless the investigative consumer reporting agency has procedure to confirm the information or the person interviewed is the best possible source of the information. Cal. Civil Code §1786.18(d).

Consumer Report: Consumer Credit Report – No consumer credit report may contain 1) bankruptcies which antedate the report by more than 10 years, or 2) suit and judgments, paid tax liens, accounts placed for collection, records of arrest, indictment, information, misdemeanor complaint, or conviction of a crime which antedate the report by more than 7 years, or 3) unlawful detainer actions where the defendant was the prevailing party or where the action is resolved by settlement agreement. Records of arrest, indictment, information, misdemeanor complaint, or conviction of a crime shall no longer be reported if at any time it is learned that a full pardon has been granted or a conviction did not result. Cal. Civil Code §1786.18(a). In 2001 this section was amended to delete any salary cap. Since this portion of the statute without a salary cap was not in effect on September 30, 1996, it is pre-empted by 15 USC §1681t(b)(1)(E). As of September 30, 1996 the statute had a $75,000 salary cap.

Employment: No employer shall ask an applicant for employment to disclose information concerning an arrest or detention that did not result in conviction, or information concerning a referral to, and participation in, any pretrial or post-trial diversion program. An employer in not prevented from asking about an arrest for which the employee or applicant is out on bail or is pending trial. Cal. Civil Code §432.7(a).

Employers are also prohibited from inquiring about 1) misdemeanors that resulted from possession of less than 28.5 (1 oz) grams of marijuana, which may have resulted in a referral to education, treatment, or rehabilitation facility without a court hearing, and 2) possession of more than 28.5 grams of marijuana which may have resulted in imprisonment in county jail. Cal Hlth & S §11357(b) and (c).

While a felony may be dismissed and sealed under Penal Code §1203.4, it appears from the Regulations issued by The Fair Employment and Housing Commission that an employer can still consider a felony conviction dismissed under Penal Code §1203.4. 2 CA ADC §7287.4

Agency Guidelines for Pre-Employment Inquiries: Department of Fair Employment and Housing, "Pre-Employment Inquiry Guidelines." A copy of these guidelines can be found at the California State Univ. at Long Beach website at www.csulb.edu/depts/oed/resources/pubs3b.htm.

State Statutes and Codes: www.leginfo.ca.gov/calaw.html

Legislative Bill Search: www.leginfo.ca.gov/bilinfo.html

California State Criminal Records Agency

Department of Justice, Records Security Section, PO Box 903417, Sacramento, CA 94203-4170, (courier address: 4949 Broadway, Sacramento, CA 95820.)

Phones: Dept of Justice- 916-227-3460; General Info- 916-227-3849; **Fax:** 916-227-4815
Web: www.caag.state.ca.us

Access to Records is Restricted

Penal Code Sec. 11105.3 limits access to searches involving child care, the elderly, the handicapped and mentally impaired. The subject can obtain their own copy, but the record cannot be used for employment or licensing. Entities must be authorized before records can be requested. 99% of arrest records are fingerprint supported, entered from final disposition. Those entities authorized to obtain records must submit a completed fingerprint card, a letter explaining why the record is needed, and address of the authorized agency where record will be sent.

Who Can Access: *Though not open to the public, there are exceptions.* Entities must be authorized before records can be requested. 99% of arrest records are fingerprint supported, entered from final disposition. If for a statutorily-required employment check, only records with dispositions are released. However, certain social service agencies may be eligible for all arrest records. Include the following in your request-fingerprints, full name; also helpful DOB and SSN. Those entities authorized to obtain records must submit a completed fingerprint card, a letter explaining why the record is needed, and address of the authorized agency where record will be sent.

California Sexual Offender Registry

Department of Justice , Sexual Offender Program, PO Box 903387, Sacramento, CA 94203-3870, (courier address: 4949 Broadway, Rm H-216, Sacramento, CA 95820.) **Phones:** 916-227-4974; Tracking- 916-227-4199; **Fax:** 916-227-4345 **Web:** www.meganslaw.ca.gov/

Online Searching: The web page offers online searching by a sex offender's specific name or by geographic location including ZIP Code, county or within a predetermined radius of a selected address, park, or school. This site will provide access to information on more than 63,000 persons required to register in California as sex offenders. Search specific home addresses displayed on more than 33,500 offenders. Email questions to MegansLaw@doj.ca.gov.

California Incarceration Records Agency

Dept of Corrections , Corrections & Rehabilitation ID Unit, PO Box 942883, Sacramento, CA 94283-0001 **Phones:** Inmate Check Line (Media Only)- 916-557-5933; Identt Unit (Public Inquiry)- 916-445-6713; **Fax:** 916-327-1988 **Web:** www.cdcr.ca.gov

California State Court System

Court Administrator: Administrative Office of Courts, 455 Golden Gate Ave, San Francisco, CA, 94102; 415-865-4200. www.courtinfo.ca.gov.

Court Structure: In 1998, the judges in individual counties were given the opportunity to vote on unification of superior and municipal courts within their respective counties. By late 2000, all counties had voted to unify these courts. Courts that were formally Municipal Courts are now known as Limited Jurisdiction Superior Courts. In some counties, superior and municipal courts were combined into one superior court. It is important to note that Limited Courts may try minor felonies not included under our felony definition.

Find Felony Records: Superior Court

Misdemeanor Records: Superior Court and Limited Jurisdiction Superior Court

Online Access: There is no statewide online computer access available. However, a number of counties have developed their own online access sytems and provide internet access at no fee. Los Angeles County has an extensive free and fee-based online system at www.lasuperiorcourt.org.

The website at www.courtinfo.ca.gov offers access to all opinions from the CA Supreme Court and Appeals Courts from 1850 to present. Opinions not certified for publications are available for the last 60 days. This site also contains very useful information about the state court system, including opinions from the Supreme Court and Appeals Courts.

Searching Hints: If there is more than one court of a type within a county, where the case is tried and where the record is held depends on how a citation is written, where the infraction occurred, or where the filer chose to file the case.

Some courts now require signed releases from the subject in order to perform criminal searches and will no longer allow the public to conduct such searches. Fees are set by statute.

Colorado

Colorado Statutes & Related Employer Restrictions

General Rule: Except for records of official actions, all criminal justice records may be open to inspection by any person. CRSA §24-72-304(1).

Expunged Record: Upon the entry of an order to seal criminal records, the subject of the record may state that no such record exists. CRSA §24-72-308(1)(d). Record may be sealed upon application with 15 years of no offenses. Id., (1)a)(III)(B)

Consumer Report: A consumer reporting agency may furnish a consumer report to a person which the agency has reason to believe intends to use the information for employment purposes if the applicant or employee is first informed and consented in writing. CRSA §12-14.3-103(1)(c).

No consumer reporting agency may disclose 1) bankruptcies which antedate the report by more than 10 years, or 2) suits and judgments, records of arrest, indictment, or conviction of a crime, any other adverse information which antedates the report by more than 7 years. CRSA §12-14.3-105.3(1). However this provision was added by SB 97-133 §3, effective August 1, 1997. Under 15 U.S.C. §1681t(b)(1)(E), this section is pre-empted by the FCRA 1681t

However, that does not apply to a consumer report used in the connection with the employment of an individual whose salary equals $75,000 or more. CRSA §12-14.3-105.3(2). This is the same as the FCRA and there is no conflict.

Employment: Employers, educational institutes, state and local government agencies shall not in any application or interview require an applicant to disclose any information contained in sealed records. Such applicant may not be denied solely because of the applicant's refusal to disclose arrest and criminal record information that has been sealed. CRSA §24-72-308(1)(f)(1).

Agency Guidelines for Pre-Employment Inquiries: Colorado Civil Rights Division, Publications, "Preventing Job Discrimination" is available online at www.dora.state.co.us/civil-rights/Publications/JobDiscrim2001.pdf.

State Statutes and Codes: www.michie.com/colorado/lpext.dll?f=templates&fn=main-h.htm&cp=

Legislative Bill Search: www.leg.state.co.us/Clics/CLICS2008A/csl.nsf/MainBills?openFrameset

Colorado State Criminal Records Agency

Bureau of Investigation, State Repository, Identification Unit, 690 Kipling St, Suite 3000, Denver, CO 80215 **Phone:** 303-239-4208; **Fax:** 303-239-5858 **Web:** http://cbi.state.co.us

Search Note: Records are available to the general public. The requester must sign a disclaimer stating "This record shall not be used for the direct solicitation of business for pecuniary gain." Include the following in your request-full name, date of birth, and disclaimer. The SSN, race, and gender are optional. Fingerprints are optional unless statutorily-required. Records are 100% fingerprint supported. If charged after fingerprinted, the practice of notifying the state is becoming more common, though this not yet statewide.

What Is Released: All records or arrests are released, including those without dispositions, except sealed records, juvenile records and pending mental comps. Records are available from early 1950s. Records prior to 1967 are in on-site computer archives. 17% of all arrests in database have final dispositions recorded, over 78% for those arrests within last 5 years.

Access Methods: mail, in person, online.

Online Searching: See https://www.cbirecordscheck.com/CBI_New/CBI_newIndex.asp. Requesters must use a credit card, an account does not need to be established. However, account holders may set up a batch system. The fee is $6.85 per record.

Colorado Sexual Offender Registry

Colorado Bureau of Investigation , SOR Unit, 690 Kipling St, Suite 3000, Denver, CO 80215 **Phone:** 303-239-4222; **Fax:** 303-239-4661 **Web:** http://sor.state.co.us

Note: Each police or sheriff's agency is required to maintain a list of convicted sex offenders in their jurisdiction and may release that information to the public. Requesters are screened for purpose, they must be at least 18 years of age.

Online Searching: The website gives access to only certain high-risk registered sex offenders in the following categories: Sexually Violent Predator (SVP), Multiple Offenses, Failed to Register, and adult felony conviction.

Colorado Incarceration Records Agency

Colorado Department of Corrections , Offender Records Customer Support, 2862 South Circle Dr. #418, Colorado Springs, CO 80906-4195 **Phones:** ; Locator Service- 719-226-4880; **Fax:** 719-226-4899 **Web:** www.doc.state.co.us

Online Searching: Search the Inmate Locater for only active offenders and parolees at https://exdoc.state.co.us/inmate_locator/offender_search_splash.php.   This   is   not   a historical search. Also, one may email locator requests to pio@doc.state.co.us.

Colorado State Court System

Court Administrator:	State Court Administrator, 1301 Pennsylvania St, Suite 300, Denver, CO, 80203; 303-861-1111. www.courts.state.co.us.
Court Structure:	District and County Courts are combined in most counties. Combined courts usually search both civil or criminal indexes for a single fee, except as indicated in the profiles. Municipal courts only have jurisdiction over traffic, parking, and ordinance violations.
Find Felony Records:	District Courts
Misdemeanor Records:	County Courts
Online Access:	LexisNexis CourtLink was appointed to act as agent for the Colorado Judicial Department to act as the conduit for the ICON (Integrated Colorado Online Network) and provide access to vendors and to the

general public. The vendors permit users to look at a name index - the Register of Actions - to court filings and appearance dates. There is a fee. The name search includes viewing all of the Registers of Actions related to that name. Images or copies of documents are not available from any of the commercial sites and may only be obtained by contacting the individual court where the documents were filed.

Opinions from the Court of Appeals are available from the website at www.courts.state.co.us/.

Searching Hints: November 15, 2001, Broomfield City & County came into existence, derived from the counties of Adams, Boulder, Jefferson and Weld. A District and County Court was established.

Connecticut
Connecticut Statutes & Related Employer Restrictions

General Rule: Conviction information shall be available to the public for any purpose. CGSA §54-142K(c)(k)(b). Any person may authorize in writing an agency holding non-conviction information pertaining directly to such person to disclose it to his attorney at law. CGSA §54-142K(d). Otherwise, non-conviction information may only be release 1) for the purpose of research, or 2) if there is a specific agreement with a criminal justice agency. CGSA §54-142(m).

Definitions: CGSA §54-142(g)

Conviction Information – criminal history record information which has not been erased, and which discloses that a person has pleaded guilty, or nolo contendere to, or was convicted of any criminal offense, and the terms of the sentence.

Non-conviction Information – means 1) criminal history record information that has been erased; 2) information relating to person granted youthful offender status; 3) continuances which are more than thirteen months old.

Expunged Record: Whenever the accused is found not guilty of the charge, or the charge is dismissed, all police records and records of the state attorney pertaining to such charge shall be erased. Erasure does not apply to persons found not guilty by reason of mental disease or guilty but not criminally responsible by reason of mental disease. CGSA §54-142a(a). Youthful offenders may have police and court records erased if there are no further offenses within the time frames (2-4 years) depending upon the type of the original offense. CGSA §46b-146.

Caveat: No employer may require an employee or prospective employee to disclose erased records. Employers may not deny employment to a prospective employee because of the existence of an erased record. CGSA §31-51i(b) and (d).

Consumer Report: CRA must give notice to consumer if criminal record information is sought for employment purposes and provide name of entity requesting the report. Further, only current Connecticut criminal records may be furnished – no database records. 2008 Senate Bill 705.

State Statutes and Codes: www.cga.ct.gov/asp/menu/Statutes.asp

Legislative Bill Search: www.cga.ct.gov/asp/menu/Search.asp

Connecticut State Criminal Records Agency

Department of Public Safety, Bureau of Identification, 1111 Country Club Rd, Middletown, CT 06457 **Phone:** 860-685-8480; **Fax:** 860-685-8361 **Web:** www.ct.gov/dps/site/default.asp

Search Notes: DPS-846-C Form "State Police Bureau of Identification Request" can be downloaded from the website. Records are open to the public using a name search. Fingerprint searches are not available to the public. Pending case information is available. Include the following in your request-date of birth Request forms may be downloaded from the website. Approximately 90% of the records on file are fingerprint supported.

What Is Released: The records released to the public contain guilty pending and nolles if the nolle has not reached 13 months. Nolle over 13 months can appear if part of an indictment that contains a disposition. Records are available from the 1950's on. Records were first computerized in 1983. The following data is not released: dismissals or juvenile records. After receiving, it takes about 30 days before new records are available for inquiry.

Access Methods: mail, in person.

Connecticut Sexual Offender Registry

Department of Public Safety , Sex Offender Registry Unit, PO Box 2794, Middletown, CT 06757-9294, (courier address: 1111 Country Club Rd, Middleton, CT 06457.) **Phone:** 860-685-8060; **Fax:** 860-685-8349

Web: www.ct.gov/dps/cwp/view.asp?a=2157&Q=294474&dpsNav=|

Online Searching: The website has two searches: those convicted of a CT law, and those offenders who violated a law in a different state but are living or working in CT. Search by name or town, ZIP Code, or entire list. Record data can be purchased in bulk. Email questions to sex.offender.registry@po.state.ct.us.

Connecticut Incarceration Records Agency

Connecticut Department of Corrections , Public Information Office, 24 Wolcott Hill Rd, Wethersfield, CT 06109 **Phone:** Locater- 860-692-7780; **Fax:** 860-692-7783
Web: www.ct.gov/doc/site/default.asp

Search Notes: Direct questions to DOC.PIO@po.state.ct.us. Records are open to the public using a name search. Location, conviction and sentencing information, bond, and release dates are released. An FOI request must be submitted to access records for inmates not currently incarcerated.

Online Searching: Current inmates may be searched at www.ctinmateinfo.state.ct.us/searchop.asp.

Connecticut State Court System

Court Administrator:	Chief Court Administrator, 231 Capitol Av, Hartford, CT, 06106; 860-757-2100. www.jud.ct.gov/.
Court Structure:	The Superior Court is the sole court of original jurisdiction for all causes of action. The state is divided into 15 Judicial Districts, 20 Geographic Area Courts, and 14 Juvenile Districts. When not combined, the Judicial District Courts handle felony and civil cases while the Geographic Area Courts handle misdemeanors.
Find Felony Records:	Judicial District Court
Misdemeanor Records:	Geographic Area Courts
Online Access:	The Judicial Branch offers web look-up to docket information at www.jud.ct.gov/jud2.htm. The criminal and motor vehicle case docket data is available on cases where a disposition or bond forfeiture occurred on or after 1/1/2000. To search statewide, leave the location field blank.
	Opinions from the Supreme and Appellate courts are available at www.jud.state.ct.us/opinions.htm..
Searching Hints:	The State Record Center in Enfield, CT is the repository for criminal and some civil records. Case records are sent to the Record Center from 3 months to 5 years after disposition by the courts. These records are then maintained 10 years for misdemeanors and 20+ years for felonies. If a requester is certain that the record is at the Record Center, it is quicker to direct the request there rather than to the original court of record. Only written requests are accepted. Search requirements: full defendant name, docket number, disposition date, and court action. Fee is $5.00 for each docket. Direct Requests to: Connecticut Record Center, 111 Phoenix Ave., Enfield CT 06082, 860-741-3714.

Delaware

Delaware Statutes & Related Employer Restrictions

General Rule: The Bureau may furnish information pertaining to the identification and conviction data of any person to individuals and agencies for the purpose of employment of the person whose record is sought.   11 Del. C §8513(c).

Definitions: 11 Del. C §8502.

> Conviction Data - criminal history record information relating to an arrest which has led to a conviction or other disposition adverse to the subject. This also includes dismissal entered after a period of probation, suspension, or deferral of a sentence. It does not include decisions not to prosecute, dismissals, or acquittals.

> Disposition - includes trial verdicts of guilty or not guilty, nolle prosequis, Attorney General probations, pleas of guilty or nolo contendere, dismissals, incompetence to stand trial, findings of delinquency or non-delinquency, and initiation and completion of appellate proceedings.

Expungement: If a person is charged with the commission of a crime and is acquitted or nolle prosequi is taken, the person may file a petition requesting expungment of the police and court records. 11 Del. C §4372.

> An offense for which records have been expunged shall not have to be disclosed by the person as an arrest for any reason.   11 Del. C §4374(e).

Exception: An employment application as an employee of a law enforcement agency. 11 Del.C. §4374(a)

State Statutes and Codes: http://delcode.delaware.gov/

Legislative Bill Search: http://legis.delaware.gov/

Delaware State Criminal Records Agency

Delaware State Police, State Bureau of Identification, PO Box 430, Dover, DE 19903-0430, (courier address: 1407 N Dupont Highway, Dover, DE 19901.) **Phone:** 302-739-2134; **Fax:** 302-739-5888   **Web:** http://dsp.delaware.gov/default.shtml

Search Notes: Records are available to the general public, but must have a signed release from the subject for the fingerprint search and release of information. Include the following in your request-fingerprints, full name, signed release.

What Is Released: Records are available from 1935. If the disposition is not known by this agency, the record will say "disposition not known." Will only release records with dispositions to pre-employment screeners. 94% of all arrests in database have final dispositions recorded, 92% for arrests within last 5 years.

Access Methods: mail, in person.

Delaware Sexual Offender Registry

Delaware State Police , Sex Offender Central Registry, PO Box 430, Dover, DE 19903-0430, (courier address: 1407 N Dupont Highway, Dover, DE 19901.) **Phone:** 302-672-5306; **Fax:** 302-739-5888 **Web:** http://sexoffender.dsp.delaware.gov/

Note: There are three Tiers or Levels of offenders in the state. The public is only made aware of Tiers 2 and 3 via the Internet through public notification programs by local law enforcement. Door-to-door is used for Tier 3 notification. Name searching is not available in the state except through the web page.

Online Searching: Statewide registry can be searched at the website. The site gives the ability to search by last name, Development, and city or Zip Code. Any combination of these fields may be used; however, a search cannot be performed if both a city and Zip Code are entered. Email questions to soffender@state.de.us.

Delaware Incarceration Records Agency

Delaware Department of Corrections , Director of Central Offender Records, 245 McKee Rd, Dover, DE 19904 **Phone:** 302-857-5490; **Fax:** 302-739-7486 **Web:** http://doc.delaware.gov/

The Department of Correction does not offer the public access to an automated database of offender information. But escapees and death row convicts are listed. However, the public may receive basic information about an offender, including whether the individual is incarcerated in Delaware, where the individual is incarcerated and, how to contact an offender, by calling the number above. Escapees and death penalty lists are available online at http://doc.delaware.gov/escapees/escapees.shtml.

Delaware State Court System

Court Administrator:	Administrative Office of the Courts, Supreme Court of Delaware, 500 N King St, #11600, Wilmington, DE, 19801; 302-255-0090, 8:30AM-5PM. http://courts.delaware.gov.
Court Structure:	Superior Courts have jurisdiction over felonies and all drug offenses, the Court of Common Pleas has jurisdiction over all misdemeanors. Justice of the Peace Court hears certain misdemeanors and most motor vehicle cases (excluding felonies) and the Justices of the Peace may act as committing magistrates for all crimes.
Find Felony Records:	Superior Court
Misdemeanor Records:	Court of Common Pleas

Online Access: Chancery, Superior, Common Pleas, and Supreme Courts opinions and orders are available free online at http://courts.state.de.us/opinions. Supreme, Superior, and Common Pleas Courts calendars are available free at http://courts.delaware.gov/calendars.

District of Columbia

District Statutes & Related Employer Restrictions

General Rule: The Mayor shall keep records of general complaint files, records of lost, stolen, or missing property . . . and arrest books which contain information about the offense with which the person was arrested and the disposition of the case. DC ST §5-113.01. Those records shall be open to the public when not in actual use. DC ST §5-113.06.

Exception: It is illegal to make the subject of the record pay to produce the record. Such "arrest records" without a conviction shall only contain listings of convictions and forfeitures of collateral that have occurred within 10 years of the time at which such record is requested. DC ST §2-1402.66.

State Statutes and Codes: http://government.westlaw.com/linkedslice/default.asp?SP=DCC-1000
Legislative Bill Search: www.dccouncil.us/lims/default.asp

District of Columbia Criminal Records Agency

Metropolitan Police Dept., Henry J Daley Bldg, Identification and Records Section, 300 Indiana Ave NW, Rm 3055, Washington, DC 20001 **Phone:** 202-727-4245, 202-727-4357; **Fax:** 202-442-4247 **Web:** http://mpdc.dc.gov/mpdc/site/default.asp

Search Notes: Records are available to the general public. Records are referred to as Police Clearances. Include the following in your request-signed, notarized release from subject, full name (middle initial), date and place of birth, year. Use of the PD70 Application (Criminal History Request) is suggested. The SSN, race, current address and case number, if known, are helpful. Although 80% of the records are fingerprint supported, fingerprints searches are not available.

What Is Released: Records are available for 10 years. The only records released to the public contain convictions. 46% of all arrests in database have final dispositions recorded, 84% for those arrests within last 5 years.

Access Methods: mail, in person.

District of Columbia Sexual Offender Registry

Metropolitan Police Department , Sex Offender Registry Unit, 300 Indiana Ave NW, Rm 3009, Washington, DC 20001 **Phone:** 202-727-4407; **Fax:** 202-727-9292 **Web:** http://mpdc.dc.gov/mpdc/site/default.asp

Note: In general, an offense requiring registration is a felony sexual assault (regardless of the age of the victim); an offense involving sexual abuse or exploitation of minors; or sexual abuse of wards, patients, or clients. Searchers can visit any police station and inspect a public registry that will contain current information on all registered sex offenders in the District of Columbia.

Online Searching: A list of Class A & B registered sex offenders is provided on the website. Under "Services" click on Sex Offender Registry.

District of Columbia Incarceration Records

District of Columbia Department of Corrections , DC Jail Records Office, 1901 D Street SE, Washington, DC 20003 **Phones:** 202-673-8257; VINE Inmate Information Line- 202-673-8136 option; **Fax:** 202-671-2043 **Web:** www.doc.dc.gov/doc/site/default.asp

Dictrict of Columbia Local Court System

Court Administrator: Executive Office, 500 Indiana Av NW, Room 1500, Washington, DC, 20001; 202-879-1700. www.dccourts.gov/dccourts/index.jsp.

Court Structure: The Superior Court in DC is divided into 17 divisions, one of which is criminal.

Find Felony Records: Superior Court

Misdemeanor Records: Superior Court

Online Access: The Superior Court and Court of Appeals offer access to opinions at www.dcbar.org.

Florida

Florida Statutes & Related Employer Restrictions

General Rule: Persons in the private sector and non-criminal justice agencies may be provided criminal history information upon tender of fees. Access is without regard to quantity or category of criminal history record information requested.   FSA §943.053.

Person may not be disqualified from employment by the state, any of its agencies or political subdivisions, nor shall a person whose civil rights have been restored be disqualified to practice, pursue, or engage in any occupation, trade, vocation, profession, or business for which a license, permit, or certificate is required to be issued by the state because of a prior conviction of a crime.   FSA §112.011(1)(a) and (b).

Above rule is not applicable if:
1. prior conviction of a felony or first-degree misdemeanor and directly related to the position of employment sought   FSA §112.011(1)(a) and (b).
2. Law enforcement or correctional agency   FSA §112.011(2)(a).
3. Fire Department   FSA §112.011(2)(b).
4. Positions deemed to be critical to security or public safety   FSA §112.011 (2)(c).

Definitions: FSA §943.045

> Criminal History Information – includes information about arrests, detentions, indictments, or other formal criminal charges and the disposition thereof.
>
> Expunction of a Criminal Record – court-ordered physical destruction or obliteration of a record.
>
> Sealing of a Criminal Record – preservation of a record in a way that it is secure and inaccessible to any person not having a legal right to access it.

Minors: Minor who is a serious or habitual offender – retain criminal history record for 5 years after offender reaches 21 at which time the record is expunged. FSA §943.0515(1)(a). Minor who is NOT a serious or habitual offender – retain record for 5 years after offender reaches 19 at which time the record is expunged. FSA §943.0515(1)(b).

> If person 18 and charged with or convicted of forcible felony and juvenile record has not been destroyed – person's juvenile record is merged and becomes apart of person's adult record.
> FSA §943.0515(2)(a).
>
> If at any time minor adjudicated as an adult for forcible felony – criminal record prior to the time of adult adjudication is merged with record as an adjudicated adult. FSA §943.0515(2)(b).

Expunction: Any criminal record of a minor or an adult, which is ordered expunged by a court, must be physically destroyed. FSA §943.0585(4).

> The person whose record is expunged may lawfully deny or fail to acknowledge the arrests covered by the expunged record, except 1) a candidate for employment with a criminal justice agency, 2) a defendant in a criminal prosecution, 3) candidate for admission to the Florida Bar, 4) person seeking employment who would have direct contact with children, the developmentally disabled, the aged, or the elderly, or 5) a person seeking employment at a school, any district school board, or any government entity that licenses child care facilities. FSA §943.0585(4)(a).

State Statutes and Codes: www.flsenate.gov/Statutes/index.cfm?submenu=-1&Tab=statutes

Legislative Bill Search: www.flsenate.gov/Welcome/index.cfm

Florida State Criminal Records Agency

Florida Department of Law Enforcement, User Services Bureau/Public Records, PO Box 1489, Tallahassee, FL 32302, (courier address: 2331 Phillip Rd, Tallahassee, FL 32308.) **Phones:** 850-410-8109, 850-410-8107; **Fax:** 850-410-8201   **Web:** www.fdle.state.fl.us

Search Notes: Records are available to the general public. Include the following in your request-date of birth, race, sex, name. SSN is helpful You can submit fingerprints, for the same fee, but it is not required. 100% of the arrest records are fingerprint-supported.

What Is Released: All records are released, including those without dispositions except sealed or expunged records, juvenile records prior to 10/94 if felony, 06/30/96 if misdemeanor. Records are available from the early 1930's. The SSN is suppressed except for the last 4

digits. 70% of all felony arrests in database have final dispositions recorded; 63% of misdemeanors. 68% of all records within last 5 years include dispositions.

Access Methods: mail, in person, online.

Online Searching: Criminal history information may be ordered over the Department Program Internet site at www2.fdle.state.fl.us/cchinet. A $23.00 fee applies. Juvenile records from 10/1994 forward are also available. Credit card ordering will return records to your screen or via email. A great webpage profiling this agency's various records and services is at www.fdle.state.fl.us/criminalhistory/. Search state's wanted list at www3.fdle.state.fl.us/fdle/wpersons_search.asp.

Florida Sexual Offender Registry

Florida Department of Law Enforcement , Offender Regsitration and Tracking Srvs, PO Box 1489, Tallahassee, FL 32302, (courier address: 2331 Phillips Rd, Tallahassee, FL 32308.) **Phone:** 888-357-7332, 850-410-8572; **Fax:** 850-410-8599 **Web:** http://offender.fdle.state.fl.us/offender/homepage.do

Note: Chapter 97-299, Laws of Florida, requires certain sex offenders to directly register with law enforcement or to have information compiled by the Department of Corrections, with the information to be provided to FDLE. Under Chapter 119, Florida Statutes, the Public Records Law, any of the public records of the Department of Law Enforcement are available for review upon request, subject to statutorily-authorized editing of exempt or confidential information.

Online Searching: Search the registry from the web page. Searching can be done by name or by geographic area.

Florida Incarceration Records Agency

Florida Department of Corrections , Central Records Office, 2601 Blair Stone Rd, Tallahassee, FL 32399-2500 **Phones:** 850-488-2533; Records- 850-488-1503; **Fax:** 850-413-8302 **Web:** www.dc.state.fl.us

Note: Full records are housed at the individual institutions, though inmate information available through this agency and the website should sufficiently fulfill most searches. Location, DOC number, physical identifiers, conviction information, and release dates released.

Online Searching: Extensive search capabilities are offered at www.dc.state.fl.us/inmateinfo/inmateinfomenu.asp. Click on Inmate Population Information Search. Bulk data may be purchased on a CD.

Florida State Court System

Court Administrator: Office of State Courts Administrator, Supreme Court Bldg, 500 S Duval, Tallahassee, FL, 32399-1900; 850-922-5081. www.flcourts.org.

Court Structure: Many counties have combined Circuit and County Courts. Circuit courts have general trial jurisdiction over matters not assigned by statute to the county courts and also hear appeals from county court cases.

Find Felony Records: Circuit Court

Misdemeanor Records: County Court

Online Access: Search Supreme Court dockets online at http://jweb.flcourts.org/pls/docket/ds_docket_search. Many courts offer online access to the public, usually through the Clerk of the Circuit Court. Fees are involved when ordering copies; save $1.50 per record by becoming a subscriber. Visit www.flcourts.org/gen_public/stratplan/privacy.shtml for the latest information regarding the electronic release of court records in Florida.

Searching Hints: All courts have one address and switchboard; however, the divisions within the court(s) are completely separate. Requesters should specify which court and which division – e.g., Circuit Criminal, County Criminal, etc. – the request is directed to, even though some counties will automatically check both with one request.

Georgia

Georgia Statutes & Related Employer Restrictions

General Rule: Georgia Crime Information Center shall make criminal history records available to private persons and businesses. Private individuals and businesses must provide a fingerprint or a signed consent of the person. When identifying information provided is sufficient to identify person whose records are requested electronically, the center may disseminate electronically criminal history records of in-state felony convictions, pleas, and sentences without consent of the person whose records are requested. Records of arrest, charges, and sentences for crimes relating to first offender in which the offender has been exonerated and discharged without court adjudication of guilt may not be released. Ga. Code Ann. §35-3-34(a).

Exceptions to allow release of records of exoneration include if the person was exonerated or discharged on or after July 1, 2004, and

1. Person applied for employment with a school, child welfare agency, or entity that provides care for minor children and the record pertained to alleged child

molestation, sexual battery, enticing a child for indecent purposes, sexual exploitation of a child, pimping, pandering, or incest; or

2. Person applied for employment with a nursing home, personal care home, or entity which provides care for the elderly and the record pertained to alleged sexual battery, pimping, pandering, or incest; or

3. Person applied for employment with a facility that provides services to the mentally ill and the record pertained to alleged sexual battery, pimping, pandering, or incest. Ga. Code Ann. §35-3-34.1

Caveat: In the event an adverse employment decision is made against the person whose record was obtained, the person must be notified by the business of all the information pursuant to that decision. Ga. Code Ann. §35-3-34(b).

Definitions: Ga. Code Ann. §35-3-30

Criminal History Record Information – includes notations of arrest, detentions, indictments, accusations, information, or other formal charges, and any disposition arising there from, sentencing, correctional supervision, and release.

State Statutes and Codes: www.lexis-nexis.com/hottopics/gacode/default.asp

Legislative Bill Search: www.legis.state.ga.us

Georgia State Criminal Records Agency

Georgia Bureau of Investigation, Attn: GCIC, PO Box 370748, Decatur, GA 30037-0748, (courier address: 3121 Panthersville Rd, Decatur, GA 30034.) **Phone:** 404-244-2639; **Fax:** 404-270-8529 **Web:** www.ganet.org/gbi/

Search Notes: GCIC is the central criminal records repository for the State. But anyone with a signed release may make a record request at any local law enforcement office and the statewide record will be provided. Fees for this may vary; the maximum fee is $20.00.

Records are available to employers, government agencies including licensing agencies, and adoption and foster care providers. 100% of arrest records are fingerprint supported. Include the following in your request-name, set of fingerprints, date of birth, sex, race, SSN. Certain law enforcement agencies, who are online, and local agencies may access and retrieve records for investigative/background purposes. These agencies have the option of requesting a signed release from subject or including a set of fingerprints.

What Is Released: Information released includes arrest, disposition, and custodial information for offenses designated as fingerprintable by the State AG. Records without dispositions are released. Records are available from 1972 forward. The following data is not released: juvenile records, traffic ticket information or out-of-state or federal charges. After receiving, it takes 1-3 days before new records are available for inquiry. 70% of all arrests in database have final dispositions recorded, 82% for those arrests within last 5 years.

Access Methods: mail, in person.

Georgia Sexual Offender Registry

Georgia Bureau of Investigations , GCIC - Sexual Offender Registry, PO Box 370808, Decatur, GA 30037, (courier address: 3121 Panthersville Rd, Decatur, GA 30037.) **Phones:** ; 24 Hour Line to GBI- 404-244-2600; **Fax:** 404-270-8452

Web: http://services.georgia.gov/gbi/gbisor/disclaim.html

Online Searching: Search at http://services.georgia.gov/gbi/gbisor/disclaim.html. Earliest records go back to 07/01/96. Close to 80% of registered offenders have photographs on the web site. Searches may be conducted for sex offenders, absconders, and predators.

Georgia Incarceration Records Agency

Georgia Department of Corrections , Inmate Records Office - 6th Fl, East Tower, 2 Martin Luther King, Jr. Drive, S.E., Atlanta, GA 30334-4900 **Phone:** 404-656-4569; **Fax:** 404-463-6232 **Web:** www.dcor.state.ga.us

Online Searching: The website has an extensive array of search capabilities.

Georgia State Court System

Court Administrator: Court Administrator, 244 Washington St SW, Suite 550, Atlanta, GA, 30334; 404-656-5171,. www.georgiacourts.org.

Court Structure: Georgia's Superior Courts are arranged in 49 circuits of general jurisdiction, and these assume the role of a State Court if the county does not have one. The 69 State Courts, like Superior Courts, can conduct jury trials, but are limited jurisdiction. Magistrate Courts can issue arrest warrants and set bond on all felonies. Probate courts can, in certain cases, issue search and arrest warrants, and hear miscellaneous misdemeanors.

Find Felony Records: Superior Court

Misdemeanor Records: Superior, State, Magistrate, and Municipal Courts

Online Access: A limited number of county courts offer online access to court records, but there is no statewide online access available statewide. Search the dockets of the Court of Appeals at www.gaappeals.us/. Search dockets of the Supreme Court at www.gasupreme.us/computer docket.php. Make online purchases of certificates of admission and good standing ($3.00), Supreme Court opinions ($5.00), and certified copies of Supreme Court opinions ($8.00).

Searching Hints: In most Georgia counties, the courts will not perform criminal record searches. An in-person search or the use of a record retriever is required.

Hawaii

Hawaii Statutes & Related Employer Restrictions

Employment: A person shall not be disqualified from public office or employment by the State or be disqualified to practice, pursue, or engage in any occupation, trade, vocation, profession or business for which a license, permit, or certificate is required by the State solely by reason of a prior conviction of a crime. HRS 831-3.1(a). Employer may consider convictions not arrests. HRS 378-2.5.

An employer may inquire about and consider an individual's criminal conviction record, within the most recent 10 years since the date of conviction or release from prison, provided that the conviction record bears a rational relationship to the duties and responsibilities of the position. HRS §378-2.5(a).

Inquiry into and consideration of conviction for prospective employee is allowed only after the prospective employee has received a conditional offer of employment.

Expunged Record: The person who has his or her criminal records expunged shall be treated as not having been arrested, and may state no record exists. HRS §831-3.2.

Agency Guidelines for Pre-Employment Inquiries: Hawaii Civil Rights Commission "Guide to Pre-Employment Inquiries" is available online at www.state.hi.us/hcrc/forms/pre-empinquire.pdf

State Statutes and Codes: www.capitol.hawaii.gov/site1/hrs/default.asp

Legislative Bill Search: www.capitol.hawaii.gov/site1/docs/docs.asp?press1=docs

Hawaii State Criminal Records Agency

Hawaii Criminal Justice Data Center, Criminal Record Request, 465 S King St, Room 101, Honolulu, HI 96813 **Phone:** 808-587-3279 **Web:** http://hawaii.gov/ag/hcjdc/

Search Notes: Include the following in your request- any aliases. Also helpful are gender, date of birth, Social Security Number. Submission of fingerprints is an option. Per a US DOJ Study in 2003, 99% of the records are fingerprint-supported.

What Is Released: Only records with convictions are released to the public. Records without dispositions are not released. Records are available from the 1930's. After receiving, it takes 1 to 20 days before new records are available for inquiry. Per a US DOJ Study in 2003, 90% of all arrests in database have final dispositions recorded, 91% for those arrests within last 5 years.

Access Methods: mail, in person, online.

Online Searching: Online access is available view eCrim at http://ecrim.ehawaii.gov/ahewa/. There is no fee to view the results of your search; the option is available to purchase a certified copy of the record for $13.00. Registration is required. Questions are directed to 808-587-4220.

Hawaii Sexual Offender Registry

Hawaii Criminal Justice Data Center , Sexual Offender Registry, 465 S King St, Room 101, Honolulu, HI 96813 **Phone:** 808-587-3100; **Fax:** 808-857-3024 **Web:** http://sexoffenders.hawaii.gov/index.html

Note: Information regarding covered offenders is permitted pursuant to Chapter 846E. Public access to this information is based solely on the fact of each offender's criminal conviction and is not based on an estimate of the offender's level of dangerousness. The following information about offenders is available to the public: name, prior names, aliases, photograph, residence address, personal vehicles(s) driven, street name of employment, college/university affiliation, and crime for which convicted.

Online Searching: Search at http://sexoffenders.ehawaii.gov/sexoff/search.jsp?. Search by name, street or ZIP Code.

Hawaii Incarceration Records Agency

Hawaii Department of Public Safety , Inmate Classification, 919 Ala Moana Blvd #401, Honolulu, HI 96814 **Phone:** 808-587-2567; **Fax:** 808-587-2568 **Web:** www.hawaii.gov/ag/hcjdc/

Hawaii State Court System

Court Administrator: Administrative Director of Courts, Judicial Branch, 417 S King St, Honolulu, HI, 96813; 808-539-4900. www.courts.state.hi.us/index.jsp.

Court Structure: Hawaii's trial level is comprised of Circuit Courts (with Family Courts) and District Courts. These trial courts function in four judicial circuits: First (Oahu), Second (Maui/Molokai/Lanai), Third (Hawaii County), and Fifth (Kauai/Niihau). The Fourth Circuit was merged with the Third in 1943. Circuit Courts are general jurisdiction and handle all jury trials and felony cases. The District Court handles criminal cases punishable by a fine and/or less then 1-yr imprisonment, also DUI cases.

Find Felony Records: Circuit Court

Misdemeanor Records: District Court

Online Access: Free online access to all Circuit Court and family court records is available at the website www.courts.state.hi.us (click on "Search Court Records"). Search by name or case number. These records are not considered "official" for FCRA compliant searches. Most courts have access back to mid 1980's. Also, opinions from the Appellate Court are available from the home page.

Searching Hints: Most Hawaii state courts offer a public access terminal to search records at the courthouse.

Idaho

Idaho Statutes & Related Employer Restrictions

General Rule: A person, private or public agency upon written application may obtain a copy of a person criminal history record. A record of an arrest that does not contain a disposition after twelve months from the date of the arrest may only be disseminated by the department to criminal justice agencies, the subject of the record, or a person requesting the criminal history information who has a signed release from the subject of the record. A person, private or public agency shall not disseminate criminal history information to a person that is not a criminal justice agency without a signed release from the subject of the record. ID ST §67-3008(2)(b).

Definitions: ID ST §67-3001

> Criminal History Record – includes arrests, prosecutions, disposition of cases by court, sentencing, probation and parole, and information from correctional agencies.

Agency Guidelines for Pre-Employment Inquiries: Idaho Human Rights Commission, "Pre-Employment Inquiries" is available online at www.jobservice.us/lawintvw3.htm.

State Statutes and Codes: www.legislature.idaho.gov/statutesrules.htm

Legislative Bill Search: www3.state.id.us/legislat/legtrack.html

Idaho State Criminal Records Agency

State Repository, Bureau of Criminal Identification, PO Box 700, Meridian, ID 83680-0700, (courier address: 700 S Stratford Dr, Meridian, ID 83642.) **Phone:** 208-884-7130; **Fax:** 208-884-7193 **Web:** www.isp.state.id.us

Search Notes: A signed release is not required, but suggested. Include the following in your request-name, DOB. SSN and alias will aid in identification. Fingerprints are optional but may be required to establish positive identification Fingerprint searches take 1-3 days. 100% of records are fingerprint-supported.

What Is Released: A record of an arrest without disposition after 12 months from date of arrest will only be given if signed release presented. Requests without the release will receive only records with dispositions. Records are available from 1960 or until person reaches 99. The following data is not released: juvenile records unless charged as an adult. 66% of all arrests in database have final dispositions recorded, and at least 67% for those arrests within last 5 years.

Access Methods: mail, in person.

Idaho Sexual Offender Registry

State Repository , Central Sexual Offender Registry, PO Box 700, Meridian, ID 83680-0700, (courier address: 700 S Stratford Dr, Meridian, ID 83642.) **Phone:** 208-884-7305; **Fax:** 208-884-7193 **Web:** www.isp.state.id.us

Online Searching: Access from the web page is available to the public. Make inquires by name, address, or by county or ZIP Code. Mapping is also available. Questions may be directed by email to idsor@isp.idaho.gov. Requests may be made on a named individual or a list of registered sex offenders by ZIP Code or county.

Idaho Incarceration Records Agency

Idaho Department of Corrections , Records Bureau, 1299 N. Orchard Street, Suite 110, Boise, ID 83706 **Phone:** 208-658-2000; **Fax:** 208-327-7444 **Web:** www.idoc.idaho.gov/

Online Searching: Search at https://www.accessidaho.org/public/corr/offender/search.html Provides information about offenders currently under Idaho Department of Correction jurisdiction: those incarcerated, on probation, or on parole. Names of individuals who have served time and satisfied their sentence will appear - their convictions will not.

Idaho State Court System

Court Administrator:	Administrative Director of Courts, Supreme Court Building, PO Box 83720, Boise, ID, 83720-0101; 208-334-2246. www.isc.idaho.gov.
Court Structure:	The District Court oversees felony and most civil cases, and appeals of decisions of the Magistrate Division. The Magistrate Division hears initial felony proceedings through the preliminary hearing, criminal misdemeanors, infractions.
Find Felony Records:	District Court
Misdemeanor Records:	District Court
Online Access:	The statewide computer system at www.idcourts.us offers free online access to court records back to at least 1995, from the state Supreme Court Data Repository. Online results include identifiers year of birth and middle initial. All courts provide public access terminals onsite. Also, appellate and supreme court opinions are available at www.isc.idaho.gov/opinions/.
Searching Hints:	A statewide court administrative rule states that record custodians do not have a duty to "compile or summarize information contained in a record, nor ... to create new records for the requesting party." Under this rule, some courts will not perform searches. Many courts require a signed release for employment record searches.

Illinois

Illinois Statutes & Related Employer Restrictions

General Rule: All conviction information shall be open to public inspection in the State of Illinois. All persons, state agencies, and unit of local government shall have access to inspect, examine, and reproduce such information. 20 ILCS 2635/5.

A requestor shall submit a request to the department and maintain on file for at least 2 years a release signed by the individual to whom the information pertains. 20 ILCS 2635/7.

A requester shall only permit the subsequent dissemination of conviction information furnished by the department for a 30-day period immediately following receipt of the info. 20 ILCS 2635/13.

Definitions: 20 ILCS 2635/3

Conviction Information – data reflecting a judgment of guilt or nolo contendere. Includes prior and subsequent criminal history event directly relating to such judgments such as arrest, charges filed, sentence imposed, fine imposed, all related probation, parole, and release information. Information is not conviction information when a judgment of guilt is reversed or vacated.

Requestor – any private individual, corporation, organization, employer, employment agency, labor organization, or non-criminal justice agency that has made a request pursuant to this Act to obtain conviction information.

State Statutes and Codes: www.ilga.gov/legislation/ilcs/ilcs.asp

Legislative Bill Search: www.ilga.gov/legislation/default.asp

Illinois State Criminal Records Agency

IL State Police Bureau of Identification, Civil Processing Unit, 260 N Chicago St, Joliet, IL 60432-4075 **Phones:** 815-740-5160; Forms- 815-740-5216 **Web:** www.isp.state.il.us/crimhistory/crimhistoryhome.cfm

Search Note: Requester must use the Uniform Conviction Information Form ISP6-405B. Personal requests are honored per Illinois statute. 100% of arrest records are fingerprint supported. Include the following in your request-name, date of birth, sex, race. Fingerprint cards are an option; a fingerprint search using Form ISP6-404B is recommended in order to assure proper identification. All forms can be ordered (but not downloaded) at the website. Maiden names must be submitted as a separate request, fee.

What Is Released: Records are available from 1932 forward. No records are released without a disposition of conviction. The following data is not released: records with warrants only, juvenile records unless juvenile convicted by an adult court of law. 52% of all arrests in database have final dispositions recorded, 52% for those arrests within last 5 years.

Access Methods: mail, in person, online.

Online Searching: Online access costs $10 per name or $16 if fingerprints submitted electronically ($20 if fingerprints submitted manually); discounts for quantities. Upon signing an interagency agreement with ISP and establishing an escrow account, users can submit inquiries by email. Responses are sent back in 24 to 48 hours by either email or fax. Visit www.isp.state.il.us/services/convictioninquiries.cfm to enroll.

Illinois Sexual Offender Registry

Illinois State Police , SOR Unit, 201 E Adams, Springfield, IL 62701 **Phone:** 217-785-0653 **Web:** www.isp.state.il.us/sor/

Note: Persons required to register as Sex Offenders are persons who have been charged of an offense listed in Illinois Compiled Statutes 730 ILCS 150/2. This office address is temporary due to storm. Will change in April 14, 2008. Illinois Compiled Statutes (730 ILCS 152/115 (a) and (b)) mandate that the Illinois State Police ("ISP") establish and maintain a statewide Sex Offender Database, accessible on the Internet. A status field indicates if offender listed as "COMPLIANT" are in good standing with the Sex Offender Registration Laws. Offenders listed as "NON-COMPLIANT" have failed to maintain accurate registration information.

Online Searching: The website provides an online listing of sex offenders required to register in the State of Illinois. The database is updated daily and allows searching by name, city, county, and ZIP Code.

Illinois Incarceration Records Agency

Illinois Department of Corrections , PO Box 19277, Springfield, IL 62794-9277, (courier address: 1301 Concordia Court, Springfield, IL 62794.) **Phone:** 217-522-2666 x2008; **Fax:** 217-524-6856 **Web:** www.idoc.state.il.us

Online Searching: Click on Inmate Search at the website or at www.idoc.state.il.us/subsections/search/default.asp.   A CD of data since 1982 may be purchased for $45. Send request to FOIA Officer at address above.

Illinois State Court System

Court Administrator: Administrative Office of Courts, 3101 Old Jacksonville Road, Springfield, IL 62704; 217-558-4490. www.state.il.us/court/.

Court Structure: Illinois is divided into 22 judicial circuits; 3 are single county: Cook, Du Page (18th Circuit) and Will (12th Circuit). The other 19 circuits consist of 2 or more contiguous counties. The Circuit Court of Cook County is the largest unified court system in the world. Its 2300-person staff handles approximately 2.4 million cases each year.

Find Felony Records:	Circuit Court
Misdemeanor Records:	Circuit Court
Online Access:	While there is no statewide public online system available, other than Appellate Court and Supreme Court opinions from the website. A number of Illinois Circuit Courts offer online access, many through a vendor at www.judici.com.
Searching Hints:	At least 90% of the courts offer public access terminals to look-up docket data. The search fee is set by statute and has three levels based on the county population. The higher the population, the larger the fee.

Indiana

Indiana Statutes & Related Employer Restrictions

General Rule: Law enforcement agencies shall release or allow inspection of a limited criminal history to non-criminal justice organizations or individuals if the subject of the request has applied for employment with a non-criminal justice organization or individual. IC 10-13-3-27

Limited criminal history records may not be disclosed which are over 15 years old if the person on record petitioned to limit access to his or her limited criminal history. IC 35-38-5-5.

Juvenile: Department may not release a person's juvenile history data to any person or agency unless the requestor is the juvenile of record or the juvenile's parents, guardian, or custodian. IC 10-13-4-12.

Definitions:

Criminal History Data – includes notations of arrests, indictments, information or other formal charges, information regarding a sex and violent offender, and any disposition, including sentencing, correctional system intake, transfer, and release. IC 10-13-3-5.

Limited Criminal History – information about any arrest or criminal charge which must include disposition. However it does include information about any arrest or criminal charge that occurred less than one year before the date of a request even if no disposition has been entered. IC 10-13-3-11

State Statutes and Codes: www.in.gov/legislative/ic/code/

Legislative Bill Search: www.in.gov/apps/lsa/session/billwatch/billinfo

Indiana State Criminal Records Agency

Indiana State Police, Criminal History Records, PO Box 6188, Indianapolis, IN 46206-6188
Phone: 317-232-5424; **Fax:** 317-233-8813   **Web:** www.IN.gov/isp/

Search Note: Include the following in your request-full name, date of birth, sex, race. Use State Form 8053 is required for mail or in-person requests. Go to www.in.gov/ai/appfiles/isp-lch/ for the link. Submitting fingerprints is an option, but if requesting record on oneself. 100% of the records are fingerprint-supported.

What Is Released: The release of records is governed by IC 10-13-3-27. A "Limited Criminal History" is available to designated entities including employers, licensing agencies, schools, and certain other designates. Record will show all activity, including arrests, dismissals, and convictions. But, if a charge is over a year old with no disposition, then the record will not be released. Records are available from 1935. The following data is not released: ISP case reports and arrests over 1 year with no disposition. After receiving, it takes 10 days before new records are available for inquiry. Approximately 45% of all arrests in database have final dispositions recorded, over 50% for those arrests within last 5 years. This agency now is notified when charges are made after fingerprints are submitted.

Access Methods: mail, in person, online.

Online Searching: A Limited Criminal History with only felonies and class A misdemeanor arrests is available at www.in.gov/ai/appfiles/isp-lch//. Using a credit card, the search fee is $16.32. Subscribers to accessIndiana can obtain records for $15.00 per search or for no charge if statutorily exempt, or $7.00 with a government exemption. Response of No Records Found is an official search result. The state Attorney General's Office has a searchable web page of companies that have violated consumer laws. Visit http://atgindsha01.atg.in.gov/cpd/enforcement/search.aspx.

Indiana Sexual Offender Registry

Sex and Violent Offender Directory Manager , Indiana Government Center South, E334, 302 W. Washington Street, Indianapolis, IN 46204   **Phone:** 317-232-1232; **Fax:** 317-233-1474
Web: www.insor.org/insasoweb/

Online Searching: The website has a searching capabilities by name and city or county at www.insor.org/insasoweb/. Email questions to svor@cji.in.gov.

Indiana Incarceration Records Agency

Indiana Department of Correction, IGCS , Supervisor of Records, Room E-334, 302 W. Washington Street, Indianapolis, IN 46204   **Phone:** 317-232-5765; **Fax:** 317-232-5728
Web: www.in.gov/idoc/

Online Searching: At the website, click on Offender Locator or visit www.in.gov/apps/indcorrection/ofs/.

Indiana State Court System

Court Administrator: State Court Administrator, 30 South Meridian St, Suite 500, Indianapolis, IN, 46204; 317-232-2542. www.in.gov/judiciary.

Court Structure: There are 92 judicial circuits with Circuit Courts or Combined Circuit and Superior Courts. In addition, there are 48 City Courts and 25 Town Courts. Trial courts have different names primarily due to accidents of legislative history and local custom, not true differences in the nature or purpose of the courts. County Courts are gradually being restructured into divisions of the Superior Courts.

Find Felony Records: Circuit or Superior or County Courts

Misdemeanor Records: Circuit, Superior, County, City, and Town Courts

Online Access: Implementation of an online record search system available for the public, called Odyssey, began with all Monroe County Courts and the Marion County Washington Township Small Claims Court. An additional 9 counties will be integrated into the system by the end of 2008.Visit http://mycase.in.gov/default.aspx.

Also, a vendor is working closely with many counties to provide electroinc access. An expanding limited free search of open case index is available at www.doxpop.com/prod/welcome.jsp. Fees are involveded.

The home page gives free access to an index of docket information for Supreme, Appeals, and Tax Court cases.

Searching Hints: The Circuit Court Clerk/County Clerk in a county is the same individual and is responsible for keeping all county judicial records. However, we recommend that, when requesting a record, the request indicate which court heard the case (Circuit, Superior, or County). Many courts do not perform criminal searches, based on a 7/8/96 statement by the State Board of Accounts.

Iowa

Iowa Statutes and Related Employer Restrictions

General Rule: The Department may provide copies of Criminal History Data to a person or public or private agency. ICA §692.2 (1)(b).

Criminal History Data that does not contain any disposition after eighteen month from the date of arrest, or successful completion of probation following a deferred judgment, may only be disseminated by the Department to a person requesting the Criminal History Data with a signed release from the subject of the Criminal History Data. ICA §692.2 (1)(b)(3) and (4).

Records of acquittals or dismissals by reason of insanity and records of adjudication of mental incompetence to stand trial in cases in which physical or mental injury or an attempt to commit physical or mental injury to another was alleged shall not be disseminated to persons or agencies other than criminal or juvenile justice agencies. ICA §692.2 (1)(b)(6).

Juvenile: Juvenile court records are confidential and may not be inspected or disclosed. ICA §232.47(1).

Definitions: ICA §692.1

Criminal History Data – includes arrest data, conviction data, disposition data, correctional data, adjudication data, and custody data.

Custody Data – means information pertaining to the taking into custody a juvenile for a delinquent act which would be a serious or aggravated misdemeanor or felony if committed by an adult, and includes the date, time, place, facts, and circumstances of the delinquent act.

Agency Guidelines for Pre-Employment Inquiries: Iowa Civil Rights Commission, "Successfully Interviewing Job Applicants" is available online at www.iowaworkforce.org/region1/succcessinter.htm

Legislative Bill Search: www.legis.state.ia.us

Iowa State Criminal Records Agency

DPS - Division of Criminal Investigations, Records Unit, 215 E 7th St, Des Moines, IA 50319
Phone: Records- 515-725-6066; **Fax:** 515-725-6073

Web: www.dps.state.ia.us/DCI/index.shtml

Search Note: Iowa law requires employers to pay the fee for potential employees record checks. (This is normal operating procedure when an employer uses a pre-employment screening company in compliance with FCRA.).

Search Requirements: A signed release or waiver is not required but suggested (see below), nor are fingerprints. Include the following in your request-full name, date of birth, sex. The SSN and middle name are helpful. Be sure to give the full name. Request form is required for each surname. Obtain form from- web, by fax, mail, or in person.

What Is Released: If a waiver is included, the report will show any arrest over 18 months old without a disposition, otherwise not. Email questions to cchinfo@dps.state.ia.us. A signed release by subject entitles requester to all records including those without dispositions (up to 4 years old). If the subject's signed release is not presented, then no arrest records over 18 months old without dispositions are released.Records are available until the person is 80 years old or passes away. There is a computerized index going back to 1935. 100% of arrest records are fingerprint supported. 95% of all arrests in database have final dispositions recorded, 84% for those arrests within last 5 years. Records are normally destroyed after If DCI does not receive a fingerprint card and/or a disposition form, arrest information will be purged from DCI files. This is why DCI does not guarantee/certify a person has not been convicted in an IA court.

Access Methods: mail, fax, in person.

Iowa Sexual Offender Registry

Division of Criminal Investigations , SOR Unit -, 215 East 7th St, Des Moines, IA 50319-0041 **Phone:** 515-725-6050; **Fax:** 515-725-6040 **Web:** www.iowasexoffender.com/

Online Searching: The website permits name searching, enables a requester to be notified on the movement of an offender, and provides a map of registrants.

Iowa Incarceration Records Agency

Iowa Department of Corrections , 510 E 12th Street, Des Moines, IA 50319 **Phone:** 515-725-5701 **Web:** www.doc.state.ia.us

Online Searching: At the agency website, click on Offender Information for an inmate search.

Iowa State Court System

Court Administrator:	State Court Administrator, Judicial Branch Bldg, 1111 East Court Ave, Des Moines, IA, 50319; 515-281-5911. www.judicial.state.ia.us.
Court Structure:	The District Court is the court of general jurisdiction and handles all court matters. There are no limited jurisdiction courts.
Find Felony Records:	District Court
Misdemeanor Records:	District Court
Online Access:	District criminal is available from all 99 Iowa counties at www.iowacourts.state.ia.us/ESAWebApp/SelectFrame. Name searches are available on either a statewide or specific county basis. Names of juveniles who are 10 to 17 will only appear for completed cases with a guilty verdict. There is no fee for basic information. A $25 per month pay system is offered for more detailed requests. Although records are updated daily, the historical records offered are not from the same starting date on a county-by-county basis. From the home page www.judicial.state.ia.us one may access Supreme Court and Appellate Court opinions.
Searching Hints:	Most courts do not do searches and recommend either in person searches or use of a record retriever. Most courts have a public access terminal for access to that court's records.

Kansas

Kansas Statutes & Related Employer Restrictions

Employment: An employer may require a job applicant or prospective independent contractor to sign a release allowing the employer to access the applicant's criminal history record for determining the applicant's fitness for employment. If denied employment, the information must reasonably bear upon the applicant's trustworthiness or the safety or well being of the employer's employees or customers. KSA §22-4710

Expunged Record: A person who has had criminal records expunged may state that he or she has never been arrested or convicted of such an offense. KSA §12-4516(g).

Consumer Report: A consumer reporting agency may not disclose 1) bankruptcy that antedates the report by more than 14 years, and 2) suits and judgments, records of arrest, indictment, or conviction of a crime, paid tax liens, accounts placed for collection, or any other adverse item of information that antedate the report by more than 7 years. KSA §50-704(a).

Exception: Employment of an individual at an annual salary that equals $20,000 or more. KSA §50-704(b)(3).

Agency Guidelines for Pre-Employment Inquiries: Kansas Human Rights Commission "Guidelines on Equal Employment Practices: Preventing Discrimination in Hiring" is available online at www.khrc.net/hiring.html

State Statutes and Codes: www.kslegislature.org/legsrv-statutes/index.do

Legislative Bill Search: www.kslegislature.org/legsrv-legisportal/bills.do

Kansas State Criminal Records Agency

Kansas Bureau of Investigation, Criminal Records Division, 1620 SW Tyler, Crim. History Record Sec., Topeka, KS 66612-1837 **Phone:** 785-296-8200; **Fax:** 785-368-7162 **Web:** www.accesskansas.org/kbi/

Search Note: Records are available to the general public. The criminal history information maintained by the KBI includes felony and misdemeanor arrests, prosecution data, court dispositions and information of incarceration in state-operated confinement facilities. Include the following in your request-full name, sex, race, date of birth, Social Security Number. Each request must be on a separate "Records Check Request Form." Fingerprints are optional. Approximately 85% of records are fingerprint supported; approximately 50% of records are automated. Agencies dealing with children, the elderly or disabled clientele may qualify for reduced fees for record checks. These accounts are known as Caretaker accounts.

What Is Released: Records of arrests within the past 12 months are also released when the records of disposition have not yet been received. Records released include court convictions for violations of law that are felonies or class A or class B misdemeanors as well as municipal ordinances or county resolutions that are equivalent to class A or class B misdemeanors under state statute. Class C misdemeanor assaults are also part of the database. Records are available from 1939 to present. The following data is not released: expunged records, non-convictions or juvenile records except to Criminal justice agencies and agencies required by law. 50% of all arrests in database have final dispositions recorded, 65% for those arrests within last 5 years.

Access Methods: mail, fax, online.

Online Searching: Anyone may obtain non-certified criminal records online at www.accesskansas.org/kbi/criminalhistory/. The system is also available for premium subscribers of accessKansas. The fee is $17.50 per record; credit cards accepted online. The system is unavailable between the hours of midnight and 4 AM daily. A Kansas "Most Wanted" list is available at www.accesskansas.org/kbi/mw.htm.

Kansas Sexual Offender Registry

Kansas Bureau of Investigation , Offender Registration, 1620 SW Tyler, Topeka, KS 66612-1837 **Phone:** 785-296-2841; **Fax:** 785-296-6781 **Web:** www.kansas.gov/kbi/ro.shtml

Note: There are over 4,370 offenders registered in the state. Further information on any registered offender in the file can be obtained from the sheriff's office in the registrant's county of residence.

Online Searching: Searching is available at the website. All open registrants are searchable. The information contained in a registration entry was provided by the registrant. Neither the Kansas Bureau of Investigation (KBI) nor the sheriff's office can guarantee the accuracy of this information.

Kansas Incarceration Records Agency

Kansas Department of Corrections , Public Information Officer, 900 SW Jackson, 4th floor, Topeka, KS 66612-1284 **Phone:** 785-296-3310, 785-296-5873; **Fax:** 785-296-0014 **Web:** www.dc.state.ks.us/

Online Searching: Web access to the database known as KASPER gives information on offenders who are: currently incarcerated; under post-incarceration supervision; and, who have been discharged from a sentence. The database does not have information available about inmates sent to Kansas under the provisions of the interstate compact agreement. Go to www.dc.state.ks.us/kasper. Also, one may view the escapee list at www.dc.state.ks.us/kasper/index.htm. Bulk lists are available on CD for $.01 per record. General questions can be sent to kdocpub@kdoc.dc.state.ks.us.

Kansas State Court System

Court Administrator: Judicial Administrator, Kansas Judicial Center, 301 SW 10th St, Topeka, KS, 66612; 785-296-3229. www.kscourts.org.

Court Structure:	The District Court is the court of general jurisdiction. There are 110 courts in 31 districts in 105 counties. If an individual in Municipal Court wants a jury trial, the request must be filed de novo in a District Court.
Find Felony Records:	District Court
Misdemeanor Records:	District Court
Online Access:	Commercial online access for civil and criminal records is available for District Court records in all counties. To open an account, visit www.accesskansas.org. An initial $95.00 subscription is required, access fees are also involved. The system also provides state criminal records and motor vehicle records among other records. For additional information or a registration packet, telephone 800-4-KANSAS (800-452-6727) or visit the web page.
	The Kansas Appellate Courts offer free online access to case information at www.kscourts.org. Published opinions from the Appellate Courts and Supreme Court are also available.
Searching Hints:	Five counties - Cowley, Crawford, Labette, Montgomery and Neosho - have two hearing locations, but only one record center.
	Many Kansas courts do not do criminal record searches and will refer any criminal requests to the Kansas Bureau of Investigation.

Kentucky

Kentucky Statutes & Related Employer Restrictions

General Rule: All public records shall be open for inspection by any person. KRS § 61.872.

Exceptions: Expunged records are not open to the public. KRS §197.025(5). Proceedings relating to the adjudication of a juvenile as delinquent or in need of supervision cannot be released without a court order. 502 KAR 30:060. Non-conviction data can only be released to 1) criminal justice agencies for criminal justice purposes and criminal justice employment. 502 KAR 30:060.

An employer may request records involving any felony, pornography misdemeanor, sexual offense misdemeanor, controlled substance misdemeanor committed within five years immediately preceding the application, or any conviction for Driving Under the Influence committed within five years immediately preceding the application of a person who applies for employment or volunteers for a position in which he or she would have supervisory or disciplinary power over a minor. KRS §17.10(1).

Definitions: 502 KAR 30:010

Criminal History Record Information – includes information on arrests, detentions, indictments, information, and other criminal charges, and any disposition arising there from, including sentencing, correctional supervision, and release.

Consumer Report: Consumer Reporting Agencies are prohibited from maintaining criminal records, that are non-conviction records, from any Kentucky court. KRS §367.310.

State Statutes and Codes: http://lrc.ky.gov/statrev/frontpg.htm

Legislative Bill Search: www.lrc.ky.gov/record_search.htm

Kentucky State Criminal Records Agency

Kentucky State Police, Criminal Identification & Records Branch, 1250 Louisville Rd, Frankfort, KY 40601 **Phone:** 502-227-8713; **Fax:** 502-226-7422 **Web:** www.kentuckystatepolice.org

Search Note: Records are available to all requesters as long as a signed release is submitted. Special forms are suggested for certain employment purposes such as nursing, schools, lottery, EMT, YMCA, daycare, and adoptive/foster parent background searches. Include the following in your request-signed release from subject with witness signature, full name, date of birth, SSN, reason for information request. Certain authorized searches require fingerprints to be submitted. Request forms may be downloaded from webpage. Statistical information about criminal offenses and accidents is available from 1971 on.

What Is Released: Records without dispositions, including pending and dismissed cases, are not released. Records are available from 1952 on for criminal records. The following data is not released: when individual tried as a juvenile. 69% of all arrests in database have final dispositions recorded, 59% for those arrests within last 5 years. Nearly 95% of records are automated. 75% of arrest records are fingerprint supported.

Access Methods: mail, in person.

Kentucky Sexual Offender Registry

Kentucky State Police , Criminal Identification and Records Branch, 1250 Louisville Rd, Frankfort, KY 40601 **Phones:** 502-227-8700; Alert Line- 866-564-5652; **Fax:** 502-226-7419 **Web:** http://kspsor.state.ky.us

Note: The Alert Line is open 24 hours daily. Sex offenders must register their location for a minimum of ten years or a maximum of their lifetime, depending on crime. Only offenders convicted of statutorily covered crimes who are convicted after July 15, 1994 or incarcerated or sentenced after July 15, 1998 are listed.

Online Searching: Access is available via the website; all registrants are listed. Online searches must provide one of the following fields: Last Name, City, ZIP, County.

Kentucky Incarceration Records Agency

Kentucky Department of Corrections , Offender Information Services, PO Box 2400, Frankfort, KY 40602-2400, (courier address: 275 E. Main, Room 619, Frankfort, KY 40602.) **Phones:** 502-564-2433; Victim Notification Line- 800-511-1670; **Fax:** 502-564-1471 **Web:** www.corrections.ky.gov

Online Searching: The website http://apps.corrections.ky.gov/KOOL/ioffsrch.asp provides current inmate information on the Kentucky Online Offender Lookup (KOOL) system as a service to the public. It can take as long as 120 days for the data to be current. The IT Dept has the database on CD available for $50.00; call 502-564-4360.

Kentucky State Court System

Court Administrator:	Administrative Office of Courts, Pre-Trial Services Records Unit, 100 Mill Creek Park, Frankfort, KY, 40601; 502-573-1682. http://courts.ky.gov/.
Court Structure:	The Circuit Court is the court of general jurisdiction and the District Court is the limited jurisdiction court and felony prelims. Most of Kentucky's counties combined the courts into one location and records are co-mingled.
Find Felony Records:	Circuit Courts
Misdemeanor Records:	District Courts
Online Access:	There is a free access to limited criminal record info at http://apps.kycourts.net/CourtRecords/. Search daily court calendars by county for free at http://apps.kycourts.net/dockets. KY Bar attorneys may register to use the KCOJ court record index data at http://apps.kycourts.net/courtrecordsKBA/, this is a fee system. Search online opinons and case information for the Supreme Court and Court of Appeals at http://courts.ky.gov/research/.
Searching Hints:	Until 1978, county judges handled all cases; therefore, in many cases, District and Circuit Court records go back only to 1978. Records prior to that time are archived.
	The AOC offers a service of providing statewide criminal background checks via fax, standard mail, walk-in, or drive-thru service. Their CourtNet Criminal History database contains records of all misdemeanor and traffic cases for at least the last five years, and for felonies dating back to 1978, from all 120 counties. The required Release Form is available from the AOC at the number above. A SASE and a second postage-attached envelope must accompany the request.

Louisiana

Louisiana Statutes & Related Employer Restrictions

General Rule: Any person of the age of majority may inspect or copy any public record. LSA-RS 44:31.

Exception: Disclosure is not required for 1) records pertaining to pending criminal litigation, 2) identity of a confidential source, 3) records of a person's arrest until a final judgment of conviction or the acceptance of a guilty plea. LSA-RS 44:3.

Employment: A person shall not be disqualified to engage in any trade, occupation, or practice solely because of a prior criminal record unless he or she was convicted of a felony that directly relates to the position sought. LSA-RS 37:2950(A).

This rule does not apply to 1) any law enforcement agency, 2) Louisiana State Board of Medical Examiners, 3) Louisiana State Board of Dentistry, 4) Louisiana State Board of Nursing, 5) Louisiana State Board of Practical Nurse Examiners, 6) State Racing Commission, 7) State Athletic Commission, 8) State Bar Association, 9) State Board of Pharmacy, 10) Louisiana Professional Engineering and Land Surveying Board, 11) State Board of Architectural Examiners, 12) State Board of Private Investigator Examiners, 13) State Board of Embalmers and Funeral Directors, and 13) Office of Alcohol and Tobacco Control of the Department of Revenue, 14) State Board of Elementary and Secondary Education LSA-RS 37:2950(D).

State Statutes and Codes: www.legis.state.la.us/searchlegis.htm

Legislative Bill Search: www.legis.state.la.us

Louisiana State Criminal Records Agency

State Police, Bureau of Criminal Identification, 7919 Independence Blvd, Baton Rouge, LA 70806 **Phone:** 225-925-6095; **Fax:** 225-925-7005   **Web:** www.lsp.org/index.html

Access to Records is Restricted

Though not open to the public, there are exceptions. Records are available for employment or licensing purposes but only as state law dictates, and usually only for occupational licensing baords and government use. Authorized forms are available from this department. 100% of the records are fingerprint-supported. Only records with convictions are released.

Louisiana Sexual Offender Registry

State Police , Sex Offender and Child Predator Registry, PO Box 66614, Box A-6, Baton Rouge, LA 70896 **Phone:** 225-925-6100, 800-858-0551; **Fax:** 225-925-7005 **Web:** http://lasocpr1.lsp.org

Search Note: The Sex Offender and Child Predator Registry program is statutorily provided through La. R. S. 15:542 & 15:542.1, et. seq., of the Louisiana Criminal Code. This agency does not answer search requests made directly from the public; to search, you must make your request via a local law enforcement agency, who must make the request on their official letterhead. Email add'l questions to SOCPR@dps.state.la.us.

Online Searching: Search by name, ZIP Code, or view the entire list at the website. Also search by city, school area or parish. Also, email requests are accepted, use SOCPR@dps.state.la.us.

Louisiana Incarceration Records Agency

Department of Public Safety and Corrections , PO Box 94304, Attn: Office of Adult Services, Baton Rouge, LA 70804   **Phones:**   225-342-6642; Locator- 225-342-9711; **Fax:** 225-342-3349 **Web:** www.corrections.state.la.us

Online Searching: Access is online, but limited to schedules for upcoming Parole Board hearings, as well as decisions from previous Parole Board hearings. Go to www.corrections.state.la.us/Offices/paroleboard/paroledockets.htm.   Also, view the system's fugitive, escapee, and absconder lists free at www.doc.louisiana.gov/Fugitives Escapees Absconders/escapees.htm.

Louisiana State Court System

Court Administrator: Judicial Administrator, Judicial Council of the Supreme Court, 400 Royal St, Suite 1190, New Orleans, LA, 70130; 504-310-2550. www.lasc.org.

Court Structure: A District Court Clerk in each Parish holds all the records for that Parish. Each Parish has its own clerk and courthouse. In criminal matters, City Courts generally have jurisdiction over ordinance violations and misdemeanor violations of state law.   Parish Courts exercise jurisdiction in criminal cases punishable by fines of $1,000 or less, or imprisonment of six months or less. Cases are appealable from the Parish Courts directly to the courts of appeal. A municipality may have a Mayor's Court; the mayor may hold trials, but nothing over $30.00, and there are no records.

Find Felony Records: District Courts

Misdemeanor Records: City and Parish Courts, and the New Orleans City Courts

Online Access: Search opinions from the state Supreme Court at www.lasc.org/opinion search.asp. Online records go back to 1995. There is no statewide system open to the public for trial court dockets, but a number of parishes offer online access.

Searching Hints: The courts vary widely in terms of fees. 80% of the courts offer a public access terminal.

Maine

Maine Statutes & Related Employer Restrictions

Public Records General Rule: Every person shall have the right to inspect and copy any public record. 1 MRSA § 408. Records of persons detained, except for records of juvenile detention, are public records. 16 MRSA §612-A(3).

Conviction Data may be disseminated to any person for any purpose. 16 MRSA § 615. Non-conviction data may only be disseminated to 1) criminal justice agencies for criminal justice purposes, 2) express authorization by statute, or court order, 3) specific agreement with criminal justice agency to provide services for the criminal justice agency, and 4) research activities. 16 MRSA § 613.

Definitions: 16 MRSA § 611

Conviction Data – means criminal history information other than non-conviction data

Non-conviction Data – means 1) arrests without disposition if one year has elapsed from the date of arrest and no active prosecution charge is pending, 2) information that the police have elected not to refer a matter to the prosecutor, 3) information that the prosecutor has elected not to pursue criminal proceedings, 4) information that the criminal proceedings have been indefinitely postponed, 5) a dismissal, 6) an acquittal, except one because of mental disease, and 7) information disclosing that a person has been granted a full pardon or amnesty.

Employers General Rule: A state licensing agency may take into consideration criminal history record information from Maine or elsewhere which have not been set aside or for which a full and free pardon has not been granted. The existence of such information shall not operate as an automatic bar to being licensed. 5 MRSA § 5301(1).

A licensing agency may use criminal history record information for 1) convictions in which incarceration for one year or more may be imposed, 2) convictions in which incarceration for less that one year may be imposed and which involved dishonesty, was directly related to the trade, or involved sexual misconduct, and 3) convictions in which no incarceration may be imposed but directly relates to the trade or occupation. 5 MRSA §5301(2). Licensing agency may deny, suspend, or revoke a license for one of the previous criminal history record information ONLY if the licensing agency determines that the applicant has not been sufficiently rehabilitated. 5 MRSA § 5302(1).

Limitations - Consideration of prior criminal convictions as an element of fitness shall apply for three years. After three years, the applicant must be considered equivalent to applicants with no prior criminal conviction. 5 MRSA § 5303(1).

Applicants to the Board of Medicine, Osteopathic, Dental Examiners, Psychologists, Social Workers, Nursing, Chiropractic, Criminal Justice Agency, Physical Therapy, and Medical Services Board shall have a ten-year limit for the consideration of prior criminal conviction as an element of fitness. 5 MRSA § 5303(2).

Consumer Reports General Rule: A consumer reporting agency may furnish a consumer report to a person that the consumer reporting agency has reason to believe intends to use the information for employment purposes. 10 MRSA §1313-A(1)(C)(2).

Consumer must authorize in writing the procurement of the report. 10 MRSA §1313-A(2)(B)(2).

A consumer reporting agency may not disclose 1) bankruptcy that antedates the report by more than 10 years and 2) civil suits, civil judgments and records of arrest, paid tax liens, accounts placed for collection, any other adverse item of information, other than records of conviction of crimes that antedate the report by more than 7 years. 10 MRSA § 1313-B(1).

Exception: Employment of an individual at an annual salary that equals $75,000 or more. 10 MRSA § 1313-B(2)

State Statutes and Codes: http://janus.state.me.us/legis/statutes/

Legislative Bill Search: http://janus.state.me.us/legis/LawMakerWeb/search.asp

Maine State Criminal Records Agency

Maine State Police, State Bureau of Identification, State House Station #42, Augusta, ME 04333-0042, (courier address: 45 Commerce Dr #1, Augusta, ME 04330.) **Phone:** 207-624-7240; **Fax:** 207-287-3421   **Web:** http://www10.informe.org/PCR/

Search Note: Records are available to the general public. Requests must be in writing. Will only do FBI fingerprint checks as authorized by Maine Statutes. Records are updated as often as records are submitted to this agency. All convictions and all pending cases less than 1 year old are reported, or if the case has not yet been adjudicated in court. Include the following in your request-name, date of birth, any aliases. Fingerprints are optional Include maiden name for females. Also include purpose of the inquiry and name and address of requester. 63% of the records are fingerprint-supported. Fingerprints generally are submitted with arrest information to this agency by the police.

What Is Released: All convictions and all pending cases less than 1 year old are reported, or if the case has not yet been adjudicated in court. Records are available from 1937 on. The following data is not released: limited juvenile records. 90% of all arrests in database have final dispositions recorded for those arrests within last 5 years.

Access Methods: mail, in person, online.

Online Searching: One may request a record search from the web. Results are usually returned via e-mail in 2 hours. Fee is $25, unless requester is an in-state subscriber to InforME, then fee is $15 per record. There is a $75 annual fee to be a subscriber.

Maine Sexual Offender Registry

State Bureau of Investigation , Sex Offender Registry, State House Station #42, Augusta, ME 04333-0042 **Phone:** 207-624-7270; **Fax:** 207-287-3421 **Web:** http://sor.informe.org/sor/

Note: Once a request is made and a specific subject is brought up, the requester can ask this agency for more information, including personal information, the description of the offense, dates, and sentence imposed. Direct question to maine_SOR.help@maine.gov.

Online Searching: Search at the web page. Information is only provided for those individuals that are required to register pursuant to Title 34-A MRSA, Chapter 15. Records date to 01/01/82 and forward. The date of the last address verification is indicated next to the registrant's address.

Maine Incarceration Records Agency

Maine Department of Corrections , Inmate Records, 111 State House Station, Augusta, ME 04333 **Phone:** 207-287-4376; **Fax:** 207-287-4370 **Web:** www.maine.gov/corrections/

Note: One may also do a search by sending an email to Corrections.Webdesk@maine.gov. Include your full name, address, and reasons for the search. Public information is provided.

Maine State Court System

Court Administrator:	State Court Administrator, PO Box 4820, Portland, ME, 04112; 207-822-0792. www.state.me.us/courts.
Court Structure:	The Superior Court is the court of general jurisdiction. Both Superior and District Courts handle "misdemeanor" and "felony" cases, with jury trials being held in Superior Court only. Superior Court has exclusive jurisdiction over pleas or trials for murder cases.
Find Felony Records:	Superior Court, District Court
Misdemeanor Records:	Superior Court, District Court
Online Access:	The website offers access to Maine Supreme Court opinions and administrative orders, but not all documents are available online. Also, the website offers access to trial court schedules by region and case type. Some county level courts are online through a private vendor.
Searching Hints:	Some courts offer a free search if only one name is submitted. Most mail requests of a name search for full criminal history record information are returned to the sender, referring them to the State Bureau of Investigation. Mail requests that make a specific inquiry related to an identified case are responded to in writing. You must also include all appropriate copy and attestation fees. Aroostook County has two Superior Courts.

Maryland

Maryland Statutes & Related Employer Restrictions

Public Records General Rule: Except in accordance with applicable federal law and regulations, a criminal justice unit and the central Repository may not disseminate criminal history record information. MD Code §10-219. A person or his or her attorney, with written authorization, may inspect criminal history record information about the person. MD Code Crim. Pro. §10-222.

A person may not open or review an expunged record, or disclose to another person any information from that record without a court order. MD Code Crim. Pro. §10-108.

Consumer Reports General Rule: A consumer reporting agency may furnish a consumer report to a person which the agency has reason to believe intends to use the information for employment purposes. MD Code Commercial Law, 14-1202.

A consumer reporting agency may not disclose 1) bankruptcy that antedates the report by more than 10 years and 2) Suits and judgments, paid tax liens, accounts placed for collection, records of arrest, indictment, or conviction of a crime, and any other adverse item of information that antedate the report by more than 7 years. MD Code §14-1203(a). **Exception:** employment of an individual at an annual salary that equals $20,000 or more. MD Code Crim. Pro. §14-1203(b)(3).

Caveat: An employer may not require a person to inspect or challenge any criminal history record information relating to that person for the purpose of obtaining a copy of the person's record to qualify for employment. MD Code §10-228.

State Statutes and Codes: http://mlis.state.md.us/#stat

Legislative Bill Search: http://mlis.state.md.us/#gena

Maryland State Criminal Records Agency

Criminal Justice Information System, Public Safety & Correctional Records, PO Box 32708, Pikeville, MD 21282-5743, (courier address: 6776 Reisterstown Rd, Rm 102, Baltimore, MD 21215.) **Phone:** 410-764-4501, 888-795-0011; **Fax:** 410-653-5690 **Web:** www.dpscs.state.md.us

Search Notes: Release of criminal records is restricted. All private parties must first write/fax/phone this office and request a "petition package," then apply for a petition number. Employers are eligible to request a petition number; 3rd parties may not, directly. Include the following in your request-set of fingerprints. A signed release is not necessary but is helpful. When applying for fingerprinting, a photo ID is required. 100% of records are fingerprint-supported. All searches require fingerprints and all require an authorization number including government. Investigators and all 3rd parties are considered as agents of employers and must use employer's authorization. You may link to Customer Service Unit via the website in order to download a petition for authorization and return the petition via fax or mail.

What Is Released: All records released to law enforcement; public receives records with conviction data only. Records with dispositions of acquittal are not released to private entities. Records are available from 1978. It takes 10 days if not submitted electronically. before new records are available for inquiry. 90% of all arrests in database have final dispositions recorded, 97% for arrests within last 5 years.

Maryland Sexual Offender Registry

Criminal Justice Information System , PO Box 32708, SOR Unit, Pikeville, MD 21282-5743, (courier address: 6776 Reisterstown Rd, Baltimore, MD 21215.) **Phone:** 410-585-3649, 866-368-8657; **Fax:** 410-653-5690 **Web:** www.socem.info/

Online Searching: Online access is free at www.socem.info/. Search by name or ZIP Code. An interactive map is also available. Access to the Sexual Offender Registry can be requested by email at websiteresponse@dpscs.state.md.us. A printout is available of partial or complete SOR. Request must be in writing.

Maryland Incarceration Records Agency

Dept of Public Safety and Correctional Services , Maryland Division of Corrections, 6776 Reistertown Road, Suite 310, Baltimore, MD 21215-2342 **Phone:** 410-585-3351; **Fax:** 410-764-4220 **Web:** www.dpscs.state.md.us

Note: For an inmate's DOC # and location contact Data Processing by phone or email to cwood@dpscs.state.md.us. To obtain any other information than DOC number you must contact individual institutions. Only location and DOC number are released from this agency.

Online Searching: Search inmates online at www1.dpscs.state.md.us/inmate/. The Locator may not list some short sentenced inmates who, although committed to the Commissioner of Correction, are in fact housed at Division of Pretrial and Detention Services facilities.

Maryland State Court System

Court Administrator:	Court Administrator, Administrative Office of the Courts, 580 Taylor Ave, Annapolis, MD, 21401; 410-260-1400, 410-260-1488. www.courts.state.md.us.
Court Structure:	The Circuit Court is the highest court of record. Certain categories of minor felonies are handled by the District Courts. However, all misdemeanors and felonies that require a jury trial are handled by Circuit Courts, and when the penalty may be confinement for three years or more or a fine of $2,500 or more.
Find Felony Records:	Circuit Court, District Court (minor)
Misdemeanor Records:	Circuit Court, District Court

Online Access: Appellate opinions are available from www.courts.state.md.us/opinions.html. There is a free search of dockets from the trial courts at http://casesearch.courts.state.md.us/inquiry/inquiry-index.jsp. The search includes all district courts and circuit courts. Records are updated daily, but note that case information from Montgomery and Prince George's counties are always lagging one day behind.

Maryland's dial-up (non-Internet) system is being phased out and should be completely shut down in the first quarter of 2008. For info call 410-260-1031 or visit www.courts.state.md.us/courtrecords.html.

Plans are underway for subscribing parties to access statewide Case Search bulk data and data extracts through a standards-based interface in XML format. Also, there is an attorney Calendar Service that displays information related to an Attorney's trial and hearing schedule.

Searching Hints: The CJIS Central Repository in Pikesville serves as a statewide criminal court record provider, phone 888-795-0011 or 410-764-4501.

Massachusetts

Massachusetts Statutes & Related Employer Restrictions

General Rule: Any person may examine or inspect any public record. MGLA 66 § 10.

Expunged Record: Records may be sealed by the court when the defendant has been found not guilty, a finding of no probable cause, a nolle prosequi has been entered, or a dismissal has been entered. An applicant with a sealed record on file may answer "no record" with respect to an inquiry of prior arrests or criminal court appearances. MGLA 276 § 100C.

Employment: An employer may not discriminate against an employee for employment purposes regarding 1) an arrest, detention, or disposition in which a conviction did not result, 2) a first conviction for drunkenness, simple assault, speeding, minor traffic violations, affray, or disturbance of the peace, or 3) any conviction of a misdemeanor that occurred 5 years or more from the date of application unless there has been an intervening conviction for another offense. MGLA 151B § 4.

Consumer Report: No consumer reporting agency may disclose in a consumer report 1) bankruptcy that antedates the report by more than 14 years and 2) Suits and judgments, paid tax liens, accounts placed for collection, records of arrest, indictment, or conviction of a crime, and any other adverse item of information that antedate the report by more than 7 years. MGLA 93 § 52. **Exception:** employment of an individual at an annual salary that equals $20,000 or more. MGLA 93 § 52(b)(3).

State Statutes and Codes: www.mass.gov/legis/laws/mgl/index.htm

Legislative Bill Search: www.mass.gov/legis/ltsform.htm

Massachusetts State Criminal Records Agency

Criminal History Systems Board, CORI, 200 Arlington Street, #2200, Chelsea, MA 02150
Phone: 617-660-4640; **Fax:** 617-660-4613   **Web:** www.mass.gov/chsb/

Search Notes: These CORI searches are offered: 1) Personal, 2) Certified Agency, 3) Publicly Accessible (PUBAC). Certified Agency requests are pre-approved via statute or the Board. PUBAC is open to the public; data is limited.

PUBAC requesters are limited to adult records; the crime must include a sentence of 5 years or more OR sentenced and convicted for any term if, at the time of request, the subject is on probation or has been released within 2 years of felony conviction. Include the following in your request-name, date of birth; please include SSN in request for record matching purposes; SSNs are not shown in results. The Personal request (on one's self) requires a notarized signature. A "certified agency" search is for employers, screening companies, care providers, and others approved by CHSB. Any employer may be approved. CRAs must fill out a Non-Disclosure form.

What Is Released: A Certified Agency record includes all conviction and all open or pending actions. A PUBAC record contains only convictions. Records are available for at least 50 years. 100% of PUBAC records have final dispositions recorded. This agency does not conduct FBI fingerprint searches. Unit provides CORI to Board certified, non-criminal justice agencies such as schools, day care centers, home health aides, youth athletic coaches, and municipal government agencies.

Access Methods: mail, online.

Online Searching: Certified agencies may order $15.00 records online. This limited to 'true employers' and pre-approved agencies. Consumer Reporting Agencies who represent employers are not currently permitted access online, but plans are underway to permit access.

Massachusetts Sexual Offender Registry

Sex Offender Registry Board , PO Box 4547, Salem, MA 01970
Phone: 978-740-6400; **Fax:** 978-740-6464 **Web:** www.mass.gov/sorb/

Note: Information about a sex offender is available to the public only if subject has been classified by the Board as a Level 2 or a Level 3 Offender. In person requests should be conducted at local law enforcement offices. Requests to this office must be in writing or online access is available from the Internet site.

Online Searching: Search free from links found at the home page. Pursuant to M.G.L. C. 6, §§ 178C - 178P, the individuals who appear on the web page have been designated a Level 3 Sex Offenders by the Sex Offender Registry Board.

Massachusetts Incarceration Records Agency

Massachusetts Executive Office of Public Safety , Department Of Corrections, 50 Maple Street, Suite 3, Chelsea, MA 02150 **Phone:** 617-660-4640 **Web:** www.mass.gov/doc/

Online Searching: No searching online is offered by this agency; however this agency promotes a private company offers free web access to DOC offenders at https://www.vinelink.com/vinelink/siteInfoAction.do?siteId=20000.

Massachusetts State Court System

Court Administrator: Chief Justice for Administration and Management, 2 Center Plaza, Room 540, Boston, MA, 02108; 617-742-8575. www.mass.gov/courts/admin/index.html.

Court Structure: The various court sections are called "Departments." In addition to misdemeanors, the District Courts and Boston Municipal Courts have jurisdiction over certain minor felonies.

Find Felony Records: Superior Court, District Court

Misdemeanor Records: District Court, Boston Municipal Court, Housing Court

Online Access: Online access to records on the statewide Trial Courts Information Center website with both criminal and civil superior court cases is available to attorneys and law firms only at www.ma-trialcourts.org/tcic/welcome.jsp. Access is free but BBO number is a requisite. Middlesex, Suffolk, Worcester indices go back to 1990s; other counties go back to active cases as of 2000-2001. The system plan is to have all courts online in 2008. For more information, contact Peter Nylin by email at nylin_p@jud.state.ma.us or Victoria Palmarcci at victoria.palmacci@jud.state.ma.us. Site updated daily.

Opinions from the Supreme Court and Appellate Courts can be found at http://massreports.com.

Searching Hints: In Massachusetts courts, "attestation" is the term for what is known as certification in other states. In Massachusetts, a "certificate" is a separate authentification page with a gold seal.

Michigan

Michigan Statutes & Related Employer Restrictions

General Rule: A person has the right to inspect, copy, or receive copies of a public record of a public body. MCLA 15.233(1). Investigative records complied for law enforcement purposes may not be released if it would 1) interfere with law enforcement proceedings, 2) deprive a person of a fair trail, 3) constitute an unwarranted invasion of privacy, 4) disclose the identity of a confidential source, 5) disclose law enforcement investigative techniques, or 6) endanger the life or physical safety of law enforcement personnel. MCLA 15.243 (1)(b).

Expunged Record: A person who is convicted of not more than one offense may file an application with the convicting court for the entry of an order setting aside the conviction. MCLA 780.621. If the order is granted, the conviction record becomes non-public except for a few circumstances, such as employment for a law enforcement agency. MCLA 780.623.

Employment: An employer may not request, make, or maintain a record of information regarding a misdemeanor arrest, detention, or disposition where a conviction did not result. MCLA 37.2205 a (1).

Agency Guidelines for Pre-Employment Inquiries: Michigan Civil Rights Commission, "Pre-Employment Inquiry Guide" is available online at http://ses.cmich.edu/ses-new-webpage/seshand book/student-supervisors'-handbook/MI-Dept-of-Civil-Rights-Inquiry-Guide.htm

State Statutes and Codes: www.legislature.mi.gov

Legislative Bill Search: www.legislature.mi.gov

Michigan State Criminal Records Agency

Michigan State Police, Criminal History Section, Criminal Justice Information Center, 7150 Harris Dr, Lansing, MI 48913 **Phone:** 517-322-1956; **Fax:** 517-322-0635 **Web:** www.michigan.gov/msp

Search Notes: All felonies and serious misdemeanors that are punishable by over 93 days are required to be reported to the state repository by law enforcement agencies, prosecutors, and courts in all 83 Michigan counties. A SSN or maiden name/previous name is very helpful. Records can be searched with or without a fingerprint card.

What Is Released: Records are available until the subject's DOB indicates 99 years or a death is reported. Since 2/2006, the general public may receive information on arrest records that do not have a conviction attached. Information regarding warrants and suppressed records are not released. Prior to that date only conviction data was released. Include the following in your request-full name, sex, race, date of birth. It takes up to 30 days before new records are available for inquiry. 80% of all arrests in database have final dispositions recorded, 87% for arrests within last 5 years.

Access Methods: mail, online.

Online Searching: Access is available at http://apps.michigan.gov/ICHAT/Home.aspx. Results are available in seconds; fee is $10.00 per name. Call 517-322-1377. This is a non-fingerprint search. You are also allowed up to three variations on one name search. Use of a MasterCard or VISA is required. This is the only method available for a non-fingerprint search.

Michigan Sexual Offender Registry

Michigan State Police , SOR Section, 7150 Harris Dr, Lansing, MI 48913 **Phone:** 517-322-4938; **Fax:** 517-322-4957 **Web:** www.mipsor.state.mi.us

Note: The agency recommends in person searchers to visit local law enforcement offices. Only those offenders who have been convicted of a listed offense on or after October 1, 1995 or convicted prior to that date who were still incarcerated, on parole or probation for a listed offense on 10/1/1995 are listed.

Online Searching: One may search the registry at the website, no charge.

Michigan Incarceration Records Agency

Michigan Department of Corrections , Central Records Office, PO Box 30003, Lansing, MI 48909, (courier address: 206 E. Michigan Ave., Lansing, MI 48909.) **Phone:** 517-373-3651; **Fax:** 517-373-2558 **Web:** www.michigan.gov/corrections

Online Searching: The online access found at www.state.mi.us/mdoc/asp/otis2.html has many search criteria capabilities. There is also a DOC Most Wanted list at www.state.mi.us/mdoc/MostWanted/MostWanted.asp. Bulk sales of database information is available.

Michigan State Court System

Court Administrator: State Court Administrator, 309 N. Washington Sq, PO Box 30048, Lansing, MI, 48909; 517-373-0130. http://courts.michigan.gov/scao/.

Court Structure: The Circuit Court is the court of general jurisdiction. District Courts and Municipal Courts have jurisdiction over certain minor felonies and handle all preliminary hearings.

Six counties (Barry, Berrien, Iron, Isabella, Lake, and Washtenaw) and the 46th Circuit Court are participating in a project designed to streamline court services and consolidate case management. These courts may refer to themselves as County Trial Courts.

Find Felony Records: Circuit Court

Misdemeanor Records: District Court, Municipal Court

Online Access: There is a wide range of online computerization of the judicial system from "none" to "fairly complete," but there is no statewide court records network. Some Michigan courts provide public access terminals in clerk's offices, and some courts are developing off-site electronic filing and searching capability. A few offer remote online to the public. The Criminal Justice Information Center (CJIC), the repository for MI criminal record info, offers online access, but the requester must be a business. Also, subscribe to email updates of appellate opinions at http://courtofapp eals.mijud.net/resources/subscribe.htm. There is no fee.

Searching Hints: Court records are considered public except for specific categories: controlled substances, spousal abuse, Holmes youthful trainee, parental kidnapping, set aside convictions and probation, and sealed records. Courts will, however, affirm that cases exist and provide case numbers. Some courts will not perform criminal searches, rather they refer requests to the State Police. Courts search requirements and procedures vary widely because each jurisdiction may create its own administrative orders.

Minnesota
Minnesota Statutes & Related Employer Restrictions

General Rule: All government data collected, created, received, maintained, or disseminated by a state agency, political subdivision, or statewide system shall be public unless classified as non-public, protected non-public, private, or confidential. MSA §13.03(1).

Arrest data, such as the charge, arrest, search warrant, date and time for any release from custody or incarceration, and criminal investigative data that has become inactive is open to the public. MSA 13.82(2) and (7).

Correction and detention data on individuals are classified as private to the extent that 1) it would endanger an individual's life, 2) endanger the effectiveness of an investigation, 3) identify a confidential informant, or 4) disclose medical, psychological or financial information not related to their lawful confinement. MSA §13.85.

Expunged Record: Records may be sealed for first time drug offenders and juveniles, and become a not public record. Non-conviction records may be sealed on application. A finding of not guilty due to mental illness is not a resolution in favor of the petitioner. Further offenses which require registration as a sexual offender may not be expunged. MSA §609A.02.

Employment: No person shall be disqualified from public employment, nor disqualified from pursuing, practicing, or engaging in any occupation for which a license is required solely or in part because of a prior conviction, unless the crime for which convicted directly relates to the position of employment sought. MSA §364.03(1).

A person who has been convicted of a crime that directly relates to the public employment sought shall not be disqualified from consideration if that person can show evidence of sufficient rehabilitation. MSA §364.03(3).

Records of arrest without a valid conviction, convictions which have been annulled or expunged, and misdemeanor convictions for which no jail sentence can be imposed can not be used, distributed, or disseminated by the state of Minnesota in connection with any application for public employment nor in connection with an application for a license. MSA §364.04.

However, the restriction does not apply to applicants seeking admission to the bar, peace officers, fire protection agencies, law enforcement agencies, private detectives, school bus drivers, special transportation service, commercial driver training instructors, emergency medical services personnel, taxicab drivers, and doctors. MSA §364.09.

Consumer Report: A person may not obtain a consumer report on a consumer for employment purposes unless the person clearly and accurately discloses to the consumer that a consumer report may be obtained. This statute does not apply to a consumer report to be used for employment purposes for which the consumer has not specifically applied, or a consumer report used for an investigation of a violation of a criminal or civil statute by a current employee for which the employer may be liable. MSA §13C.02(1) and (4).

Agency Guidelines for Pre-Employment Inquiries: Minnesota Department of Human Rights, "Hiring, Job Interviews and the Minnesota Human Rights Act" available online at www.humanrig hts.state.mn.us/employer_hiring.html

State Statutes and Codes: https://www.revisor.leg.state.mn.us/pubs/

Legislative Bill Search: www.leg.state.mn.us/leg/legis.asp

Minnesota State Criminal Records Agency

Bureau of Criminal Apprehension, CJIS - Criminal History Access Unit, 1430 Maryland Ave E, St Paul, MN 55106 **Phone:** 651-793-2400; **Fax:** 651-793-2401 **Web:** www.bca.state.mn.us/CJIS/Documents/cjis-intro.html

Search Note: State statutes require all law enforcement agencies to report juvenile felony and gross misdemeanor arrests, and adult felony, gross misdemeanor, enhanced gross misdemeanor and targeted misdemeanor arrests to BCA. Other misdemeanors are sometimes reported.

For most requesters, to obtain the entire adult history, including all arrests, you must have a notarized release form signed by person of record. To get a 15-year record of convictions only, a consent form is not required. Include the following in your request-name, date of birth, and sex. Include signed release for a complete record. Fingerprint searches are not permitted. However, 100% of records are fingerprint-supported.

What Is Released: With consent, all records are released, including those without dispositions. If no consent then only conviction records released. Targeted misdemeanors (violent, DV, DUI, etc, where a jail sentence may be imposed) are released; other misdemeanors are if received. Records are available from 1924. The following data is not released: juvenile records. Per a U.S. DOJ Survey, 41% of all arrests in database have final dispositions recorded, 55% for those arrests within last 5 years.

Access Methods: mail, in person, online.

Online Searching: Access to the public criminal history record (15 year, no consent) is available free at https://cch.state.mn.us/SearchOffenders.aspx. A public database is available on CD-ROM. Monthly updates can be purchased. Data is in ASCII format and is raw data. Call for fees.

Minnesota Sexual Offender Registry

Bureau of Criminal Apprehension , Minnesota Predatory Offender Program, 1430 Maryland Ave E, St Paul, MN 55106 **Phone:** 651-793-7070, 888-234-1248; **Fax:** 651-793-7071 **Web:** https://por.state.mn.us/

Note: This is not a notification state. The state does not permit public access to this information beyond the Level 3 names and non-compliant offenders age 16 and older found on the web. This means local law enforcement offices cannot give the public access to all names.

Online Searching: Offenders and non-compliant offender if 16 or older may be searched at https://por.state.mn.us/OffenderSearch.aspx.

Minnesota Incarceration Records Agency

Minnesota Department of Corrections , Records Management Unit, 1450 Energy Park Drive, Suite 200, St. Paul, MN 55108 **Phone:** 651-361-7200; **Fax:** 651-643-3588 **Web:** www.corr.state.mn.us

Online Searching: Search at the web to retrieve public information about adult offenders who are still under this agency's jurisdiction (i.e. in prison, or released from prison and still under supervision). Search by name, with or without DOB, or by OID number at http://info.doc.state.mn.us/publicviewer/main.asp. Also, there is a separate search for Level 3 offender/predatory information.

Minnesota State Court System

Court Administrator: State Court Adminstrator, 135 Minn. Judicial Center, 25 Constitution Ave, St Paul, MN, 55155; Telephone: 651-296-2474. www.mncourts.gov/default.aspx.

Court Structure: There are 97 District Courts comprising 10 Judicial Districts in the state.

Find Felony Records:	District Court
Misdemeanor Records:	District Court
Online Access:	Appellate and Supreme Court opinions are available from the website. There is an online system in place that allows internal and external access, but only for government personnel.

Minnesota offers the Trial Court Public Access (MPA) at http://pa.courts.state.mn.us/default.aspx. Search statewide or by county. Records available include criminal, civil, family, and probate. Searches can be performed using a case number or by name.

But there are a number of caveats - certain publicly-accessible case records cannot be viewed online.

Electronic copies of public documents filed by parties also cannot be viewed online. Name searches for criminal case records will not return pre-conviction criminal records. A statewide case inquiry may exclude district courts that have not yet converted to the system. Also, the public access terminals found at the courthouses do not use this system. For example, party street address and name searches on criminal pre-conviction case records are publicly accessible and available at the courthouse, but not online. The federal Violence Against Women Act (VAWA) also prevents the state from displaying harassment and domestic abuse case records online, but these are available at the courthouse. Comment fields for all case types are not available online but are available at the courthouse. Online users are not notified when such public data is restricted from online viewing.

The bottom line is the public access terminals found at courthouses are still the most accurate searching locations. In Judicial Districts (arranged by number and often covering several counties) many court's public access terminals contain court records for that entire district. The online system is supplemental at best.

The state provides free access to Appellate and Supreme Court opinions at www.mncourts.gov/default.aspx?page=1650. An approved bail bond agent list search is also free. Calenders looked-up by district at www.mncourts.gov/default.aspx?page=512.

Searching Hints:	An exact name is required to search, e.g., a request for "Robert Smith" will not result in finding "Bob Smith." The requester must request both names and pay two search and copy fees. But most Judicial Districts no longer perform criminal record name searches for the public.

Mississippi

Mississippi Statutes & Related Employer Restrictions

General Rule: All public records are public property and any person has the right to inspect, copy or obtain a reproduction of any public record. MS ST §25-61-5(1).

Unless specifically authorized by statute, records maintained by the Mississippi Justice Information Center Database are exempt from the Public Records Act. MS ST §45-27-19(1).

Expunged Records: If participant completes all requirements imposed upon him by a drug court, and any person who is arrested, issued a citation, or held for any misdemeanor and not formally charged or prosecuted with an offense within 12 months of arrest, or upon dismissal of the charge, may have the matter expunged. MS ST §§99-15-59 and 9-23-23.

If a person successfully completes deferment of a drug or narcotics charge before the age of 26 or the person is a first time offender convicted of a misdemeanor, he or she may petition the court to expunge the record. The effect of the expunged record shall be to restore that person to the status he or she had before the conviction and he or she shall not be guilty of perjury for denying or failure to recite the conviction later. MS ST §§99-19-71(1) and 41-29-150(d)(2).

Employment: State conviction information and arrest information less than one year old, which is contained in the Mississippi Justice Information Center Database, shall be made available to any non-governmental entity or any employer authorized by the subject of the record in writing or by state or federal law. MS ST §45-27-12(1)(b).

State Statutes and Codes: www.sos.state.ms.us/ed_pubs/mscode/

Legislative Bill Search: http://billstatus.ls.state.ms.us/

Mississippi State Criminal Records Agency

Criminal Information Center, Dept. of Public Safety, Bureau of Investigation, PO Box 958, Jackson, MS 39205, (courier address: 3891 Highway 468W, Pearl, MS 39208.) **Phone:** 601-933-2600; **Fax:** 601-933-2660

Web: www.dps.state.ms.us/dps/dps.nsf/Divisions/ci?OpenDocument

Search Note: CIC permits access to their state criminal records with the subject's expressed written consent on the state's Release Form, and to entities with purposes provided for by state statute, in health care, banking/finance, military, childcare and schools.

Approved requestors must submit fingerprint cards, the subject need not. The agency, which is not equipped to handle large numbers of subject requests, still suggests employers and public obtain information at the county level. Include the following in your request- name, current address, SSN, DOB, race, sex, subject's phone number, and witness to subject's signature, notary preferred. Specify if the background check is to be fingerprint-based or name-based. Send Release Information request form to the attention of the Special Process Unit. The subject may specify to whom and where to send the results.

What Is Released: All charges and convictions shown on results - all criminal records information in the possession of or accessible by the Justice Information Center. Dispositions are available for less than half of records; a county-level court search may be necessary. Records on file are 100% fingerprint supported. Only 40% of the records contain dispositions.

Access Methods: mail, fax.

Mississippi Sexual Offender Registry

DPS- MS Bureau of Investigations , Sexual Offender Registry, PO Box 958, Jackson, MS 39205 **Phone:** 601-987-1540; **Fax:** 601-933-2695 **Web:** www.sor.mdps.state.ms.us

Note: Questions may be directed to msor@mdps.state.ms.us. Searches may also be directed to the local sheriff's office.

Online Searching: The state Sex Offender Registry can be accessed at the website. Search by last name, city, county, or ZIP Code.

Mississippi Incarceration Records Agency

Mississippi Department of Corrections , Records Department, 421 W Pascagoula, Jackson, MS 39205 **Phone:** Central Records Office- 601-933-2889 **Web:** www.mdoc.state.ms.us

Online Searching: Search online by name only from the website. Click on Inmate Search. Also, search the Parole Board records (click on Parole Board and follow instructions).

Mississippi State Court System

Court Administrator:	Court Administrator, Supreme Court, PO Box 117, Jackson, MS, 39205; 601-354-7406. www.mssc.state.ms.us
Court Structure:	The court of general jurisdiction is the Circuit Court with 70 courts in 22 districts. Justice Courts were first created in 1984, replacing Justice of the Peace Courts. Prior to 1984, records were kept separately by each Justice of the Peace, so the location of such records today is often unknown. Jasper County added a 2nd Justice Court in 5/2008; it is located in City of Paulding.
Find Felony Records:	Circuit Court
Misdemeanor Records:	County Court, Justice Court, Municipal Court
Criminal Notes:	The Administrative Office of Courts offers a statewide search via fax requesting with a in by 4 p.m., out by 9 a.m. turnaround time. There is a start-up fee and a name search fee. Call 601-576-4635 or fax 601-576-4639 for details.

Online Access:	A statewide online computer system is in use internally for court personnel. The website offers searching of the MS Supreme Court and Court of Appeals Decisions and dockets.
Searching Hints:	A number of Mississippi counties have two Circuit Court Districts. A search of either court in such a county will include the index from the other court.
	Full name is a search requirement for all courts. DOB and SSN are very helpful for differentiating between like-named individuals.

Missouri

Missouri Statutes & Related Employer Restrictions

General Rule: All state, county and municipal records shall at all reasonable times be open for a personal inspection by any citizen of Missouri. VAMS 109.180.

All incident reports and arrest reports shall be open records. Investigative reports of all law enforcement agencies are closed records until the investigation becomes inactive. If any person is arrested and not charged with an offense against the law within 30 days of the person's arrest, the arrest report shall be a closed record. VAMS 610.100. However, arrest records with no charge that are older than 30 days will be available to criminal justice agencies for criminal justice purposes, criminal justice employment, and child, elderly, or disabled care employment. VAMS 610.120.

Definitions: VAMS 610.100

Arrest report – a record of a law enforcement agency of an arrest and any detention or confinement incident and the charge

Incident report – a record of a law enforcement agency consisting of the date, time, specific location, name of the victim, and immediate facts and circumstances surrounding the initial report of a crime.

Expunged Record: Any record of arrest may be expunged if there is no probable cause, no charges will be pursued, subject of the arrest has no prior or subsequent misdemeanor or felony convictions, the subject did not receive a suspended sentence, and no civil action is pending. VAMS 610.122.

The official records shall be closed if a person arrested is charged, but the case is subsequently nolle prossed, dismissed, the accused is found not guilty, or the imposition of sentence is suspended. If the accused is found not guilty due to mental disease, the records shall be closed except to law enforcement agencies, childcare agencies, and in home services provider agencies. VAMS 610.105.

Employment: No board or other agency may deny a license to an applicant upon the basis that a felony or misdemeanor conviction of the applicant precludes the applicant from demonstrating good moral character, where the conviction resulted in the applicant's incarceration and the applicant has been released by pardon, parole, or the applicant has been placed on probation and there in no evidence the applicant has violated his probation. The board or agency may consider the conviction as some evidence of an absence of good moral character, but shall consider other factors when making its decision. VAMS 314.200.

Agency Guidelines for Pre-Employment Inquiries: Commission on Human Rights, Missouri Department of Labor and Industrial Relations, "Pre-Employment Inquiries." More information can be found at www.dolir.state.mo.us/HR/interview.htm.

State Statutes and Codes: www.moga.state.mo.us/STATUTES/STATUTES.HTM

Legislative Bill Search: www.house.mo.gov/billcentral.aspx

Missouri State Criminal Records Agency

Missouri State Highway Patrol, Criminal Record & Identification Division, 1510 E Elm St, Jefferson City, MO 65102 **Phone:** 573-526-6153; **Fax:** 573-751-9382 **Web:** www.mshp.dps.missouri.gov/MSHPWeb/Root/index.html

Search Note: Records are available to the general public. Youth service providers must have signature of the subject. Include the following in your request-full name, date of birth, sex, race, Social Security Number. Fingerprints are an option. A request form can be downloaded from the website. Records are 100% fingerprint-supported.

What Is Released: Records are available from 1970 on. Open records are accessible by the public; these are convictions or arrests less than 30 days old unless charges are sought, or suspended imposition of sentence during probation period. Certain entities may access closed record files in accordance with state statute, with submission of fingerprints and required fee. Per a 2003 DOJ Study, 76% of all arrests in database have final dispositions recorded, 54% for those arrests within last 5 years.

Access Methods: mail, in person. Bulk/multiple requests can be submitted on diskette; prior arrangement and agency approval required. Alias or maiden names require separate search.

Missouri Sexual Offender Registry

Missouri State Highway Patrol , Sexual Offender Registry, PO Box 9500, Jefferson City, MO 65102-0568, (courier address: 1510 E Elm St, Jefferson City, MO 65102.) **Phone:** 573-526-6153, 888-767-6747; **Fax:** 573-751-9382 **Web:** www.mshp.dps.mo.gov/CJ38/search.jsp

Note: The Revised Statutes of Missouri, Sections 589.400 to 589.425 and 43.650, RSMO., mandate that the Missouri State Highway Patrol shall maintain a sex offender database and a website on the Internet that is accessible to the public. Registry information is available from the sheriff (or CLEO) in the county, or city not within a county, where the offender resides. The county list may be released to any person upon request. A myriad of information about the offender is available including photograph and physical description of offender, physical description of vehicles owned by offender, any known alias, and nature of all offenses.

Online Searching: The name index can be searched at the website, by name, county or ZIP Code. The web page also gives links lists to the county sheriffs who have online access. Look at bottom of disclaimer page for access to spreadsheet.

Missouri Incarceration Records Agency

Missouri Department of Corrections , Probation and Parole, 1511 Christy Dr., Jefferson City, MO 65101 **Phone:** 573-751-8488; **Fax:** 573-522-8739 **Web:** www.doc.missouri.gov

Online Searching: No Internet searching is available from this agency. However, you may email a single request to probation&parole@doc.mo.gov or constituentservices@doc.mo.gov. Spell the full name correctly. An email response will be provided to you, usually within 24 hours of receipt during regular business hours. This is limited to general search information. Department does not provide search data to companies conducting background checks.

Missouri State Court System

Court Administrator:	State Court Administrator, 2112 Industrial Dr., PO Box 104480, Jefferson City, MO 65109; 573-751-4377. www.courts.mo.gov
Court Structure:	The Circuit Court is the court of general jurisdiction. There are 45 circuits comprised of 115 county Circuit Courts and one independent City Court. There are also Associate Circuit Courts with limited jurisdiction. A growing trend is to form Combined Courts (23 consolidated 2005/2008). Municipal Courts only have jurisdiction over traffic and ordinance violations.
Find Felony Records:	Circuit Court
Misdemeanor Records:	Associate Circuit Court
Online Access:	Available at www.courts.mo.gov/casenet/cases/searchCases.do is Missouri Casenet, an online system for access to docket data. The system includes all Circuit Courts, City of St. Louis, the Eastern, Western, and Southern Appellate Courts, the Supreme Court, and Fine Collection Center. Some counties only offer probate case data. Cases can be searched case number, filing date, or litigant name.
	Search Supreme Court and Appellate Court opinions at the home page.
Searching Hints:	Many Circuit Courts and Associate Courts no longer accept mail or fax requests to perform criminal record searches. Instead, the courts instruct requesters to mail criminal search request to the MO State Highway Patrol Criminal Records Division.

Montana

Montana Statutes & Related Employer Restrictions

General Rule: Every citizen has a right to inspect and take a copy of any public writings of this state. MCA 2-6-102. There are no restrictions on the dissemination of public criminal justice information. MCA 44-5-301.

Non-public criminal history information may be disseminated with the consent of the individual, court order, or for statistical purposes. MCA 44-5-302.

An individual may inspect any criminal history record information about that individual or transfer copies of that information to any other person. MCA 44-5-214. Dissemination of confidential criminal justice information is restricted to criminal justice agencies. MCA 44-5-303.

Definitions: MCA 44-5-103

Confidential Criminal Justice Information – means criminal investigative information, criminal intelligence information, fingerprints and photographs, criminal justice information made confidential by law, and any other criminal justice information not clearly defined as public criminal justice information.

Criminal History Record Information – consists of descriptions and notations of arrest, detentions, filing of complaints, indictments, or information, and dispositions arising therefrom, sentences, correctional status, and release. Does not include records of traffic offenses or court records.

Disposition – includes conviction at trial, plea of guilty, acquittal, acquittal by reason of mental disease, acquittal by reason of mental incompetence, sentence imposed and all conditions attached, deferred sentence, nolle prosequi, nolo contendere, deferred prosecution, bond forfeiture, death, release, dismissal, revocation of probation or parole, and correctional placement on probation.

Expunged Record: Upon completion of a deferred sentence, the court may allow the defendant to withdraw a plea of guilty or nolo contendere or may strike the verdict of guilty from the record and order that the charge or charges against the defendant be dismissed. After the charge is dismissed, all records and data relating to the charge are confidential criminal justice information, and public access to the information may only be obtained by district court order upon showing good cause. MCA 46-18-204.

Consumer Report: A consumer reporting agency may furnish a consumer report to a person it has reason to believe intends to use the information for employment purposes. MCA 31-3-111(3)(b).

A person may not procure or cause to be prepared or distributed an investigative consumer report on any consumer unless the report is to be used for employment purposes for which the consumer applied. MCA 31-3-113(b).

No consumer reporting agency may report bankruptcies which antedate the report by more that 14 years, nor suits and judgments, paid tax liens, accounts placed for collection or charged to profit and loss, records of arrest, indictments, or conviction of crime, or any other adverse action which antedates the report by more than 7 years. MCA 31-3-112.

State Statutes and Codes: http://data.opi.mt.gov/bills/mca_toc/index.htm

Legislative Bill Search: http://leg.mt.gov/css/research/laws.asp

Montana State Criminal Records Agency

Department of Justice, Criminal Records, PO Box 201403, Helena, MT 59620-1403, (courier address: 303 N Roberts, 4th Floor, Helena, MT 59620.) **Phone:** 406-444-3625; **Fax:** 406-444-0689 **Web:** http://doj.mt.gov/

Search Notes: Records are available to the general public. Account status available to approved screening firms. Include the following in your request-name, alias, date of birth. The Social Security Number and any aliases are helpful. Place written requests on letterhead. Fingerprint searches are optional. 100% of records are fingerprint-supported. Direct questions to dojitsdpublicrecords@mt.gov.

What Is Released: Records are available from 1950's on and are 100% computerized. All felonies and misdemeanors (except traffic violations) are released. Records without dispositions are released; the agency attempts to locate the disposition prior to public release. Deferred impositions that have been dismissed are not released. 85% of all arrests in database have final dispositions recorded.

Access Methods: mail, in person, online.

Online Searching: Access is available for "public users" or "registered users" at https://app.mt.gov/choprs/. Fee is $11 per record. Registered users must pay a $75 annual fee and have access to other data. Search using the name and DOB. The SSN is helpful but not required. Results include up to 4 aliases, dispositions, detentions, sentences, and correctional status.

Montana Sexual Offender Registry

Department of Justice , Sexual and Violent Offender Registry, PO Box 201417, Helena, MT 59620-1417   **Phone:**   406-444-2497,   406-444-9479;   **Fax:** 406-444-2759 **Web:** http://doj.mt.gov/svor/search.asp

Note: There are over 3,900 registered offenders in the database. There are three Tier Levels of offenders, 1 being the lowest and 3 being the highest. Level 3 also indicates the offender is a sexually violent predator.

Online Searching: The state sexual offender list is available at the website. You can search for this information by name, by city or county, or by ZIP Code Also, the entire database may be purchased as a download for $300.00. Submit questions to dojsvor@mt.gov.

Montana Incarceration Records Agency

Montana Department of Corrections , Directors Office, PO Box 201301, Helena, MT 59620-1301, (courier address: 1539 11th Ave, Helena, MT 59620.) **Phones:** 406-444-3930; Information Officer- 406-444-7461; **Fax:** 406-444-4920 **Web:** www.cor.state.mt.us

Online Searching: Search current or former inmates on the ConWeb system at http://app.mt.gov/conweb/. Search by ID# or name. **Other Access:** Entire offender database is available for purchase for $100.00; call Discovering Montana, 406-449-3468. Academic or social researchers can acquire the same database for no charge.

Montana State Court System

Court Administrator:	Court Administrator Park Avenue Building, Room 328 (PO Box 203005), Helena, MT, 59620; 406-444-2621. http://courts.mt/gov
Court Structure:	The District Court is the court of general jurisdiction. There are Limited Jurisdiction Courts (also known as Justice Courts), City Courts and one Municipal Court. Many Montana Justices of the Peace maintain case record indexes on their personal PCs, which does speed the retrieval process.
Find Felony Records:	District Court
Misdemeanor Records:	Limited Jurisdiction Court, City Court, Municipal Court
Online Access:	Supreme Court opinions, orders, and recently filed briefs may be found http://searchcourts.mt.gov. There is no statewide access to docket information from the trial courts.

Nebraska

Nebraska Statutes & Related Employer Restrictions

General Rule: Complete criminal history record information shall be a public record open to inspection and copying by any person. NE ST §29-3520. Posters for apprehending fugitives, police blotters, court records of any judicial proceeding, and records of traffic offenses shall be classified as public records. NE ST §29-3521.

Notations of arrest that antedate a criminal record history request by one year shall not be disseminated unless the subject of record has made a notarized request for the release of such record. NE ST §29-3523(1)(c).

Definitions

> Complete – with reference to criminal history record information, complete means that arrest records shall show the subsequent disposition of the case. NE ST §29-3507.

> Criminal History Record information – includes arrest warrants, arrests, detentions, indictments, other formal charges, and any disposition arising from such arrest, charges, sentencing, correctional supervision, and release. NE ST §29-3506.

> Disposition – information disclosing that criminal proceedings have been concluded, including if the police elect not to refer the matter to a prosecutor or that the prosecutor has elected not to commence criminal proceedings. NE ST §29-3511.

Expunged Record: Any person arrested due to an error of a law enforcement agency may petition the court to expunge the criminal history record information.   NE ST §29-3523(2).

State Statutes and Codes: http://uniweb.legislature.ne.gov/QS/laws.html

Legislative Bill Search: www.unicam.state.ne.us/web/public/home

Nebraska State Criminal Records Agency

Nebraska State Patrol, CID, PO Box 94907, Lincoln, NE 68509-4907, (courier address: 233 S 10th St, Lincoln, NE 68508.) **Phone:** 402-471-4545; **Fax:** 402-479-4002 **Web:** www.nsp.state.ne.us

Search Note: Records are available to the general public. Include the following in your request-full name, disposition, date of birth, SSN, sex, race. Fingerprints required for certain state occupation checks; this includes an FBI fingerprint search. State keeps record of requesters and will inform the person of record if asked. 100% of records are fingerprint-supported. Felonies are required to be submitted this agency, though not all misdemeanors are. Agency will refer you to the proper county.

What Is Released: Records are available from 1937 to present. Records without dispositions are not released, except if an arrest without disposition is less than one year old. The following data is not released: juvenile records. 62% of all arrests in database have final dispositions recorded, 57% for those arrests within last 5 years.

Access Methods: mail, fax, in person.

Nebraska Sexual Offender Registry

Nebraska State Patrol , Sexual Offender Registry, PO Box 94907, Lincoln, NE 68509-4907, (courier address: 1500 Nebraska Highway 2, Lincoln, NE 68502.) **Phone:** 402-471-8647; **Fax:** 402-471-8496 **Web:** www.nsp.state.ne.us/sor/

Online Searching: A Level 3 sexual offender registry search is available at the website. The records may be searched by either ZIP Code, last name, city, or county. Search or review the entire list of names.

Nebraska Incarceration Records Agency

Nebraska Department of Correctional Services , Central Records Office, PO Box 94661, Lincoln, NE 68509-4661 **Phone:** 402-479-5273; **Fax:** 402-479-5913 **Web:** www.corrections.state.ne.us

Online Searching: Click on Inmate Records at the website for a search of inmates incarcerated after 1977.

Nebraska State Court System

Court Administrator:	Court Administrator, PO Box 98910, Lincoln, NE, 68509-8910; 402-471-3730. http://court.nol.org/
Court Structure:	District courts have original jurisdiction in all felony cases. District Courts also have appellate jurisdiction in certain matters arising out of County Courts. County Courts have original jurisdiction in violations of city or village ordinances, preliminary hearings in felony cases, and eminent domain proceedings. The county courts have concurrent jurisdiction in criminal matters classified as misdemeanors or infractions. Nearly all misdemeanor cases are tried in County Courts.
Find Felony Records:	District Court
Misdemeanor Records:	County Court
Online Access:	An online access subscription service is available for Nebraska District Courts and County courts, except Douglas County District Court. Case details, all party listings, payments, and actions taken for criminal, civil, probate, juvenile, and traffic is available. Users must be registered with Nebraska.gov; there is a start-up fee. The fee is $.60 per record or a flat rate of $300.00 per month. Also, for $15.00 fee per search, you may access the JUSTICE Court Case System statewide at https://www.nebraska.gov/justicecc/ccname.cgi. Go to www.nebraska.gov/faqs/justice or call 402-471-7810 for more info and info on how far back records go per county. Supreme Court opinions are available from http://court.nol.org/opinions.
Searching Hints:	Most Nebraska courts require the public to do their own in-person searches and will not respond to written search requests. The State Attorney General has recommended that courts not perform searches because of the time involved and concerns over possible legal liability.

Nevada

Nevada Statutes & Related Employer Restrictions

General Rule: All public books and public records of a government entity must be open to inspection by any person, and may be copied. NRS 239.101.

No criminal justice agency in Nevada may disseminate any record of criminal history relating to a felony or gross misdemeanor without first making inquiry of the central repository to obtain the most current information available. NRS 179A.090.

Any record, which only reflects conviction or which pertains to an incident for which a person is currently within the system, may be disseminated by a criminal justice agency without any restrictions. NRS 179A.100(1).

No person who receives criminal history information may disseminate it further without express authority of law or court order. NRS 179A.110.

Definitions: NRS 179A.070

Record of Criminal History – identifies the subject and notations of warrants, arrest, citations for misdemeanors, detentions, decisions not to prosecute, indictments, dispositions of the charges, dismissals, acquittals, convictions, sentences, parole, and probation. Does not include information concerning juveniles, court decisions or opinions, records of traffic violations or records of traffic offenses.

Expunged Record: If the court orders a record sealed, all proceedings in the record are deemed to have never occurred and the person may answer accordingly to any inquiry. NRS 179.285(1)(a).

Employment: Any record which only reflects convictions or which pertains to an incident for which a person is currently within the system may be disseminated by a criminal justice agency to a prospective employer. NRS 179A.100(3). The Central Repository can provide additional criminal record information, including arrest information on sexual offenses to an employer which obtains the written consent of the applicant/employee. NRS 179a.110(5).

Consumer Report: A "consumer report" is limited under Nevada law to a communication regarding a consumer's payment history, credit worthiness, credit standing or credit capacity. The report may be used for credit, employment or any other FCRA permissible purpose. NRS 598C.060. A "reporting agency" (someone who provides "consumer reports", NRS 598C.100) must purge bankruptcies older than 10 years and criminal records older than 7 years. NRS 598C.150. Thus a FCRA "consumer reporting agency" that does not provide credit related information is not affected by this statutory limitation.

State Statutes and Codes: www.leg.state.nv.us/NRS/

Legislative Bill Search: www.leg.state.nv.us

Nevada State Criminal Records Agency

DPS-Records & Technolgy Div, Records Bureau, 333 W Nye Lane, #100, Carson City, NV 89706 **Phone:** 775-684-6262; **Fax:** 775-684-6265   **Web:** www.nvrepository.state.nv.us

Search Note: Records are available if you provide fingerprints and consent of subject. This repository maintains all retainable criminal charges as defined by state statute including DUI and domestic violence. 100% of arrest records are fingerprint supported. Include the following in your request-set of fingerprints, signed release, full name, DOB, SSN, sex and race.

What Is Released: Records are available from 1987 and are on computer. Records are maintained indefinitely, unless sealed due to court order or on the death or 100th birthday of the individual. Records without dispositions are released.The following data is not released: sealed records or juvenile records. According to a U.S. DOJ study in 2003 37% of all arrests in database have final dispositions recorded, approximately 30% for those arrests within last 5 years.

Access Methods: mail, in person.

Nevada Sexual Offender Registry

Records and Identification Bureau , Sex Offender Registry, 333 W Nye Lane, #100, Carson City, NV 89706 **Phone:** 775-684-6256; **Fax:** 775-684-6266 **Web:** www.nvsexoffenders.gov

Online Searching: Information available on the website is extensive, including aliases, photograph (where available), injury and conviction information, and latest registered address. Information is provided for sex offenders with a risk assessment score of a TIER Level 3 or TIER Level 2. Search by name, ZIP Code, license plate number. Email questions to sorhelp@dps.state.nv.us.

Nevada Incarceration Records Agency

Nevada Department of Corrections , Attn: Records, PO Box 7011, Carson City, NV 89702, **Phone:** 775-887-3285; **Fax:** 775-687-6715 **Web:** www.doc.nv.gov

Online Searching: Access information from the web page. This will allow you to look up information about a particular individual. If you prefer, you may click on Download Information to obtain text files of all the information available via the Inmate Search. This system contains information about current inmates and those discharged in the past 18 months.

Nevada State Court System

Court Administrator: Supreme Court of Nevada, Administrative Office of the Courts, Capitol Complex, 201 S Carson St #250, Carson City, NV, 89701; 775-684-1700. www.nvsupremecourt.us/index.php

Court Structure: There are 17 District Courts within 9 judicial districts. The 45 Justice Courts are named for the township of jurisdiction. Note that, due to their small populations, some townships no longer have Justice Courts. The Justices of the Peace also preside over felony and gross misdemeanor arraignments and conduct preliminary hearings to determine if sufficient evidence exists to hold criminals for trial at District Court

Find Felony Records: District Court

Misdemeanor Records: District Court, Justice Court

Online Access: Some Nevada Courts have internal online computer systems, but only Clark and Washoe counties offer online access to the public. A statewide court automation system is being implemented. The Supreme Court website gives access to opinions.

Searching Hints: Many Nevada Justice Courts are small and have very few records. Their hours of operation vary widely and contact is difficult. It is recommended that requesters call ahead for information prior to submitting a written request or attempting an in-person retrieval.

New Hampshire

New Hampshire Statutes & Related Employer Restrictions

General Rule: Every citizen has the right to inspect all public records. NH ST §91-A:4. Records of grand and petit juries, parole and pardon boards, personal school records of pupils, teacher certification records, records pertaining to preparing and carrying out emergency functions, and otherwise confidential records are exempt from the general rule. NH ST §91-A:5.

Criminal conviction records are not open to the public unless the subject of the record has provided authorization in writing, signed and notarized, allowing the requestor to receive the information. NH ST §106-B:14.

Information available for noncriminal justice purposes is limited to conviction data. NH ADC SAF-C 5703.04.

Expunged Record: The record of arrest, conviction, and sentence of any person may be annulled by the sentencing court. NH ST §651:5(I). One may petition to have their record annulled after various periods of time passing without a subsequent conviction, other than DUI, depending upon the seriousness of the crime: 1 year for "offenses" up to 10 years for Class A felonies, sexual assault, etc. The person whose record is annulled shall be treated in all respects as if he had never been arrested, convicted, or sentenced. NH ST §651:5(X)(a).

Employment: In any application for employment, license, or other civil right or privilege, a person may be questioned about a previous criminal record only in terms such as "Have you ever been arrested for or convicted of a crime that has not been annulled by a court?" NH ST §651:5(X)(c).

Consumer Report: No consumer reporting agency shall disclose 1) bankruptcies which antedate the report by 14 years, or 2) suits and judgments, paid tax liens, accounts placed for collection, records of arrest, indictment, or conviction of a crime, or any other adverse action which antedates the report by more than 7 years. NH ST §359-B:5(I).

Exception: The reporting prohibition does not apply to the employment of an individual at an annual salary of $20,000 or more. NH ST §359-B:5(II)

State Statutes and Codes: http://gencourt.state.nh.us/rsa/html/indexes/default.html

Legislative Bill Search: http://gencourt.state.nh.us/index/

New Hampshire State Criminal Records Agency

State Police Headquarters, Criminal Records, James H. Hayes Bldg,, 33 Hazen Dr, Concord, NH   03305   **Phone:**   603-271-2538;   **Fax:** 603-271-2339
Web: www.nh.gov/safety/divisions/nhsp/forms.html

Search Note: There is no specific web page devoted to criminal record ordering and procedures. Instead, you must click on "Documents and Forms" and then open the forms to obtain general information.

Records are available to the general public. Requester must have "authorization in writing, duly signed and notarized, explicitly allowing the requester to receive such information." Also specify exactly what information is needed. Statutorily-required fingerprint searches include FBI check. Include the following in your request-notarized release, full name, date of birth, any aliases, sex, race. Fingerprint searches are required for certain occupations (i.e. teachers) per state statute. 75% of the records are fingerprint supported.

What Is Released: Records are available from circa 1900. Records without convictions are not released. 80% of all arrests in database have final dispositions recorded, 87% for those arrests within last 5 years.

Access Methods: mail, in person.

New Hampshire Sexual Offender Registry

State Police Headquarters , Special Investigations Unit-SOR, James H. Hayes Bldg, 33 Hazen Dr, Concord, NH 03305 **Phone:** 603-271-6344 **Web:** www.egov.nh.gov/nsor/

Online Searching: For web access, click on the Offenders Against Children link. This list only contains certain information about registered offenders who have committed certain criminal offenses against children. The list also contains outstanding arrest warrants for any sexual offender or offender against children who did not register.

New Hampshire Incarceration Records Agency

New Hampshire Department of Corrections , Offender Records Office, PO Box 14, Concord, NH 03302 **Phone:** 603-271-1825; **Fax:** 603-271-1867 **Web:** www.nh.gov/nhdoc/

Online Searching: An inmate locator is available on their web page. The inmate locator displays the offender's current controlling sentence and does not show concurrent sentences also being served or consecutive sentences that have yet to be served.

New Hampshire State Court System

Court Administrator: Administrative Office of the Courts, Supreme Court Bldg, 2 Charles Doe, Concord, NH 03301; Phone 603-271-2521. www.courts.state.nh.us

Court Structure: The Superior Court is the court of General Jurisdiction. Felony cases include Class A misdemeanors.

Find Felony Records: Superior Court

Misdemeanor Records: District Court

Online Access: While there is no statewide access available for trial court records, the web page has a lot of useful information, including opinions and directives form Supreme Courts, Superior Courts, and District Courts.

Searching Hints: Fees for searching, copies, certification are set by NH Supreme Court.

New Jersey

New Jersey Statutes & Related Employer Restrictions

General Rule: A person or non-governmental entity of any state, who seeks to directly engage the services of the subject of the record, is authorized to obtain from the State Bureau of Identification all New Jersey criminal history record information for purposes of determining the subject's qualifications for employment or volunteer work. NJ ADC 13:59-1.2(a)(2).

Regardless of the subject's age, all records of pending arrests and charges for violations of New Jersey laws will be released, unless such records have been expunged. NJ ADC 13:59-1.2(a). Expunged records are deemed not to have occurred. NJSA 2C:52-27.

State Statutes and Codes: http://lis.njleg.state.nj.us/cgi-bin/om_isapi.dll?clientID=37640657
Legislative Bill Search: www.njleg.state.nj.us

New Jersey State Criminal Records Agency

Division of State Police, Records and Identification Section, PO Box 7068, West Trenton, NJ 08628-0068   **Phones:**   609-882-2000 x2991;   Crim   Info   Unit- 609-882-2000 x2918; **Fax:** 609-530-5780   **Web:** www.njsp.org/about/serv_chrc.html

Search Note: Record access is limited to attorney firms, employers, private investigators, and the subject. Records may be ordered with or without fingerprints, except if ordered by the subject then fingerprints are required. Include the following in your request-date of birth, Social Security Number. Requesters must use form 212B. Attorney firms may submit a subpoena instead of the form. The name must match exactly. 100% of the records are fingerprint supported. Fingerprints are required with a request made by the subject.

What Is Released: Records are available from 1951 forward. Records destroyed upon verification that subject is no longer alive. Only convictions and naked arrests are provided, unless the request is fingerprint-based and then the entire criminal history is provided. Juvenile records are restricted. Dismissals, acquittals, not-guilty verdicts are excluded to PIs and employers. 84% of all arrests in database have final dispositions recorded, 72% for arrests within last 5 years.

Access Method: mail.

New Jersey Sexual Offender Registry

Division of State Police , Sexual Offender Registry, PO Box 7068, West Trenton, NJ 08628-0068 **Phone:** 609-882-2000 x2886; **Fax:** 609-538-0544   **Web:** www.njsp.org

Online Searching: At the website click on NJ Sex Offender Registry. There are a variety of searches available including geographic, individual, advanced, and fugitives.

New Jersey Incarceration Records Agency

New Jersey Department of Corrections , Central Reception & Assignment Facility, PO Box 7450, Trenton, NJ 08628   **Phone:**   609-777-5753,   609-984-2695;   **Fax:** 609-777-8369 **Web:** www.state.nj.us/corrections/index.shtml

Note: There are three possible physical locations for records. Processing can take longer if records must be obtained at one of the other 2 locations. Location, DOC number, physical identifiers, conviction info, and release dates released.

Online Searching: Extensive search capabilities are offered from the website; click on "Offender   Search"   or   visit   https://www6.state.nj.us/DOC_Inmate/inmatefinder?i=I. Offenders on Work Release, Furlough, or in a Halfway House are not necessarily reflected as such in their profile.

New Jersey State Court System

Court Administrator: Admin. Office of the Courts, RJH Justice Complex, Courts Bldg 7th Fl, PO Box 037, Trenton, NJ, 08625; Phone: 609-984-0275. www.judiciary.state.nj.us

Court Structure: Each of the 21 Superior Courts have 2 divisions; one is for the Criminal Division. Search requests should be addressed separately to each division.

Find Felony Records: Superior Court

Misdemeanor Records: Municipal Court

Online Access: No online criminal record access; a useful website giving decisions is maintained by the Rutgers Law School at http://lawlibrary.rutgers.edu/search.shtml. Supreme and Appellate case data is found at www.judiciary.state.nj.us/opinions/index.htm.

Originally developed for county prosecutors, the **Promis/Gavel** is an automated criminal case tracking system that provides the function of docketing, indexing, noticing, calendaring, statistical reporting, and case management reporting, etc. Promis/Gavel is interactive with the courts as well as with the NJSP. **But rules do not allow the public to access the complete Promis/Gavel system—only a filtered Promis/Gavel Public Access (PGPA) system is available to the public on the public access terminals in the courts.** Also, the PGPA does not include contain offenses or petty offenses recorded in 530+ municipal courts, unless they are filed with indictables. The more serious of these petty offenses include drug offenses, violence, theft, sexual assault, and pedophilia. An AOC press release about the PGPA states, "The court records obtained from Promis/Gavel do not constitute a criminal history records check, which must be obtained through law enforcement." However, because of the simplicity of access and cost, the PGPA is the system of choice for most screening companies.

Searching Hints: Criminal searches may be done in person at the courts on their public access terminals, but the Superior Court now directs non-in person searches to the New Jersey State Police Records and ID Section at 609-882-2000, x2991 or x2918. State Police records are fingerprint-based searches. For information on purchase of the statewide public access criminal records databases, telephone 609-882-2000.

Note that Cape May County offices are located in City of Cape May Court House, and not in City of Cape May."

New Mexico

New Mexico Statutes & Related Employer Restrictions

General Rule: Every person has a right to inspect public records of this state except records classified as confidential or law enforcement records that would reveal confidential sources. NMSA 1978 §14-2-1.

Records of arrest not followed by a valid conviction and misdemeanor convictions not involving moral turpitude shall not be distributed in connection with an application for any public employment or license. NMSA 1978 §28-2-3(B).

Expunged Records: A person may petition and expunge arrest records. An arrest record includes cases not prosecuted, dismissals referral to diversion programs, placement on probation or in position of a fine. NMSA 29-3-8.1.

Employment: In determining eligibility for employment with the state or for a license, permit, or certificate to engage in any trade, business or profession, the board may take convictions into consideration. The conviction shall not operate as an automatic bar to obtaining employment or license. NMSA 1978 §28-2-3(A).

Additionally, the state licensing board may refuse to grant a license if the applicant has 1) been convicted of a felony or misdemeanor involving moral turpitude, and the conviction relates directly to the employment sought, 2) been convicted of a felony or misdemeanor involving moral turpitude, and the conviction does not directly relate to the employment sought but the board determines the applicant has not been sufficiently rehabilitated, or 3) the applicant has been convicted of trafficking controlled substances, criminal sexual penetration, related sexual offenses, or child abuse, and the applicant is seeking employment involving children. NMSA 1978 §28-2-4(A).

Consumer Report: A credit bureau (defined as any business engaged in furnishing credit information - thus if a CRA does not provide credit reports as part of its business they are not covered by state restrictions) may not disclose 1) bankruptcies which antedate the report more than 14 years, or 2) accounts placed for collection, suit and judgments, paid tax liens, arrests and indictment pending trial, conviction of a crime, or any other data not otherwise specified which antedate the report by more than 7 years. NMSA 1978 §56-3-6.

State Statutes and Codes: www.conwaygreene.com/NewMexico.htm

Legislative Bill Search: http://legis.state.nm.us/lcs/BillFinder.asp

New Mexico State Criminal Records Agency

Department of Public Safety, Criminal Records Bureau, PO Box 1628, Santa Fe, NM 87504-1628, (courier address: 4491 Cerrillos Rd, Santa Fe, NM 87504.) **Phone:** 505-827-9181; **Fax:** 505-827-3388 **Web:** www.dps.nm.org

Search Note: Records are available to the general public. Fingerprint search requests are not available except for checks for children or elderly-related occupations mandated by state statute, and an FBI search can be done for those groups. The state's records are 100%

fingerprint-supported. Include the following in your request-date of birth, Social Security Number, full name, DPS notarized signed release by subject. Download the release form at the web page.

What Is Released: Records are available from 1935 on. All records are released, including those without dispositions. This includes arrest record information on persons arrested in New Mexico for felony, misdemeanor (offenses punishable by 6 months or more imprisonment) and DWI offenses. Juvenile records are not released. After receiving, it takes 2 to 4 weeks before new records are available for inquiry. 32% of all arrests in database have final dispositions recorded, 35% for arrests within last 5 years.

Access Methods: mail, in person.

New Mexico Sexual Offender Registry

Department of Public Safety , Records Bureau, PO Box 1628, Santa Fe, NM 87504-1628, (courier address: 4491 Cerrillos Rd, Santa Fe, NM 87504.) **Phone:** 505-827-9297, 505-827-9193; **Fax:** 505-827-3399 **Web:** www.nmsexoffender.dps.state.nm.us

Online Searching: The website offers a variety of search methods including by name, county, city, and ZIP Code. The site also offers a complete state list, also an absconder list.

New Mexico Incarceration Records Agency

New Mexico Corrections Department , Central Records Unit, PO Box 27116, Santa Fe, NM 87502 **Phone:** 505-827-8674; **Fax:** 505-827-8821 **Web:** http://corrections.state.nm.us

Online Searching: To search at the website, you must first click on Offender Information, then on Offender Search.

New Mexico State Court System

Court Administrator: Admin. Office of the Courts, Judicial Information Division, 2905 Rodeo Park Dr East, Bldg #5, Santa Fe, NM, 87505; 505-476-6900. www.nmcourts.com

Court Structure: The 30 District Courts in 13 districts are the courts of general jurisdiction. Municipal Courts handle petty misdemeanors, DWI/DUI, traffic violations, and other municipal ordinance violations.

Find Felony Records: District Court

Misdemeanor Records: Magistrate Court, Bernalillo Metropolitan Court in Bernalillo County

Online Access: The home page offers free access to District Courts and Magistrate Courts case information (except Bernalillo Metropolitan Court, see below). In general, records are available from June, 1997 forward. The site also offers a DWI Offender History tool for researching an individual's DWI history. Search by name.

Research Supreme Court opinions at www.supremecourt.nm.org.

A commercial online service is available for the Metropolitan Court of Bernalillo County. There is a $35.00 set up fee, a connect time fee based on usage. Call 505-345-6555 for more information.

Searching Hints: There are some "shared courts" in low-populated counties in New Mexico, with one county handling cases arising in another.

New York
New York Statutes & Related Employer Restrictions

General Rule: Each agency shall make available for public inspection and copying all records, except that such agency may deny access to records or portions thereof. NY PUB OFF §87(2).

No agency may disclose any record or personal information unless such disclosure is pursuant to a written request by or the voluntary written consent of the data subject, provided that such request or consent is limited by its terms and specifically describes the personal information requested, the requestor of the information, and the uses of the information requested. NY PUB OFF §96(1)(a).

Expunged Record: All official records relating to a youthful offender are confidential and are not available to any person or public or private agency. NY CRIM PRO §720.35(2). A youthful offender is defined as someone aged 16. 17 or 18. There are several qualifications. NY CRIM PRO §720.10.

Employment: It is unlawful for any person, agency, bureau, corporation, or association to deny any license or employment to an individual by reason of his or her being convicted of one or more criminal offenses, or to conclude a lack of "good moral character" based on his or her being convicted of one or more criminal offenses. NY EXEC §296(15).

An employer may consider the conviction if 1) there is a direct relationship between the previous criminal offense and the employment or license sought or 2) the issuance of the license or granting employment would involve unreasonable risk to property or to the safety or welfare of a specific individual or the general public. NY CORRECTION §752.

It is also illegal to make inquiry about or to act adversely to the individual involved, any criminal accusation not then pending which was followed by a termination of the criminal action in favor of the individual, in connection with licensing or employing the individual. However, this does not apply to the regulation of deadly weapons, or an application for employment as a police officer. NY EXEC §296(16).

Credit Report: A consumer reporting agency may furnish a consumer report to a person whom it has reason to believe intends to use the information for employment purposes. NY GEN BUS §380-b(a)(3)(ii).

No consumer reporting agency can report information about an arrest or criminal charge unless there has been a criminal conviction or the charges are still pending. NY GEN BUS §380-j(a)(1).

A consumer reporting agency may collect information about a detention of an individual by a retail mercantile establishment providing that the individual admitted wrongdoing, received notice that the information will be reported, and the receiver of the information will only use the information for employment purposes. NY GEN BUS §380-j(b).

No consumer report may disclose 1) bankruptcies which antedate the report by more than 14 years, 2) judgments for seven years or longer if statute of limitations allows, but a satisfied judgment may only be reported for 5 years from the entry of satisfaction with the court, or 3) paid tax liens, accounts placed for collection, records of criminal convictions, information regarding drug or alcohol addiction, information relating to past confinement in a mental institute, or any other adverse action which antedate the report by more than 7 years. NY GEN BUS §380-j(f)(1). However, the above information is not prohibited from disclosure for the employment of any individual at an annual salary of $25,000 or more. NY GEN BUS §380-j(f)(2).

No person may procure an investigative consumer report unless the consumer has received notice and the consumer has authorized the procurement of the investigative report. NY GEN BUS §380-c(a).

If an applicant refuses to authorize the procurement of an investigative consumer report, the prospective employer may decline to grant employment. NY GEN BUS §380-c(d).

Agency Guidelines for Pre-Employment Inquiries: NY State Division of Human Rights, "Rulings on Inquiries (Pre-employment)" available on SUNY education system at http://naples.cc.sunysb.edu/Admin/HRSForms.nsf/0/510e45e64ead755885256d280 0561042/$FILE/HRSD0010.pdf

State Statutes and Codes:
http://public.leginfo.state.ny.us/menugetf.cgi?COMMONQUERY=LAWS

Legislative Bill Search: http://public.leginfo.state.ny.us/menuf.cgi

New York State Criminal Records Agency

Division of Criminal Justice Services, Record Review Unit, 4 Tower Place, Stuyvesant Plaza, Albany, NY 12203 **Phone:** 518-457-6043, 518-485-7675; **Fax:** 518-457-6550 **Web:** www.criminaljustice.state.ny.us

Access to Records is Restricted

Records are only released pursuant to court order, subpoena, to entities authorized by statute, or to person of record. The public must search at the county court level and via the state OCA system. One may obtain their own personal criminal history record review by requesting a Record Review Packet from DCJS, and following the directions for the completion and submission of a fingerprint card to DCJS, along with a fee of $50. Email questions to RecordReview@dcjs.state.ny.us.

Though not open to the public, there are exceptions. One may obtain his own personal criminal history record review by requesting a Record Review Packet from DCJS, and following the directions for the completion and submission of a fingerprint card to DCJS, along with a fee of $50. Misdemeanor convictions older than 5 years cannot be considered unless another crime has been committed during that time. 85% of records have dispositions. 99% of records are fingerprint supported. Include the following in your request-name, DOB, SSN, and fingerprints. The following data is not released: sealed records and confidential records pursuant to the Criminal Procedure Law or Family Court Act.

New York Sexual Offender Registry

Division of Criminal Justice Srvs , Sexual Offender Registry, 4 Tower Place, Rm 604, Albany, NY 12203 **Phones:** Main Number- 518-457-3167; Search- 800-262-3257; **Fax:** 518-485-5805 **Web:** www.criminaljustice.state.ny.us/nsor/index.htm

Online Searching: The sex offender registry Level 3 can be searched at the website. Requesters are required to register. Email questions to infodcjs@dcjs.state.ny.us.

New York State Incarceration Records Agency

New York Department of Correctional Services , Building 2 - Central Files, 1220 Washington Ave, Albany, NY 12226-2050 **Phones:** 518-457-5000; Contact phone- 518-457-8126; **Fax:** 518-457-4966 **Web:** www.docs.state.ny.us

Written requests should be directed to FOIA Unit. Location, DIN number, conviction and sentencing info, and release dates are provided.

Online Searching: Computerized inmate information is available from the Inmate Lookup at http://nysdocslookup.docs.state.ny.us/kinqw00 or follow "inmate lookup" link at main site. Records go back to early 1970s. To acquire inmate DIN number, you may call 518-457-5000. The site has state DOC data but not data from all counties.

New York State Court System

Court Administrator: New York State Unified Court System, Office of Court Administration, 4 ESP, Suite 201, Empire State Plaza, Albany, NY 12223. There is also a New York City Office of Court Administration, 25 Beaver St, New York, NY 10004, 212-428-2700. www.courts.state.ny.us

Court Structure: New York State has two sites for Administration; an Albany office and a New York City office (addresses and phone numbers below).

"Supreme & County Courts" are the highest trial courts in the state, equivalent to Circuit or District Courts in other states. New York's Supreme and County Courts may be administered together or separately. County Courts handle felony cases, and in many New York counties, these County Courts also handle misdemeanors.

City Courts handle misdemeanors. Not all counties have City Courts, thus cases there fall to the Supreme and County Courts respectively, or, in a many counties, to the small Town and Village Courts, which can number in the dozens within a county.

The staff at NY Superior, County, and City Courts are NY state employees. However, in some counties (usually smaller NY counties), the clerk for Supreme and County Courts may also be the "County Clerk" - these duo-role clerks are employed partly by the county, and partly by the state, which creates a question of whose "directives" and rules do they follow in regard to court record search procedures.

Records for Supreme and County Courts are maintained by the County Clerks, who are county employees. There are exceptions. In New York City - with its five boroughs - the courts records are administered directly by the state OCA (Office of Court Administration). Also, there are a small number of upstate counties where the Supreme Court OR County Court records are maintained by their court clerk (state employee), and only an index list of cases and defendants is provided to the County Clerk (county employee).

In some NY counties, the address for the County Clerk is the same as for the Supreme and County Courts. Note also that, due to limitations in the receiving of records from the Chief Court Clerks, the County Clerk may only be able to do a civil record search, or, rarely, only a criminal record search. Each county is going to be different.

City Courts - While all City Courts are administered by state employees, there are a few City Courts that will do a city-only record check despite the edict to state employees that they must direct record searches to the OCA for the statewide record check. Records from City Courts do not go to the County Clerk. Records from City Courts go directly to the OCA.

In at least 20 New York Counties, misdemeanor records are only available at city, town, or village courts. You may also conclude that an accurate search for misdemeanor records is nearly impossible as there are over 1200 Town and Village Courts in NY which may or may not be accurately reporting their case records.

Find Felony Records: County Court (Supreme & County Court), City Court

Misdemeanor Records: City Court, District Court, City of NY Criminal Court, Town and Village Justice Courts

Criminal Notes: OCA will perform an electronic search for criminal history information from a database of criminal case records from all boroughs and all counties including Supreme Courts, County Courts, and City Courts. At press time, it is not clear that all City Courts submit all misdemeanors to this database. The search fee, payable by check, is $55.00 per name. The search is available by mail or in person (6 to 24-hour turnaround time), or high volume requesters may order online with email return (same day if ordered by 2:30 pm). The Criminal History Record Search Unit can be reached at 212-428-2943 or www.nycourts.gov/apps/chrs.

Direct mail and in person requests to: Office of Court Administration (OCA), Criminal History Search, 25 Beaver St, 8th Fl, NY, NY 10004.

Please note that nearly all the City Courts no longer do criminal record searches and send misdemeanor record requesters to the OCA for the $55.00 statewide record search

Many Counties Still Offer a Countywide Criminal Record Search -

In counties outside of NYC, as cases are closed, the general rule is that the files are given to the County Clerk who is responsible for the public record. Each county has a County Clerk employed by the county (and in rare instances, the clerk may be both the state's Chief Court Clerk and the County's County Clerk). State edicts aside, the reality is that either type of clerk may "sell" county criminal and/or civil records. The County Clerk can because they are not state employees, and the Chief Court Clerk can - though they are told not to and seldom do - because it just makes life easier for everyone.

Public Access Terminals- The County Clerks, since they already handle real estate, judgments, and lien records, can also provide access to these records AND the civil records (received from the Supreme Court Clerk) on their public access terminals. You will find, however, that there are far, far fewer County Clerks who offer access to criminal records on the county-owned public access terminals.

City Courts- The City Courts throughout the state do not provide public access terminals. However, plans are to add public access terminals at City Courts, but there is no promise on that nor is there a set timetable for plugging the public in.

County Courts- You will find that rarely does a County Court provide public access terminals where you can view their criminal records. It is also rare to find County Court criminal records on the County Clerk's public access terminal. In some counties, the County Court provides the County Clerk with only a paper record of criminal indexes.

Online Access: In addition to the $55 statewide mail or in-person record search, which is explained above, the OCA offers online access to "approved requesters" for criminal records. Requesters receive information back via email. Call the OCA for details on how to set up an account.

Visit https://iapps.courts.state.ny.us/caseTrac/jsp/ecourt.htm. This site provides access to a number of records, including WebCrims to criminal case dockets with future appearance dates in 13 counties, open landlord tenant cases from NYC, and open family court cases from all 62 counties. Also from here access or monitor Supreme Court and Family Court case information on open cases for all 62 New York counties. Appellate decisions available at www.nycourts.gov/ctapps/latdec.htm

Searching Hints: Almost all County Courts (felony records) will provide a Certificate of Disposition. This Certificate is a certified document from the court that indicates the disposition of a case. The fee for a Certificate of Disposition is either $5.00 or $6.00, depending upon the county. To obtain a Certificate of Disposition, you must prepay, you must include the name and an exact as possible date (either the disposition date or the arrest date - this requirement varies from county to county), or provide the case number. Some counties also ask for a signed release.

North Carolina

North Carolina Statutes & Related Employer Restrictions

General Rule: Public records and public information is the property of the people and the people may obtain copies. NCGSA §132-1(b). Records of criminal investigation or criminal intelligence information are not public records. NCGSA §132-1.4(a).

Records and evidence compiled by the director of the Dept. of Justice, State Bureau of Investigation, are not public records and will not be made available to the public unless ordered by a court of competent jurisdiction. 12 NCAC 3B.0401.

The North Carolina Attorney General's Office is responsible for determining what persons or agencies are entitled by law/authorized to receive criminal history record information. 12 NCAC 3B.0502(b). An authorized requestor is any person approved to receive state and national criminal history data by virtue of being 1) a member of an approved law enforcement agency, 2) any person from Division of Criminal Information, or 3) National Crime Information Center authorized non-criminal justice agency. 12 NCAC 4E.0104(3).

Criminal History Record Information disseminated to the requesting person or agency for a purpose other than the administration of justice will consist of arrest data, which includes a final disposition to the arrest, and arrest data without a final disposition if the date of arrest is within one year or less from the date of request. 12 NCAC 3B.0502(g).

Additional persons/agencies authorized by statute to obtain criminal record check if they obtain the individual's consent include:

1) Hospitals and child placing agencies for providers of treatment for services to children, the elderly, mental health patients, the sick and disabled. NCGSA §114-19.3

2) Division of Social Services, Department of Health and Human Services for a prospective foster or adoptive parent. NCGSA §114-19.4

3) Division of Child Development for any child care provider. NCGSA §114-19.5.

4) Department of Health and Human Services or Department of Juvenile Justice and Delinquency Prevention for an applicant for employment or current employee in a position to care for a client, patient, student, resident, or ward of the Department. NCGSA §114-19.6.

5) NC Auctioneers Commission for an applicant for an auctioneer's license. NCGSA §114-19.8.

6) Nursing Homes, Adult Care Homes, Home Care Agencies, Area Mental Health, Developmental, disabilities, and substance abuse services authorities. NCGSA §114-19.10.

7) North Carolina Board of Nursing for any applicant seeking licensure as a registered nurse or licensed practical nurse. NCGSA §114-19.11.

8) Fire Department for a paid or volunteer position and Emergency Medical Services. NCGSA §114-19.12.

9) North Carolina Manufactures Housing Board for any applicant for licensure as a manufactured home manufacturer, dealer, salesperson, or set-up contractor. NCGSA §114-19.13.

10) The City for any person seeking employment with the city. NCGSA §114-19.14.

11) North Carolina Locksmith Licensing Board for any applicant seeking licensure as a locksmith or apprentice. NCGSA §114-19.15.

Employment: Employers for the Fire Department, Department of Health and Human Services, or Department of Juvenile Justice and Delinquency Prevention may use a person's conviction of certain felonies and misdemeanors as just cause for not selecting the person for employment, or for dismissing the person from current employment. However, the conviction shall not automatically prohibit employment. The employer must take into consideration the seriousness of the crime, date of the crime, age of the person at the time of conviction, nexus between the crime and the job duties, and the subsequent commission of a crime.   NCGSA §§114-19.6(d) and 114-19.12(d).

Expunged Record: No person who has had a record expunged will be guilty of perjury or guilty of otherwise giving a false statement or response to any inquiry made for any purpose, by reason of his failure to recite or acknowledge any expunged records. NCGAS §15A-146(a).

State Statutes and Codes: www.ncleg.net/gascripts/Statutes/Statutes.asp

Legislative Bill Search: www.ncleg.net

North Carolina State Criminal Records Agency

State Bureau of Investigation, C.I.I.S., PO Box 29500, Raleigh, NC 27626, (courier address: 3320 Garner Rd, Raleigh, NC 27626-0500.) **Phones:** 919-662-4500; Customer Svc Dept.- 919-662-4509 x6266; **Fax:** 919-662-4380   **Web:** www.ncsbi.gov/default.jsp

Access to Records is Restricted

Search Note: Not Record access is limited to criminal justice and other government agencies authorized by law. Employers are denied access unless subject is in a business designated to receive records (i.e. health or child care). Contact agency for proper paperwork. This agency will direct you to the Admin. Office of the Courts (AOC) for online access to statewide Clerk of Court criminal records. Private companies offering NC criminal records are listed at www.nccourts.org/Citizens/GoToCourt/Default.asp?topic=1. The subject can request their record for $14.00 cert check or M.O.; mandatory to include a FD-258 fingerprint card. Send to- Attn: Applicant Unit. The result is returned to the subject only - this agency will not forward it to a third party.

North Carolina Sexual Offender Registry

State Bureau of Investigation , Criminal Information & Ident Sect - SOR Unit, PO Box 29500, Raleigh, NC 27626-0500, (courier address: 3320 Garner Rd, Raleigh, NC 27626-0500.) **Phone:** 919-662-4500 x6257; **Fax:** 919-662-4619 **Web:** http://ncfindoffender.com/disclaimer.aspx

Note: Records are available for public inspection; name, sex, address, physical description, picture, conviction date, offense for which registration was required, the sentence imposed as a result of the conviction, and registration status. This office only releases information online. They suggest to submit a written request for the information to the county sheriff. The identity of the victim cannot be released. A sheriff may charge a reasonable fee.

Online Searching: Search Level 3 records at the website. Search by name or geographic region. Agency can provide data on CD-Rom.

North Carolina Incarceration Records Agency

North Carolina Department of Corrections , Combined Records, 2020 Yonkers Road, 4226 MSC, Raleigh, NC 27699-4226 **Phone:** 919-716-3200; **Fax:** 919-716-3986 **Web:** www.doc.state.nc.us

Online Searching: The web access allows searching by name or ID number for public information on inmates, probationers, or parolees since 1973. Go to http://webapps6.doc.state.nc.us/apps/offender/menu1.

North Carolina State Court System

Court Administrator: Administrative Office of the Courts, Justice Bldg, PO Box 2448, Raleigh, NC, 27602; 919- 890-1000. www.nccourts.org

Court Structure: The Superior Court is the court of general jurisdiction, the District Court is limited. The counties combine the courts, thus searching is done through one court, not two, within the county.

Find Felony Records: Superior Court

Misdemeanor Records: District Court

Online Access: The state AOC has public access for approved requesters on its Virtual Private Network. Charges are based on screens viewed rather than a specific fee per name. A lesser valued product known as the Criminal Extract is available, but does not have the depth and quality as the Virtual Private Network. Call 919-716-5088 for details. the District and Superior Court Query system for current criminal defendants at www1.aoc.state.nc.us/www/calendars/CriminalQuery.html. There are also queries for Impaired Driving, Citations, and Current Civil and Criminal Calendars. Appellate and Supreme Court opinions are at www.aoc.state.nc.us/www/public/html/opinions.htm.

Searching Hints: Many courts have archived their records prior to 1968 in the Raleigh State Archives, 919-807-7280. Companies offering NC online criminal records are listed online at www.nccourts.org/Citizens/GoToCourt/Documents/WebsiteListing.pdf.

North Dakota

North Dakota Statutes & Related Employer Restrictions

General Rule: Only the bureau may disseminate criminal history record information to parties other than criminal justice agencies, courts, or pursuant to a judicial, legislative, or administrative agency subpoena issued in North Dakota. The dissemination may only be made if the information 1) has not been purged or sealed, 2) the information is of a conviction, or notwithstanding any disposition following a deferred sentence, or information is a reportable event occurring within one year of the request, 3) the request is written and contains sufficient information to identify the subject, and 4) the identifying information does not match more than 1 individual. NDCC 12-60-16.6.

If the bureau disseminates information to a non-criminal justice agency, the bureau must mail notice to the record subject, unless the request was accompanied by an authorization. NDCC 12-60-16.8.

Definitions:

Reportable Event – an interaction with a criminal justice agency for which a report is required to be filed. The term includes only those events in which the subject of the event is an adult or a juvenile adjudicated as an adult. NDDC 12-60-16.1.

Reportable Events – each criminal justice agency shall report to the bureau for each felony and reportable offense the following: fingerprints, charges, description of person arrested, decision not to refer the arrest for prosecution, all charges filed, all final dispositions, judgments of not guilt, judgments of guilt and the sentence, discharges, dismissals in the trial court, reverse or remand of a reported conviction, order to vacate or modify sentence, other information concerning the receipt, escape, death, release, pardon, conditional pardon of an individual who has been sentenced to the North Dakota state penitentiary or other correctional facility. NDDC 12-60-16.2.

Employment: A person may not be disqualified to practice, pursue, or engage in any occupation, trade, or profession for which a license, permit, or certificate is required from any state agency, board or commission solely because of a prior conviction. However, the applicant may be denied a license if the licensing board has determined that the applicant has not been sufficiently rehabilitated, or that the offense has a direct bearing upon a person's ability to serve the public in the specific occupation. NDCC 12.1-33-02.1.

Consumer Report: A consumer reporting agency may not provide or sell data or list that include any information that in whole or in part was submitted in conjunction with an insurance inquiry about a consumer's credit information or a request for a credit report or insurance score. NDCC 26.1-25.1-09.

Consumer Report, Definitions: NDCC 26.1-25.1-02

Consumer Reporting Agency – any person that for a monetary fee regularly engages in whole or in part in the practice of assembling or evaluating consumer credit information for the purposes of furnishing consumer reports to third parties.

Consumer Report: any written, oral or other communication of information by a consumer reporting agency bearing on a consumer's creditworthiness, credit standing, or credit capacity which is used or expected to be used for the purpose of serving as a factor to determine personal insurance premiums, eligibility for coverage, or tier placement.

Agency Guidelines for Pre-Employment Inquiries: North Dakota Department of Labor, Human Rights Division "Employment Applications and Interviews" is available online at www.state.nd.us/la bor/publications/docs/brochures/005.pdf

State Statutes and Codes: www.legis.nd.gov/information/statutes/cent-code.html

Legislative Bill Search: www.legis.nd.gov/assembly/59-2005/leginfo/bill-inquiry/index.html

North Dakota State Criminal Records Agency

Bureau of Criminal Investigation, Criminal Records Section, PO Box 1054, Bismarck, ND 58502-1054, (courier address: 4205 State St, Bismarck, ND 58501.) **Phone:** 701-328-5500; **Fax:** 701-328-5510   **Web:** www.ag.state.nd.us/BCI/CHR/CHR.html

Search Note: Records are available to the general public. Subject will be notified of the request if a signed release is not submitted. A request form and an authorization form are both downloadable from the web. After three years, only records with convictions are released. Include the following in your request-either the signed release from subject or the address of subject, name, DOB, current address, SSN. Fingerprint searches are available to public. 100% of the records are fingerprint-supported. Direct questions to bcinfo@state.nd.us.

What Is Released: Records are available from 1930 to present. Charges that are dismissed or sealed are not released as well as Jail or prison custody records that are more than three years old. 86% of all arrests in database have final dispositions recorded, including those arrests within last 5 years.

Access Methods: mail, in person.

North Dakota Sexual Offender Registry

Bureau of Criminal Investigation , SOR Unit, PO Box 1054, Bismarck, ND 58502-1054, (courier address: 4205 N State St, Bismarck, ND 58501.) **Phone:** 701-328-5500; **Fax:** 701-328-5510 **Web:** www.sexoffender.nd.gov/

Online Searching: All searching must be performed from the web page. Information on all offenders with a registration requirement (including moderate and low risk offenders) can be downloaded. Look for the Printable List of All Offenders at www.sexoffender.nd.gov/PublicListing.aspx.

North Dakota Incarceration Records Agency

Department of Corrections and Rehabilitation , Records Clerk, PO Box 5521, Bismarck, ND 58506, (courier address: 3100 E Railroad Ave, Bismarck, ND 58506.) **Phone:** 701-328-6122; **Fax:** 701-328-6640 **Web:** www.nd.gov/docr/

Employees of the Prisons Division may not disclose inmate information except as granted in North Dakota Century Code 12-47-36. Location, conviction and sentencing information, and release dates are provided.

North Dakota State Court System

Court Administrator: State Court Administrator, North Dakota Judiciary, 600 E Blvd, 1st Floor Judicial Wing, Dept. 180, Bismarck, ND, 58505-0530; 701-328-4216, Fax: 701-328-2092. www.ndcourts.com

Court Structure: The District Courts are general jurisdiction over criminal, civil, and juvenile matters. Municipal courts in North Dakota have jurisdiction of all violations of municipal ordinances, with some exceptions. At one time there were County Courts, but these courts merged with the District Courts statewide in 1995. These older County Court records are held by the 53 District Court Clerks in the seven judicial districts.

Find Felony Records: District Court

Misdemeanor Records: District Court

Online Access: Access district court criminal index on the state system at www.ndcourts.gov/publicsearch/contactsearch.aspx. This includes nine municipal courts as well. Each counties index only goes back to their month of computerization. Also, you may now search North Dakota Supreme Court dockets and opinions at www.ndcourts.com. Search by docket number, party name, or anything else that may appear in the text. Records are from 1982 forward. Email notification of new opinions is also available. A statewide computer system for internal use only is in operation for most North Dakota counties.

Searching Hints: For search request that are to go back to 1995 or further, it is recommended you state "include all County Court cases" in the request.

Ohio

Ohio Statutes & Related Employer Restrictions

General Rule: All public records shall be promptly prepared and made available for inspection to any person. OH ST §149.43(B)(1). Information and materials collected by the superintendent of Criminal Identification and Investigation, such as records of felony convictions, misdemeanor convictions that would be felonies upon a second conviction, photographs, and fingerprints, are not public records. OH ST §109.57(D).

Criminal Record History Information may be disseminated to employers for applicants who have contact with children, mentally retarded, medical patients, and disabled or elderly adults. OH ST §109.57(F)(2)(a).

Expunged Record: Records sealed upon a finding that the person was a first offender or an unruly child may be sealed and considered not to have occurred. OH ST §§2953.32(C)(2) and 2151.358(C).

Employment: The business of pre-employment background investigation means, and is limited to, furnishing for hire, in person or through a partner or employees, the conducting of limited background investigations, in person interviews, telephone interviews, or written inquires that pertain only to a client's prospective employee, and the employee's employment, and that are engaged in with the prior written consent of the prospective employee. OH ST §4749.01(H)(3)(c).

In application for employment, license, or other right or privilege, an applicant may only be questioned about convictions not sealed, and bail forfeitures not expunged or sealed, unless the question bears a direct and substantial relationship to the position sought. OH ST §2953.33(B).

State Revised Code: http://codes.ohio.gov/orc

Legislative Bill Search: www.legislature.state.oh.us/search.cfm

Ohio State Criminal Records Agency

Ohio Bureau of Investigation, Civilian Background Section, PO Box 365, London, OH 43140, (courier address: 1560 State Rte 56, London, OH 43140.) **Phones:** General Info- 740-845-2000; Civilian Background Cks- 740-845-2375; **Fax:** 740-845-2633

Web: www.ag.state.oh.us/business/fingerprint/index.asp

Search Note: Records are available to the general public. All out-of-state record requests must include a fingerprint card: name searches are not performed. In state requesters are access to use the web service, which also entails fingerprints. Include the following in your request- witnessed signed release from subject, fingerprints, name DOB, SSN. 100% of the records are fingerprint supported.

What Is Released: Records are available from 1921 on. Records from 1960's on are computerized and the agency is in the process of computerizing older records. Records without dispositions are not released. Escalating misdemeanors are released; these are any offense classified as a misdemeanor on the 1st offense and felony on subsequent offense. 65% of all arrests in database have final dispositions recorded, 85% for those arrests within last 5 years.

Access Methods: mail, online

Online Searching: Civilian Background Checks (WebCheck) is a web-based system for all in-state record requests. Results are NOT returned via the Internet. Agencies can send fingerprint images and other data via the Internet using a single digit fingerprint scanner and a driver's license magnetic strip reader. Hardware costs are involved.

Ohio Sexual Offender Registry

Ohio Bureau of Investigation , Sexual Offender Registry, PO Box 365, London, OH 43140, (courier address: 1560 State Rte 56 SW, London, OH 43140.) **Phone:** 866-406-4534; **Fax:** 740-845-2021 **Web:** www.esorn.ag.state.oh.us/Secured/p1.aspx

O.R.C. 2950.13 requires that the public eSORN database contain information on every person convicted as an adult and registered in the state registry of sex offenders and child-victim offenders. The database that contains information regarding all registered sex offenders in the State of Ohio is known as eSORN. The individual county sheriff's representatives are best situated to provide local sex offender and registration information.

Online Searching: Search online eSORN at www.esorn.ag.state.oh.us/Secured/p21 2.aspx. Users can search by offender name, zip code, county and/or school district. The site is linked to all 88 of Ohio's sheriff's offices.

Ohio Incarceration Records Agency

Ohio Department of Rehabilitation and Correction , Bureau of Records Management, 978 Freeway Drive, N., Columbus, OH 43229 **Phones:** 614-752-1076; Inmate Records- 614-752-1159 x3; **Fax:** 614-752-1086 **Web:** www.drc.state.oh.us

Online Searching: From the website, in the Select a Destination box, select Offender Search or see www.drc.state.oh.us/OffenderSearch/Search.aspx. You can search by name or inmate number. The Offender Search includes all offenders currently incarcerated or under some type of Department supervision (parole, post-release control, or transitional control).

Ohio State Court System

Court Administrator:	Administrative Director, Supreme Court of Ohio, 65 S Front St, Columbus, OH 43215; 614-387-9000. www.supremecourtofohio.gov
Court Structure:	The Court of Common Pleas is the general jurisdiction court and County Courts have limited jurisdiction.
Find Felony Records:	Court of Common Pleas
Misdemeanor Records:	County Court, Municipal Court, Mayor's Court
Online Access:	There is no statewide computer system, but a great number courts offer online access. Appellate and Supreme Court opinions may be researched from the Supreme Court website.
Searching Hints:	Over 80% of the Ohio courts offer a public access terminal to view a docket index.

Oklahoma

Oklahoma Statutes & Related Employer Restrictions

General Rule: All records of public body and officials shall be open to any person for inspection, copying and/or mechanical reproduction. 51 OSA §24A.5.

Law enforcement agencies shall make available for public inspection arrestee description, facts concerning the arrest, conviction information, disposition of all warrants, crime summary, radio logs, and jail registers. 51 OSA §24A.8(A).

Expunged Record: Employers shall not in any application or interview require an applicant to disclose any information contained in sealed records. An applicant may state that no such action ever occurred. 22 OSA §19(F).

Credit Report: If a consumer report is sought for employment purposes the requester or user must provide notice on a box for the consumer to check to receive a copy of the report sent to the requester at no charge. 24 OSA§148.   A consumer reporting agency may include information on tax liens when the information is obtained directly from the Oklahoma Tax Commission. 24 OSA §86.

State Statutes and Codes: www.lsb.state.ok.us

Legislative Bill Search: www.lsb.state.ok.us

Oklahoma State Criminal Records Agency

OK State Bureau of Investigation, Criminal History Reporting, 6600 N Harvey, Oklahoma City, OK 73116 **Phone:** 405-848-6724, 405-879-2690; **Fax:** 405-879-2503 **Web:** www.ok.gov/osbi/

Search Note: Records are available to the general public. The agency offer billing accounts for entities ordering more than 50 requests per month. Include the following in your request- Full name and DOB or approximate age, also aliases and reason for request. SSN, sex, and race are helpful and provide a better search, but not required. Fingerprints optional. A signed release is not required. 100% of the records are fingerprint-supported. A sex offender search will also be included with search but only if requested. Questions may be directed to sylvia@osbi.state.ok.us.

What Is Released: Records are available from 1925 on. Records are maintained indefinitely. Arrest records without dispositions are released if the party was fingerprinted. Computer searches include arrests without dispositions. Per a 2003 DOJ Study, 32% of all arrests in database have final dispositions recorded, 33% for those arrests within last 5 years. However, the agency is working on updating more records and the % numbers are increasing.

Access Methods: mail, fax, in person.

Oklahoma Sexual Offender Registry

Oklahoma Department of Corrections , Sex Offender Registry, 3400 Martin Luther King Ave, Oklahoma City, OK 73106 **Phone:** 405-425-2872; **Fax:** 405-425-7070 **Web:** http://docapp8.doc.state.ok.us/servlet/page?_pageid=422&_dad=portal30&_schema=P ORTAL30&id=1

Online Searching: Searching is available from the website. With a number of search options. A parole status search is available at http://gov.ok.gov/parole/parole_lookup.php. Database and bulk purchases can be requested from the IT department. Call for pricing and media.

Oklahoma Incarceration Records Agency

Oklahoma Department of Corrections , Offender Records, PO Box 11400, Oklahoma City, OK 73136, (courier address: 3400 Martin Luther King Avenue, Oklahoma City, OK 73136.) **Phone:** 405-425-2624; **Fax:** 405-425-2608 **Web:** www.doc.state.ok.us

Online Searching: At the main website, click on Offender Information or visit www.doc.state.ok.us/offenders/offenders.htm. The online system is not available between 3:15 AM to 3:20 AM Monday through Friday, and 3:15 AM to 7:00 AM Saturdays for system maintenance.

Oklahoma State Court System

Court Administrator: Administrative Director of Courts, 1915 N Stiles #305, Oklahoma City, OK, 73105; 405-521-2450. www.oscn.net

Court Structure: There are 80 District Courts in 26 judicial districts. Cities with populations in excess of 200,000 (Oklahoma City and Tulsa) have municipal criminal courts of record. Cities with less than 200,000 do not have such courts.

Find Felony Records: District Court

Misdemeanor Records: District Court, Municipal Court of Record

Online Access: Free Internet access to criminal docket information is available for District Courts in 13 counties and all Appellate courts at www.oscn.net. Also, search the Oklahoma Supreme Court Network from the website. Case information is available in bulk form for downloading to computer; for info, call Admin. Director of Courts, 405-521-2450.

Also, the Oklahoma District Court Records free website at www.odcr.com offers searching for over 60 District Courts. More counties are being added as they are readied. The hope is to eventually feature all Oklahoma District Courts. Please note few counties in this system do not go back seven years.

Searching Hints: About 75% of the courts charge $5.00 for a name search. 80% offer a public access terminal.

Oregon

Oregon Statutes & Related Employer Restrictions

General Rule: The Department of State Police shall deliver to the person or agency making the request of criminal offender information the following information, regarding any convictions, and any arrest less than one year old on which the records show no acquittal or dismissal: 1) date of arrest, 2) offenses for which arrest was made, 3) arresting agency, 4) court of origin, and 5) disposition including sentence imposed, date of parole and parole revocations. ORS §181.560(1)(b).

If the department does not have any information on the individual or the information consists only of non-conviction data, the department shall respond that the individual has no criminal record and shall not release any further information. ORS §181.560(2).

Employment: An entity may request from an authorized agency a criminal record check for the purposes of evaluating the fitness of a subject individual as an employee, contractor, or volunteer. ORS §181.533(2).

The employer must first advise the employee or prospective employee that such information might be sought, and shall state upon making the request that the individual has been so advised and the manner in which so advised. ORS §181.555(2)(b).

Except for applicants seeking employment as a teacher or a license with the Health Licensing Office, no licensing board or agency shall deny, suspend, or revoke an occupational or professional license solely for the reason that the applicant or licensee has been convicted of a crime. It may consider the relationship of the facts that support the conviction and all intervening circumstance to the specific occupational or professional standards in determining the fitness of the person to receive or hold the license or certificate. ORS §670.280.

It is an unlawful employment practice for an employer, state agency, or licensing board to refuse to employ or discharge from employment an individual because of a juvenile record that has been expunged. ORS §§659A.030(1)(a) and 670.290.

Agency Guidelines for Pre-Employment Inquiries: Oregon Bureau of Labor and Industries, Civil Rights Division, Fact Sheets, "Pre-Employment Inquiries" is available online at www.oregon.gov/bdi/ta/ifaq_tdpreemp.shtrel

State Statutes and Codes: www.leg.state.or.us/ors/home.htm

Legislative Bill Search: www.leg.state.or.us/bills_laws/

Oregon State Criminal Records Agency

Oregon State Police, Unit 11, Identification Services Section, PO Box 4395, Portland, OR 97208-4395, (courier address: 3772 Portland Rd NE, Bldg C, Salem, OR 97301.) **Phone:** 503-378-3070; **Fax:** 503-378-2121 **Web:** http://egov.oregon.gov/OSP/ID/

Search Notes: Three types of searches exist: open records search, own record search, and statutorily-required search. The latter can include an FBI fingerprint check for an additional $24.00 fee. Include the following in your request-(for open records) name, date of birth, last known address. Submitting the SSN is helpful, but not required. Fingerprints are required only when subject submits the request. For an open record request, if record exists, person of record will be notified of the request and the record will not be released for 14 additional days.

What Is Released: Records are available from 1941 on and are computerized. Open record info includes all records with convictions and also all arrests within the past year without disposition. Statutorily-required record searches and own record searches include all records. Approximately 50% of all arrests in database have final dispositions recorded.

Access Methods: mail, fax, online.

Online Searching: A web based site is available for requesting and receiving criminal records. Website is ONLY for high-volume requesters who must be pre-approved. Results are posted as "No Record" or "In Process" ("In Process" means a record will be mailed in 14 days). Use the "open records" link to get into the proper site. Fee is $10.00 per record. Call 503-373-1808 x230 to receive the application, or visit the website.

Oregon Sexual Offender Registry

Oregon State Police , SOR Unit, 255 Capitol St NE, 4th Fl, Salem, OR 97310 **Phone:** 503-378-3720; **Fax:** 503-363-5475 **Web:** http://egov.oregon.gov/OSP/SOR/index.shtml

Note: The law allows the release of the names, DOB, photo, physical description, address or city of residence, supervising agency and phone number. Direct questions to Sexoffender.Questions@state.or.us.

Online Searching: Visit http://sexoffenders.oregon.gov/ for online searching of sex offenders who have been designated as Predatory. A mapping function is also offered. Lists by city or zip can usually be requested for no fee, a statewide list be purchased for $85.00.

Oregon Incarceration Records Agency

Oregon Department of Corrections , Offender Information & Sentence Computation, PO Box 5670, Wilsonville, OR 97070-5670, (courier address: 24499 SW Grahams Ferry Rd, Bldg Z, Wilsonville, OR 97070.) **Phones:** 503-570-6900; Search Requests- 503-570-6919; **Fax:** 503-570-6902 **Web:** www.doc.state.or.us

Search Notes: No online offender searching is available from this agency; there is a "Corrections Most Wanted" list in the pull down menu box. The agency web page mentions https://www.vinelink.com/vinelink/siteInfoAction.do?siteId=38000, a private compnay site that includes state, DOC, and most county jails. Also, use imate.info@doc.state.or.us to request by email. Bulk sale of information is available. Contact ISSD.

Oregon State Court System

Court Administrator: Court Administrator, Supreme Court Building, 1163 State St, Salem, OR, 97301-2563; 503-986-5500. www.ojd.state.or.us

Court Structure: Effective January 15, 1998, the District and Circuit Courts were combined into "Circuit Courts." At the same time, three new judicial districts were created by splitting existing ones. There are over 100 Municipal Courts and 35 Justice Courts who oversee minor misdemeanor, traffic, ordinance cases.

Find Felony Records: Circuit Court

Misdemeanor Records: Circuit Court, Justice Court, Municipal Court

Online Access: Online computer access is available through the Oregon Judicial Information Network (OJIN) which includes cases filed in the Oregon state courts. Searching is done by county, there is no statewide search available. There is a one-time setup fee of $295.00 plus usage fees of $10-13.00 per hour, plus $10 per month per user. The database contains criminal, civil, small claims, tax, domestic, usually probate when not at the county court, and some but not all juvenile records. However, it does not contain any records from municipal or county courts. For further information visit www.ojd.state.or.us/ojin, or call 800-858-9658 or 503-986-5588. Appellate opinions at www.publications.ojd.state.or.us.

Searching Hints: Many Oregon courts indicated that in person searches would markedly improve request turnaround time as court offices are understaffed or spread very thin. Most Circuit Courts that have records on computer do have a public access terminal that will speed up in-person or retriever searches. Most records offices close from Noon to 1PM Oregon time.

Pennsylvania

Pennsylvania Statutes & Related Employer Restrictions

General Rule: Criminal History record information shall be disseminated by a state or local police department to any individual or noncriminal justice agency upon request. All notations of arrest, indictments, or other information relating to the initiation of criminal proceedings where 2 years have elapsed from the date of arrest, no conviction occurred, and no proceedings are pending seeking a conviction shall be extracted from the record when disseminated to an individual or noncriminal justice agency. 18 PACSA §9121.

Expunged Record: When no disposition has been received within 18 months of arrest and no action is pending or in certain juvenile delinquency cases, the court may order records expunged. 18 PACSA §§9123 and 9122.

An expunged record is removed so that there is no trace or indication that such information existed, except for maintenance of the record for certain judicial requirements. 18 PACSA §9102.

Employment: An employer may consider felony and misdemeanor convictions only to the extent that they relate to the applicant's suitability for employment in the position for which he or she has applied and an employer is required to notify the applicant in writing if the decision was based in whole or in part on the criminal history. 18 PACSA §9125.

A licensing board may consider conviction of the applicant, but the convictions shall not preclude the issuance, certificate, registration, or permit. Records or arrest without conviction, convictions expunged, convictions of a summary offense, conviction which received a pardon, and convictions which do not relate to the applicant's suitability for the license sought shall not be used in consideration of an application for a license by the licensing board. However, a licensing board may refuse to grant or renew, or may suspend or revoke a license because of a felony conviction or a misdemeanor that relates to the trade, occupation or profession for which the license is sought. 18 PACSA §9124.

Agency Guidelines for Pre-Employment Inquiries: Pennsylvania Human Relations Commission, Publications, "Pre-Employment Inquiries" is available online at www.phrc.state.pa.us/PA Exec/PH RC/publications/literature/web preempqs.htm

State Statutes and Codes: http://members.aol.com/StatutesPA/Index.html

Legislative Bill Search: www.legis.state.pa.us/cfdocs/legis/home/session.cfm

Pennsylvania State Criminal Records Agency

State Police, Central Repository -164, 1800 Elmerton Ave, Harrisburg, PA 17110-9758
Phones: 717-783-5494, 717-783-9973; **Fax:** 717-772-3681
Web: www.psp.state.pa.us/psp/site/default.asp

Search Notes: Records are available to the general public. Must make request on Request Form SP4-164 or the request will be returned. The form can be found on web page (help menu in PATCH section) or call for form. Include the following in your request-full name, date of birth, Social Security Number, sex, race, any aliases, all on proper form. A release is not required. The record database is 100% fingerprint-supported. Statutorily-required fingerprint searches include an FBI fingerprint search.

What Is Released: Records are available from the 1920s. Records include all convictions; all charges that are less then three years from the date of arrest and the Central Repository has not received a disposition; and all charges for which a warrant of arrest has been issued and the Central Repository has been notified of such warrant. Records are available for all convictions. Per a U.S. Dept of Justice Study, 60% of all arrests in database have final dispositions recorded, 31% for those arrests within last 5 years.

Access Methods: mail, online.

Online Searching: Record checks are available for approved agencies through the Internet on the Pennsylvania Access to Criminal History (PATCH). Ongoing requesters may become registered users. This is a commercial system, the same $10.00 fee per name applies. PATCH accepts Visa, Discover, MasterCard, AmEx cards. Go to https://epatch.state.pa.us/Home.jsp or call 717-705-1768 to register. Up to 10 records may be requested at one session.

Pennsylvania Sexual Offender Registry

State Police Bureau of Records and Ident. , Megan's Law Unit, 1800 Elmerton Ave, Harrisburg, PA 17110-9758 **Phone:** 717-783-4363, 866-771-7130; **Fax:** 717-705-8839 **Web:** www.pameganslaw.state.pa.us

Online Searching: Limited information on all registered sex offenders can be viewed online from the webpage. Complete address information is listed for all active offenders. Upon opening the offender's record, you are provided tabs to click on access details such as alias, address, offense, vehicle, and physical characteristics information. This office provides no searches except via the Internet or email.

Pennsylvania Incarceration Records Agency

Pennsylvania Department of Corrections , Bureau of Inmate Services, PO Box 598, Camp Hill, PA 17001-0598 **Phones:** Records- 717-730-2721; Main- 717-975-4859; **Fax:** 717-731-7159 **Web:** www.cor.state.pa.us

Online Searching: At the website, click on Inmate Locator for information about each inmate currently under the jurisdiction of the Department of Corrections, or visit www.cor.state.pa.us/inmatelocatorweb/. The site indicates where an inmate is housed, race, date of birth, marital status and other items. The Inmate Locator does not contain information on inmates not currently residing in a state correctional institution.

Pennsylvania State Court System

Court Administrator:	Administrative Office of Pennsylvania Courts, PO Box 229, Mechanicsburg, PA, 17055; 717-795-2097. www.courts.state.pa.us
Court Structure:	The Courts of Common Pleas are the general trial courts, with jurisdiction over both civil and criminal matters and appellate jurisdiction over matters disposed of by the special courts.
	It is not necessary to check with each District Court, but rather to check with the Prothonotary for the county.
Find Felony Records:	Court of Common Pleas, Philadelphia Municipal Court
Misdemeanor Records:	Court of Common Pleas, Philadelphia Municipal Court, Pittsburgh City Magistrate Court, Magisterial District Court (Justice Court)

Online Access: The web page at http://ujsportal.pacourts.us/ offers access to a variety of the Judiciary's Electronic Services (E-Services) such as Web Docket Sheets, DA Link, Superior Court's Web Docketing Statements, etc. Web Docket provides public access to view and print case docket sheets from the criminal cases of the Courts of Common Pleas and from the Appellate Courts. Search by docket number, name or organization.

The Infocon County Access System provides a commercial direct dial-up access to court record information for at least 25 counties. There is a $25.00 base set-up fee plus a minimum $25.00 per month based on a $1.10 fee per minute. For Information, call Infocon at 814-472-6066 or visit www.infoconcountyaccess.com.

Searching Hints: Many courts will not conduct searches due to a lack of personnel or, if they do search, turnaround time may be excessively lengthy. Many courts have public access terminals for in-person searches.

Rhode Island

Rhode Island Statutes & Related Employer Restrictions

General Rule: All records maintained or kept on file by any public body shall be public records and every person or entity shall have the right to inspect and/or copy those records. RI ST §38-2-3(a).

Expunged Record: In any application for employment, a person whose conviction of a crime has been expunged may state that he or she has never been convicted of the crime, unless the applicant is applying for a teaching certificate, coaching certificate, admission to the bar, or the operator or employee of an early childhood education facility. RI ST §12-1.3-4(b).

All police records relating to the arrest, detention, apprehension, and disposition of any juvenile shall be withheld from public inspection. RI ST §14-1-64(a).

Employment: It is unlawful for any employer to include on any application a question inquiring if the applicant has ever been arrested or charged with a crime, unless the applicant seeks employment with a law enforcement agency. An employer may inquire whether an applicant has ever been convicted of a crime. RI ST §28-5-7(7).

State Statutes and Codes: www.rilin.state.ri.us/Statutes/

Legislative Bill Search: http://dirac.rilin.state.ri.us/BillStatus/webclass1.asp

Rhode Island State Criminal Records Agency

Department of Attorney General, Bureau of Criminal Identification, 150 S Main Street, Providence, RI 02903 **Phone:** 401-274-4400 x2232; **Fax:** 401-222-1331 **Web:** www.riag.ri.gov

Search Note: Criminal records are only released to law enforcement agencies, the subject, or to those with a signed notarized authorization from the subject. Include the following in your request-signed notarized release from subject, DOB, picture ID and DOB of the requester. Fingerprints and SSN are optional. They may call the Notary on the authorization for verification. 100% of records are fingerprint-supported.

What Is Released: Records are available from 1900's. All arrests and convictions are reported. 86% of all arrests in database have final dispositions recorded.

Access Methods: mail, in person. This agency does not offer online access, but the state court system does offer an information site that should not be substituted as an official search. See that profile for details.

Rhode Island Sexual Offender Registry

Sex Offender Community Notification Unit , Varley Building, 40 Howard Avenue, Cranston, RI 02920 **Phone:** 401-462-0905; **Fax:** 401-462-0916 **Web:** www.paroleboard.ri.gov/

Online Searching: Two name lists are presented at the web page for Level 2 and Level 3 offenders respectively. Email questions to parolebd@doc.ri.gov.

Rhode Island Incarceration Records Agency

Rhode Island Department of Corrections , Records, PO Box 8249, Cranston, RI 02920, (courier address: 40 Howard Avenue, Cranston, RI 02920.) **Phone:** 401-462-3900; **Fax:** 401-462-2253 www.doc.ri.gov/index.php

Online Searching: A free DOC search is available at www.doc.ri.gov/inmate_search/index.php.

Rhode Island State Court System

Court Administrator: Court Administrator, Supreme Court, 250 Benefit St, Providence, RI, 02903; 401-222-3266,. www.courts.state.ri.us

Court Structure: Rhode Island has five counties, but only four Superior/District Court Locations (2nd-Newport, 3rd-Kent, 4th-Washignton, and 6th-Prividence/ Bristol Districts). Bristol and Providence counties are completely merged at the Providence location.

Find Felony Records: Superior Court

Misdemeanor Records: District Court

Online Access: The Rhode Island Judiciary offers free access to an index of county criminal cases statewide at http://courtconnect.courts.state.ri.us. A word of caution, this website is provided as an informational service only and should not be relied upon as an official record of the court. Supreme Court and Appellate opinions available at the home page.

Searching Hints: Most records available are from the mid 1980's to the present.

South Carolina

South Carolina Statutes & Related Employer Restrictions

General Rule: Any person has a right to inspect or copy any public record of a public body. SC ST ANN §30-4-30(a).

Expunged Record: Any person who has a criminal offense discharged, dismissed, or is found guilty can have all records of the arrest destroyed and no evidence of such record shall be retained by any municipal, county, or state law enforcement agency. SC ST ANN §17-1-40.

Employment: A person may not be refused an authorization to practice, pursue, or engage in a regulated profession solely because of a prior criminal conviction unless it relates directly to the profession or occupation. A board may refuse an applicant if based on all the information available, including the applicant's record of prior conviction, it finds the applicant unfit or unsuited to engage in the profession. SC ST ANN §40-1-140.

State Statutes and Codes: www.scstatehouse.net/html-pages/research.html

Legislative Bill Search: www.scstatehouse.net/html-pages/legpage.html

South Carolina State Criminal Records Agency

South Carolina Law Enforcement Division (SLED), Criminal Records Section, PO Box 21398, Columbia, SC 29221, (courier address: 4400 Broad River Rd, Columbia, SC 29210.) **Phone:** 803-896-7043; **Fax:** 803-896-7022 **Web:** www.sled.sc.gov/

Criminal records are open without restrictions. All records are released, including those without dispositions. Include the following in your request-full name, any aliases, sex, race, and DOB. The SSN is helpful. 100% of the records are fingerprint supported. However, this agency will not do fingerprint searches without state or federal statute.

What Is Released: Records are available from the 1960s. The following data is not released: juvenile. After receiving, it takes 1 to 12 days before new records are available for inquiry.

70% of all arrests in database have final dispositions recorded, 85% for those arrests within last 5 years.

Access Methods: mail, in person, online.

Online Searching: SLED offers commercial access to criminal record history from 1960 forward on the website. Fees are $25.00 per screening or $8.00 if for a charitable organization. Credit card ordering accepted. See website or call 803-896-7219 for details.

South Carolina Sexual Offender Registry

Sex Offender Registry , c/o SLED, PO Box 21398, Columbia, SC 29221, (courier address: 4400 Broad River Rd, Columbia, SC 29210.) **Phone:** 803-896-7043; **Fax:** 803-896-2311 **Web:** http://services.sled.sc.gov/sor/

Online Searching: Access is available from the website. Click on Sexual Offender Registry. Search by name or ZIP Code, county or city. Reports may also be obtained by school name (under the Report Generator).

South Carolina Incarceration Records Agency

Department of Corrections , Inmate Records Branch, 4444 Broad River Rd, Columbia, SC 29221-1787 **Phones:** 803-896-8531; Inmate Information Line- 877-846-3472; **Fax:** 803-896-1217 **Web:** www.doc.sc.gov

Online Searching: The Inmate Search on the Internet is found at https://sword.doc.state.sc.us/incarceratedInmateSearch/index.jsp or click on Inmate search at the main website.

South Carolina State Court System

Court Administrator: Court Administration, 1015 Sumter St, 2nd Fl, Columbia, SC, 29201; 803-734-1800. www.sccourts.org

Court Structure: The 46 SC counties are divided among sixteen judicial circuits. The circuit courts are in operation at the county level and consist of a court of general sessions (criminal) and court of common pleas (civil). The over 300 Magistrate and Municipal Courts (often referred to as "Summary Courts") only handle misdemeanor cases involving a $500.00 fine and/or 30 days or less jail time.

Find Felony Records: Circuit Court

Misdemeanor Records: Circuit Court, Magistrate Court, Municipal Court

Online Access: Appellate and Supreme Court opinions available at www.sccourts.org. Also, some, not all, Circuit Court and Summary Courts records are available at www.sccourts.org/caseSearch/; counties on the state system are Anderson, Beaufort, Charleston, Cherokee, Clarendon, Dorchester, Edgefield, Florence, Georgetown, Greenville, Horry, Jasper, Lexington,

Pickens, Richland, Spartanburg, Sumter, York, with more counties to be added or hotlinked. Two counties on the system also offer access to dockets – Beaufort, Jasper. Charleston is hot-linked but has its own online court records and dockets service, including judgments, traffic.

Searching Hints: If requesting a record in writing, it is recommended that the words "request that General Session, Common Pleas, and Family Court records be searched" be included in the request.

Most South Carolina courts will not conduct searches. If a name and case number are provided, many will pull and copy the record.

South Dakota

South Dakota Statutes & Related Employer Restrictions

General Rule: The officer required to keep public records shall keep them available and open to public inspection by any person. SDCL §1-27-1. Confidential criminal justice information is not a public record. SDCL §23-5-11.

Any person may examine criminal history information filed with the Attorney General that refers to that person. The person may also authorize the Attorney General to release his criminal history information to other individuals or organizations. SDCL §23-5-12.

Definitions: SDCL §23-5-10

Criminal History information – includes arrest information, conviction information, disposition information, and correction information.

Expunged Record: Upon granting a pardon, the governor shall order all records relating to the criminal offense sealed. No person who has had records sealed will be guilty of perjury or giving a false statement by such person's failure to recite or acknowledge such arrest, indictment, or trial in response to any inquiry made for any purpose. SDCL §24-14-11.

Agency Guidelines for Pre-Employment Inquiries: South Dakota Division of Human Rights "Pre-employment Inquiry Guide" is available online at www.state.sd.us/dol/Boards/hr/preemplo.htm

State Statutes and Codes: http://legis.state.sd.us/statutes/index.aspx

Legislative Bill Search: http://legis.state.sd.us/sessions/2008/index.aspx

South Dakota State Criminal Records Agency

Division of Criminal Investigation, Identification Section, 1302 E Highway 14, Ste 5, Pierre, SD 57501-8505 **Phone:** 605-773-3331; **Fax:** 605-773-2235 **Web:** http://dci.sd.gov

Search Note: Records are available to the general public. Include the following in your request-date of birth, full name, set of fingerprints, signed release form. The form requires identifying information: color of hair and eyes, height, weight, date of birth, SSN.

What Is Released: All open records without dispositions are released. Records are available for 10 years for misdemeanors from sentence date and lifetime for felonies. The following data is not released: juvenile records, minor traffic violations or out-of-state or federal charges. 98% of all arrests in database have final dispositions recorded.

Access Methods: mail.

South Dakota Sexual Offender Registry

Division of Criminal Investigation , Identification Section - SOR Unit, 1302 E Highway 14, #5, Pierre, SD 57501 **Phone:** 605-773-3331; **Fax:** 605-773-4629 **Web:** http://sor.sd.gov/disclaimer.asp?page=search&nav=2

Online Searching: Searching is available from the web. Email questions to sdsor@state.sd.us.

South Dakota Incarceration Records Agency

SD Department of Corrections , Central Records Office, PO Box 5911, Pierre, SD 57117 **Phone:** 605-367-5140; **Fax:** 605-367-5584 **Web:** www.state.sd.us/corrections/corrections.html

South Dakota State Court System

Court Administrator: State Court Administrator, State Capitol Building, 500 E Capitol Av, Pierre, SD, 57501; 605-773-3474. www.sdjudicial.com

Court Structure: The state re-aligned their circuits from 8 to 7 effective June, 2000. The circuit courts are the general trial courts of the Unified Judicial System. Circuit courts are the only court where a criminal felony case can be tried and determined. Magistrate Courts assist the circuit courts in processing minor criminal cases and less serious civil actions. There are 66 counties, but 64 courts. Cases for Buffalo County are handled at the Brule County Circuit Court. Cases for Shannon County are handled by the Fall River County Circuit Court.

Find Felony Records: Circuit Court

Misdemeanor Records: Circuit Court, Magistrate Court

Online Access:	The Supreme Court calendar, opinions, rules and archived oral arguments may be searched from the website.
	South Dakota has a statewide criminal record search database administrated by this office. Requesters may wish to set up a commercial account by faxing a written request to Jill Gusso, Unified Court System at 605-773-8437 or email jill.gusso@ujs.state.sd.us. Accounts are billed monthly. The search fee is $15.00 per name search. State-authorized commercial accounts may order and receive records by fax, there is an additional minimum $5.00 fee unless a non-toll free line is used.
Searching Hints:	Most South Dakota courts do not allow the public to perform searches, but rather require the court clerk to do them for a fee. A special Record Search Request Form must be used and can be found at www.sdjudicial.com/downloads/prcdr/rsrf.pdf. Clerks are not required to respond to telephone or fax requests, but many courts will return records via fax to ongoing commercial accounts.
	The state asks that all mail requests be directed to any one of three processing centers; the Miner County Clerk of Court, PO Box 265, Howard SD 57349 or to Aurora County Clerk of Court, PO Box 366, Plankinton, SD 57368-0366.

Tennessee

Tennessee Statutes & Related Employer Restrictions

General Rule: All state, county, and municipal records shall be open for personal inspection by any citizen of Tennessee. TCA §10-7-503(a). The Tennessee Bureau of Investigation shall process requests for criminal background checks from any authorized person, organization or entity permitted by law to seek criminal history background checks on certain persons. TCA §38-6-109(a).

The following organizations and employers may request a criminal history background check:

- A municipality hiring for public transportation. TCA §6-54-128(b)(1).

- Applicant for license to operate an adult-oriented establishment. TCA §7-51-1122(a).

- Applicant for a permit as an entertainer at an adult oriented establishment. TCA §7-51-1122(a).

- Person seeking to obtain a public contract. TCA § 12-4-606.

- Applicant for school bus driver position.   TCA §49-6-2117

- Applicants for employment or to volunteer with adult day care centers.   TCA §71-2-403(a)(1).

- Person seeking employment as a teacher or for any other position requiring proximity to schoolchildren.   TCA §49-5-406.

Expunged Records: Expunged records are confidential and not public.   TCA §38-6-118(d).

State Statutes and Codes: www.tennessee.gov/sos/bluebook/index.htm

Legislative Bill Search: www.legislature.state.tn.us

Tennessee State Criminal Records Agency

Tennessee Bureau of Investigation, TN Open Records Information Srvs, 901 R S Gass Blvd, Nashville, TN 37216 **Phone:** 615-744-4057; **Fax:** 615-744-4289   **Web:** www.tbi.state.tn.us

Search Note: Records are available to the general public.   Include the following in your request-name, DOB, AKA's. Sex, race and current address are helpful.   The search system is called TORIS (Tennessee Open Records Information Service). A request form can be downloaded from the webpage. The agency suggests that ongoing requester be registered with an account.

What Is Released: Records are available approx. 80 years on paper. All records are released to those entitled, including those without dispositions. Juvenile records are not released. Per a recent U.S. DOJ Study, 23% of all arrests in database have final dispositions recorded, 30% for those arrests within last 5 years.

Access Methods: mail, fax, in person, online.

Online Searching: Records may be requested online via email from the website, but this is not an interactive service. Records must still me manually searched and will take several days. Also, the agency maintains a website at www.ticic.state.tn.us for searching of sexual offenders, missing children, and people placed on parole who reside in TN.

Tennessee Sexual Offender Registry

Tennessee Bureau of Investigation , Sexual Offender Registry, 901 R S Gass Blvd., Nashville, TN 37216 **Phone:** SOR Hotline- 888-837-4170; **Fax:** 615-744-4655 **Web:** www.ticic.state.tn.us

Online Searching: Search sexual offenders at www.ticic.state.tn.us/sorinternet/sosearch.aspx by last name, city, county or ZIP Code. One may also search for missing children, and people placed on parole who reside in Tennessee. A map search is found at http://tnmap.state.tn.us/sor/map.aspx.

Tennessee Incarceration Records Agency

Tennessee Department of Corrections , Rachel Jackson Building, Ground Fl, 320 6th Avenue, N., Nashville, TN 37243-0465 **Phone:** 615-741-1000; **Fax:** 615-532-1497 **Web:** www.state.tn.us/correction/

Online Searching: Extensive search capabilities are offered from the website at https://www.tennesseeanytime.org/foil/foil_index.jsp. A CD-Rom is available with only public information from current offender database; nominal fee; contact the Planning & Research Division.

Tennessee State Court System

Court Administrator: Administrative Office of the Courts, 511 Union St, Nashville City Center, #600, Nashville, TN, 37219; 615-741-2687. www.tncourts.gov

Court Structure: Criminal cases are handled by the Circuit Courts and General Sessions Courts. Generally, misdemeanor cases are heard by General Sessions, but in Circuit Court if connected to a felony. Criminal cases are tried in Circuit Court except in districts with separate Criminal Courts established by the General Assembly. Criminal Courts relieve Circuit Courts in areas where they are justified by heavy caseloads. Criminal Courts exist in 13 of the State's 31 judicial districts. Combining of Circuit Court and General Sessions Courts varies by county.

Find Felony Records: Circuit Court

Misdemeanor Records: Circuit Court, General Sessions Court, Criminal Court, Municipal Court

Online Access: Appellate Court opinions cna be found free online at www.tsc.state.tn.us/geninfo/Courts/AppellateCourts.htm.
Several counties offer online access to court records, but there is no statewide access system.

Searching Hints: Over two-thirds of the general jurisdiction courts offer public access terminals to view docket indices.

Texas

Texas Statutes & Related Employer Restrictions

General Rule: Criminal history record information maintained by the department is confidential information for the use of the department, and except as provided for, may not be disseminated by the department. TX GOVT §411.083(a).

Any person is entitled to obtain from the Department of Public Safety criminal history record information maintained by the department that relates to the conviction of or grant of deferred adjudication to a person for any criminal offense, including arrest information that relates to the conviction or grant of deferred adjudication. TX GOVT §411.135(a)(2).

A person who obtains information from the department may use the information for any purpose, or release the information to any other person. TX GOVT §411.135(c).

Expunged Records: The release, dissemination, or use of expunged records and files for any purpose, other than criminal justice purposes, is prohibited when the order to expunge records is final. TX CRIM PRO §55.03(1).

The person arrested may deny the occurrence of the arrest and the existence of the expungement order. TX CRIM PRO §55.03(2).

Employment: An agency that licenses or regulates members of a particular trade, occupation, business, vocation, or profession is entitled to obtain from the Department of Public Safety criminal history record information that relates to a person who is an applicant for a license or a holder of a license. TX GOVT §411.122(a).

A licensing authority may suspend, revoke, or disqualify a person from receiving a license on the grounds that the person has been convicted of a felony or misdemeanor that directly relates to the duties and responsibilities of the licensed occupation. TX OCCS Code § 53.021(a).

Consumer Report: A consumer reporting agency may furnish a consumer report to a person the agency has reason to believe intends to use the information for employment purposes. TX BUS & COM §20.02(a)(3)(B).

A consumer reporting agency may not furnish a report that contains 1) bankruptcies that antedate the report by more than 10 years or 2) a suit or judgment, a tax lien, a record of arrest, indictment or conviction of a crime, or another item or event that antedates the report by more than 7 years. TX BUS & COM §20.05(a). A consumer reporting agency is not restricted from reporting information if it is provided in connection with the employment of a consumer with a salary of $75,000 or more. TX BUS & COM §20.05(b)(3). However, this law was enacted in 2003 (Texas S.B. 473). This section is pre-empted by 15 USC §1681t(b)(1)(E), this negating the restriction on reporting convictions.

State Statutes and Codes: www.legis.state.tx.us/

Legislative Bill Search and Monitoring: www.legis.state.tx.us/

Texas State Criminal Records Agency

DPS - Access & Dissemination Bureau, Crime Records Service, PO Box 15999, Austin, TX 78761-5999 **Phone:** 512-424-2474; **Fax:** 512-424-5011

Web: https://records.txdps.state.tx.us/dps_web/Portal/index.aspx

Search Note: Records are available to the general public. To obtain ALL arrest information (conviction and non-conviction), must have a signed release and full set of fingerprints from the person of record. Since 1/1/93 records should include complete info regarding charge, disposition, date of conviction, and county. Data prior to this date may not be complete. Include the following in your request-fingerprint card (with full name, DOB, sex, race, SSN), reason for request, signed release, full name and address of requester. To obtain conviction and deferred adjudication data only, submit full name, sex, race, and DOB. The SSN is helpful, but not required. No letter of authorization is needed for the conviction only report.

What Is Released: Records are available from 1930 to present. Fingerprint searches show complete record; name search is conviction only and deferred adjudications. Juvenile recordsnot released. 66% of all arrests in database have final dispositions recorded.

Access Methods: mail, in person, online.

Online Searching: The Texas Department of Public Safety offers two websites for accessing criminal records. One is for the public. The other is for eligible entities (authorized by law). Public requesters may use a credit card and establish an account to pre-purchase credits. The fee established by the Department (Sec. 411.135(b)) is $3.15 per request plus a $.57 handling fee. These checks are instantaneous and provide convictions and deferred adjudications only.

Texas Sexual Offender Registry

Dept of Public Safety , Sex Offender Registration, PO Box 4143, Austin, TX 78765-4143
Phone: 512-424-2800; **Fax:** 512-424-5666

Web: https://records.txdps.state.tx.us/DPS_WEB/Sor/index.aspx

Online Searching: Sex offender data is available at the web page. Search by name or city/ZIP or by map.

Texas Incarceration Records Agency

Texas Department of Criminal Justice , Bureau of Classification and Records, PO Box 99, Huntsville, TX 77342, (courier address: 861 IH 45 North, Huntsville, TX 77320.)
Phones: Offender Locator- 936-295-6371; In State Parole Status line- 800-535-0283; **Fax:** 936-437-6227 **Web:** www.tdcj.state.tx.us

Online Searching: Name searching is available from this agency at http://168.51.178.33/webapp/TDCJ/index2.htm. You may also send an email search request to classify@tdcj.state.tx.us.

Texas State Court System

Court Administrator: Office of Court Administration, PO Box 12066, Austin, TX, 78711; 512-463-1625. www.courts.state.tx.us

Court Structure: The legal court structure for Texas is explained extensively in the "Texas Judicial Annual Report." Generally, Texas District Courts have general civil jurisdiction and exclusive felony jurisdiction; there can be several districts in one courthouse County Courts handle misdemeanors and general civil cases. In 69 counties, District Court and County Court are combined. The County Clerk is responsible for records in every county.

Find Felony Records: District Court

Misdemeanor Records: County Court, Justice of the Peace Court, Municipal Court

Online Access: A number of local county courts offer online access to their records but there is no statewide system of local level court records. Case records of the Supreme Court can be searched at www.supreme.courts.state.tx.us. Appellate Court case information is searchable free at the website of each Appellate Court, reached online from www.courts.state.tx.us/courts/coa.asp. Court of Criminal Appeals opinions are found at www.cca.courts.state.tx.us.

Searching Hints: Often, a record search is automatically combined for two courts, for example a District Court with a County Court, or both County Courts. Less than half the courts have public access terminals to view docket indices.

Utah

Utah Statutes & Related Employer Restrictions

General Rule: Dissemination of information from a criminal history record or warrant of arrest information from the Criminal Investigation and Technical Services Division is limited to a qualifying entity for employment background checks for their own employees and persons who have applied for employment with the qualifying entity. UT ST §53-10-108(1)(g).

A qualifying entity is a business, organization, or governmental entity that employs people who deal with national security interest, care, custody, or control of children, fiduciary trust over money, or health care to children or vulnerable adults. UT ST §53-10-102(19).

Before requesting information, a qualifying entity must obtain a signed waiver from the person whose information is requested. UT ST §53-10-108(3)(a).

If a person has no prior criminal conviction record, criminal history information contained in the file may not include arrest or disposition data concerning an individual who has been acquitted, his charges dismissed, or when no complaint has been filed against him. UT ST §53-10-108(5).

Employment: Employers are prohibited from inquiring about arrest records. Employers may ask whether the applicant has been convicted of a felony, however it is advised only if the inquiry is job related. UAC R606-2(V).

The Division of Occupational and Professional Licensing may refuse to issue a license to an applicant if the applicant has engaged in unprofessional conduct. UT ST §58-1-401(2)(a).

Unprofessional conduct includes engaging in conduct that results in conviction, a plea of nolo contendere, or a plea of guilty with respect to a crime of moral turpitude or any crime that bears a reasonable relationship to the applicant's ability to safely or competently practice the occupation or profession. UT ST 58-1-501(2)(c).

Agency Guidelines for Pre-Employment Inquiries: Utah Labor Division Anti-Discrimination Rules, Rule R6062. "Pre-Employment Inquiry Guide" is available free at www.rules.utah.gov/publi cat/code/r606/r606-002.htm

State Statutes and Codes: http://le.utah.gov/Documents/code_const.htm

Legislative Bill Search: http://le.utah.gov/Documents/bills.htm

Utah State Criminal Records Agency

Bureau of Criminal Identification, Records Supervisor, Box 148280, Salt Lake City, UT 84114-8280, (courier address: 3888 West 5400 South, Salt Lake City, UT 84118.) **Phone:** 801-965-4555; **Fax:** 801-965-4749   **Web:** http://bci.utah.gov

Access to Records is Restricted

Records are not open to the public nor to employers not identified by statute even with notarized release from prospective employee. signature. Those agencies authorized by law do not need to submit fingerprints, but still must have subject's notarized signature.

Utah Sexual Offender Registry

Sex Offenders Registration Program , 14717 S Minuteman Dr, Draper, UT 84020 **Phone:** 801-545-5916; **Fax:** 801-545-5659 **Web:** www.corrections.utah.gov

Online Searching: The Registry may be searched from the web page. Records are searchable by name, ZIP Code, or name and ZIP Code. The information released includes photos, descriptions, addresses, vehicles, offenses, and targets. Also, requests and questions may be emailed to registry@utah.gov

Utah Incarceration Records Agency

Utah Department of Corrections , Records Bureau, 14717 Minuteman Dr, Draper, UT 84020 **Phones:**   801-545-5500; Phone of Service Vendor   877-884-8463; **Fax:** 801-545-5702 **Web:** www.cr.ex.state.ut.us

Search Note: No direct online access available. Direct questions to corrections@utah.gov. Location, conviction and sentencing information, and release dates are provided. Records are released in bulk on tape or CD. Call 801-545-5625 for details. The Utah Most Wanted List is found at www.cr.ex.state.ut.us/community/mostwanted/index.html.

Utah State Court System

Court Administrator: Court Administrator, 450 S State St, Salt Lake City, UT, 84114; 801-578-3800. www.utcourts.gov

Court Structure: 41 District Courts are arranged in eight judicial districts. Branch courts in larger counties, such as Salt Lake, which were formerly Circuit Courts and now elevated to District Courts have full jurisdiction over felony as well as misdemeanor cases. Justice Courts are established by counties and municipalities and have the authority to deal with class B and C misdemeanors, violations of ordinances, and infractions committed within their territorial jurisdiction. The Justice Court shares jurisdiction with the Juvenile Court over minors 16 or 17 years old who are charged with certain traffic offenses– automobile homicide, alcohol or drug related traffic offenses, reckless driving, fleeing an officer, and driving on a suspended license are excepted.

Find Felony Records: District Court

Misdemeanor Records: District Court, Justice Court

Online Access: Case information from all Utah District Court locations is available online through Xchange; however, misdemeanor B's, C's, Infractions and Small Claims cases are often filed in limited jurisdiction courts and not available through this site. Fees include $25.00 registration and $30.00 per month which includes 200 searches. Information about XChange and the subscription agreement can be found at www.utcourts.gov/records.

One may search for supreme or appellate opinions at the main website.

Searching Hints: The Salt Lake District Court has an automated information phone line that provides court appearance look-ups, outstanding fine balance look-ups, and judgment/divorce decree lookups. Call 801-238-7830.

Vermont

Vermont Statutes & Related Employer Restrictions

General Rule: Any person may inspect or copy any public record or document of a public agency. I VSA §316(a). Records, which by law may only be disclosed to specifically designated persons, are exempt from public inspection. VSA §317(c)(2).

Employment: An employer may obtain from the Vermont Criminal Information Center a Vermont criminal conviction record and those employers who care for children, the elderly or disabled may also obtain an out-of-state criminal record from the Center for any applicant who has given written authorization on a release form. 20 VSA §2056c (c) (1)(B) (b).

The employer may obtain the criminal record only after a conditional offer of employment has been made to the applicant. 20 VSA §2056c(c) (1 (A); and a report on a volunteer may be obtained after a position is offered. 20 USA§2056c(c)1(B).

State Statutes and Codes: www.leg.state.vt.us/statutes/statutes2.htm

Legislative Bill Search: www.leg.state.vt.us/database/database2.cfm

Vermont State Criminal Records Agency

Criminal Record Check Section, Vermont Criminal Information Center, 103 S. Main St., Waterbury, VT 05671-2101 **Phone:** 802-244-8727; **Fax:** 802-241-5552 **Web:** www.dps.state.vt.us

Search Note: Until July 1, 2008, the Legislation permitted this agency to only provide record access to employers after a conditional offer of employment is made. But, since July 1, 2008, records are open to the public. 35% of records are fingerprint supported. Include the following in your request-subject's notarized signature, DOB, SSN, telephone number. The requester must have a User Agreement in place. Copies of the User Agreement and the Request Form may both be downloaded from the web page. A copy of the record must be given by the employer to the hiree within 10 days. The employer may be represented by an agency or third party.

What Is Released: Only conviction data is released, unless requester is law enforcement. Charges arraigned in Family Court, the Traffic Ticket Bureau or the Municipal Ordinance Bureau are not reported. Juvenile records not released unless the juvenile was prosecuted in District Court as an adult. 96% of records in the state database have dispositions.

Access Methods: mail.

Vermont Sexual Offender Registry

State Repository , Vermont Criminal Information Center, 103 S. Main St., Waterbury, VT 05671-2101 **Phone:** 802-244-8727, 802-241-5400; **Fax:** 802-241-5552 **Web:** www.dps.state.vt.us/cjs/s_registry.htm

Online Searching: The webpage gives access to the high-risk offenders only. The requestor must also acknowledge a statement which specifies the conditions under which the registry information is being released. The complete record database is not publicly available and is accessible only by those authorized by law (employers with employees working with children, elderly, or disabled) or by the subject. Otherwise, requesters must search at local level.

Vermont Incarceration Records Agency

Vermont Department of Corrections , Inmate Information Request, 103 S. Main Street, Waterbury, VT 05671-1001 **Phone:** 802-241-2276; **Fax:** 802-241-2565 **Web:** www.doc.state.vt.us

Online Searching: The website provides an Incarcerated Offender Locator to ascertain where an inmate is located. Click at the top of main page, or go directly to www1.doc.state.vt.us/offender/. The search results gives name, DOB, location and case worker. This is not designed to provide complete inmate records nor is it a database of all inmates past and present in the system.

Vermont State Court System

Court Administrator: Administrative Office of Courts, Court Administrator, 109 State St, Montpelier, VT, 05609-0701; 802-828-3278. www.vermontjudiciary.org

Court Structure: On rare occasions the Superior Court hears hears criminal cases, but the District Court hears predominantly criminal cases.

Find Felony Records: District Court

Misdemeanor Records: District Court

Online Access: Vermont Courts Online provides access to civil and small claim cases and court calendar information from 12 of the county Superior Courts. Access is not offered for Chittenden and Franklin counties. Go to https://secure.vermont.gov/vtcdas/user. Records are in real-time mode. There is a $12.50 activation fee plus a fee of $.50 per case for look-up after the 1st 5 cases.

Supreme Court opinions are available from the main website and are also maintained by Vermont Dept. of Libraries at http://dol.state.vt.us.

Virginia

Virginia Statutes & Related Employer Restrictions

General Rule: Criminal history record information shall be disseminated only to individuals or organizations specifically authorized by statute. Criminal justice information disseminated to non-criminal justice agencies and individuals may not include information concerning the arrest of an individual if a year has passed from the date of arrest, no disposition of the charge has been recorded, and no active prosecution charges is pending. VA ST §19.2-389(2).

Expunged Record: It is unlawful for any person to disclose any information about an expunged record to another person without a court order. VA ST §19.2-392.3(A).

Employment: An employer shall not require an applicant to disclose information concerning any arrest or criminal charge against him that has been expunged. VA ST §19.2-392.4(A).

An applicant for a license from any licensing board may not be denied solely because of the applicant's refusal to disclose information concerning any arrest or criminal charge against him that has been expunged. VA ST §19.2-392.4(B).

State Statutes and Codes: http://leg1.state.va.us/000/src.htm

Legislative Bill Search: http://leg1.state.va.us/051/bil.htm

Virginia State Criminal Records Agency

Virginia State Police, CCRE, PO Box 85076, Richmond, VA 23261-5076, (courier address: 7700 Midlothian Turnpike, Richmond, VA 23235.) **Phone:** 804-674-6750; **Fax:** 804-674-8529 **Web:** www.vsp.state.va.us Direct questions to Thomas.Turner@vsp.virginia.gov.

Search Notes: Records are available to the general public. Include the following in your request-full name, date of birth, sex, race. The SSN is optional. The general public and employers not covered by statute must have a signed release from person of record, including notarized signatures for both subject and requester. These requesters must use form "SP-167" - which is downloadable from website.

What Is Released: Records are available from 1966. ection 19.2-389 Code of Virginia outlines that non-criminal entities can receive conviction only records. Certain agencies may receive complete records. The website gives complete details. Certain agencies receive complete records; non-criminal justice entities receive conviction only records. The following data is not released: dismissals, nolled pressed, whenever the disposition is missing, or if not guilty 84% of all arrests in database have final dispositions recorded.

Access Methods: mail, online.

Online Searching: Certain entities, including screening companies, are can apply for online access via the NCJI System. The system is ONLY available to IN-STATE accounts and allows you to submit requests faster. Fees are same as manual submission-$15 per record or $20 SOR record search. Username and password required. There is a minimum usage requirement of 10 requests per month. Turnaround time is 24-72 hours.

Virginia Sexual Offender Registry

Virginia State Police - Criminal records , Sex Offender and Crimes Against Minors Registry, PO Box 85076, Richmond, VA 23261-5076 **Phone:** 804-674-6750; **Fax:** 804-674-8529 **Web:** http://sex-offender.vsp.virginia.gov/sor/index.htm

Online Searching: Search by name, city, county or ZIP Code, or from a map at http://sex-offender.vsp.virginia.gov/sor/html/search.htm. Email questions to Lt.CJIS@vsp.virginia.gov.

Virginia Incarceration Records Agency

Virginia Department of Corrections , Records Unit, PO Box 26963, Richmond, VA 23261-6963, (courier address: 6900 Atmore Drive, Richmond, VA 23225.) **Phone:** 804-674-3131; **Fax:** 804-674-3598 **Web:** www.vadoc.state.va.us

Online Searching: Visit www2.vipnet.org/cgi-bin/vadoc/doc.cgi for an Inmate Status/Locator to ascertain where an inmate is located. This is not designed to provide complete inmate records nor is it a database of all inmates past and present in the system. Requesters can email requests to clasrec@vadoc.state.va.us. A DOC wanted/fugitives list is found at www.vadoc.virginia.gov/offenders/wanted/fugitive.shtm.

Virginia State Court System

Court Administrator: Executive Secretary, Admin. Office of Courts, 100 N 9th St, 3rd Fl, Supreme Court Building, Richmond, VA, 23219; 804-786-6455. www.courts.state.va.us

Court Structure: The Circuit Courts in 31 districts are the courts of general jurisdiction. There are 132 District Courts of limited jurisdiction. Please note that a district can comprise a county or a city. The General District Court decides all criminal offenses involving ordinances laws, and by-laws of the county or city where it is located and all misdemeanors under state law. A misdemeanor is any charge that carries a penalty of no more than one year in jail or a fine of up to $2,500, or both.

Find Felony Records: Circuit Court

Misdemeanor Records: District Court

Online Access: There are 3 available state systems. Each county must be searched separately. Cases from 132 General District Courts are accessible at www.courts.state.va.us/courts/gd.html and searched free at http://epwsgdp1.courts.state.va.us/gdcourts/caseSearch.do?index=index. Also. you can search records from over 120 Circuit Courts at www.courts.state.va.us/courts/circuit.html. These 2 online systems usually include partial DOBs in criminal results, and civil results sometimes include addresses. Also, a dial-up access system known as LOPAS (Law Office & Public Access System) is available free with District and Circuit Court records. Results include full name and address. Call Marguerite Steele, 804-786-6455 for LOPAS details. Also, the web page www.courts.state.va.us offers access to Supreme Court and Appellate opinions.

Searching Hints: Fifteen independent cities share the Clerk of Circuit Court with the county - Bedford, Covington (Alleghany County), Emporia (Greenville County), Fairfax, Falls Church (Arlington or Fairfax County), Franklin (Southhampton County), Galax (Carroll County), Harrisonburg (Rockingham County), Lexington (Rockbridge County), Manassas and Manassas Park (Prince William County), Norton (Wise County), Poquoson (York County), South Boston (Halifax County), and Williamsburg (James City County). Charles City and James City are counties, not cities. The City of Franklin is not in Franklin County but is its own separate jurisdiction. The City of Richmond is not in Richmond County but is its own separate jurisdiction. The City of Roanoke is not in Roanoke County but is its own separate jurisdiction.

Washington

Washington Statutes & Related Employer Restrictions

General Rule: The Washington state patrol must furnish a conviction record upon the request of any employer if the employer's purpose for the information is:

- to secure a bond required for employment, or
- conduct a pre-employment or postemployment evaluation of an employee or prospective employee who may in the course of their employment have access to information affecting national security, trade secrets, confidential or proprietary business information, money, or items of value, or
- used to investigate employee misconduct that might constitute a criminal offense. RCWA 43.43.815(1).

If an employer obtains a conviction record, they must notify the employee within 30 days of receiving it, and must allow the employee time to examine it. RCWA 43.43.815(2)

If an employer asks an employee or prospective employee about arrests, they must ask whether the arrest occurred within the last ten years and whether the charges are still pending, have been dismissed, or led to a conviction of a crime that would adversely affect job performance. Wash. Admin. Code 162-12-140.

Employers may ask employees or prospective employees about convictions or imprisonment if they are required by business necessity. A business necessity exists if the crimes reasonably relate to the duties of the job and the conviction occurred within the last ten years.

If a conviction record is cleared or vacated, an employee or prospective employee may answer questions as though the conviction never occurred. RCWA §§ 9.94A.640, 9.96.060.

Definitions

"'Conviction record' means criminal history record information relating to an incident which has led to a conviction or other disposition adverse to the subject." RCWA § 10.97.030(3).

State Statutes and Codes: www1.leg.wa.gov/LawsAndAgencyRules/

Legislative Bill Search: http://apps.leg.wa.gov/billinfo/

Washington State Criminal Records Agency

Washington State Patrol, Identification and Criminal History Section, PO Box 42633, Olympia, WA 98504-2633, (courier address: 3000 Pacific Ave. SE #204, Olympia, WA 98501.) **Phones:** 360-705-5100; WATCH or CHRI Info- 360-534-2000; **Fax:** 360-570-5277
Web: www.wsp.wa.gov

Search Note: Two types of records available: General Conviction - all convictions and arrests less than one year pending disposition; and Child & Adult Abuse record - all conviction and crimes against person, pending disposition (1 yr or less). The Child & Adult Abuse record is available for non-profits. Include the following in your request-date of birth, Social Security Number, sex, race, name and address of subject. Fingerprints are optional. Records are 100% fingerprint-supported. Mail requests are directed to the WSP or e-mail to crimhis@wsp.gov.

What Is Released: Records are available from 1974. Criminal history information is retained at the Identification and Criminal History Section until the offender is age seventy, or ten years from the last date of arrest, whichever is longer. Records without dispositions not released unless the arrest is less than 1 year old. 79% of all arrests in database have final dispositions recorded, 70% for arrests within last 5 years.

Access Methods: mail, in person, online.

Online Searching: WSP offers access through a system called WATCH, which can be accessed from their website. The fee per name search is $10.00. The exact DOB and exact spelling of the name are required. Credit cards are accepted online. Add $5.00 for notarize seal (fax requests accepted for these). To set up a WATCH account, call 360-705-5100 or email watch.help@wsp.wa.gov. Non-profits can request a fee-exempt account. WATCH stands for Washington Access To Criminal History. See the State Court Administrator's office for information about their criminal records database (JIS-Link).

Washington Sexual Offender Registry

Washington State Patrol , SOR, PO Box 42633, Olympia, WA 98504-2633, (courier address: 3000 Pacific Ave. SE #204, Olympia, WA 98501.) **Phone:** 360-534-2000 x3; **Fax:** 360-534-2072 **Web:**

Online Searching: In cooperation with the Washington Assoc. of Sheriffs and Police Chiefs, free online access to Level II and Level III sexual offenders is available at http://ml.waspc.org/.

Washington Incarceration Records Agency

Washington Department of Corrections , Office of the Secretary, 410 W. 5th, MS-41118, Olympia, WA 98504-1118 **Phones:** Headquarters- 360-725-8213; Public Disclosure- 360-725-8852; **Fax:** 360-664-4056 www.doc.wa.gov

Other Access: No online searching provided; however, email requests can be directed to docpublicdisclosureunit@doc1.wa.gov. A private company provides access to the statewide SAVIN (victim notification) System but it excludes Pierce and King county jails; search free at https://www.vinelink.com/vinelink/siteInfoAction.do?siteId=48626. Data is available by subscription for bulk users; for information, contact the Contracts Office at 360-725-8363.

Washington State Court System

Court Administrator:	Court Administrator, Temple of Justice, PO Box 41174, Olympia, WA, 98504; 360-753-3365. www.courts.wa.gov
Court Structure:	Superior Court is the court of general jurisdiction, but District Courts have criminal jurisdiction over misdemeanors, gross misdemeanors, and criminal traffic cases. Many Municipal Courts combine their record keeping with a District Court housed in the same building.
Find Felony Records:	Superior Court
Misdemeanor Records:	District Court, Municipal Court
Online Access:	The web offers free look-up of docket information at http://dw.courts.wa.gov/. Search by name or case number. This is an unofficial search. For more detailed case data, the AOC provides facilities that allow one to access information in the Judicial Information System's (JIS) statewide computer. This program of services is called JIS-Link. JIS-Link provides access to all counties and court levels. Case records include criminal, civil, domestic, probate, and judgments. Fees include a one-time $100.00 per site, a transaction fee of $.065. A $6.00 per month minimum. Call 360-357-3365 or www.courts.wa.gov/jislink.
	Supreme and Appellate opinions are at www.courts.wa.gov/appellate%5Ftrial%5Fcourts/. The page offers a notification service also. There is a Request for Information form at

http://dw.courts.wa.gov/datadis/request.doc which can be mailed, faxed or emailed to dda@courts.wa.gov. Fees are listed on the form.

Searching Hints: District Courts retain civil records for ten years from date of final disposition, then the records are destroyed. District Courts retain criminal records forever. An SASE is required in most courts that respond to written requests.

West Virginia
West Virginia Statutes & Related Employer Restrictions

General Rule: Every person has a right to inspect or copy any public record of a public body in this state. WV ST §29B-1-3(1).

Records of law enforcement agencies that deal with the detection and investigation of crime and the internal records and notations of such law enforcement agencies, which are maintained for internal use for matters relating to law enforcement, are exempt from disclosure. WV ST §29B-1-4(a)(4).

Records of a juvenile proceeding are not public records and shall not be disclosed. WV ST §49-5-17(a).

Expunged Records: Upon expungment, the proceedings in the matter shall be deemed to never have occurred. The court and other agencies shall reply to any inquiry that no record exists on the matter. The person whose record was expunged shall not have to disclose the fact of the record or any matter relating to it on an application for employment, credit, or other application. WV ST §61-11-25(e).

Employment: The following may deny an application for a license, suspend a license, or revoke a license upon proof that the applicant has been convicted of a felony:

State Board of Accountancy. WV ADC §1-3-4.

Board of Chiropractic Examiners. WV ADC §4-5-4.

Board of Hearing Aid Dealers. WV ADC §8-3-4.

Board of Optometry. WV ADC §14-4-4.

Board of Physical Therapy. WV ADC §16-3-4.

Board of Examiners of Psychologists. WV ADC §17-4-4.

Board of Examiners for Radiologic Technologists. WV ADC §18-4-4.

Nursing Home Administrator Board. WV ADC §21-2-4.

Board of Examiners of Land Surveyors. WV ADC §23-1-8.

Board of Osteopathy. WV ADC §24-6-4.

Board of Veterinary Medicine. WV ADC§26-2-4.

Board of Speech-Language Pathology and Audiology. WV ADC §29-4-4.

Board of Respiratory Care. WV ADC §30-4-3.

Massage Therapy Licensure Board. WV ADC §194-3-4.

Board of Registration for Foresters. WV ADC §200-3-4.

Agency Guidelines for Pre-Employment Inquiries: Bureau of Employment Programs "Pre-Employment Inquiry Guide" is available at www.wvbep.org/bep/bepeeo/empinqu.htm

State Statutes and Codes: www.legis.state.wv.us/WVCODE/Code.cfm

Legislative Bill Search: www.legis.state.wv.us/Bill_Status/bill_status.cfm

West Virginia State Criminal Records Agency

State Police, Criminal Records Section, 725 Jefferson Rd, South Charleston, WV 25309
Phones: Records- 304-746-2179; Information- 304-746-2178; **Fax:** 304-746-2209
Web: www.wvstatepolice.com

Search Online: Records are available to the general public. All searches require fingerprints, also FBI fingerprint checks. Include the following in your request-subject's signed release, SSN, DOB, race, sex, full fingerprints set. Use a WV Fingerprint Card and authorization. All records are returned by mail. Search can be initiated in person, results mailed. 100% of the records are fingerprint-supported. FBI checks only available if there is statutory authorization.

What Is Released: Records are available from 1938 on computer or until person reaches 80. All records are released, including those without dispositions. 40% of all arrests in database have final dispositions recorded, 90% for arrests within last 5 years. The state will also sell an "incident report" of a specific criminal action for $20.00, call 304-746-2178 or use Form WVSP-141 www.wvstatepolice.com/traffic/wvsp141.pdf. This is for a single incident only.

Access Methods: mail.

West Virginia Sexual Offender Registry

State Police Headquarters , Sexual Offender Registry, 725 Jefferson Rd, South Charleston, WV 25309 **Phone:** 304-746-2133; **Fax:** 304-746-2402 **Web:** www.wvstatepolice.com/sexoff/

Online Searching: Online searching is available from website, search by county or name, or by most wanted. Email questions to registry@wvsp.state.wv.us. You can also search the offender database to determine if a specific email address or username used on the internet belongs to a registered sex offender and has been reported.

West Virginia Incarceration Records Agency

West Virginia Division of Corrections , Records Room, 112 California Ave, Bldg 4, Room 300, Charleston, WV 25305 **Phone:** 304-558-2037; **Fax:** 304-558-5934 **Web:** www.wvdoc.com/wvdoc/

Online Searching: This agency offers a free search from www.wvdoc.com/wvdoc/OffenderSearch/tabid/117/Default.aspx

West Virginia State Court System

Court Administrator: Administrative Office, Supreme Court of Appeals, 1900 Kanawha Blvd, Bldg 1, Rm E 100, State Capitol, Charleston, WV, 25305; 304-558-0145. www.state.wv.us/wvsca.

Court Structure: The trial courts of general jurisdiction are the Circuit Courts which handle civil cases at law over $300 or more or in equity, felonies and misdemeanor and appeals from the Family Courts. The Magistrate Courts, which are akin to small claims courts, issue arrest and search warrants, hear misdemeanor cases, conduct preliminary examinations in felony cases. Magistrates also issue emergency protective orders in cases involving domestic violence.

Find Felony Records: Circuit Court

Misdemeanor Records: Magistrate Court

Online Access: Supreme Court of Appeals Opinions and Calendar are available at the web page. Supreme Court of Appeals Opinions/Calendar is available at the web page. 18 circuit courts have accessible records at www.swcg-inc.com/products/circuit_express.html. Fees are involved. Records are from 02/1997.

Searching Hints: There is a statewide requirement that search turnaround times not exceed five business days. However, most courts do far better than that limit. Release of public information is governed by WV Code Sec.29B-1-1 et seq. Find court forms at www.wvcourtnet.org/public.asp.

Wisconsin

Wisconsin Statutes & Related Employer Restrictions

General Rule: It is a violation of Wisconsin's civil rights laws to discriminate against a properly qualified employee or prospective employee by reason of their arrest or conviction record. Wis. Stat. §§ 111.31-111.335.

Employers may not ask about an arrest record except an employer may ask about a pending charge. Wis. Stat. § 111.335.

If a pending charge substantially relates to the circumstances of the particular job, employers may discriminate against an employee or prospective employee on that basis. An employer may also discriminate against an employee or prospective employee because of a conviction record if the charges substantially relate to the circumstances of the particular job or licensed activity, or if the individual is unable to be bonded because of the conviction.

Special Situations: It is not employment discrimination to refuse to employ or revoke the license or permit of an individual that has been convicted of a felony if the employ or license is for an installer of burglar alarms, private security guard, or a private detective. Wis. Stat. § 111.335.

In addition, it is not employment discrimination to revoke, suspend, or refuse to renew a license or permit involving alcoholic beverages if the individual has been involved in a crime involving the manufacturing, distribution, or delivery of controlled substances.

Definitions

Arrest record - includes, but is not limited to, information indicating that an individual has been questioned, apprehended, taken into custody or detention, held for investigation, arrested, charged with, indicted or tried for any felony, misdemeanor or other offense pursuant to any law enforcement or military authority." Wis. Stat. § 111.32.

Conviction record - includes, but is not limited to, information indicating that an individual has been convicted of any felony, misdemeanor or other offense, has been adjudicated delinquent, has been less than honorably discharged, or has been placed on probation, fined, imprisoned, placed on extended supervision or paroled pursuant to any law enforcement or military authority."

Agency Guidelines for Pre-Employment Inquiries: Wisconsin Department of Workforce Development, Civil Rights Division Publications, "Fair Hiring & Avoiding Loaded Interview Questions" is available at www.dwd.wisconsin.gov/er/discrimination_civil_rights/publication_erd_4825_pweb.htm

State Statutes and Codes: www.legis.state.wi.us/rsb/stats.html

Legislative Bill Search: www.legis.state.wi.us

Wisconsin State Criminal Records Agency

Wisconsin Department of Justice, Crime Information Bureau, Record Check Unit, PO Box 2688, Madison, WI 53701-2688, (courier address: 17 W Main St, Madison, WI 53703.) **Phones:** 608-266-5764; Online Questions- 608-266-7780; **Fax:** 608-267-4558 **Web:** www.doj.state.wi.us/dles/cib/crimback.asp

Search Note: Criminal record information is open to the public per statute 3-21-91. Certain statutorily-required searches require fingerprints. Include the following in your request-sex, race, full name, date of birth. Fingerprints are optional. All requests must be in writing. You must have an account with CIB in order to submit fingerprint cards. The account application can be downloaded from the web, as are request forms.

What Is Released: Records are available from July 1971 (when the agencies were required to save records) and are computerized. For fingerprint requests, all records are released, including those without dispositions. Arrests without supporting fingerprints are not included in the criminal history database search. Juvenile records are not released. 77% of all arrests in database have final dispositions recorded, 83% for arrests within last 5 years.

Access Methods: mail, fax, in person, online.

Online Searching: The agency offers Internet access at http://wi-recordcheck.org. Access 1) with an account with PIN is required, or 2) pay as you go with Visa/MC credit card. Records must be "picked up" at the website within 10 days. They are not returned by mail. Fee is $13 per request, $2 if a non-profit, and $5 if a government agency. Only daycare centers and other caregivers can receive immediate online response but pay an additional $3.00 per record request. Email account set-up questions to wi-recordcheck-account@doj.state.wi.us or to INTCH@doj.state.wi.us to answer general online questions. There is a free Internet service for access to the state's Circuit Courts' records, except for Portage county. Visit http://wcca.wicourts.gov/index.xsl.

Wisconsin Sexual Offender Registry

Department of Corrections , Sex Offender Registry Program, PO Box 7925, Madison, WI 53707-7925, (courier address: 3099 E Washington Avenue, Madison, WI 53704.) **Phone:** 608-240-5830; **Fax:** 608-240-3355 **Web:** http://offender.doc.state.wi.us/public/

Online Searching: Search offenders at the web by either name or location.

Wisconsin Incarceration Records Agency

Wisconsin Department of Corrections , Attn: Records, PO Box 7925, Madison, WI 53707-1921, (courier address: 3099 E Washington Ave, Madison, WI 53704.) **Phone:** Records Office-608-240-3750; **Fax:** 608-240-3306 **Web:** www.wi-doc.com

Search Note: The agency sells a raw database file of inmates for $100 on CD. The CD is published twice a year. Call for details.

Wisconsin State Court System

Court Administrator: Director of State Courts, Supreme Court, PO Box 1688, Madison, WI, 53701; 608-266-6828. http://wicourts.gov

Court Structure: The Circuit Court is the court of general jurisdiction, with 74 courts in 69 circuits. There are over 225 Municipal Courts in the state; the majority of cases involve traffic and ordinance matters

Find Felony Records: Circuit Court

Misdemeanor Records: Circuit Court

Online Access: Wisconsin Circuit Court Access (WCCA) allows users to view Circuit Court case information on the Wisconsin court system website at http://wcca.wicourts.gov. Data is available from all counties except Portage. Searches can be conducted statewide or county-by-county. WCCA provides detailed information about circuit cases and for civil cases, the program displays judgment and judgment party information. WCCA also offers the ability to generate reports. Due to statutory requirements, WCCA users will not be able to view restricted cases.

Appellate Courts and Supreme Court opinions are available from the main web page.

Searching Hints: Public access terminals are available at each court. There is normally no search fee charged for in-person searches.

Wyoming
Wyoming Statutes & Related Employer Restrictions

General Rule: Criminal history record information may be disseminated if the person seeking such information submits proof that the individual whose record is being checked consents to the release of the information to that person, the application is made through a criminal justice agency in Wyoming that is authorized to access criminal history record information, and a fee is paid. Wyo. Stat. §7-19-106(k).

The information may also be accessed in conjunction with a background check into employees of substitute care providers, state institutions, department of family services or department of health who have access to minors, those suffering from mental or developmental disabilities, or the elderly. Wyo. Stat. § 7-19-201.

Definitions

Criminal history record information - means information, records and data compiled by criminal justice agencies on individuals for the purpose of identifying criminal offenders consisting of identifiable descriptions of the offenders and notations or a summary of arrests, detentions, indictments, information, pre-trial proceedings, nature and disposition of criminal charges, sentencing, rehabilitation, incarceration, correctional supervision and release. Criminal history record information is limited to information recorded as the result of the initiation of criminal proceedings. It does not include intelligence data, analytical prosecutorial files, investigative reports and files, or statistical records and reports in which individual identities are not ascertainable, or any document signed by the governor granting a pardon, commutation of sentence, reprieve, remission of fine or forfeiture, or a restoration of civil rights by the governor or restoration of voting rights by the state board of parole.   Wyo. Stat. § 7-19-103(a)(ii).

Criminal justice agency - means any agency or institution of state or local government other than the office of the public defender which performs as part of its principal function, activities relating to:

- The apprehension, investigation, prosecution, adjudication, incarceration, supervision, or rehabilitation of criminal offenders;

- The collection, maintenance, storage, dissemination, or use of criminal history record information.   Wyo. Stat. §§ 7-19-103(a)(iii).

State Statutes and Codes: http://legisweb.state.wy.us/titles/statutes.htm
Legislative Bill Search: http://legisweb.state.wy.us/sessions/legsess.htm

Wyoming State Criminal Records Agency

Division of Criminal Investigation, Criminal Record Unit, 316 W 22nd St, Cheyenne, WY 82002   **Phone:**   307-777-7523;   **Fax:** 307-777-7301
Web: http://attorneygeneral.state.wy.us/dci/index.html

Search Notes: Records are available to the general public. First, obtain a Request for Criminal Record Packet from the address above or by telephoning this agency. Records include all felony and major misdemeanor arrests and convictions. Include the following in your request-notarized waiver from subject, name, set of fingerprints, date of birth, Social Security Number, number of years to search. Use the WY standard 8" x 8" orange fingerprint card. All requests are fingerprint based. Must also complete all information and waiver is on the back of this office's fingerprint card.

What Is Released: Records are available from 1941 on. A record inquiry includes all reported felonies, high misdemeanors and other specified misdemeanors, but not municipal ordinance violations. Juvenile records not released if no guardian consent. 73% of all arrests in database have final dispositions recorded, 65% for those arrests within last 5 years.

Access Methods: mail, in person.

Wyoming Sexual Offender Registry

Division of Criminal Investigation , ATTN: WSOR, 316 W 22nd St, Cheyenne, WY 82002-0001   **Phone:**   307-777-7809;   **Fax:** 307-777-7301
Web: http://wysors.dci.wyo.gov/sor/home.htm

Online Searching: The Internet is the search method offered by this agency to the public. Search is by last name, street name, city, county or ZIP. Data includes name including AKA, physical address, date and place of birth, date and place of conviction, crime for which convicted, photograph and physical description.

Wyoming Incarceration Records Agency

Wyoming Department of Corrections , 700 W. 21st Street, Cheyenne, WY 82002 **Phone:** 307-777-7405, 307-777-7208; **Fax:** 307-777-7479 **Web:** http://corrections.wy.gov/

Wyoming State Court System

Court Administrator:	Court Administrator, 2301 Capitol Av, Supreme Court Bldg, Cheyenne, WY, 82002; 307-777-7583. www.courts.state.wy.us
Court Structure:	Prior to 2003, for their "lower" jurisdiction court some counties have Circuit Courts and others have Justice Courts. Thus each county has a District Court ("higher" jurisdiction) and either a Circuit or Justice Court.
	Effective January 1, 2003 all Justice Courts become Circuit Courts and follow Circuit Court rules. Three counties have two Circuit Courts each: Fremont, Park, and Sweetwater. Cases may be filed in either of the two court offices in those counties, and records requests are referred between the two courts.
	Municipal courts operate in all incorporated cities and towns; their jurisdiction covers all ordinance violations. The Municipal Court judge may assess penalties of up to $750 and/or six months in jail
Find Felony Records:	District Court
Misdemeanor Records:	Circuit Court, Justice of the Peace, Municipal Court
Online Access:	Wyoming's statewide case management system is for internal use only. Planning is underway for a new case management system that will ultimately allow public access. Supreme Court opinions listed by date at the home page.

Appendix 1

FCRA Summaries

Appendix F to Part 698 - General Summary of Consumer Rights

The prescribed form for this summary is a disclosure that it substantially similar to the Commission's model summary with all information clearly and prominently displayed. The list of federal regulators that is included in the Commission's prescribed summary may be provided separately so long as this is done in a clear and conspicuous way. A summary should accurately reflect changes to those items that may change over time (e.g., dollars amounts, or telephone numbers and addresses of federal agencies) to remain in compliance. Translation of this summary will be in compliance with the Commission's prescribed model, provided that the translation is accurate and that it is provided in a language used by the recipient consumer.

A Summary of Your Rights Under the Fair Credit Reporting Act

Para informatcion en espanol, visite www.ftc.gov/credit o escribe a la FTC Consumer Response Center, Room 130-A 600 Pennsylvania Ave. N.W., Washington, DC 20580.

The federal Fair Credit Reporting Act (FCRA) promotes promote accuracy, fairness and privacy of information in the files of consumer reporting agencies There are many types of consumer reporting agencies, including credit bureaus and specialty agencies (such as agencies that sell information about check writing histories, medical records, and rental history records). Here is a summary of your major rights under the FCRA For more information, including information about additional rights, go to www.ftc.gov/credit or write to: Consumer Response Center, Room 130-A, Federal Trade Commission, 600 Pennsylvania Ave. N.W., Washington, DC 20580.

- **You must be told if information in your file has been used against you.** Anyone who uses a credit report or another type of consumer report to deny your application for credit, insurance, or employment – or to take another adverse action against you – must tell you, and must give you the name, address and phone number of the CRA that provided the information.

- **You have the right to know what is in your file.** You may request and obtain all the information about you in the files of a consumer reporting agency (your "file disclosure"). You will be required to provide proper identification, which may include your Social Security number. In many cases, the disclosure will be free. You are entitled to a free file disclosure if:
    - o a person has taken adverse action against you because of information in your credit report;
    - o you are a victim of identity theft and place a fraud alert in your file; your file contains inaccurate information as a result of fraud;
    - o you are on public assistance;
    - o you are unemployed but expect to apply for employment within 60 days.
- In addition, by September 2005 all consumers will be entitled to one free disclosure every 12 months upon request from each nationwide credit bureau and from nationwide specialty consumer reporting agencies. See www.ftc.gov/credit for additional information.
- **You have the right to ask for a credit score.** Credit scores are numerical summaries of your credit worthiness based on information from credit bureaus. You may request a credit score from consumer reporting agencies that create scores or distribute scores used in residential real property loans, but you will have to pay for it. In some mortgage transactions, you will receive credit score information for free from the mortgage lender.
- **You have the right to dispute incomplete or inaccurate information.** If you identify information in your file that is incomplete or inaccurate and report it to the consumer reporting agency, the agency must investigate unless your dispute is frivolous. See www.ftc.gov/credit for an explanation of dispute procedures.
- **Consumer reporting agencies must correct or delete inaccurate, incomplete, or unverifiable information.** Inaccurate, incomplete or unverifiable information must be removed or corrected, usually within 30 days. However, a consumer reporting agency may continue to report information it has verified as accurate.
- **Consumer reporting agencies may not report outdated negative information.** In most cases, a consumer reporting agency may not report negative information that is more than seven years old, or bankruptcies that are more than 10 years old.
- **Access to your file is limited.** A credit reporting agency may provide information about you only to people with a valid need -- usually to consider an application with a creditor, insurer, employer, landlord, or other business. The FCRA specifies those with a valid need for access.
- **You must give your consent for reports to be provided to employers.** A consumer reporting agency may not give out information about you to your

employer, or a potential employer, without your written consent given to the employer. Written consent generally is not required in the trucking industry. For more, go to www.ftc.gov/credit.

- **You may limit "prescreened" offers of credit and insurance you get based on information in your credit report.** Unsolicited "prescreened" offers for credit and insurance must include a toll-free phone number you can call if you choose to remove your name and address from the lists these offers are based on. You may opt-out with the nationwide credit bureaus at 1-800-XXX-XXXX.

- **You may seek damages from violators.** If a consumer reporting agency, or, in some cases, a user of consumer reports or a furnisher of information to a consumer reporting agency violates the FCRA, you may be able to sue in state or federal court.

- **Identity Theft victims and active duty military personnel have additional right.** For more information, visit www.ftc.gov.credit.

State may enforce the FCRA, and many states have their own consumer reporting laws. In some cases, you may have more rights under state law. For more information, contact your state or local consumer protection agency or your state Attorney General. Federal enforcers are:

TYPE OF BUSINESS:	CONTACT:
Consumer reporting agencies, creditors and others not listed below	**Federal Trade Commission: Consumer Response Center - FCRA,** Washington, DC 20580; 1-877-382-4357
National banks, federal branches/agencies of foreign banks (word "National" or initials "N.A." appear in or after bank's name)	**Office of the Comptroller of the Currency** Compliance Management, Mail Stop 6-6, Washington, DC 20219; 1-800-613-6743
Federal Reserve System member banks (except national banks and federal branches/agencies of foreign banks)	**Federal Reserve Board Division of Consumer & Community Affairs,** Washington, DC 205551 202-452-3693
Savings associations and federally chartered savings banks (word "Federal" or initials "F.S.B." appear in the federal institution's name)	**Office of Thrift Supervision** Consumer Complaints, Washington, DC 20552; 800-842-6929
Federal credit unions (words "Federal Credit Union" appear in institution's name)	**National Credit Union Administration** 1775 Duke St, Alexandria, VA 22314; 703-519-4600
State-chartered banks that are not members of the Federal Reserve System	**Federal Deposit Insurance Corporation,** Consumer Response Center, 2345 Grand Ave, Suite 100, Kansas City, MO 64108-2638; 1-877-275-3342
Air, surface, or rail common carriers regulated by former Civil Aeronautics Board of Interstate Commerce Commission	**Department of Transportation,** Office of Financial Management, Washington, DC 20590; 202-366-1306
Activities subject to the Packers and Stockyards Act of 1921	**Department of Agriculture,** Office of Deputy Administrator - GIPSA, Washington, DC 20590; 202-720-7051

Appendix G to Part 698 – Notice of Furnisher Responsibilities

The prescribed form for this disclosure is a separate document that is substantially similar to the Commission's model notice with all information clearly and prominently displayed. Consumer reporting agencies may limit the disclosure to only those items that they know are relevant to the furnisher that will receive notice.

> All furnishers subject to the Federal Trade Commission's jurisdiction must comply with all applicable regulations, including regulation promulgated after this notice was prescribed in 2004. Information about applicable regulations currently in effect can be found at the Commission's website, www.ftc.gov/credit. Furnishers who are not subject to the Commission's jurisdiction should consult with their regulators to find any relevant regulations.

Notices to Furnishers of Information: Obligations of Furnishers Under The FCRA

The federal Fair Credit Reporting Act (FCRA), 15 U.S.C. 1681-1681y, imposes responsibilities on all persons who furnish information to consumer reporting agencies (CRAs). These responsibilities are found in Section 623 of the FCRA, 15 U.S.C. 1681s-2. State law may impose additional requirements on furnishers. All furnishers of information to CRAs should become familiar with the law and may want to consult with their counsel to ensure that they are in compliance. The text of the FCRA is set forth in full at the website of the Federal Trade Commission (FTC): www.ftc.gov/credit.

Section 623 imposes the following duties upon furnishers:

Accuracy Guidelines

The banking and credit union regulators and the FTC will promulgate guidelines and regulations dealing with the accuracy of information provided to CRAs by furnishers. The regulations and guidelines issued by the FTC will be available at www.ftc.gov/credit when they are issued. Sections 623(e).

General Prohibition on Reporting Inaccurate Information

The FCRA prohibits information furnishers from providing information to a CRA that they know or have reasonable cause to believe is inaccurate. However, the furnisher is not subject to this general prohibition if it clearly and conspicuously specifies an address to which consumers may write to notify the furnisher that certain information is inaccurate. Sections 623(a)(1)(A) and (a)(1)(C).

Duty to Correct and Update Information

If at any time a person who regularly and in the ordinary course of business furnishes information to one or more CRAs determines that the information provided is not complete or accurate, the furnisher must promptly provide complete and accurate information to the CRA. In addition, the furnisher must notify all CRAs that received the information of any corrections, and must thereafter report only the complete and accurate information. Section 623(a)(2).

Duties After Notice of Dispute from Consumer

If a consumer notifies a furnisher, at an address specified by the furnisher for such notices, that specific information is inaccurate, and the information is, in fact, inaccurate, the furnisher must thereafter report the correct information to CRAs. *Section 623(a)(1)(B)*

If a consumer notifies a furnisher that the consumer disputes the completeness or accuracy of any information reported by the furnisher, the furnisher may not subsequently report that information to a CRA without providing notice of the dispute. *Section 623(a)(3)*

The federal banking and credit union regulators and the FTC will issue regulations that will identify when an information furnisher must investigate a dispute made directly to the furnisher by a consumer. Once these regulations are issued, furnishers must comply with them and complete and investigation within 30 days (or 45 days, if the consumer later provides relevant additional information) unless the disputer is frivolous or irrelevant or comes from a "credit repair organization." The FTC regulations will be available at www.ftc.gov/credit. Section 623(a)(8).

Duties After Notice of Dispute from Consumer Reporting Agency

If a CRA notifies a furnisher that a consumer disputes the completeness or accuracy of information provided by the furnisher, the furnisher has a duty to follow certain procedures. The furnisher must:

- Conduct an investigation and review all relevant information provided by the CRA, including information given to the CRA by the consumer. Sections 623(b)(1)(A) and (b)(1)(B).

- Report the results to the CRA that referred the dispute, and, if the investigation establishes that the information was, in fact, incomplete or inaccurate, report the results to all CRAs to which the furnisher provided the information that compile and maintain files on a nationwide basis. Sections 623(b)(1)(C) and (b)(1)(D).

- Complete the above steps within 30 days from the date the CRA receives the dispute (or 45 days, if the consumer later provides relevant additional information to the CRA). Section 623(b)(2).

- Promptly modify or delete the information, or block its reporting. Section 623(b)(1)(E).

Duty to Report Voluntary Closing of Credit Accounts

If a consumer voluntarily closes a credit account, any person who regularly and in the ordinary course of business furnishes information to one or more CRAs must report this fact when it provides information to CRAs for the time period in which the account was closed. *Section 623(a)(4)*

Duty to Report Dates of Delinquencies

If a furnisher reports information concerning a delinquent account placed for collection, charged to profit or loss, or subject to any similar action, the furnisher must, within 90 days after reporting the information, provide the CRA with the month and the year of the commencement of the delinquency that immediately preceded the action, so that the agency will know how long to keep the information in the consumer's file. *Section 623(a)(5)*

Any person, such as a debt collector, that has acquired or is responsible for collecting delinquent accounts and that reports information to CRAs may comply with the requirements of Section 623(a)(5) (until there is a consumer dispute) by reporting the same delinquency date previously reported by the creditor. If the creditor did not report this date, they may comply with the FCRA by establishing reasonable procedures to obtain and report delinquency dates, or, if a delinquency date cannot be reasonably obtained, by following reasonable procedures to ensure that the date reported precedes the date when the account was place for collection, charged to profit or loss, or subject to any similar action. Section 623(a)(5).

Duty of Financial Institutions When Reporting Negative Information

Financial Institutions that furnish information to "nationwide" consumer reporting agencies, as defined in Section 603(p), must notify consumers in writing if they may furnish or have furnished negative information to a CRA. Section 623(a)(7). The Federal Reserve Board has prescribed model disclosures, 12 CFR Part 222, App. B.

Duty When Furnishing Medical Information

A furnisher whose primary business is providing medical services, products, or devices (and such furnisher's agents or assignees) is a medical information furnisher for the purposes of the FCRA and must notify all CRAs to which it reports of this fact.

Section 623(a)(9). This notice will enable CRAs to comply with their duties under Section 604(g) when reporting medical information.

Duties When ID Theft Occurs

All furnishers must have in place reasonable procedures to respond to notifications from CRAs that information furnished is the result of identity theft, and to prevent refurnishing the information in the future. A furnisher may not furnish information that a consumer has identified as resulting from identity theft unless the furnisher subsequently knows or is informed by the consumer that the information is correct. Section 623(a)(6). If a furnisher learns that it has furnished inaccurate information due to identity theft, it must notify each consumer reporting agency of the correct information and must thereafter report only complete and accurate information. Section 623(a)(2). When any furnisher of information is notified pursuant to the procedures set forth in section 605B that a debt has resulted from identity theft, the furnisher may not sell, transfer, or place for collection the debt except in certain limited circumstances. Section 615(f).

The FTC's website, www.ftc.gov/credit, has more information about the FCRA, including publications for business and the full text of the FCRA.

Appendix H to Part 698 - Notice of User Responsibilities

The prescribed form for this disclosure is a separate document that is substantially similar to the Commission's notice with all information clearly and prominently displayed. Consumer reporting agencies may limit the disclosure to only those items that they know are relevant to the furnisher that will receive notice.

> All users subject to the Federal Trade Commission's jurisdiction must comply with all applicable regulations, including regulations promulgated after this notice was prescribed in 2004. Information about applicable regulations currently in effect can be found at the Commission's website, www.ftc.gov/credit. Persons not subject to the Commission's jurisdiction should consult with their regulators to find any relevant regulations.

Notice to Users of Consumer Reports: Obligations of Users Under the FCRA

The federal Fair Credit Reporting Act (FCRA), 15 U.S.C. 1681-1691y, requires that this notice be provided to inform users of consumer reports of their legal obligations. State law may impose additional requirements. The text of the FCRA is set forth in full at the Federal Trade Commission website at www.ftc.giv/credit. Other information about user duties is also available at the Commission's website. **Users must consult the relevant provisions of the FCRA for details about their obligations under the FCRA.**

This first section of this summary sets forth the responsibilities imposed by the FCRA on all users of consumer reports. The subsequent sections discuss the duties of users of reports that contain specific types of information, or that are used for certain purposes, and the legal consequences of violations. If you are a furnisher of information to a consumer reporting agency (CRA), you have additional obligations and will receive a separate notice from the CRA describing your duties as a furnisher.

I. OBLIGATIONS OF ALL USERS OF CONSUMER REPORTS

A. Users Must Have a Permissible Purpose

Congress has limited the use of consumer reports to protect consumers' privacy. All users must have a permissible purpose under the FCRA to obtain a consumer report. Section 604 of the FCRA contains a list of the permissible purposes under the law. These are:

- As ordered by a court or a federal grand jury subpoena. Section 604(a)(1).

- As instructed by the consumer in writing. Section 604(a)(2).

- For the extension of credit as a result of an application from a consumer, or the review or collection of a consumer's account. Section 604(a)(3)(A).

- For employment purposes, including hiring and promotion decisions, where the consumer has given written permission. Sections 604(a)(3)(B) and 604(b).

- For the underwriting of insurance as a result of an application from a consumer. Section 604(a)(3)(C).

- When there is a legitimate business need, in connection with a business transaction that is initiated by the consumer. Section 604(a)(3)(F)(i).

- To review a consumer's account to determine whether the consumer continues to meet the terms of the account. Section 604(a)(3)(F)(ii).

- To determine a consumer's eligibility for a license or other benefit granted by a governmental instrumentality required by law to consider an applicant's financial responsibility or status. Section 604(a)(3)(D).

- For use by a potential investor or servicer, or current insurer, in a valuation or assessment of the credit or prepayment risks associated with an existing credit obligation. Section 604(a)(3)(E).

- For use by state and local officials in connection with the determination of child support payments, or modifications and enforcement thereof. Sections 604(a)(4) and 604(a)(5).

In addition, creditors and insurers may obtain certain consumer report information for the purpose of making "prescreened" unsolicited offers of credit or insurance. Section 604(c). The particular obligations of users of "prescreened" information are described in Section VII below.

B. Users Must Provide Certifications

Section 604(f) prohibits any person from obtaining a consumer report from a consumer reporting agency (CRA) unless the person has certified to the CRA the permissible purpose(s) for which the report is being obtained and certifies that the report will not be used for any other purpose.

C. Users Must Notify Consumers When Adverse Actions Are Taken

The term "adverse action" is defined very broadly by Section 603 of the FCRA. "Adverse actions" include all business, credit, and employment actions affecting consumers that can be considered to have a negative impact as defined by Section 603(k) of the FCRA – such as denying or canceling credit or insurance, or denying employment or promotion. No adverse action occurs in a credit transaction where the creditor makes a counteroffer that is accepted by the consumer.

1. Adverse Actions Based on Information Obtained From a CRA

If a user takes any type of adverse action as defined by the FCRA that is based at least in part on information contained in a consumer report, Section 615(a) requires the user to notify the consumer. The notification may be done in writing, orally, or by electronic means. It must include the following:

- The name, address, and telephone number of the CRA (including a toll-free telephone number, if it is a nationwide CRA) that provided the report.

- A statement that the CRA did not make the adverse decision and is not able to explain why the decision was made.

- A statement setting forth the consumer's right to obtain a free disclosure of the consumer's file from the CRA if the consumer requests the report within 60 days.

- A statement setting forth the consumer's right to dispute directly with the CRA the accuracy or completeness of any information provided by the CRA.

2. Adverse Actions Based on Information Obtained From Third Parties Who Are Not Consumer Reporting Agencies

If a person denies (or increases the charge for) credit for personal, family, or household purposes based either wholly or partly upon information from a person other than a CRA, and the information is the type of consumer information covered by the FCRA, Section 615(b)(1) requires that the user clearly and accurately disclose to the consumer his or her right to be told the nature of the information that was relied upon if the consumer makes a written request within 60 days of notification. The user must provide the disclosure within a reasonable period of time following the consumer's written request.

3. Adverse Actions Based on Information Obtained From Affiliates

If a person takes an adverse action involving insurance, employment, or a credit transaction initiated by the consumer, based on information of the type covered by the FCRA, and this information was obtained from an entity affiliated with the user of the information by common ownership or control, Section 615(b)(2) requires the user to notify the consumer of the adverse action. The notice must inform the consumer that he or she may obtain a disclosure of the nature of the information relied upon by making a written request within 60 days of receiving the adverse action notice. If the consumer makes such a request, the user must disclose the nature of the information not later than 30 days after receiving the request. If consumer report information is shared among affiliates and then used for an adverse action, the user must make an adverse action disclosure as set forth in I.C.1 above.

D. Users have Obligations When Fraud and Active Duty Military Alerts are in Files

When a consumer has placed a fraud alert, including one relating to identity theft, or an active duty military alert with a nationwide consumer reporting agency as defined in Section 603(p) and resellers, 605A(h) imposes limitation on users of reports obtained from the consumer reporting agency in certain circumstances, including the establishment of a new credit plan and the issuance of additional credit cards. For the initial fraud alerts and active duty alerts, the user must have reasonable policies and procedures in place to form a belief that the user knows the identity of the applicant or contact the consumer at a telephone number specified by the consumer; in the case of extended fraud alerts, the user must contact the consumer in accordance with the contact information provided in the consumer's alert.

E. Users Have Obligations When Notified of an Address Discrepancy

Section 605(h) requires nationwide CRAs, as defined in Section 603(p), to notify users that request reports when the address for a consumer provided by the user in requesting the report is substantially different from the addresses in the consumer's file. When this occurs, users must comply with regulations specifying the procedures to be followed, which will be issued by the Federal Trade Commission and the banking and credit union regulators. The Federal Trade Commission's regulations will be available at www.ftc.gov/credit.

F. Users Have Obligations When Disposing of Records

Section 628 requires that all users of consumer report information have in place procedures to properly dispose of records containing this information. The Federal Trade Commission, the Securities and Exchange Commission, and the banking and credit union regulators have issued regulations covering disposal. The Federal Trade Commission's regulations may be found at www.ftc.gov/credit.

II. CREDITORS MUST MAKE ADDITIONAL DISCLOSURES

If a person uses a consumer report in connection with an application for, or a grant, extension, or provision of, credit to a consumer on material terms that are materially less favorable than the most favorable terms available to a substantial proportion of consumers from or through that person, based in whole or in part on a consumer report, the person must provide a risk-based pricing notice to the consumer in accordance with regulations to be jointly prescribed by the Federal Trade Commission and the Federal Reserve Board.

Section 609(g) requires a disclosure by all persons that make or arrange loans secured by residential real property (one to four units) and that use credit scores. These persons must provide credit scores and other information about credit scores to applicants, including the disclosure set forth in section 609(g)(1)(D)("Notice to the Home Loan Applicant").

III. OBLIGATIONS OF USERS WHEN CONSUMER REPORTS ARE OBTAINED FOR EMPLOYMENT PURPOSES

A. Employment Other Than in the Trucking Industry

If information from a CRA is used for employment purposes, the user has specific duties, which are set forth in FCRA Section 604(b). The user must:

- Make a clear and conspicuous written disclosure to the consumer before the report is obtained, in a document that consists solely of the disclosure, that a consumer report may be obtained.
- Obtain from the consumer prior written authorization. Authorization to access reports during the term of employment may be obtained at the time of employment.

- Certify to the CRA that the above steps have been followed, that the information being obtained will not be used in violation of any federal or state equal opportunity law or regulation, and that, if any adverse action is to be taken based on the consumer report, a copy of the report and a summary of the consumer's rights will be provided to the consumer.

- **Before** taking an adverse action, the user must provide a copy of the report to the consumer as well as the summary of the consumer's rights. (The user should receive this summary from the CRA.) A Section 615(a) adverse action notice should be sent after the adverse action is taken.

An adverse action notice also is required in employment situations if credit information (other than transactions and experience data) obtained from an affiliate is used to deny employment. Section 615(b)(2).

The procedures for investigative consumer reports and employee misconduct investigations are set forth below.

B. Employment in the Trucking Industry

Special rules apply for truck drivers where the only interaction between the consumer and the potential employer is by mail, telephone, or computer. In this case, the consumer may provide consent orally or electronically, and an adverse action may be made orally, in writing, or electronically. The consumer may obtain a copy of any report relied upon by the trucking company by contacting the company.

IV. OBLIGATIONS OF USERS OF INVESTIGATIVE CONSUMER REPORTS

Investigative consumer reports are a special type of consumer report in which information about a consumer's character, general reputation, personal characteristics, and mode of living is obtained through personal interviews by an entity or person that is a consumer reporting agency. Consumers who are the subjects of such reports are given special rights under the FCRA. If a user intends to obtain an investigative consumer report, Section 606 requires the following:

- The user must disclose to the consumer that an investigative consumer report may be obtained. This must be done in a written disclosure that is mailed, or otherwise delivered, to the consumer at some time before or not later than three days after the date on which the report was first requested. The disclosure must include a statement informing the consumer of his or her right to request additional disclosures of the nature and scope of the investigation as described below, and the summary of consumer rights required by Section 609 of the FCRA. (The summary of consumer rights will be provided by the CRA that conducts the investigation.)

- The user must certify to the CRA that the disclosures set forth above have been made and that the user will make the disclosure described below.

- Upon the written request of a consumer made within a reasonable period of time after the disclosures required above, the user must make a complete disclosure of the nature and scope of the investigation. This must be made in a written statement that is mailed, or otherwise delivered, to the consumer no later than five days after the date on which the request was received from the consumer or the report was first requested, whichever is later in time.

V. SPECIAL PROCEDURES FOR EMPLOYEE INVESTIGATIONS

Section 603(x) provides special procedures for investigations of suspected misconduct by an employee or for compliance with Federal, state or local laws and regulations or the rules of a self-regulatory organization, and compliance with written policies of the employer. These investigations are not treated as consumer reports so long as the employer or its agent complies with the procedures set forth in Section 603(x), and a summary describing the nature and scope of the inquiry is made to the employee if an adverse action is taken based on the investigation.

VI. OBLIGATIONS OF USERS OF MEDICAL INFORMATION

Section 604(g) limits the use of medical information obtained from consumer reporting agencies (other than payment information that appears in a coded form that does not identify the medical provider). If the report is to be used for an insurance transaction, the consumer must give consent to the user of the report or the information must be coded. If the report is to be used for employment purposes – or in connection with a credit transaction (except as provided in regulations issued by the banking and credit union regulators) – the consumer must provide specific written consent and the medical information must be relevant. Any user who receives medical information shall not disclose the information to any other person (except where necessary to carry out the purpose for which the information was disclosed, or as permitted by statute, regulation, or order.)

VII. OBLIGATIONS OF USERS OF "PRESCREENED LISTS"

The FCRA permits creditors and insurers to obtain limited consumer report information for use in connection with unsolicited offers of credit or insurance under certain circumstances. Sections 603(l), 604(c), 604(e), and 615(d). This practice is known as "prescreening" and typically involves obtaining from a CRA a list of consumers who meet certain pre-established criteria. If any person intends to use prescreened lists, that person must (1) before the offer is made, establish the criteria that will be relied upon to make the offer and to grant credit or insurance, and (2) maintain such criteria on file for a three-year period beginning on the date on which the offer is made to each consumer. In addition, any user must provide with each written solicitation a clear and conspicuous statement that:

- Information contained in a consumer's CRA file was used in connection with the transaction.

- The consumer received the offer because he or she satisfied the criteria for credit worthiness or insurability used to screen for the offer.

- Credit or insurance may not be extended if, after the consumer responds, it is determined that the consumer does not meet the criteria used for screening or any applicable criteria bearing on credit worthiness or insurability, or the consumer does not furnish required collateral.

- The consumer may prohibit the use of information in his or her file in connection with future prescreened offers of credit or insurance by contacting the notification system established by the CRA that provided the report. The statement must include the address and the toll-free telephone number of the appropriate notification system.

In addition, once the Federal Trade Commission by rule has established the format, type size, and manner of the disclosure required by Section 615(d), users must be in compliance with the rule. The FTC's regulations will be at www.ftc.gov/credit.

VIII. OBLIGATIONS OF RESELLERS

A. Disclosure and Certification Requirements

Section 607(e) of the FCRA requires any person who obtains a consumer report for resale to take the following steps:

- Disclose the identity of the end-user to the source CRA.
- Identify to the source CRA each permissible purpose for which the report will be furnished to the end-user.
- Establish and follow reasonable procedures to ensure that reports are resold only for permissible purposes, including procedures to obtain:
  1. the identity of all end-users;
  2. certifications from all users of each purpose for which reports will be used; and
  3. certifications that reports will not be used for any purpose other than the purpose(s) specified to the reseller. Resellers must make reasonable efforts to verify this information before selling the report.

B. Re-investigations by Resellers

Under Section 611(f), if a consumer disputes the accuracy or completeness of information in a report prepared by a reseller, the reseller must determine whether this is a result of an action or omission on its part and, if so, correct or delete the information. If not, the reseller must send the dispute to the source CRA for reinvestigation. When any CRA notifies the reseller of the results of an investigation, the reseller must immediately convey the information to the consumer.

C. Fraud Alerts and Resellers

Section 605(f) requires resellers who receive fraud alerts or active duty alerts from another consumer reporting agency to include these in their reports.

IX. LIABILITY FOR VIOLATIONS OF THE FCRA

Failure to comply with the FCRA can result in state government or federal government enforcement actions, as well as private lawsuits. Sections 616, 617, and 621. In addition, any person who knowingly and willfully obtains a consumer report under false pretenses may face criminal prosecution. Section 619.

For More Information on the FCRA

The Federal Trade Commission website is filled with information, including Staff Opinion Letters, Educational Materials, and a complete copy of the Act. Visit www.ftc.gov/os/statutes/fcrajump.htm

Appendix 2

Title VII EEOC Notices

This Appendix contains copies of four important notices written by the EEOC. These notices have set the bar so to speak on what an employer and cannot do with criminal records.

- Notice N-915.043 (July, 1989)
- Notice N-915-061 (9/7/90)
- Notice N-915 (7/29/87)
- Notice N-915 (2/4/87)

For more information about the EEOC, visit its web site at www.eeoc.gov.

Notice N-915.043 (July, 1989)

1. SUBJECT: Job Advertising and Pre-Employment Inquiries Under the Age Discrimination In Employment Ace (ADEA).

2. PURPOSE: This policy guidance provides a discussion of job advertising and pre-employment inquiries under the ADEA. Additionally, certain defenses are discussed that may be proffered by respondents when impermissible practices appear to be involved.

3. EFFECTIVE DATE: Upon receipt.

4. EXPIRATION DATE: As an exception to EEOC Order 205.001, Appendix B, Attachment 4, § a(5), this Notice will remain in effect until rescinded or superseded.

5. ORIGINATOR: ADEA Division, Office of the Legal Counsel.

6. INSTRUCTIONS: File behind § 801 of Volume II of the Compliance Manual.

7. SUBJECT MATTER:

I. JOB ADVERTISING

A: GENERAL

The ADEA makes it unlawful, unless a specific exemption applies, for an employer to utilize job advertising that discriminates on account of age against persons 40 years of age or older. Specifically, sec. 4(e) of the ADEA provides as follows:

> It shall be unlawful for an employer, labor organization, or employment agency to print of publish, or cause to be printed or published, any notice or advertisement relating to employment by such an employer or membership in or any classification or referral for employment by such a labor organization, or relating to any classification or referral for employment by such an employment agency, indicating any preference, limitation, specification, or discrimination, based on age.   29 USC. § 623(e).

The commission interpretative regulation further develops the statutory language by providing the following guidance.

> When help wanted notices or advertisements contain terms and phrases such as "age 25 to 35," "young," "college student," "recent college graduate," "boy," "girl," or others of a similar nature, such a term or phrase a violation of the Act, unless one of the exceptions applies. Such phrases as "40 to 50," "age over 65," "retired persons," or "supplement your pension" discriminate against others within the protected group and, therefore, are prohibited unless one of the exceptions applies.   29 C.F.R. S 1625.4(a).

Former Secretary of Labor, Willard Wirtz, in his 1965 report to Congress on age discrimination in employment was among the first to recognize a need to carefully assess employers' job advertisements, to assure that older workers are not arbitrarily discriminated against.

> The most obvious kind of discrimination in employment takes the form of employer policies of not haring people over a certain age, without consideration of a particular applicant's individual qualifications. These restrictive practices appear in announced employer policies (e.g., in help-wanted advertisements; or in job orders filed with employment agencies) or in dealing with applicants when they appear in the hiring office.[1]

Congress responded to this concern, in part, by enacting sec. 4(e). Covered entities are limited by sec. 4(e) of the ADEA with respect to the content of their job notices and advertisements. They must be careful to avoid not only explicit age based limitations, but also advertisements that implicitly deter older persons from applying. For example, a "job description can exert a subtle form of discrimination by setting qualifications of education that are completely appropriate for the young employee and completely irrelevant for someone with 30 years experience."[2]

---

[1] *The Older American Worker, Age Discrimination In Employment, Report of the Secretary of Labor to the Congress Under Section 715 of the Civil Rights Act of 1964*, 6 (1965)

[2] *Improving The Age Discrimination Law: A Working Paper, Senate Special Committee on Aging*, 93d Cong., 1st Sess. 6 (1973)

Although the language of sec. 4(e) is relatively straightforward, and judicial and Commission interpretations have added insight as to its application, generally there remains the need for a careful, case-by-case assessment as to whether a particular job advertisement runs afoul of sec. 4(e). The analysis requires an examination not only of the language used in the advertisement but also the context in which it is used to determine whether persons in the protected age group would be discouraged from applying.

In Hodgson v. Approved Personnel Service Inc., 529 F.2d 760 (4ᵗʰ Cir. 1975), the court examined over fifty advertisements published by the defendant, an employment agency. The court held that some of the advertisements violated the ADEA while others did not. The defendant's advertisements used such words and phrases as: "recent college graduate." "those unable to continue in college," "1-2 years out of college," "excellent first job," "any recent degree," "recent high school grad," "young executive," recent technical school grad," "junior secretary," "junior accountant," "athletically inclined," "career girls," "young office group," and "all American type."

The court's analysis of each phrase involved close scrutiny of the advertisement in its entirety to determine whether sec. 4(e) had been violated. Specifically the court stated, "we are inclined to think that the discriminatory effect of an advertisement is determined no solely by "trigger words" but rather by its context."[3] In order to determine from its context whether the advertisement is in fact discriminatory, one must read the ad in its entirety, taking into consideration the results of the ad on the employer's hiring practices. The mere presence of "trigger words: does not constitute a violation of the ADEA.

Those words and phrases found by the Hodgson court not to violate the ADEA are as follows: 1) "young executive seeks," refers to the age of the employer and does not state an age requirement for job applicants or suggest that older persons will not be considered; 2) "young office group," certainly carries an implication that an older person might not fit in but it tells the older applicant something he may want to know: that those already employed who will be his work associates are young; 3) "Athletically inclined" or "all American type," state qualifications relating to personal appearance and physical characteristics which can exist in persons at any age; 4) "junior," this adjective when applied to an employee's job description designates the scope of his duties and responsibilities. And does not carry connotations of youth prohibited by the Act; Hodgson at page 767 (Appendix). Of course, in a different context, the outcome with respect to any of the foregoing words and phrases might be different. As stated in the text, a case-by-case fact specific analysis is always required.

---

[3] Hodgson v. Approved Personnel Serv. At 765.

Read in context, "trigger words" may be innocent in some advertisements and clearly discriminatory in others. Hodgson at 765. The above concepts are demonstrated by the following examples.

> EXAMPLE 1 = CP, a 65 year old, saw an ad in the newspaper for a cashier at a local supermarket ®. R's advertisement specified that "applicant must be young, energetic, and posses excellent customer relations skills. Applicants who are selected would be required to stand long periods of time and to lift 20-30 pounds." CP contacted the Commission to institute a charge against R, local supermarket. In this case the Commission would find a violation. By use of the word "young" the ad specifically indicates a preference, limitation, specification or discrimination based on age. Such an ad would almost certainly deter many qualified older persons from applying. Note that if the same ad appeared with only the word "young" deleted, it would probably be acceptable. Persona of all ages can be energetic and possess excellent customer relations skills. Further, the need to stand for long periods and to lift 20-30 pounds are not age related criteria and, in any event, appear to be legitimate requirements for the job in question.

> EXAMPLE 2 – CP, a 57 year old graphic artist, claims that R, Advertising Firm, has discriminated against him based on age by publishing an advertisement which he feels clearly deters older persons from applying. R's ad stated, "Young-thinking, 'new wave' progressive advertising firm has openings for entry level position for graphic artist with no more than 3 years experience. We specialize in music videos and broadcast productions for a youthful audience. Our main focus is in the area of animation. Our clients include famous rock stars. If you have fresh, innovative ideas, and can relate to our audience, send your resume." While the ad does not contain explicit age limitations, read in its entirety, it does appear that persons in the protected age group would be discouraged from applying for the position. The employer contends that it does not discriminate against older persons and would hire a 75 year old applicant if he or she is qualified and willing to work for an entry level salary. However, on further investigation it was found that the employer has no employees over 30 years of age. It was also revealed that the firm recently turned down two fully qualified graphic artists X and Y, ages 47 and 67, who were willing to work at an entry level salary, though both possessed more that 3 years of experience. In this context the Commission would probably take the position that the ad is designed to deter older persons from applying. The Commission would seek to have R change the ad to read "young-thinking persons of any age with at least 3 years experience and willing to work at an entry level salary." The Commission would also attempt to contact X and Y to investigate the circumstances surrounding the denial of employment for the advertised position. The Commission has provided further specific guidance for investigating such incidents of "subtle" discriminatory advertising. See Volume I, Investigative Procedures Manual, § 8.6(b)(3)(i).

As indicated in sec. 1625.4(a), younger persons in the protected age group, for example, those individuals older than 40 but not old enough to retire, may be victimized by job advertising favoring older persons within the protected age group. The following example illustrates how this situation may occur.

> EXAMPLE 3 – CP, a 42 year old individual who is actively seeking part-time employment, contends that she was deterred from applying for a position because of the employer's ad. R, a local Laundromat, advertised in the newspaper as follows: "Opening for a person seeking to supplement pension. Part-time position available for Laundromat Attendant

from 9:00 am – 2:00 PM, Monday-Thursday. Responsibilities include dispensing products sold on premises, maintaining washer, dryer, and vending machines. Retired persons preferred." This ad limits the applicant pool by indicating a preference based on age. Persons rarely receive pensions or attain retirement status before 55 and frequently not until age 65. Thus, the ad deters younger persons within the protected age group from applying. Therefore it is a violation of sec. 4(e) unless one of the exceptions to the Act applies.

Note, however, that the Commission would be unlikely to find a violation in situations where an age-neutral advertisement encourages individuals within the protected age group to actively seek the position(s) available.[4]

EXEMPLE 4 – In response to a acute labor shortage that exists throughout the southeast region of the country, R, a large home improvement chain publishes the following advertisement:

WANTED; Individuals of all ages. Day and evening hours available. Full and part-time positions. All inquiries welcomed. Excellent secondary source of income for retirees.

While the ad mentions "retirees," the Commission would not find an illegal age-based discriminatory advertising practice in this instance. Individuals of all ages are welcomed for the employment opportunity. The reference to retirees in the ad does not, on its face, indicate a preference for this sub-grouping of the protected age group. Rather, it notifies them of an opportunity and invites them to participate. The language in this ad differs from the language used in Example 3 which suggests that only retired, pension eligible persons are considered for employment.

B. EMPLOYMENT AGENCY ADVERTISEMENTS

Some courts have fashioned an exception to the general rules when the advertising in question is done by an employment agency and is intended to acquaint persons with the agency's services.[5] The Hodgson court held that when employment agencies use such phrases as "recent grad," or others of a similar nature to appeal acquaint such individuals with the agency's services, the ADEA is not violated. However, such an advertisement would seem to clearly indicate a preference, limitation, specifications, or discrimination based on age which is prohibited by the ADEA. The Commission, therefore, would not agree with the exception fashioned in the Hodgson decision. As a general enforcement principle, the Commission will closely scrutinize all ads that use words and phrases that would deter older persons from applying, including those used by employment agencies to inform the public of their services. An employment agency could as easily advertise generally for persons looking for employment by including in

---

[4] Section 2(b) of the ADEA states in pertinent part that "[I]t is therefore the purpose of this Act to promote employment of older persons based on their ability rather than age." See also EEOC Opinion Letter – 1, December 13, 1983 (ADEA rights of retirees).

[5] See Hodgson at 766.

the advertisement language making it clear that both young and older applicants are wanted.[6]

In summary, a careful analysis of job advertising practices, whether by an employer or employment agency, is required in determining whether a violation of sec. 4(e) of the ADEA has occurred. If an ADEA charge/complaint raises the issue of an illegal age-based discriminatory advertising practice the following analytical scheme of investigation is suggested.

In some instances an advertisement may use a term or phrase which is listed in 29 C.F.R. § 1625.4(a). If an employer or employment agency resorts to the use of such terminology the advertising practice is per se illegal and a finding of a violation of sec. 4(e) of the ADEA is warranted, unless an exception (e.g., BFOQ) applies.

In many cases, however, the challenged advertisement will not contain direct age-based prohibited specifications or preferences and as such the legality of the advertising practice will depend upon the overall context, application and effect of discouraging individuals within the protected age group from applying or, in the alternative, generally limits, classifies or otherwise discriminates against an individual based on age. Specific attention in such instances should be given but not limited to charging party's/complainant's (1) explanation of why the ad served to discourage him or her from applying; (2) respondent's overall hiring practices, or; (3) a comparative analysis of respondent's applicant flow data with similar size employers using nondiscriminatory advertising practices. See generally Volume I, Investigative Procedures Manual, § 8.6(b)(3)(i)(ii).

C. BONA FIDE OCCUPATIONAL QUALIFICATION DEFENSE

Where an ad is per se discriminatory on the basis of age, a respondent may seek to invoke the :bona fide occupational qualification" defense, hereinafter referred to as "BFOQ," to justify the use of the ad.[7] If, because of the requirements of a job, an employer believes it must limit, specify, or discriminate based on age, an employer has the burden of proving that the position is a BFOQ.[8]

---

[6] C. Edelman & I. Sigler, Federal Age Discrimination in Employment Law, Slowing Down the Gold Watch, 96 (1978). The Commission, for example, would encourage the use of such phrases as "state of the art knowledge" in lieu of "recent college graduate" or recommend to employment agencies the use of a specific disclaimer such as, "While we are skilled in assisting recent grads in finding positions, we encourage applicants of all ages and levels of experience – neither this agency nor any of our clients discriminate on the basis of an applicant's age."

[7] Section 4(f)(l) of the ADEA permits an employer "to take any action otherwise prohibited under subsection (a), (b), (c), or (e) of this section where age is a bona fide occupational qualification reasonably necessary to the normal operation of the particular business."

[8] 29 C.F.R.S 1625.6(b)

There are several elements which must be met in establishing a BFOQ defense. Whenever this defense is raised an employer must <u>always</u> show that :the age limit is reasonably necessary to the essence of the business."[9] In proving that age must be used as a proxy for ability to perform the job, an employer must next show that either "all or substantially all individuals excluded from the job are in fact disqualified,"[10] or "some of the individuals so excluded possess a disqualifying trait that cannot be ascertained except by reference to age."[11]

Unless the employer can establish the existence of a BFOQ, the ad would have to be modified to eliminate any limitations based upon age.

> EXAMPLE 5 – CP, a 43 year old fashion model, contends that she has been discriminated against based on age. R, a modeling agency, advertised in the newspaper as follows:" Experienced models between 20-30 for upcoming spring collection of 'junior sportswear.' Applicants must bring a portfolio and references to our New York Office. Only those persons in the specified age category need apply." CP auditioned and was rejected when the company found out her age. During the investigation, R raises the BFOQ defense and states that the "junior collection requires applicants who have a youthful appearance. R further alleges that traditionally the "junior" fashions are targeted to younger women, generally between 20-30. However, while CP is 43, she appears to be 23. In fact, R was in the process of completing the paperwork necessary to hire CP when its personnel manager noticed the date of birth on her driver's license. R is not able to prove that persons 40 or older have a disqualifying trait that cannot be ascertained except by reference to age. R has not established the existence of a BFOQ and its discriminatory ad must be changed. R has also violated the Act by its failure to hire CP on account of her age.

In sum, the employer has the burden of proving a bona fide occupational qualification. The Commission and the courts construe this defense very narrowly. If, however, the employer satisfies the requirements of the exemption, it can continue to express appropriate age limitations in its job ads.

II. PRE-EMPLOYMENT INQUIRIES

Pursuant to sec. 4(a)(1) of the ADEA, 29 U. S. C. § 623(A)(1), "[I]t shall be unlawful for an employer to fail or refuse to hire or to discharge any individual or otherwise discriminate against any individual with respect to his compensation, terms, conditions, or privileges of employment, because of such individual's age." Although it is almost always unlawful to make employment decisions based on age, a pre-employment inquiry on the part of an employer for information such as "Date of Birth" or :State Age" on an application form is not, in itself, a violation of the ADEA.

---

[9] 29 C.F.R. S 1625.6(b)(3)

[10] 29 C.F.R.S 1625.6(b)(2)

[11] 29 C.F.R. S 1625.6(b)(1)

However, because the request that an applicant state his age may tend to deter older applicants from applying, pre-employment inquires which request such information will be closely scrutinized by the Commission to assure that the request is for a permissible purpose and not for a purpose proscribed by the Act. There must be legitimate, non-discriminatory reasons for seeking the information and the information must not be used for an impermissible purpose.

The Commission has addressed the issue of pre-employment inquiries concerning age in two separate provisions. The first provision, 29 C.F.R. § 1625.4(b), Specifically addresses requests in help-wanted notices or advertisements for age or date of birth. The Commission's position in regard to help-wanted notices and advertisements is that although inquiries regarding age will be closely scrutinized, such inquiries are not <u>per se</u> violations of the Act.

The second provision, 29 C.F.R. § 1625.5, focuses on requests for age on employment application forms. The Commission regulation at 29 C.F.R. § 1625.5 provides in part:

> A request on the art of an employer for information such as "Date of Birth" or "State Age" on an application form is not, in itself, a violation of the Act. But because the request that an applicant state his age may tend to deter older applicants or otherwise discriminate based on age, employment application forms which request such information will be closely scrutinized to assure that the request is for a permissible purpose and not for purposes proscribed by the Act. That the purpose is not one proscribed by the statute should be made known to the applicant. The term "employment applications" refers to all written inquiries about employment or application for employment or promotion including, but not limited to, resumes or other summaries of the applicant's background. It relates not only to written pre-employment inquiries, but to inquiries concerning terms, conditions, or privileges of employment as specified in section 4 of the Act.

The purpose of section 1625.5 is to insure that older applicants are judged on ability rather than age. To assure applicants in the protected age group that an inquiry as to age is for a permissible purpose, employers should include a reference on the application form stating that the employer does not discriminate on the basis of age. Another option would be to explain to each applicant the specific reason why the information concerning age is being requested. Most importantly, of course, employers must not use age related inquiries for an impermissible purpose.

> <u>EXAMPLE 6</u> – CP, a 55 year old radio announcer, sent a resume to R, WZAB, for the position of Program Director. WZAB's format is "hard rock." R responded by forwarding CP an employment application and scheduling an interview. The application requested CP to state his age, and also stated the statutory prohibition against age discrimination in employment. At the interview CP was introduced to the staff, all of whom appeared to be between the ages of 18 and 35. During the interview, CP discussed his past experience and talked at length about how the radio business had changed since he had begun his career. R asked CP if he would be opposed to having a younger supervisor and whether or not CP enjoyed working with younger people. Two days lager CP received a rejection letter from R. CP alleges that he was discriminated against based on age. It was later found that X, a

23 year old who was hired for the position of Program Director, did not submit an application and no inquiry was made as to her age. This evidence conflicted with R's statement that it was a standard practice to ascertain the age of all applicants. Despite the presence of the statutory prohibition against age discrimination on the application form, it would appear that in this particular instance, the inquiry about age was not applied uniformly and was used only to disqualify CP. Thus, even if an employer sets forth the statutory prohibition against age discrimination on the application form, when an age related inquiry is challenged, the employer must show that it has legitimate non-discriminatory reasons for seeking the information.

III. CASE RESOLUTION

The Commission's position is that employment related inquiries requesting an applicant's age or date of birth will be closely scrutinized on a case-by-case basis to assure that they are for a lawful purpose.

Pre-employment inquiries as to age which are used for the purpose of disqualifying persons in the protected age group are prohibited. When the employer's inquiry does not serve any legitimate purpose, or the practice is not uniformly adhered to, it is quite likely that the information is being sought for purposes proscribed by the ADEA.[12][13]

[Signed by Clarence Thomas on 07-02-89]

Date: _____   Signed: _____

Clarence Thomas

Chairman

---

[12]The ADEA principles and the BFOQ defense discussed in the text apply equally to Title VII. See, e.g., 29 C.F.R. S 1604.7. It should be noted, however, that the BFOQ defense under Title VII is limited to religion, sex, and national origin.

Notice N-915-061 **(9/7/90)**

1.   <u>SUBJECT</u>: Policy Guidance on the Consideration of Arrest Records in Employment Decisions under Title VII of the Civil Rights Act of 1964, as amended, 42 USC. § 2000e <u>et seq.</u> (1982).

2.   <u>PURPOSE</u>: This policy guidance sets forth the Commission's procedure for determining whether arrest records may be considered in employment decisions.

3.   <u>EFFECTIVE DATE</u>: September 7, 1990.

4.   <u>EXPIRATION DATE</u>: As an exception to EEOC Order 205.001, Appendix B, Attachment 4, § a(5), this Notice will remain in effect until rescinded or superseded.

5.   <u>ORIGINATOR</u>: Title VII/EPA Division, Office of the Legal Counsel.

6.   <u>INSTRUCTIONS</u>: File behind the last Policy Guidance § 604 of Volume II of Compliance Manual.

7.   <u>SUBJECT MATTER</u>:

I. Introduction

The question addressed in this policy guidance is "to what extent may arrest records be used in making employment decisions?" The Commission concludes that since the use of arrest records as a absolute bar to employment has a disparate impact on some protected groups, such records alone cannot be used to routinely exclude persons from employment. However, conduct which indicates unsuitability for a particular position is a basis for exclusion. Where it appears that the applicant or employee engaged in the conduct for which he was arrested and that the conduct is job-related and relatively recent, exclusion is justified.

The analysis set forth in this policy guidance is related to two previously issued policy statements regarding the consideration of conviction records in employment decisions: "Policy Statement on the Issue of Conviction Records under Title VII of the Civil Rights Act of 1964, as amended 42 U.S.C. § 2000e <u>et seq.</u> (1982)" (hereinafter referred to as the February 4, 1987 Statement) and "Policy Statement on the use of statistics in charges involving the exclusion of individuals with conviction records from employment" (hereinafter referred to ad July 29, 1987 Statement). The February 4, 1987 Statement states that nationally, Blacks and Hispanics are convicted in numbers which are disproportionate to Whites and that barring people from employment based on their conviction records will therefore disproportionately exclude those groups.[1] Due to this adverse impact, an employer may not base an employment decision on the conviction record of an applicant or an employee absent business necessity.[2] Business necessity can be established where the

---

[1] The July 29 Statement notes that despite national statistics showing adverse impact, an employer may refute this <u>prima facie</u> showing by presenting statistics which are specific to its region or applicant pool. If these statistics demonstrate that the policy has no adverse impact against a protected group, the plaintiff's <u>prima facie</u> case has been rebutted and the employer need not show any business necessity to justify the use of the policy. Statistics relating to arrests should be used in the same manner.

[2] The policy statements on convictions use the term "business necessity," as used by courts prior to the Supreme Court's decision in <u>Wards Cove Packing Co. v. Atonio</u>, 109 S. Ct. 2115 (1989). In <u>Atonio</u>, the Supreme Court adopted the term "business justification" in place of business necessity, but noted that "although we have phrased the query differently in different cases...the dispositive issue is whether a challenged practice serves, in a significant way, the legitimate employment goals of the employer, "citing, <u>inter alia</u>, <u>Griggs v. Duke Power Co.</u>, 401 US 424 (1971). 109 S. Ct. at 2125-2126.

employee or applicant is engaged in conduct which is particularly egregious or related to the position in question.

Conviction records constitute reliable evidence that a person engaged in the conduct alleged since the criminal justice system requires the highest degree of proof ("beyond a reasonable doubt") for a conviction. In contract, arrests alone are not reliable evidence that a person has actually committed a crime. Schware v. Board of Bar Examiners, 353 US 232, 241 (1957) ("[t]he mere fact that a [person] has been arrested has very little, if any, probative value in showing that he has engaged in misconduct.") Thus, the Commission concludes that to justify the use of arrest records, an additional inquiry must be made. Even where the conduct alleged in the arrest record is related to the job at issue, the employer must evaluate whether the arrest record reflects the applicant's conduct. It should, therefore, examine the surrounding circumstances, offer the applicant or employee an opportunity to explain, and, if he or she denies engaging in the conduct, make the follow-up inquiries necessary to evaluate his/her credibility. Since using arrests as a disqualifying criteria can only be justified where it appears that the applicant actually engaged in the conduct for which he/she was arrested and that conduct is job related, the Commission further concludes that an employer will seldom be able to justify making broad general inquiries about an employee's or applicant's arrests.

The following discussion is offered for guidance in determining the circumstances under which an employer can justify excluding an applicant or an employee on the basis of an arrest record.

II. Discussion

A. Adverse Impact of the Use of Arrest Records

The leading case involving an employer's use of arrest records is Gregory v. Litton Systems, 316 F. Supp. 401, 2 EPD ¶ 10,264 (C.D. Cal. 1970), modified on other grounds, 472 F.2d 631, 5 EPD ¶ 8089 (9th Cir. 1972). Litton held that nationally, Blacks are arrested more often than are Whites. Courts and the Commission have relied on the statistics presented in Litton to establish a prima facie case of discrimination against Blacks where arrest records are used in employment decisions.[3] There are, however, more recent statistics, published by the US Department of Justice, Federal Bureau of Investigation, which are consistent with the Litton finding.[4] It is desirable to use the most current available statistics. In addition, where local statistics are available, it may be helpful to use them, as the court did in Reynolds v. Sheet Metal Workers Local 102, 498 F. Supp. 952, 22 EPD ¶ 30,739 (D.C. 1980), aff'd., 702 F.2d 221, 25 EPD ¶ 31,706 (D.C. Cir. 1981). In Reynolds, the court found that the use of arrest records in employment decisions adversely affected Blacks since the 1978 Annual Report of the Metropolitan Police of Washington, D.C., stated that 85.5% of persons arrested in the District of Columbia were nonwhite while the nonwhite population constituted 72.4% of the total population. 498 F. Supp. At 960. The Commission has determined that Hispanics are also adversely affected by arrest record inquiries. Commission Decisions Nos.

---

[3] US v. City of Chicago, 385 F. Supp. 543, 556-557 (N.D. Ill. 1974), adopted by reference, 411 F. Supp. 218, aff'd in rel. part, 549 F.2d 415, 432 (7th Cir. 1977); City of Cairo v. Illinois Fair Employment Practice Commission, et al., 8 EPD ! 9682 (Ill. App. Ct. 1974); Commission Decision Nos. 78-03, 77-23, 76-138, 76-87, 76-39, 74-92, 74-90, 74-83, 74-02, CCH EEOC Decisions (1983) !! 6714, 6710, 6700, 6665, 630, 6424, 6423, 6414, 6386 and Commission Decisions Nos. 72-1460, 72-1005, 72-094 and 71-1950, CCH EEOC Decisions (1973) !! 6341, 6357 and 6274 respectively.

[4] The FBI's Uniform Crime Reporting Program reported that in 1987, 29.5% of all arrests were of Blacks. The US. Census reported that Blacks comprised 11.7% of the national population in 1980 and projected that the figure would reach 12.2% in 1987. Since the national percentage of arrest for Blacks is more that twice the percentage of their representation in the population (whether considering the 1980 figures or the 1987 projections), the Litton presumption of adverse impact, at least nationally, is still valid.

77-23 and 76-03, CCH EEIC Decisions (1983) ¶¶ 6714 and 6598, respectively.[5] However, the courts have not yet addressed this issue[6] and the FBI's Uniform Crime Reporting Program does not provide information on the arrest records (see July 29, 1987 Statement), the employer may rebut by presenting statistics which are more current, accurate and/or specific to its region or applicant pool than are the statistics presented in the prima facie case.

B. Business Justification

If adverse impact is established, the burden of producing evidence shifts to the employer to show a business justification for the challenged employment practice. Wards Cove Packing Co. v. Atonio, 109 S.Ct. 2115, 2126 (1989).[7] As with conviction records, arrest records may be considered in the employment decision as evidence of conduct which may render an applicant unsuitable for a particular position. However, in the case of arrests, not only must the employer consider the relationship of the charges to the position sought, but also the likelihood that the applicant actually committed the conduct alleged in the charges. Gregory v. Litton Systems, 316 F. Supp. 401; Carter v. Gallagher, 452 F.2d 315, 3 EPD ¶ 8335 (8th Cir. 1971), cert. Denied, 406 U.S. 950, 4 EPD ¶ 7818 (1972); Reynolds v. Sheet Metal Workers Local 102, 498 F. Supp. 952; Dozier v. Chupka, 395 F. Supp. 836 (D.C. Ohio 1975); US. V. City of Chicago, 411 F. Supp. 218 (N.D. Ill. 1974), aff'd. in rel. part, 549 F.2d 415 (7th Cir. 1977); City of Cairo v. Illinois Fair Employment Practice Commission et al., 8 EPD ¶ 9682 (Ill. App. Ct. 1974); Commission Decisions Mos. 78-03, 77-23, 76-138, 76-87, 76-54, 76-39, 76-17, 74-92, 74-83, 76-03, 74-90, 78093, 74025, CCH EEOC Decisions (1983) ¶¶ 6714, 6710, 6700, 6665, 6639, 630, 612, 6424, 6414, 6598, 6423, 6400 and Commission Decisions Nos. 72-0947, 72-1005, 72-1460, CCH EEOC Decisions (1973) ¶¶ 6357, 6350 and 6341, respectively.

1. A Business Justification Can Rarely Be Demonstrated for Blanket Exclusions on the Basis of Arrest Records

Since business justification rests on issues of job relatedness and credibility, a blanket exclusion of people with arrest records will almost never withstand scrutiny. Gregory v. Litton Systems, 316 F. Supp. 401. Litton held that employer's policy of refusing to hire anyone who had been arrested "on a number of occasions" violated Title VII because the policy disproportionately excluded Blacks from consideration and was not justified by business necessity. In Litton, an applicant for a position as a sheet metal worker was disqualified because of this arrest record. The court found no business necessity because the employer had failed to establish a business necessity for its discriminatory policy, it was enjoined from basing future hiring decisions on arrest records. Accord Carter v. Gallagher, 452 F.2d 315 (firefighter); Dozier v. Chupka, 395 F. Supp. 836 (firefighter); City of Cairo v Illinois Fair Employment Practice Commission, et al, 8 EPD ¶ 9682 (police officer).

---

[5] The statistics presented in Decision No. 77-23 pertain only to prison populations in the Southwestern United States. This data would, therefore, probably not constitute a prima facie case of discrimination for other regions of the country. In fact, there is no case law to indicate whether courts would accept this data as evidence of adverse impact for arrest records, even for cases arising in the Southwest, since all arrests do not result in incarceration. Decision No. 76-03 noted that Hispanics are arrested more frequently that are Whites, but no statistics were presented to support this statement.

[6] Cf. EEOC v. Carolina Freight Carriers, 723 F. Supp. 734, 751, 52 EPD ¶ 39, 538 (S.D. Fla. 1989) (EEOC failed to provide statistics for the relevant labor market to prove that trucking company's exclusion of drivers with, convictions for theft crimes had an adverse impact on Hispanics at a particular job site).

[7] Under Atonio, the burden of producing evidence shifts to the employer, but the burden of persuasion remains with the plaintiff at all stages of the Title VII case. 109 S.Ct. at 2116. Atonio thus modifies Griggs and its progeny.

The Commission has consistently invalidated employment policies which create a blanket exclusion of persons with arrest records. Commission Decision Nos. 78-03, 76-87, 76-39, 76-17, 76-03, 74-90, 74-25, 72-0947, 72-1005, CCH EEOC Decisions (1983) ¶¶ 6714 (laborer), 6665 (police officer), 6630 (cashier), 6612 (credit collector), 6598 (catalogue clerk), 6423 (uniformed guard commissioned by police department), 6400 (firefighter), 6357 (line worker) and 6350 (warehouse worker or driver). In several decisions, it appears that the arrest record inquiry was made on a standard company application which was used by the employer to fill various positions and there was no mention of any particular position sought. Commission Decision Nos. 76-138, 76-54, 74-82, 74-83, 74-02 and 72-1460, CCH EEOC Decisions (1983) ¶¶ 6700, 639, 6424, 6414, 6386 and 6341 and Commission Decision No. 71-1950, CCH EEOC Decisions (1973) ¶ 6274, respectively. An employer may not routinely exclude persons with arrest records based on the assumption that an arrest record will prevent an applicant from obtaining necessary credentials to perform a job without giving the applicant an opportunity to obtain those credentials. For example, in Decision 76-87, the Commission rejected an employer's assertion that employees' arrest records might hinder its ability to maintain fidelity (bond) insurance since it offered no proof to this effect.

Even where there is no direct evidence that an employer used an arrest record in an employment decision, a pre-employment inquiry regarding arrest records may violate Title VII. It is generally presumed that an employer only asks questions which he/she deems relevant to the employment decision. Gregory v. Litton Systems, 316 F. Supp. At 403-404. Noting that information which is obtained is likely to be used, the court in Litton enjoined the employer from making any pre-employment inquiries regarding arrests which did not result in convictions. Id.[8] But see EEOC f. Local 638, 532 F.2d 821 (2d Cir. 1976) (inquiry not invalidated where there was no evidence that union actually rejected applicants who had been arrested but not convicted); Jimerson v. Kisco, 404 F. Supp. 338 (E.D. Mo. 1975) (court upheld discharge for falsifying information regarding arrest record on a pre-employment application without considering the inquiry itself violated Title VII).[9] Numerous states have specifically prohibited or advised against pre-employment inquiries in their fair employment laws due to the possible misuse of this information.[10]

2. The Alleged Conduct Must Be Related to the Position Sought

As discussed above, an arrest record may be used as evidence of conduct upon which an employer makes an employment decision. An employer may deny employment opportunities to persons based on any prior conduct which indicates that they would be unfit for the position in question, whether that conduct is evidenced by an arrest, conviction or other information provided to the employer. It is the conduct, not he arrest or conviction per se, which the employer may consider in relation to the position sought. The considerations relevant to the determination of whether the alleged Conduct demonstrates unfitness for the particular job were set forth in Green v. Missouri

---

[8] Furthermore, potential applicants who have arrest records may be discouraged from applying for positions which require them to supply this information, thus creating a "chilling effect" on the Black applicant pool. Carter v. Gallagher, 452 F.2d at 330-331; Reynolds v. Sheet Metal Workers, Local 102, 498 F. Supp. At 964 n.12, 966 n.13, 967, 973; Commission Decision Nos. 76-138, 76-87, 76-17, 74-90, 74-25 and 74-02, CCH EEOC Decisions (1983) !! 6700, 6665, 612, 6423, 6400, 6386 and Commission Decision Nos. 74-1005 and 71-1950, CCH EEOC Decisions (1973) !! 6350 and 6274, respectively.

[9] Note also that in Walls v. City of Petersburg, 895 F.2d 188, 52 EPD ! 39,602 (4th Cir. 1990), the court upheld an employer's policy of making an employment inquiry regarding the arrest records of employees' immediate family members. The court determined that under Atonio, the plaintiff was obligated to show not only that Blacks were more likely to have "negative" responses to this question, but also that the employer made adverse employment decisions based on such responses.

[10] New York, Hawaii, Oregon, Wisconsin, New Jersey, Ohio, Virginia, District of Columbia, California, Maryland, Minnesota, Utah, Washington, West Virginia, Arizona, Colorado, Idaho, Massachusetts, Michigan, Mississippi.

Pacific Railroad Co., 549 F.2d 1158, 1160, 13 EPD ¶ 11, 579 (8ᵗʰ Cir. 1977) and reiterated in the February 4, 1987 Statement on Convictions, page 2:

1. the nature and gravity of the offense or offenses;

2. the time that has passed since the conviction[11] (or in this case, arrest) .; and

3. the nature of the job held or sought.

See also Carter v. Maloney Trucking and Storage Inc., 631 F.2d 40, 43, 24 EPD ¶ 31,348 (5ᵗʰ Cir. 1980) (employer refused to rehire an ex-employee who had murdered a co-worker, not solely because of his conviction, but because he was a dangerous person and friends of the murdered man might try to retaliate against him while he was on the job); Osborne v. Cleland, 620 F.2d 195, 22 EPD on a charge of "sexual procurement" was unfit to be a nursing assistant in a psychiatric ward); Lane v. Inman, 509 F.2d 184 (5ᵗʰ Cir. 1975) (city ordinance which prohibited the issuance of taxicab driver permits to persons convicted of smuggling marijuana was "so obviously job related" that "it could not be held to be unlawful race discrimination," irrespective of any adverse impact); EEOC v. Carolina Freight, 723 F. Supp. 734, 52 EPD ¶ (S.D. Fla. 1989) (criminal history was related to position of truck driver who transported valuable property); McCray v. Alexander, 30 EPD ¶ 33,219 (D. Colo. 1982), aff'd 38 EPD ¶35,509 (10ᵗʰ Cir. 1985) (supervisory guard was discharged for killing a motorist, while off-duty, in a traffic dispute because employer concluded that, despite his acquittal, the conduct showed poor judgment on the use of deadly force).

Where the position sought is "security sensitive," particularly where it involves enforcing the law or preventing crime, courts tend to closely scrutinize evidence of prior criminal conduct of applicants. US. V. City of Chicago, 411 F. Supp. 217, 11 EPD ¶ 10,597 (N.D. Ill. 1976), aff'd in rel. part, 549 F.2d 415, 13 EPD ¶ 11,380 (7ᵗʰ Cir. 1977), on remand, 437 F. Supp. 256 (N.D. Ill. 1977) (applicants for the police department were disqualified for prior convictions for "serious" offenses); Richardson v. Hotel Corporation of America, 332 F. Supp. 519, 4 EPD ¶ 7666 (E.D. La. 1971), aff'd mem., 468 F.2d 951, 4 EPD ¶ 7666 (5ᵗʰ Cir. 1972) (bellman was discharged after his conviction for theft and receipt of stolen goods was discovered since bellmen had access to guests; rooms and was not subject to inspection when carrying packages); Haynie v. Chupka, 17 FEP Cases 267, 271 (S.D. Ohio 1976) (police department permissibly made inquires regarding arrest records and other evidence of prior criminal conduct).[12] (See Examples 3 and 4.)

Even where the employment at issue is not a law enforcement position or one which gives the employee easy access to the possessions of others, close scrutiny of an applicant's character and prior conduct is appropriate where an employer is responsible for the safety and/or well being of other persons. Osborne v. Cleland, 620 F.2d 195 (8ᵗʰ Cir. 1975) (psychiatric nursing assistant); Lane v. Inman, 509 F.2d 184 (taxi driver). In these instances, the facts would have to be examined closely in order to determine the probability that an applicant would pose a threat to the safety and well being of others. (See Examples 5 and 6).

3. Evaluating the Likelihood that the Applicant Engaged in the Conduct Alleged

---

[11] But see EEOC v. Carolina Freight Carriers, 723 F. Supp. At 753 (court upheld trucking company's lifetime bar to employment of drivers who had been incarcerated for theft crimes since EEOC did not produce evidence that a 5-10 year bar would be an equally effective alternative). Note also that the court in Carolina Freight specifically rejected the Eighth Circuit's reasoning in Green, cautioning that Green could be construed too broadly. 723 F. Supp. At 752.

[12] See also Quarrels v. Brown, 48 EPD ! 38,641 (D.C. Mich. 1988) (recent conviction was related to position of corrections officer). Note however, that this action was brought under 42 USC. S 1983, rather than Title VII, and plaintiff alleged that he was discriminated against because he was an ex-offender, not because the policy adversely affected a protected group.

The cases cited above illustrate the job-relatedness of certain conduct to specific positions. In cases alleging race discrimination based on the use of arrest records as opposed to convictions, courts have generally required not only job-relatedness, but also a showing that the alleged conduct was actually committed. In <u>City of Cairo v. Illinois Fair Employment Practice Commission, et al.</u>, 8 EPD ¶ 9682, the court held that where applicants sought to become police officers, they could not be absolutely barred from appointment solely because they had been arrested, as distinguished from convicted. <u>See also</u> Commission Decision No. 76-87, CCH EEOC Decisions (1983) ¶ 6665 (potential police officer could not be rejected based on one arrest five years earlier for riding in a stolen car since there was no conviction and the applicant asserted that he did not know that the car was stolen). Similarly, in Decision No. 74083, CCH EEOC Decision (1983) ¶ 6424, the Commission found no business justification for an employer's unconditional termination of all employees with arrest records (all five employees terminated were Black), purportedly to cut down on thefts in the workplace. The employer could produce no evidence that the employee had been involved in any of the thefts or that persons who are arrested, but not convicted, are prone toward crime. Commission Decision No. 74-92, CCH EEOC Decisions (1983) ¶ 6424.

An arrest record does no more than raise a suspicion that an applicant may have engaged in a particular type of conduct.[13] Thus, the investigator must determine whether the applicant is likely to step because it requires the employer either to accept the employee's denial or to attempt to obtain additional information and evaluate his/her credibility. An employer need not conduct an informal "trial" or an extensive investigation to determine an applicant's or employee's guilt or innocence. However, the employer may not perfunctorily "allow the person an opportunity to explain" and ignore the explanation where the person's claims could easily be verified by a phone call, i.e., to a previous employer or a police department. The employer is required to allow the person a meaningful opportunity to explain the circumstances of the arrest(s) and to make a reasonable effort to determine whether the explanation is credible before eliminating him/her from employment opportunities.[14] (See Examples 1, 4, 5 and 6.)

III. Examples

The following examples are provided to illustrate the process by which arrest record charges should be evaluated.

> Example 1: Wilma, a Black female, applies to Buss Inc. in Highway City for a position as a bus driver. In response to a pre-employment inquiry, Wilma states that she was arrested two years earlier for driving while intoxicated. Bus Inc. rejects Wilma, despite her acquittal after trial. But Inc. does not accept her denial of the conduct alleged and concludes that Wilma was acquitted only because the breatholizer test which was administered to her at the time of her arrest was not administered in accordance with proper police procedures and was therefore inadmissible at trial. Witnesses at Wilma's trial testified that after being stopped for reckless driving, Wilma staggered from the car and had alcohol on her breath. Wilma's rejection is justified because the conduct underlying the arrest, driving while intoxicated, is clearly related to the safe performance of the duties of a bus driver; it occurred fairly recently; and there was no indication of subsequent rehabilitation.

Contrast Example Number 1 with the facts below.

---

[13] The employer's suspicion may be raised by an arrest record just as it would be negative comments about an applicant's conduct made by a previous employer or a personal reference.

[14] Although the number of arrests is not determinative (see <u>Litton</u>), it may be relevant in making a credibility determination.

Example 2: Lola, a Black female, applies to Buss Inc. for a position as a bus driver. In response to an inquiry whether she had ever been arrested, Lola states that she was arrested five years earlier for fraud in unemployment benefits. Lola admits that she committed the crime alleged. She explains that she received unemployment benefits shortly after her husband died and her expenses increased. During this period, she worked part-time for minimum wage because her unemployment check amounted to slightly less than the monthly rent for her meager apartment. She did not report the income to the State Unemployment Board for fear that her payments would be reduced and that she would not be able to feed her three young children. After her arrest, she agreed to, and did, repay the state. Bus Inc. rejected Lola. Lola's rejection violated Title VII. The commission of fraud in the unemployment system does not constitute a business justification for the rejection of an applicant for the position of bus driver. The type of crime which Lola committed is totally unrelated to her ability to safely, efficiently and/or courteously drive a bus. Furthermore, the arrest is not recent.

Example 3: Tom, a Black male, applies to Lodge City for a position as a police officer. The arrest rate for Blacks is substantially disproportionate to that of Whites in Lodge City. In response to an arrest record inquiry, Tom states that he was arrested three years earlier for burglary. Tom is interviewed and asked to explain the circumstances surrounding his arrest. Tom admits that although the burglary charge was dismissed for lack of sufficient evidence, he did commit the crime. He claims, however, that he is a changed man, having matured since then. Lodge City rejects Tom. Police officers are: 1) entrusted with protecting the public; 2) authorized to enter nearly and dwelling under the appropriate circumstances; and 3) often responsible for transporting valuables which are confiscated as evidence. The department is, therefore, justified in declining to take the chance that Tom has reformed. Even if the department is completely satisfied that Tom has reformed, it may reject him because his credibility as a witness in court could be severely damaged if he were asked about his own arrest and the surrounding circumstances while testifying against a person whom he has arrested. Since an essential element of police work is the ability to effect an arrest and to credibly testify against the defendant in court, the department would have two separate business justifications for rejecting Tom.

The above example is contracted with circumstances under which an arrest record would not constitute ground for rejection.

Example 4: John, a Black male, applies to Lodge City for the same position as does Tom. John was arrested three years earlier for burglary. The charges were dismissed. Lodge City eliminates John from consideration without further investigation and will not consider the surrounding circumstances of the arrest. If allowed to explain, John could establish that his arrest was a case of mistaken identity and that someone else, who superficially fit John's description, was convicted of the crime for which John was initially charged. Since the facts indicate that John did not commit the conduct alleged in the arrest record, Lodge City has not carried its burden of proving a business justification for John's rejection.

Example 5: David, a Black male, applies for a teaching position in West High School. In response to a pre-employment inquiry, David states that he was arrested two years earlier for statutory rape, having been accused of seducing a seventeen-year old student in his class when he taught at another high school The charges were dismissed. West High rejects David. David relies on <u>Litton</u> to establish a <u>prima facie</u> case of race discrimination, and West High is unable to rebut the case with more current, ac curate or specific statistics. David denies that there is any truth to the charge. West High decides to conduct a further investigation and learns that David was arrested after another teacher found him engaged in sexual activity with Ann, one of his students, in the school's locker room. This event occurred on Ann's eighteenth birthday, but in the confusion of the arrest, no one realized that Ann had just reached the age of majority. Ann's parents and other teachers believed that David had seduced Ann, who has a schoolgirl "crush" on him, prior to her eighteenth birthday. However, since Ann would not testify against David, the charges had been dismissed. West High may reject David. Irrespective of Ann's age, West High is justified in attempting to protect its students from teachers who may make sexual advances toward them. Although he might not have been guilty of statutory rape, his conduct was unbefitting a teacher.

The above example is contracted to the following circumstances.

Example 6: Paul, a Black male, applies for the same position as does David. Paul was arrested two years earlier for statutory rape, having been accused of seducing a seventeen year old student in his class at another high school. West High eliminates Paul from consideration without further investigation and refuses to consider the surrounding circumstances of the arrest. When filing his complaint, Paul states that when he taught at the other high school, he befriended a troubled student in his class, Alice, who was terrified of her disciplinarian parents. Paul insists that he never touched Alice in any improper manner and that on the day before his arrest, Alice confided in him that she had become pregnant by her seventeen-year old boyfriend, Peter, and was afraid to tell her parents for fear that her father would kill him. Paul states that the charges were dismissed because the district attorney did not believe Alice's statements. The district attorney and the principal of the high school, Ms. P., confirm Paul's assessment of Alice. Ms. P; states that Peter confided in her that he was the father of Alice's baby and that Alice had assured him that nothing sexual had ever happened between her and Paul. Ms. P. states that there were indications that Alice's father was abusive, that he had beaten her into giving him the name of someone to blame for the pregnancy and that Alice thought that Paul could handle her father better than could Peter. Since Paul denied committing the conduct alleged and his explanation was well supported by the district attorney and his former employer, West High has not demonstrated a business justification for rejecting Paul.

The examples discussed above demonstrate that whereas an employer may consider a conviction as conclusive evidence that a person has committed the crime alleged, arrests can only be considered as a means of "triggering" further inquiry into that person's character or prior conduct. After considering all of the circumstances, if the employer reasonably concludes that the applicant's or employee's conduct is evidence that he or she cannot be trusted to perform the duties of the position in question, the employer may reject or terminate that person.

_____

Date

Approved: _____

Evan J Kemp, Jr.

Chairman

Notice N-915 (7/29/87)

1. <u>SUBJECT</u>: Policy statement on the use of statistics in charges involving the exclusion of individuals with conviction records from employment

2. <u>PURPOSE</u>: This policy statement sets forth the commission's view as to the appropriate statistics to be used in evaluating an employer's policy of refusing to hire individuals with conviction records.

3. <u>EFFECTIVE DATE</u>: July 29, 1987

4. <u>EXPIRATION DATE</u>: January 29, 1988

5. <u>ORIGINATOR</u>: title VII.EPA Division, Office of Legal Counsel.

6. <u>INSTRUCTIONS</u>: insert behind §S 604 of EEOC Compliance Manual, Volume II

7. <u>SUBJECT MATTER</u>:

INTRODUCTION

<u>Green v. Missouri Pacific Railroad Company</u>, 523 F.2d 1290, 10 EPD ¶ 10,314 (8th Cir. 1975), is the leading Title VII case on the issue of conviction records. In <u>Green</u>, the court held that the defendant's policy of refusing employment to any person convicted of a crime other than a minor traffic offense had an adverse impact on Black applicants and was not justified by business necessity. In a second appeal following remand, the court upheld the district court's injunctive order prohibiting the defendant from using an applicant's conviction record as an absolute bar to employment but allowing it to consider a prior criminal record as long as it constituted a business necessity. <u>Green v. Missouri Pacific Railroad Company</u>,549 F.2d 1158, 1160, 13 EPD ¶ 11,579 (8th Cir. 1977). <u>See</u> <u>also</u> Commission Decision No. 72-1497, CCH EEOC Decisions (1973) ¶ 6352, and Commission Decision Nos. 74-89, 78-10, 78-35, and 80-10, CCH EEOC Decisions (1983) ¶¶ 6418, 6715, 6720, and 6822, respectively.

It is the Commission's position that an employer's policy or practice of excluding individuals from employment on the basis of their conviction records has an adverse impact on Blacks [1]/ and Hispanics [2]/ in light of statistics showing that they are convicted at a rate disproportionately greater than their representation in the population. Policy Statement on the Issue of Conviction Records Under Title VII (February 4, 1987). However, when the employer can present more narrowly drawn statistics showing

Either that Blacks and Hispanics are <u>not</u> convicted at a disproportionately greater rate or that there is no adverse impact in its own hiring process resulting from the convictions policy, then a no cause determination would be appropriate.

1. Where the Employer's Policy is Not Crime-Specific

An employer's policy of excluding from employment all persons convicted of any crime is likely to create an adverse impact for Blacks and Hispanics based on national and regional conviction rate

---

[1] <u>See</u>, <u>e.g.</u>, Commission Decision No. 72-1497, CCH EEOC Decisions (1973) ! 6352, and Commission Decision Nos. 74-89, 78-10, 78-35, and 80-10, CCH EEOC Decisions (1983) !! 6418, 6715, 6720, and 6822 respectively.

[2] <u>See</u> Commission Decision No. 78-03, CCH EEOC Decisions (1983) ¶ 6714.

statistics. However, it is open to the respondent/employer to present more narrow local, regional, or applicant flow data, showing that the policy probably will not have an adverse impact on its applicant pool and/or in fact does not have an adverse impact on the pool. As Supreme Court stated,

> Although a statistical showing of disproportionate impact need not always be based on an analysis of the characteristics of actual applicants, Dothard v. Rawlinson, 433 U.S. 321, 330, evidence showing that the figures for the general population might not accurately reflect the pool of qualified job applicants undermines the significance of such figures. Teamsters v. United States, 431 U.S. 324, 340 n. 20.

New York City Transit Authority v. Beazer, 440 U.S. 568, 586 n. 29, 19 EPD ¶ 9027 at p. 6315 (1979). See also Costa v. Markey, 30 EPD ¶ 33,173 at p. 27,638 (1st Cir. 1982), vacated on other grounds, 706 F.2d 796, 32 EPD ¶ 32,622 (1st Cir.), cert. denied, 104 S. Ct. 547, 32 EPD ¶ 33,955 (1983).

If the employer provides applicant flow data, information should be sought to assure that the employer's applicant pool was not artificially limited by discouragement. For example, if many Blacks with conviction records did not apply for a particular job because they knew of the employer's policy and they therefore expected to be rejected, then applicant flow data would not be an accurate reflection of the conviction policy's actual effect. See Dothard v. Rowlinson, 433 US 321, 330 (1977). (Section 608, Recruitment, of Volume II of the Compliance Manual will provide a more detailed discussion of when and how to investigate for discouragement.

2. Where the Employer's Policy is Crime-Specific

In the past, when the Commission has evaluated an employer's "no convictions' policy dealing with a subcategory of crimes; e.g., theft, robbery, or drug-related crimes; the Commission has relied upon national or regional conviction statistics for crimes as a whole. See, e.g., Commission Decision No. 73-0257, CCH EEOC Decisions (1973) ! 6372, and Commission Decision Nos. 76-110 and 80-17, CCH EEOC Decisions (1983) !! 6676 and 6809, respectively. However, these statistics only show a probability of adverse impact for Blacks and Hispanics, while more narrow data may show no adverse impact.

If the employer can present more narrow regional or local data on conviction rates for all crimes showing that Blacks and Hispanics are not convicted at disproportionately higher rates, then a no cause determination would be proper. [3]/ Alternatively, the employer may present national, regional, or local data on conviction rates for the particular crime which is targeted in its crime-specific convictions policy. If such data shows no adverse impact, then a no cause determination would be appropriate. Finally, the employer can use applicant flow data to demonstrate that its conviction policy has not resulted in the exclusion from employment of a disproportionately high number of Blacks and Hispanics.

[Signed July 29, 1987 by Clarence Thomas]

---

[3] However, if even more narrow statistics, such as regional or local crime-specific data, show adverse impact, then a cause finding would be appropriate absent a justifying business necessity.

Notice N-915 (2/4/87)

1. <u>SUBJECT</u>: Policy Statement on the Issue of Conviction Records under Title VII of the Civil Rights Act of 1964, as amended, 42 U.S.C. § 2000e <u>et seq</u>. (1982).

2. <u>PURPOSE</u>: This policy statement sets forth the Commission's revised procedure for determining the existence of a business necessity justifying, for purposes of Title VII, the exclusion of an individual from employment on the basis of a conviction record.

3. <u>EFFECTIVE DATE</u>: February 27, 1987.

4. <u>EXPIRATION DATE</u>: September 15, 1987.

5. <u>ORIGINATOR</u>: Office of Legal Counsel.

6. <u>INSTRUCTIONS</u>: File behind page 604- 36 of EEOC Compliance Manual, Volume II, Section 604, Theories of Discrimination.

7. <u>SUBJECT MATTER</u>:

At the Commission meeting of November 26, 1985, the Commission approved a modification of its existing policy with respect to the manner in which a business necessity is established for denying an individual employment because of a conviction record. The modification, which is set forth below, does not alter the Commission's underlying position that an employer's policy or practice of excluding individuals from employment on the basis of their conviction records has an adverse impact on Blacks[1] and Hispanics[2] in light of statistics showing that they are convicted at a rate disproportionately greater than their representation in the population. Consequently, the Commission has held and continues to hold that such a policy or practice is unlawful under Title VII in the absence of a justifying business necessity. [3]

However, the Commission has revised the previous requirements for establishing business necessity [4] in the following manner. Where a charge involves an allegation that the Respondent employer [5]

---

[1] See, e.g., Commission Decision No. 72-1497, CCH EEOC Decisions (1973) ¶ 6352, and Commission Decision Nos. 74-89, 78-10, 78-35, and 80-10, CCH EEOC Decisions (1983) ¶¶ 6418, 6715, 6720, and 6822, respectively.

[2] See Commission Decision No. 78-03, CCH EEOC Decisions (1983) ¶ 6714.

[3] See, e.g., Commission decisions cited supra notes 1-2.

[4] Prior to this modification, for an employer to establish a business necessity justifying excluding an individual from employment because of a conviction record, the evidence had to show that the offense for which the applicant or employee was convicted was job-related. If the offense was not job-related, a disqualification based on the conviction alone violated Title VII. However, even if the offense were determined to be job-related, the employer had to examine other relevant factors to determine whether the conviction affected the individual's ability to perform the job in a manner consistent with the safe and efficient operation of the employer's business. The factors identified by the Commission to be considered by an employer included:

    1.   The number of offenses and the circumstances of each offense for which the individual was convicted;

    2.   The length of time intervening between the conviction for the offense and the employment decision;

    3.   The individual's employment history; and

    4.   The individual's efforts at rehabilitation.

Footnote 4 continued:

failed to hire or terminated the employment of the Charging Party as a result of a conviction policy or practice that has an adverse impact on the protected class to which the Charging Party belongs, The Respondent must show that it considered these three factors to determine whether its decision was justified by business necessity:

1. The nature and gravity of the offense or offenses:

2. The time that has passed since the conviction and/or completion of the sentence; and

3. The nature of the job held or sought. [6]

This procedure condenses the Commission's previous standard for business necessity, substituting a one-step analysis for the prior two-step procedure and retaining some but not all of the factors previously considered. [7] The modification principally eliminates the need to consider an individual's employment history and efforts at rehabilitation. However, consideration is still given to the job-relatedness of a conviction, covered by the first and third factors, and to the time frame involved, covered by the second factor. Moreover, the first factor encompasses consideration of the circumstances of the offense(s) for which an individual was convicted as well as the number of offenses.

The Commission continues to hold that, where there is evidence of adverse impact, an absolute bar to employment based on the mere fact that an individual has a conviction record is unlawful under Title VII. [8] The Commission's position on this issue is supported by the weight of judicial authority [9]

See, e.g., Commission Decision No. 78-35, CCH EEOC Decisions (1983) ! 6720.

Thus, under the previous procedure, business necessity was established by means of a two-step process: first, by showing that the conviction was job-related; then, by separately demonstrating that the conviction would affect the individual's ability to safety and efficiently perform the job upon consideration of the four factors enumerated above.

[5] Although the term "employer" is used herein, the Commission's position on this issue applies to all entities covered by Title VII. See e.g., Commission Decision No. 77-23, CCH EEOC Decisions (1983) ¶ 6710 (union's policy of denying membership to persons with conviction records unlawfully discriminated against Blacks).

[6] The Commission's revised business necessity analysis follows a decision by the United States Court of Appeals for the Eighth Circuit in the Green v. Missouri Pacific Railroad Company case. Green, 523 F.2d 1290, 10 EPD ¶ 10,314 (8th Cir. 1975), it the leading Title VII case on the issue of conviction records. In that case, the court held that the defendant's absolute policy of refusing employment to any person convicted of a crime other than a minor traffic offense had an adverse impact on Black applicants and was not justified by business necessity. On a second appeal in that case, following remand, the court upheld the district court's injunctive order prohibiting the defendant from using an applicant's conviction record as an absolute bar to employment but allowing it to consider a prior criminal record as a factor in making individual hiring decisions as long as the defendant took into account "the nature and gravity of the offense or offenses, the time that has passed since the conviction and/or completion of sentence, and the nature of the job for which the applicant has applied. Green v. Missouri Pacific Railroad Company, 549 F.2d 1158, 1160, 13 EPD ¶ 11,579 (8th Cir. 1977).

[7] See discussion supra note 4.

[8] See, e.g., Commission Decision No. 78-35, CCH EEOC Decisions (1983) ¶ 6720.

[9] See Green, 523 F.2d at 1298; Carter v. Gallagher, 452 F.2d 315, 3 EPD ¶ 8335 (8th Cir. 1971), cert. denied, 406 US 950, 4 EPD ¶ 7818 (1972) (brought under 42 U.S.C. §§ 1981 and 1983); and Richardson v. Hotel Corporation of America, 332 F. Supp. 519, 4 EPD ¶ 7666 (E.D. La. 1971), aff'd mem., 468 F.2d 951, 5 EPD ¶ 8101 (5th Cir. 1972). See also Hill v. United States Postal Service, 522 F. Supp. 1283 (S.D.N.Y. 1981); Craig v. Department of Health, Education, and Welfare, 508 F. Supp. 1055 (W.D. Mo. 1981); and Cross v. United States Postal Service, 483 F. Supp. 1050 (E.D. Mo. 1979), aff'd in relevant part, 639 F.2d 409, 25 EPD ¶ 31,594 (8th Cir. 1981).

It should be noted that the modified procedure does not affect charges alleging disparate treatment on a prohibited basis in an employer's use of a conviction record as a disqualification for employment. A charge brought under the disparate treatment theory of discrimination is one where, for example, an employer allegedly rejects Black applicants who have conviction records but does not reject similarly situated White applicants.

With respect to conviction charges that are affected by this modification—that is, those raising the issue of adverse impact—Commission decisions that apply the previous standard are no longer available as Commission decision precedent for establishing business necessity. To the extent that such prior decisions are inconsistent with the position set forth herein, they are expressly overruled.

Questions concerning the application of the Commission's revised business necessity standard to the facts of a particular charge should be directed to the Regional Attorney for the Commission office in which the charge was filed.

[Signed 2-4-87 by Clarence Thomas]

_____   Approved:_____

Date   Clarence Thomas

                                                               Chairman

Federal Court Locations for Criminal Records

Identifiers and Case Files for U.S. District Court Locations

Listed in order by state are brief summaries for U.S. District Courts, and U.S. Bankruptcy Courts. Summaries include the district's website URL, the district's VCIS phone numbers if available, what personal identifiers appear on search results if any, and duration before closed case files are shipped to the Federal Records Center for archiving. Also shown are the division locations within the district. In most cases, a court's website reveals if specific counties are under its jurisdiction.

Alabama Middle District www.almd.uscourts.gov
Search results do not include DOB or SSN. **Divisions-** Dothan, Montgomery, Opelika.

Alabama Northern District www.alnd.uscourts.gov
Search results do not include SSN or DOB. Case files sent to archives 18 months after closed. **Divisions-** Birmingham, Gadsden, Huntsville, Jasper.

Alabama Southern District www.als.uscourts.gov
Search results do not include SSN, DOB. **Divisions-** Mobile (South), Selma (North).

Alaska www.akd.uscourts.gov
VCIS: 907-222-6940. Search results do not include SSN or DOB. Tried case files sent to Anchorage Records Center. If the case did not go to trial, file sent to Seattle Records Center. **Divisions-** Anchorage, Fairbanks, Juneau, Ketchikan, Nome.

Arizona www.azd.uscourts.gov
Search results do not include SSN or DOB. Case files sent to archives 5 years after closed. **Divisions-** Phoenix, Prescott, Tucson.

Arkansas Eastern District www.are.uscourts.gov
Search results do not include SSN or DOB. Case files sent to archives 4 years after closed. **Divisions-** Batesville, Helena, Jonesboro, Little Rock, Pine Bluff.

Arkansas Western District www.arwd.uscourts.gov
Search results do not include SSN or DOB. Closed cases sent to archives after 5 years. **Divisions-** El Dorado, Fayetteville, Fort Smith, Hot Springs, Texarkana.

California Central District www.cacd.uscourts.gov
Search results do not include SSN or DOB. Case files sent to archives 2-3 years after closed. **Divisions-** Los Angeles (Western), Riverside (Eastern), Santa Ana (Southern).

California Eastern District www.caed.uscourts.gov
Search results do not include SSN or DOB. Case files sent to archives at varying intervals, usually as time permits. **Divisions-** Fresno, Sacramento.

California Northern District www.cand.uscourts.gov
Search results do not include SSN or DOB, but office can confirm or deny. Case files sent to archives 6 months after closed. **Divisions-** Oakland, San Francisco, San Jose.

California Southern District www.casd.uscourts.gov
Search results do not include SSN or DOB. When local space becomes unavailable, closed cases are transferred to archives. **Location -** San Diego.

Colorado www.co.uscourts.gov
Search results do not include SSN or DOB. Closed records sent to archives at irregular intervals. **Location-** Denver.

Connecticut www.ctd.uscourts.gov
Search results do not include SSN or DOB. **Divisions-** Bridgeport, Hartford, New Haven.

Delaware www.ded.uscourts.gov
Search results do not include SSN or DOB. Closed cases are not sent to the archives for a minimum of 6 months. **Location-** Wilmington.

District of Columbia www.dcd.uscourts.gov
Search: Criminal search results include DOB; civil returns name only. Case files sent to archives 5 years after closed.

Florida Middle District www.flmd.uscourts.gov
Search results do not include SSN or DOB. Case files sent to archives 3 years after closed. **Divisions-** Fort Myers, Jacksonville, Ocala, Orlando, Tampa.

Florida Northern District www.flnd.uscourts.gov
Search results do not include SSN or DOB. Closed cases sent to archives depending on case type. **Divisions-** Gainesville, Panama City, Pensacola, Tallahassee.

Florida Southern District www.flsd.uscourts.gov
Search: Recent cases do not include SSN or DOB. Case files sent to archives 5 years after closed, then sent to Atlanta Records Center. **Divisions-** Fort Lauderdale, Fort Pierce, Key West, Miami, West Palm Beach.

Georgia Middle District www.gamd.uscourts.gov
Search results do not include SSN or DOB. Case files sent to archives 2 years after closed. **Divisions-** Albany/Americus, Athens, Columbus, Macon, Thomasville, Valdosta.

Georgia Northern District www.gand.uscourts.gov
Search results include last 4 SSN digits. **Divisions-** Atlanta, Gainesville, Newnan, Rome.

Georgia Southern District www.gasd.uscourts.gov
Search results do not include SSN or DOB. **Divisions-** Augusta, Brunswick, Savannah.

Guam www.gud.uscourts.gov
Search results include last 4 SSN digits only. All closed case records maintained here.

Hawaii www.hid.uscourts.gov
Search results do not include SSN or DOB. Case files sent to archives 1 year after closed.

Idaho www.id.uscourts.gov
Search results do not include SSN or DOB. **Divisions-** Boise, Coeur d' Alene, Moscow, Pocatello.

Illinois Central District www.ilcd.uscourts.gov
Search results do not include SSN or DOB; court will confirm if identifiers provided in request. Case files sent to archives 5-7 years after closed. **Divisions-** Peoria, Rock Island, Springfield, Urbana.

Illinois Northern District www.ilnd.uscourts.gov
Search results do not include SSN or DOB. Case files sent to archives 1-5 years after closed. **Divisions-** Chicago (Eastern), Rockford (Western).

Illinois Southern District www.ilsd.uscourts.gov
Search results do not include SSN or DOB. Case files sent to archives as deemed necessary. **Divisions-** Benton, East St Louis.

Indiana Northern District www.innd.uscourts.gov/fortwayne.shtml
Search results do not include SSN or DOB. **Divisions-** Fort Wayne, Hammond, Lafayette, South Bend.

Indiana Southern District www.insd.uscourts.gov
Search results include SSN or DOB year for criminal cases; civil includes only last 4 SSN digits. **Divisions-** Evansville, Indianapolis, New Albany, Terre Haute.

Iowa Northern District www.iand.uscourts.gov
Search results do not include SSN or DOB or any personal identifiers. **Divisions-** Cedar Rapids (Eastern), Sioux City (Western).

Iowa Southern District www.iasd.uscourts.gov
Search results do not include SSN or DOB. Case files are all electronic; never purged. **Divisions-** Council Bluffs (Western), Davenport (Eastern), Des Moines (Central).

Kansas www.ksd.uscourts.gov
Search results do not include SSN or DOB. Case files sent to archives 12 months after closed. **Divisions-** Kansas City, Topeka, Wichita.

Kentucky Eastern District www.kyed.uscourts.gov
Search results do not include SSN or DOB. Case files sent to archives 5 years after closed. **Divisions-** Ashland, Covington, Frankfort, Lexington, London, Pikeville.

Kentucky Western District www.kywd.uscourts.gov
Search results do not include SSN or DOB. **Divisions-** Bowling Green, Louisville, Owensboro, Paducah.

Louisiana Eastern District www.laed.uscourts.gov
Search results do not include SSN or DOB. Case files sent to archives 6 months after closed. **Location-** New Orleans.

Louisiana Middle District www.lamd.uscourts.gov
Search results do not include SSN or DOB but pre-2003 crim recs may have DOBs. Case files sent to archives 1 year after closed. **Location-** Baton Rouge.

Louisiana Western District www.lawd.uscourts.gov
Search results do not include SSN or DOB. Cases files now all electronic; never purged. **Divisions-** Alexandria, Lafayette, Lake Charles, Monroe, Shreveport.

Maine www.med.uscourts.gov
Search results include partial DOB; no SSN. There is no set date when closed case files sent to archives. **Divisions-** Bangor, Portland.

Maryland Northern District www.mdd.uscourts.gov
Search results do not include SSN or DOB. Case files sent to archives 3 years after closed. **Location-** Baltimore.

Maryland Southern District www.mdd.uscourts.gov
Search results do not include SSN or DOB. Case files sent to archives 3 years after closed. **Location-** Greenbelt.

Massachusetts www.mad.uscourts.gov
Search results do not include SSN or DOB. Criminal case files sent to archives 4 years after closed; 3 years for civil. **Divisions-** Boston, Springfield, Worcester.

Michigan Eastern District www.mied.uscourts.gov
Search results do not include SSN or DOB. Closed cases are kept electronically; paper files sent to archives. **Divisions-** Ann Arbor, Bay City, Detroit, Flint.

Michigan Western District www.miwd.uscourts.gov
Search results do not include SSN or DOB. Closed electronic cases not purged. **Divisions-** Grand Rapids, Kalamazoo, Lansing, Marquette-Northern.

Minnesota www.mnd.uscourts.gov
Search results do not include SSN or DOB. **Divisions-** Duluth, Minneapolis, St Paul.

Mississippi Northern District www.msnd.uscourts.gov
Search results do not include SSN or DOB. Civil cases sent to archives 5 years after disposition; 10 years for criminal. **Divisions-** Aberdeen-Eastern, Delta, Greenville, Oxford-Northern.

Mississippi Southern District www.mssd.uscourts.gov
Search results do not include SSN or DOB. **Divisions-** Eastern, Hattiesburg, Jackson, Southern, Western.

Missouri Eastern District www.moed.uscourts.gov
Search results do not include SSN or DOB, but they may verify over phone. Case files sent to archives 4 years after closed. **Divisions-** Cape Girardeau, St Louis.

Missouri Western District www.mow.uscourts.gov
Search results do not include SSN or DOB. Case files sent to archives as deemed necessary. **Divisions-** Jefferson City - Central, Joplin - Southwestern, Kansas City - Western, Springfield-Southern, St Joseph.

Montana www.mtd.uscourts.gov
Search results do not include SSN or DOB. Case files sent to archives 4-5 years after closed. **Divisions-** Billings, Butte, Great Falls, Helena, Missoula.

Nebraska www.ned.uscourts.gov
Search results do not include SSN or DOB or gender; Pre-2004 cases may provide some identifiers. Case files sent to archives approx. 1 year after closed. **Divisions-** Lincoln, North Platte, Omaha.

Nevada www.nvd.uscourts.gov
Search results do not include SSN or DOB. **Divisions-** Las Vegas, Reno.

New Hampshire www.nhd.uscourts.gov
Search results do not include SSN or DOB. Paper case files sent to archives 1 years after closed; electronic maintained indefinitely **Location-** Concord.

New Jersey www.njd.uscourts.gov
Search: Court will examine identifiers for possible match. Closed case files sent to archives irregularly. **Divisions-** Camden, Newark, Trenton.

New Mexico www.nmcourt.fed.us/web/DCDOCS/dcindex.html
Search results do not include SSN or DOB on civil; older criminal cases may include last 4 SSN digits. Case files sent to archives 6 months after closed. **Location-** Albuquerque.

New York Eastern District www.nyed.uscourts.gov
Search results do not include SSN or DOB after 2003 **Divisions-** Brooklyn, Central Islip.

New York Northern District www.nynd.uscourts.gov
Search results include last 4 SSN digits, also birth year. Results do not include SSN or DOB if case after 2003. Case files sent to archives 1 year after closed. **Divisions-** Albany, Binghamton, Syracuse, Utica.

New York Southern District www.nysd.uscourts.gov
Search results do not include SSN or DOB, though DOB may appear on records prior to 2004. Case files sent to archives 5 years after closed (due to construction, closed cases were recently purged.) **Divisions-** New York City, White Plains.

New York Western District www.nywd.uscourts.gov
Search results do not include SSN or DOB. Closed electronic cases are not purged. **Divisions-** Buffalo, Rochester.

North Carolina Eastern District www.nced.uscourts.gov
Search results do not include SSN or DOB. Civil records retained 2 years. All criminal records after 1979 forwarded to Raleigh. **Divisions-** Eastern, Northern, Southern, Western.

North Carolina Middle District www.ncmd.uscourts.gov
Search results do not include SSN or DOB, only case numbers and cases found. Closed electronic cases not purged. **Divisions-** Greensboro.

North Carolina Western District www.ncwd.uscourts.gov
Search results do not include SSN or DOB. Closed cases sent to archives after 5 years. **Divisions-** Asheville, Bryson City, Charlotte, Statesville.

North Dakota www.ndd.uscourts.gov
Search results do not include SSN or DOB. Records posted after 11/2005 are retained indefinitely. **Divisions-** Bismarck-Southwestern, Fargo-Southeastern, Grand Forks-Northeastern, Minot-Northwestern.

Ohio Northern District www.ohnd.uscourts.gov
Search results include full name and case number only. Case files sent to archives 5 years after closed. **Divisions-** Akron, Cleveland, Toledo, Youngstown.

Ohio Southern District www.ohsd.uscourts.gov
Search results do not include SSN or DOB. Closed cases sent to archives after 5 years. **Divisions-** Cincinnati, Columbus, Dayton.

Oklahoma Eastern District www.oked.uscourts.gov
Search results do not include SSN or DOB. Case files sent to archives 3-5 years after closed. **Location-** Muskogee.

Oklahoma Northern District www.oknd.uscourts.gov
Search results do not include SSN or DOB. Case files sent to archives 1 year after closed. **Location-** Tulsa.

Oklahoma Western District www.okwd.uscourts.gov
Search results do not include SSN or DOB. Closed civil case files sent to archives 5 years after closed, 7 for criminal. **Location-** Oklahoma City.

Oregon www.ord.uscourts.gov
Search results do not include SSN or DOB. The Documentation index may have DOBs on judgments. Case files sent to archives 3-5 years after closed. **Divisions-** Eugene, Medford, Portland.

Pennsylvania Eastern District www.paed.uscourts.gov
Search results do not include SSN or DOB. Closed electronic cases not purged. **Divisions-** Allentown/Reading, Philadelphia.

Pennsylvania Middle District www.pamd.uscourts.gov
Search results do not include SSN or DOB. Closed electronic cases not purged. **Divisions-** Harrisburg, Scranton, Williamsport.

Pennsylvania Western District www.pawd.uscourts.gov
Search results do not include SSN or DOB. Closed electronic cases not purged. **Divisions-** Erie, Johnstown, Pittsburgh.

Puerto Rico www.prd.uscourts.gov
Search results do not include SSN or DOB, but judgments may have SSN. Case files sent to archives 1 year after closed.

Rhode Island www.rid.uscourts.gov
Search results do not include SSN or DOB. Case files maintained at court 25 years after closed.

South Carolina www.scd.uscourts.gov
Search results do not include SSN or DOB. **Divisions-** Anderson, Beaufort, Charleston, Columbia, Florence, Greenville, Greenwood, Spartanburg.

South Dakota www.sdd.uscourts.gov
Search results do not include SSN or DOB. Case files sent to archives 6 months after closed. **Divisions-** Aberdeen, Pierre, Sioux Falls, Western Div - Rapid City.

Tennessee Eastern District www.tned.uscourts.gov
Search results do not include SSN or DOB. Closed electronic cases not purged. **Divisions-** Chattanooga, Greeneville, Knoxville, Winchester.

Tennessee Middle District www.tnmd.uscourts.gov
Search results do not include SSN or DOB. Case files sent to archives 1 year after closed. **Divisions-** Columbia, Cookeville, Nashville.

Tennessee Western District www.tnwd.uscourts.gov
Search results do not include SSN or DOB. **Location-** Jackson, Memphis.

Texas Eastern District www.txed.uscourts.gov
Search results do not include SSN or DOB. Case files sent to archives 1 year after closed. **Divisions-** Beaumont, Lufkin, Marshall, Sherman, Texarkana, Tyler.

Texas Northern District www.txnd.uscourts.gov
Search results do not include SSN or DOB. Closed case files sent to archives yearly. **Divisions-** Abilene, Amarillo, Dallas, Fort Worth, Lubbock, San Angelo, Wichita Falls.

Texas Southern District www.txs.uscourts.gov
Search results do not include SSN or DOB. Case files sent to archives 6 months after closed. **Divisions-** Brownsville, Corpus Christi, Galveston, Houston, Laredo, McAllen, Victoria.

Texas Western District www.txwd.uscourts.gov
Search results do not include SSN or DOB. Case files kept a minimum 2 years before sending to archives. **Divisions-** Austin, Del Rio, El Paso, Midland, Pecos, San Antonio, Waco.

Utah www.utd.uscourts.gov
Search results do not include SSN or DOB; will include case number and date of sentencing. Case files sent to archives 3-4 years after closed.

Vermont www.vtd.uscourts.gov
Search results do not include SSN or DOB. Closed electronic cases not purged. **Divisions-** Burlington, Rutland.

Virginia Eastern District www.vaed.uscourts.gov
Search results do not include SSN or DOB. Closed electronic cases not purged. **Divisions-** Alexandria, Newport News, Norfolk, Richmond.

Virginia Western District www.vawd.uscourts.gov
Search results may include last 4 SSN digits. Case files sent to archives 1 year after closed. **Divisions-** Abingdon, Big Stone Gap, Charlottesville, Danville, Harrisonburg, Lynchburg, Roanoke.

Washington Eastern District www.waed.uscourts.gov
Search results do not include SSN or DOB. Case files sent to archives 6 months after closed. **Divisions-** Spokane, Yakima.

Washington Western District www.wawd.uscourts.gov
Search: Most results do not include SSN or DOB. Case files sent to archives 2-3 years after closed. **Divisions-** Seattle, Tacoma.

West Virginia Northern District www.wvnd.uscourts.gov
Search results do not include SSN or DOB. Civil cases sent to archives every 5 years; every 10 years for criminal. **Divisions-** Clarksburg, Elkins, Martinsburg, Wheeling.

West Virginia Southern District www.wvsd.uscourts.gov
Search results do not include SSN or DOB. Paper case files sent to archives as deemed necessary. **Divisions-** Beckley, Bluefield, Charleston, Huntington, Parkersburg.

Wisconsin Eastern District www.wied.uscourts.gov
Search results include last 4 SSN digits, also birth year. Case files sent to archives 3 years after closed. **Location-** Milwaukee.

Wisconsin Western District www.wiwd.uscourts.gov
Search results do not include SSN or DOB. Closed electronic cases not purged. **Location-** Madison.

Wyoming www.wyd.uscourts.gov
Search results do not include SSN or DOB. Case files sent to archives when the right number of boxes filled. **Location-** Cheyenne.

Federal Records Centers and the National Archives

After a federal case is closed, the documents are held by the federal courts location for a predetermined number of years. This can be as little as six months, or, rarely, until the court reaches its capacity to store files. The closed cases are then sent to and stored at a designated Federal Records Center (FRC). After 20 to 30 years, the records are then transferred from the FRC to the regional archives offices. All of these offices are administered by the National Archives and Records Administration (NARA).

Each court has its own transfer cycle and determines access procedures to its case records even after they have been sent to the FRC.

When case records are sent to an FRC, the boxes of records are assigned accession, location, and box numbers. These numbers, which are called *case locator information*, must be obtained from the originating court and are necessary to retrieve documents from the FRC. Some courts will provide case locator information over the telephone, but other courts may require a written request. In certain judicial districts this information is now available on PACER.

The NARA web page at www.archives.gov has detailed information regarding documents, images, and how to research. To find all the NARA locations, visit www.archives.gov/locations. The Federal Records Center location for each state is shown below.

Federal Record Center Locater Table

State	Circuit	Appeals Court	Federal Records Center
AK	9	San Francisco, CA	Anchorage (Some records are in temporary storage in Seattle)
AL	11	Atlanta, GA	Atlanta
AR	8	St. Louis, MO	Fort Worth
AZ	9	San Francisco, CA	Los Angeles
CA	9	San Francisco, CA	Los Angeles (Central & Southern CA) San Francisco (Eastern & Northern CA)
CO	10	Denver, CO	Denver
CT	2	New York, NY	Boston
DC		Washington, DC	Washington, DC
DE	3	Philadelphia, PA	Philadelphia
FL	11	Atlanta, GA	Atlanta
GA	11	Atlanta, GA	Atlanta
GU	9	San Francisco, CA	San Francisco
HI	9	San Francisco, CA	San Francisco
IA	8	St. Louis, MO	Kansas City, MO
ID	9	San Francisco, CA	Seattle
IL	7	Chicago, IL	Chicago

State	Circuit	Appeals Court	Federal Records Center
IN	7	Chicago, IL	Chicago
KS	10	Denver, CO	Kansas City, MO
KY	6	Cincinnati, OH	Atlanta
LA	5	New Orleans, LA	Fort Worth
MA	1	Boston, MA	Boston
MD	4	Richmond, VA	Philadelphia
ME	1	Boston, MA	Boston
MI	6	Cincinnati, OH	Chicago
MN	8	St. Louis, MO	Chicago
MO	8	St. Louis, MO	Kansas City, MO
MS	5	New Orleans, LA	Atlanta
MT	9	San Francisco, CA	Denver
NC	4	Richmond, VA	Atlanta
ND	8	St. Louis, MO	Denver
NE	8	St. Louis, MO	Kansas City, MO
NH	1	Boston, MA	Boston
NJ	3	Philadelphia, PA	New York
NM	10	Denver, CO	Denver
NV	9	San Francisco, CA	Los Angeles (Clark County, NV) San Francisco (Other NV counties)
NY	2	New York, NY	New York
OH	6	Cincinnati, OH	Chicago (Dayton has some bankruptcy)
OK	10	Denver, CO	Fort Worth
OR	9	San Francisco, CA	Seattle
PA	3	Philadelphia, PA	Philadelphia
PR	1	Boston, MA	New York
RI	1	Boston, MA	Boston
SC	4	Richmond, VA	Atlanta
SD	8	St. Louis, MO	Denver
TN	6	Cincinnati, OH	Atlanta
TX	5	New Orleans, LA	Fort Worth
UT	10	Denver, CO	Denver
VA	4	Richmond, VA	Philadelphia
VI	3	Philadelphia, PA	New York
VT	2	New York, NY	Boston
WA	9	San Francisco, CA	Seattle
WI	7	Chicago, IL	Chicago
WV	4	Richmond, VA	Philadelphia
WY	10	Denver, CO	Denver

Appendix 4

Common Criminal Record Terms

Archaeological Dig Uncovers Ancient Race of Skeleton People
—Headline from *The Onion*

Sometimes like white bones in black rock, criminal record information is right there in black and white. A criminal record is obtained, there is some activity on the report, but terms used are unfamiliar or the information is so abbreviated that the bare bones information must be fleshed out. With thousands of criminal record jurisdictions using thousands of terms, some unique, interpretation of information can present a challenge.

Many of these terms and abbreviations are taken from the Department of Justice Uniform Crime Reporting program that created the National Incident-Based Reporting System (NIBRS). NIBRS has the following goals:

- To enhance the quantity, quality, and timeliness of crime statistical data collected by the law enforcement community.

- To improve the methodology used for compiling, analyzing, auditing, and publishing the collected crime data.

Other terms were obtained through law dictionaries. You should consider the context in which the word is used and also watch for the use of "degrees," such as: first, second, and third; voluntary or involuntary; and petty or grand. In many cases, these are assigned for purposes of applying fines or punishment and may be relevant to you in making your employment decision.

Notwithstanding the above, this list should be used only as a guide in interpreting criminal record information. Some jurisdictions interpret some of the terms provided differently. Further, this list is obviously not all-inclusive. If you have a question on any term you find, check with your record provider, the jurisdiction from which the record was received or your legal counsel.

A

Abduction	Taking away by violence or fraud and persuasion; kidnapping. Usually a female or wife, child or ward.
Abet	See Aiding and Abetting.
Abstraction	Taking away with intent to harm or deceive.
Accessory	Not the perpetrator of the crime but in some way involved without being present in the commission of the crime.
Accessory After the Fact	One who helps a criminal to elude arrest.
Accessory Before the Fact	One who induces another to commit a crime.
Accusation	1) Charging someone with a crime by legal indictment via a Grand Jury or filing of charges by a District Attorney; 2) statement that a named person committed a crime or wrong.
Acquittal	A not-guilty verdict absolving an accused party of guilt. Release or absolution.
Adjudication	The legal process by which a case or claim is settled. May also be the final pronouncement of judgment in a case or claim.
Adjudication Withheld	The court will withhold a decision until a future date. Usually some sort of probation is added and if the defendant complies with the conditions for a specified period of time, the case will be dismissed.
Affidavit	A voluntarily, written statement of fact, confirmed by oath.
Affray	Brawl or disturbance. Not premeditated.
Aggravated (assault, battery, arson, etc.)	Circumstances surrounding the commission of a crime or tort which increase or add to its injurious consequences.
Aiding and Abetting	To assist and/or incite another to commit a crime.
Alias	False name used in substitution of a legal name on official documents and for official purposes. Nicknames are not considered aliases. May be noted as AKA (Also Known As) on criminal records.
Allegation	Statement of 'claimed fact' contained in a criminal charge, complaint, or an affirmative defense.
Amnesty	Government's blanket abolition of an offense, with the legal result those convicted/charged are unbound and freed from the charge and/or sentence.
Antitrust Acts or Laws	Laws to protect trade and commerce from unlawful practice.

Appeal... A complaint to a superior court to review the decision of a lower court.

Appellant.. One who makes a complaint to a superior court to review the decision of a lower court.

Appellate Court....................................... A court having jurisdiction of appeal and review. Not a trial court.

Appropriate .... To take something from another for one's own use or benefit.

Archive/Archives.................................... The place where records are stored after a certain specified period of time. The period of time a record is held at a court of record may differ between courts and states.

Arraignment .... A call to the accused to come before the court to hear charges or enter a plea.

Arrest .... The taking of an individual into custody by law enforcement personnel for the purpose of charging them with an illegal act.

Arrest Record... An official form completed by the police department when a person is arrested. Also, a cumulative record of all instances in which a person has been arrested.

Arson.. To unlawfully and intentionally damage or attempt to damage any real or personal property by fire or incendiary device.

Assault .... An unlawful attack by one person upon another.

Aggravated Assault.................... An unlawful attack by one person upon another wherein the offender uses a weapon or displays it in a threatening manner, or the victim suffers obvious severe or aggravated bodily injury involving apparent broken bones, loss of teeth, possible internal injury, severe laceration, or loss of consciousness. This also included assault with a disease (as in cases when the offender is aware that he/she is infected with a deadly disease and deliberately attempts to inflict the disease by biting, spitting, etc.). This usually includes offenses such as Pointing and Presenting a Firearm, Brandishing a Firearm, etc. A severe laceration is one that should receive medical attention. A loss of consciousness must be the direct result of force inflicted on the victim by the offender.

Simple Assault........................... An unlawful physical attack by one person upon another where neither the offender displays a weapon, nor the victim suffers obvious severe or aggravated bodily injury involving apparent broken bones, loss of teeth, possible internal injury, severe laceration, or loss of consciousness.

Intimidation .... To unlawfully place another person in reasonable fear of bodily harm through the use of threatening words and/or other conduct but without displaying a weapon or subjecting the victim to actual physical attack. (This offense includes stalking).

B

Bad Checks .... Knowingly and intentionally writing and/or negotiating checks drawn against insufficient or nonexistent funds.

Bail .... An amount of money set by a judge at an initial appearance to ensure the return of the accused at subsequent proceedings.

Battery .... Non-consensual, unlawful contact, such as touching, beating or wounding of another. See Assault.

Bench Trial .... Trial by judge, without jury.

Bench Warrant .... A process delivered by the court directing a law enforcement agency to bring a specified individual before the court.

Bind Over .... To put under bond to appear in court. The term is also used when a case is shifted from a lower court to a higher court.

Blackmail .... An illegal demand for money or property under threat of harm or exposure of undesirable acts.

Bond .... A certificate of obligation, either unsecured or secured with collateral, to pay a specified amount of money within a specified period of time.

Bond Forfeiture .... Bond forfeiture occurs when a case has been disposed and a fine is to be, or has been paid. If it is a first offense, it is listed on the record but not classified as a conviction; any other time it is classified as a conviction.

Bookmaking .... An operation with the purpose of placing, registering, paying off or collecting debts for bets.

Bribery .... The offering, giving, receiving, or soliciting of anything of value (i.e., a bribe, gratuity, or kickback) to sway the judgment or action of a person in a position of trust or influence.

Burglary/Breaking and Entering .... The act of entering a premises, without the privilege to enter, with the purpose of committing a crime. States may classify as first, second, or third degree burglary.

C

Capias .... The Latin meaning is "That You Take". This is the name for several types of writs which require that a law enforcement official take a named defendant into custody.

Capital Case/Crime .... Case or crime for which the death penalty may be imposed.

Capital Punishment .... Punishment by death for capital crime.

Carnal .... Sexual, sensual. Carnal knowledge is sexual intercourse.

Cause of Action .... One or more related charges combined and made against a defendant for wrongs committed.

Charge .... In criminal law, a charge is an allegation that an individual has committed a specific offense.

Citation .... An order issued by a law enforcement officer requiring appearance in court to answer a charge. Bail is not accepted in lieu of appearance.

Circuit .... Judicial division of the United States or of an individual state.

Circuit Courts .... Courts whose jurisdiction extends over several counties or districts. (There are thirteen judicial circuits wherein the U.S. Courts of Appeals reside).

City Court .... Courts that try persons accused of violating municipal ordinances. City courts may have jurisdiction over minor civil or criminal cases, or both.

Civil Disorder .... A violent public disturbance by three or more people which causes danger, damage or injury to property or persons.

Co-defendant .... One of a group of two or more people charged in the same crime.

Coercion .... The use of physical force or threats to compel someone to commit an act against their will.

Collusion .... When two persons - or a business via their officers or employees - enter into a deceitful agreement, usually secret, to defraud or gain an unfair negotiating advantage over a 3rd party, competitor, or consumers.

Commutation; Commute a Sentence ..... When an individual presently incarcerated and serving an active sentence has their sentence 'commuted' or reduced 1) by any length of time, 2) to make parole eligible, 3) to time served which would immediately release the individual.

Compounding Crime .... The receipt by an individual of consideration in exchange for an agreement not to prosecute or inform on someone who they know has committed a crime.

Concurrent Sentences .... Two or more terms of imprisonment served simultaneously.

Conditional Discharge.............................. A conviction. Court issues the discharge from the jail and requires defendant to comply with some conditions. Regardless whether defendant complies with rules or not, he/she is still convicted (GUILTY) and case can never be expunged.

Conditional Release.............................. The release from a correctional facility before full sentence has been served which is conditioned on specific behavior. If conditions are not met, the individual may be returned to the facility.

Consecutive Sentences .... Multiple sentences, served one after the other.

Conspiracy... The coming together of two or more people for the purpose of committing an unlawful act or to commit a lawful act by unlawful means.

Contempt of Court .... An act committed which serves to obstruct the court in its administration or authority.

Controlled Substance .... A drug whose availability is restricted by law.

Conversion... The unauthorized taking of another's property.

Conviction .... Guilty verdict in a criminal trial.

Count/Charge .... An offense named in a cause of action. A cause of action may contain multiple counts or charges, each relating to the others but identifying a separate offense.

Counterfeiting/Forgery........................... The altering, copying, or imitation of something, without authority or right, with the intent to deceive or defraud by passing the copy or thing altered or imitated as that which is original or genuine or the selling, buying or possession of an altered, copied, or imitated thing with the intent to deceive or defraud.

Court of Record .... The court where the permanent record of all proceedings is held.

Credit Card Fraud.................................. Use, or attempted use of a credit card to purchase goods or services with the intent to avoid payment of such.

Crime Against Nature .... Deviate sexual intercourse.

Criminal Nonsupport.............................. Failure to pay child support

Culpability .... Blame, or degree of responsibility for a crime. This may be in degrees of purposeful, knowingly, recklessly or by negligence.

Cumulative Sentence............................. A sentence that takes effect after a prior sentence is completed for crimes tried under the same cause of action.

Curfew/Loitering/Vagrancy .... The violation of a court order, regulation, ordinance, or law requiring the withdrawal of persons from the streets or other specified areas; prohibiting persons from remaining in an area or place in an idle or aimless manner; or prohibiting persons from going from place to place without visible means of support. (Includes begging.)

D

Dangerous Weapon .... Something that is capable, though not designed to cause serious injury or death.

De Novo .... Latin for "anew" or "afresh". Usually used as Trial De Novo. New trial or one that is held for a second time, as if there had been no previous trial or decision.

Dead Docket .... The case never went to trial. The case can be reopened if new evidence is submitted.

Deadly Weapon .... A weapon designed to cause serious injury or death.

Defendant .... A person against whom a cause of action is taken.

Deferred Adjudication of Guilt .... The final judgment is delayed for a period of time. Can be likened to probation before a final verdict. If "probation" is completed without incident, the charges are usually dropped and the case is dismissed. During the "probationary period" the disposition is not necessarily considered a conviction.

Deferred Discharge .... Dismissed and considered a non-conviction.

Deferred Probation .... The judge doesn't make a finding of guilt; he assigns probation. If probation is completed without incident, the charges are usually dropped.

Deferred Sentence .... Postponement of the pronouncement of the sentence.

Defraud .... Knowingly misrepresenting facts to cheat or trick.

Degree (First, Second, or Third, A, B or C) . Classification assigned to a crime, depending on circumstances, for purposes of determining punishment. First degree is considered most serious than third; A is more serious than C. Degrees may be assigned to the actual crime (IE: murder in the first or second degree) or the class of crimes (IE: felony or misdemeanor).

Destruction/Damage/Vandalism (Property) Willfully or maliciously destroy, damage, deface, or otherwise injure real or personal property without the consent of the owner or the person having custody or control of it. (The crime of arson is not included in this definition.)

Directed Verdict .... A determination by a jury, made at the direction of the judge. A directed verdict happens in cases where there has been a lack of evidence, an overwhelming amount of evidence, or where the law is in favor of one of the parties.

Dismissal .... Finally disposing of the cause without further consideration. May be voluntary or involuntary. When involuntary, there is usually lack of prosecution or failure to produce sufficient evidence.

Dismissal Without Leave After Deferred
Prosecution .... Charges dismissed after specified time (90 days to 1 year) provided certain conditions have been met such as participating in specified program of anger control or drug counseling or providing community service, etc.

Disorderly Conduct .... Any behavior that tends to disturb the public peace or decorum, scandalize the community, or shock the public sense of morality.

Disposed/Disposition .... The final settlement in the matter. Examples of disposed cases are those with a finding of guilt (conviction), innocence, or acquittal.

Diversion Program .... To set aside. A court direction which calls a defendant, who has been found guilty, to attend a work or educational program as part of probation. May include some type of anger management, drug rehab, etc. If the condition of program is met, charge may be considered non-conviction.

Diversity of Citizenship .... A crime or claim which extends between citizens of different states. This is one of the grounds that can be used to invoke the jurisdiction of the U.S. Federal District Court.

Docket Record .... A court's official record of proceedings and calendar of upcoming cases.

Double Jeopardy .... Placing someone on trial a second time for an offense for which they have been acquitted previously. This is specifically prohibited by the U.S. Constitution, even if new incriminating evidence is unearthed.

Driving Under the Influence .... Driving or operating a motor vehicle or common carrier while mentally or physically impaired as the result of consuming an alcoholic beverage or using a drug or narcotic. Complete intoxication is not required. Individual state statutes specify the blood alcohol content at which a person is presumed to be under the influence of intoxicating liquor.

Drug/Narcotic Offenses .... The violation of laws prohibiting the production, distribution, and/or use of certain controlled substances and the equipment or devices utilized in their preparation and/or use. This may include the unlawful cultivation, manufacture, distribution, sale, purchase, use, possession, transportation, or importation of any controlled drug or narcotic substance.

Drunkenness.. To drink alcoholic beverages to the extent that one's mental faculties and physical coordination are substantially impaired. This includes Drunk and Disorderly.

Due Diligence .... A reasonable and expected measure of attention taken for a particular action. Not measurable by an absolute standard, but dependant on the situation.

Due Process of Law............................... Procedures followed by law enforcement and courts to insure the protection of an individual's rights as assigned by the Constitution.

E

Embezzlement .... The unlawful misappropriation by an offender to his/her own use or purpose of money, property, or some other thing of value entrusted to his/her care, custody, or control, usually through employment.

Ex parte .... Means on one side only. When an act is one for one party only. For example, in an Ex parte proceeding, only one party to the case is heard.

Expunge/Expunged .... When a record of an offense is expunged it will not appear on a released criminal history. The record may be destroyed or sealed after a certain period of time. Records may be expunged in juvenile cases, or upon satisfactory completion of a court-ordered probation and/or class(es).

Extortion/Blackmail .... To unlawfully obtain money, property, or any other thing of value, either tangible or intangible, through the use of threat of force, misuse of authority, threat of criminal prosecution, threat of destruction or reputation or social standing, or through other coercive means.

Extradition... The surrender of an individual accused or convicted of a crime by one state to another.

F

Family Offenses, Nonviolent................... Unlawful, nonviolent acts by a family member (or legal guardian) that threaten the physical, mental, or economic well-being or morals of another family member and that are not classifiable as other offenses such as Assault, Incest, Statutory Rape, etc. Examples include: Abandonment, Desertion, Neglect and nonsupport.

FCRA .... Fair Credit Reporting Act.

Felonious .... Describing an offense which is done with malicious, villainous criminal intent. IE: felonious assault.

Felony .... A serious offense carrying a penalty of incarceration from one year to life in a state prison, to the death penalty.

Felony Conversion
(Fraudulent Conversion) .... Similar to embezzlement or theft. An example of felony conversion is if someone sold goods for a company, and kept the money instead of turning it in to the company. (North Carolina)

Forcible Entry .... Entering or taking possession of property with force, threats or menacing conduct.

Fraud .... The intentional perversion of the truth for the purpose of inducing another person or other entity in reliance upon it to part with something of value or to surrender a legal right.

> False Pretenses/Swindle/Confidence Game— The intentional misrepresentation of existing fact or condition or the use of some other deceptive scheme or device to obtain money, goods, or other things of value.

> Credit Card/Automatic Teller Machine Fraud— The unlawful use of a credit (or debit) card or automatic teller machine for fraudulent purposes.

> Impersonation—Falsely representing one's identity or position and acting in the character or position thus unlawfully assumed to deceive others and thereby gain a profit or advantage, enjoy some right or privilege, or subject another person or entity to an expense, charge, or liability that would not have otherwise been incurred.

> Welfare Fraud—The use of deceitful statement, practices, or devices to unlawfully obtain welfare benefits.

> Wire Fraud—The use of an electric or electronic communications facility to intentionally transmit a false and/or deceptive message in furtherance of a fraudulent activity.

G

Gambling Offenses .... To unlawfully bet or wager money or something else of value; assist, promote, or operate a game of chance for money or some other stake; possess or transmit wagering information; manufacture, sell, purchase, possess, or transport gambling equipment, devices, or goods; or tamper with the outcome of a sporting event or contest to gain a gambling advantage.

    Betting/Wagering—To unlawfully stake money or something else of value on the happening of an uncertain event or on the ascertainment of a fact in dispute.

    Operating/Promoting/Assisting Gambling—To unlawfully operate, promote, or assist in the operation of a game of chance, lottery, or other gambling activity.

    Gambling Equipment Violations—To unlawfully manufacture, sell, buy, possess, or transport equipment, devices, and/or goods used for gambling purposes.

    Sports Tampering—To unlawfully alter, meddle in, or otherwise interfere with a sporting contest or event for the purpose of gaining a gambling advantage.

Grand Jury .... A body of persons with the authority to investigate and accuse, but not to try cases. The grand jury will listen to and review evidence to see if it there are sufficient grounds to bring an individual to trial.

Grand Larceny .... The theft of property over a specified value. Dollar amounts vary by state.

Gross .... Flagrant, out of measure.

Gross Misdemeanor .... Serious misdemeanor.

Guilt/Guilty .... Final disposition. Having committed a crime.

H

Habeas Corpus .... A writ requesting a trial or the release of a prisoner.

Habitual Violator .... To have committed the same offence three times. Can also be charged as a habitual offender.

Hearsay .... Second-hand verbal evidence - a witness is not telling what they know personally, but what others have said.

Hijacking .... To take control of a vehicle by intimidation, force or threatened force. Also, the theft of goods while in transit, as when transported in trucks.

Homicide .... The killing of another human being by another. "Justifiable homicide" occurs in cases such as during the enforcement of law, and/or occurs without evil intent. "Excusable homicide" may occur by accident or in self-defense. "Felonious homicide" is the killing of another without justification. This type has two degrees – manslaughter and murder, depending on circumstances or intent. See Manslaughter; Murder.

Hung Jury .... A hung jury is one in which all jurors cannot reach a consensus required for a verdict.

I

Illegal Immigrant .... An alien/non-citizen who entered the US without government permission or stayed beyond the termination date of a visa.

Illicit .... Prohibited or unlawful.

Impersonation .... Falsely representing one's identity or position and acting in the character or position assumed in order to deceive others and thereby gain a profit or advantage, enjoy some right or privilege, or subject another person or entity to an expense, charge, or liability.

Incendiary .... One who intentionally set fires. Arsonist.

Incorrigible .... One who is incapable of reform.

Indictment .... A formal, written accusation made by the grand jury.

Infraction .... Violation of local ordinance or state statute usually resulting in a fine or limited period of incarceration. Term usually used in traffic offenses.

Injunction .... A court order which prohibits a person from doing a specified act for a specified period of time.

Insider Trading .... Using confidential information about transactions or a business gained through employment there or through a stock brokerage to buy or sell stocks/bonds based on private knowledge the value will go up or down.

Instrument .... 1) as evidence, an object used to perform some action, often in an assault. 2) a written legal document - a contract, lease, deed, will, bond.

Intent .... The frame of mind or attitude of the person at the time an act was committed. See Culpability.

Intoxicate, Intoxication .... Reduction of physical or mental capabilities caused by the ingestion of an intoxicating substance such as alcohol or drugs.

Involuntary Dismissal .... Dismissed due to lack of prosecution or lack of evidence.

J

Jeopardy .... Danger of being charged with or convicted of a particular crime.

Judgment .... The final decision of the court regarding a claim or case.

Jurisdiction .... The power of a court to question facts, apply law, make decisions and judgments.

K

Kidnapping/Abduction .... The unlawful seizure, transportation, and/or detention of a person against his/her will or of a minor without the consent of his/her custodial parent(s) or legal guardian.

L

Larceny .... The unlawful taking of another person's property. Larceny is commonly classified as "petty" or "grand" depending on the value of the property. Dollar values to establish classifications of "petty" and "grand" may vary from state to state.

Pocket-picking—The theft of articles from another person's physical possession by stealth where the victim usually does not become immediately aware of the theft.

Purse-snatching—The grabbing or snatching of a purse, handbag, etc., from the physical possession of another person.

Shoplifting—The theft by someone other than an employee of the victim of goods or merchandise exposed for sale.

Theft from Motor Vehicle—The theft of articles from a motor vehicle, locked or unlocked.

Legal Malice .... An act, committed without just cause or excuse, intended to inflict harm or cause death.

Lesser-included Offense .... Crime that is proved by same facts as a more serious crime.

Lewd and Lascivious .... Obscene, indecent.

Libel .... Defamation of another person through print, pictures, or signs.

Lis Pendens .... A pending suit.

M

Magistrate .... Public officials, including judicial officers who have limited jurisdiction in criminal cases and civil causes.

Mail Fraud .... The use of the mail system to commit a fraud.

Malfeasance; Misfeasance .... Intentionally doing something either legally or morally wrong, with no right to do so; involves dishonesty, illegality or knowingly exceeding authority for improper reasons. Misfeasance is committing a wrong or error by mistake, negligence or inadvertence, but not by intentional wrongdoing.

Malice Aforethought.............................. Planning to commit an unlawful act without just cause or excuse.

Manslaughter .... The unpremeditated killing of a person. Can be voluntary or involuntary, determined by circumstances. The feature distinguishing involuntary manslaughter from voluntary is the absence of intent to cause death or commit an act that might be expected to produce death or harm. Voluntary manslaughter is homicide that is committed during an act in the heat of passion.

Negligent Manslaughter—The killing of another person through negligence.

Mayhem .... The intentional infliction of injury on another which causes amputation, disfigurement or impairs the function of any part of the body.

Medical Sanction .... Identifies an individual or employers who have had sanctions brought against them for crimes that committed in associations with certain state or government funded agencies. Parties with sanctions against them are excluded from billing Medicare, Medicaid, child care and social services, and may also be excluded from Federal health care programs.

Misdemeanor .... Crime punishable by a fine and/or county jail time for up to one year; not a felony.

Mistrial.. A trial which is terminated or declared invalid. Reasons for mistrial include misconduct on the part of the jury, defense team or the court, or illness on the part of the judge, jury or defendant. May be followed by a retrial on the same charges.

Motor Vehicle Theft.............................. The theft of a motor vehicle. This includes a self propelled vehicle that runs on the surface of land and not on rails and that fits one of the following property descriptions: automobiles, buses, recreational vehicles, trucks, and other vehicles such as motorcycles, snowmobiles or golf carts.

Murder.. Unlawful killing with malice aforethought. Murder is willful, deliberate and premeditated, or done during the commission of a crime. This classification of crime is generally divided by degrees, murder in the first degree and murder in the second degree, for the purpose of imposing penalties.

N

Negligence.. Flagrant and reckless disregard of the safety of others. Willful indifference.

Negotiated Plea .... See Plea Bargain.

No Bill or No True Bill .... The decision by a grand jury that it will not bring indictment against the accused on the basis of the allegations and evidence presented by the prosecutor.

No Contest.. A plea in which the defendant does not contest the charge. This has the same effect as a guilty plea except the conviction cannot be used against the defendant in a civil suit.

No Papered... Charges were not pursued. (This is a legal term in Washington, D.C.)

No Probable Cause .... There was not sufficient reason to bring case to trial.

Nolle Pros or Nolle Prosequi .... Latin phrase used by the district attorney or plaintiff when they do not wish to prosecute or proceed with the action.

Nolo Contendre...................................... Latin phrase used by a defendant to say "I do not wish to contest." This plea in a criminal case has the legal effect of pleading guilty. See No Contest.

O

Obstruction of Justice .... Attempt to interfere with law enforcement officers or the judicial system, including threatening witnesses, improper talk with jurors, hiding evidence, interfering with an arrest.

Obtain Property under False Pretense ... The misrepresentation of the value of something. Passing bad check.

Offense Qualifier.................................... Indicates what role the offender played in the commission of a crime. 11 possibilities are-principal, attempted, conspiracy to attempt, conspiracy, accessory before the fact, accessory to attempt, Aid and Abet, accessory after fact, solicit, solicit to attempt, unknown.

Official Search .... Search performed at the record location and certified to be true and correct, with an attesting seal or official's signature.

P

Pander	To provide products or services which cater to the sexual gratification of others. To entice another into prostitution.
Parole	To release from confinement after serving part of a sentence, usually with terms and conditions provided in the parole order.
Parole Violation	An act that does not conform to the terms of parole.
Partial Verdict	Trial result where the jury finds the defendant guilty of one or more charges but not guilty of all.
Peeping Tom	To secretly look through a window, doorway, keyhole, or other aperture for the purpose of voyeurism.
Penalty	1) amount agreed in advance to be paid if payment or performance is not made on time. 2) after conviction for a crime, money fine or forfeiture of property ordered by the judge.
Pending Charge or Case	Charge for an offense not yet been disposed of by the court.
Perjury	Intentionally making a false statement under oath.
Pilferage	Theft of little things usually from shipments or baggage.
Piracy	Crime of robbery of ships or boats, now applied also to theft of intellectual property.
Plea	The defendant's formal answer to a charge.
Plea Bargain	A plea of guilt to a lesser offense in return for a lighter sentence.
Pornography/Obscene Material	The violation of laws or ordinances prohibiting the manufacture, publishing, sale, purchase, or possession of sexually explicit material, e.g., literature or photographs.
Prayer for Judgment, 1st Offense (NC)	Asking the court to give leniency. No finding of guilt by the court.
Preliminary Hearing	Meeting before the judge to determine if a person charged with a felony should be tried for that crime, based on some substantial evidence that they committed the crime. Preliminary hearing are held in the lowest local court but only if the prosecutor has filed the charge without asking the Grand Jury for an indictment.
Premeditation	Plotting, planning, deliberating before doing something. Is an important consideration in murder.

Preponderance of the Evidence .... Based on the more convincing evidence and its probable truth or accuracy, and not on the amount of evidence as commonly believed.

Presumption of Innocence .... Fundamental protection for a person accused of a crime that requires the prosecution prove its case beyond a reasonable doubt.

Pre-Sentence Diagnostic .... When an offender has been convicted of a crime but not sentenced, a diagnostic report is prepared at the request of the court to help determine the appropriate sentence.

Pre-Trial Intervention .... An extensive background check to help determine if charges will be pressed.

Privilege Against Self Incrimination .... Right to refuse to testify against oneself in any legal proceeding where testimony may be used against them.

Probation .... Relief of all or part of a sentence on the promise of proper conduct.

Prostitution .... To unlawfully engage in sexual relations for profit.

Q

Quash/Quashed .... Declined to prosecute but with the option to reopen the case.

R

Racketeering .... An organized conspiracy for the purpose of committing crimes of extortion or coercion.

Rape .... Sex without consent. May be forcible or by intoxication, with a person who is underage and unable to give consent, or with a person with diminished mental and/or physical capabilities.

Reckless Endangerment .... An act which does or could cause injury to another, not necessarily with intent.

Refused .... Charges were not accepted by the District Attorney's Office.

Remand .... To return an individual to custody pending further trial, or to return a case from an appellate to a lower court for further proceedings.

Restraining Order .... An order prohibiting a specified action until such time that a hearing on an application for an injunction can be held.

Retired (as Disposition) .... The case can be brought up within the next year if the individual is arrested for anything. It is the judge's decision and only he can take action. If the individual remains "clean," then the case can be dismissed.

RICO Act.. Racketeer Influenced and Corrupt Organizations Act.

Robbery .... The taking or attempting to take anything of value under confrontational circumstances from the control, custody, or care of another person by force or threat or violence and/or by putting the victim in fear of immediate harm.

S

Sealed Records .... Court records or decisions that a judge orders kept from public view.

Secreting Lien Property .... Hiding property that has a lien filed against it.

Sedition.. Advocating the overthrow or reform of a government by unlawful means.

Sentence.. A judgment of punishment for a criminal act.

Serious Misdemeanor............................ Having a more severe penalty than other misdemeanors.

Simple Assault .... Unlawful physical attack on another person where neither the offender displays a weapon, nor the victim suffers obvious severe or aggravated bodily injury or loss of consciousness.

Slander... Defamation verbal communication. Making false and malicious statements about another.

Sodomy.. Oral or anal sexual intercourse with another person, forcibly and/or against that person's will or not forcibly against the person's will in instances where the victim is incapable of giving consent because of his/her youth or because or his/her temporary or permanent mental or physical incapacity.

Solicitation .... Asking, urging or enticing.

Status: Closed .... No further action will occur on this case; cannot be reopened at later date.

Statute of Limitations .... Law that sets the maximum period one can wait before filing a lawsuit. There are statutes of limitations on bringing criminal charges, too (homicide generally has no time limitation.)

Statutory Rape....................................... Sexual activity by an adult with a person under the age of consent.

Stricken... To eliminate or expunge.

Successive Sentences........................... Imposition of the penalty one after the other for each of several crimes, as compared to concurrent sentences which happen at the same time.

Suspended Sentence .... Deferment of punishment usually over a period of probation.

T

Theft of Services .... Obtaining services without consent through deception, threat, tampering, etc.

Theft/unauthorized .... Means the person used someone else's information, credit card, check, or something similar.

Time Served .... Period a criminal defendant has been in jail, often while awaiting bail or awaiting trial. Often a judge will give a defendant credit for time served.

Trespassing .... To unlawfully enter land, a dwelling, or other real property.

Truncated Files .... Destroyed or partially destroyed. Unable to obtain more information.

U

Under the Influence of Intoxicating
Liquor or Drugs .... Any condition where the nervous system, brain or muscles are impaired to an appreciable degree by an intoxicating substance.

Usury .... Charging more interest than is permitted by law for a loan.

Unlawful Entry .... Entry without force and without permission by means of fraud or other wrongful act.

Uttering .... To forge another's name.

V

Vacate (Judgment) .... To make void; to cancel.

Vehicular Homicide .... Death of another caused by the intentional, unlawful or negligent operation of a motor vehicle.

Venue .... The geographic area where the case or claim occurred, within which a court with jurisdiction can hear and determine a case. A change of venue, or the moving of a case from one court to another may be granted for such reasons as when the court does not think the defendant can get a fair trial in that area or for the convenience of the parties in a civil case.

Verdict .... The formal, final decision or finding made by a jury or judge.

Voluntary Dismissal .... The court or district attorney dismisses the charges.

W

Waiver by Magistrate .... Charges are waived after the defendant agrees to pay a fine. The defendant is not prosecuted on this charge.

Waiver of Jury .... The right to a jury trial is waived and the judge makes the decision of guilt or innocence.

Wanton .... Reckless, malicious. Without regard for the rights of others, indifferent to consequences to health, life or the reputation of another. Usually done without intent, but an act so unreasonable the perpetrator should know that harm will result.

Warrant .... Court order authorizing a law enforcement official to arrest or perform search and seizure.

Weapons Offenses .... The unlawful sale, distribution, manufacture, alteration, transport, possession or use of a deadly or dangerous weapon.

White Collar Crime .... General term for crimes involving insider trading, commercial fraud, swindles, cheating consumers, embezzlement and other dishonest business schemes.

With Specifications .... When W/S is listed after a charge, it is usually followed with a description of violence involved with the charge.

Withheld .... Adjudication withheld.

Wobblers .... Offenses that can be tried as either a felony or a misdemeanor.

Writ .... A written court order, or a judicial process.

Wrongful Entrustment .... Allowing an unlicensed driver to operate a motor vehicle.

Y

Youthful Offender .... Classification of youths and young adults, generally older then juveniles. In the 18 to 25 year age group, these individuals are sometimes given special sentencing consideration for the purpose of rehabilitation, sometimes through education and counseling.

Youthful Training Act .... Usually a non-conviction. Used for juvenile first-time offenders. It may be reported on a criminal record. If the juvenile complies with the sentence, case will be dropped from the record when the offender reaches adulthood.

Common Criminal Record Abbreviations

I've got two words for you: "Keep it real!" And that's two because "it" is just an abbreviation!

— Ali G in the movie *Ali G Indahouse*

Especially mystifying — and aggravating — is obtaining a criminal record and the offense appears to be an acronym or abbreviation. The challenge is more than simply understanding the definition of the offense, but understanding what offense to which they are referring.

What follows are some of the more common abbreviations, but keep in mind two things:

1. The abbreviations shown below are not universally used and agreed upon by different jurisdictions. For example if you obtain a criminal record with an offense of "A" as shown below, do not automatically assume it is referring to an "assault" if there is no supporting evidence. Some jurisdictions abbreviate burglary as "B." Some jurisdictions abbreviate "B" as "Breaking." Contact your record provider or the jurisdiction to investigate unclear abbreviations.

2. There are many more abbreviations in use that provided here.

A

A	Assault
A ARMED	Assault, Armed
A INT MAIM	Assault with Intent to Maim
A TO K (or MAIM, MUR, RAPE, ROB)	Assault to Kill (or Maim, Murder, Rape, Rob)
A & B	Assault and Battery
A & ROB (armed)	Assault and Robbery (armed)
AA/DW	Aggravated Assault with a Deadly Weapon
AA/PO	Aggravated Assault Police Officer (Dallas County)
AA/SBI	Aggravated Assault / Serious Bodily Injury

AAWW	Aggravated Assault With Weapon
ABC Act	Alcohol Beverage Control Act
ABD	Abduction
ABNDN or ABNDNT	Abandon or Abandonment
ABST	Abstraction
ABUS LANG	Abusive Language
ABWIK	Assault and Battery With Intent to Kill
ACAF	Accessory After the Fact
ACBF	Accessory Before the Fact
ACC	Accessory
ACC AFT FACT REC	Accessory After the Fact, Receiving
ACC BURG	Accessory to Burglary
ACC TO ISS CHK	Accessory to Issuing Check
ACC TO JL BRK	Accessory to Jail Break
ACC TO L	Accessory to Larceny
ACC TO MUR	Accessory to Murder
ACC TO ROB	Accessory to Robbery
ACCOMP DD	Accompanying Drunken Driver
ACCPL	Accomplice
ACCPT BRB	Accepting a Bribe
ADJ	Adjudication
ADLTY	Adultery
ADW	Assault with Deadly Weapon
ADW/FIREARM	Assault with Deadly Weapon/Firearms
AFA	Alien Firearms Act
AFCF	After Former Conviction of a Felony
AFDVT	Affidavit
AFFR	Affray
AFFR WDW	Affray With Deadly Weapon
AFO	Assaulting a Federal Officer
AGG A	Aggravated Assault
AID & ABET LOTT	Aiding and Abetting Lottery
AID & HAR ESC PR	Aiding and Harboring an Escaped Prisoner
AID PR TO ESC	Aiding a Prisoner to Escape
AIDA	Automobile Information Disclosure Act
AKA	Also Known As
ALIEN POSS FIREARMS	Alien in Possession of Firearms
ALLOW DR W/O PRMT	Allowing One to Drive Without a Permit
ALT	Altering

ANNOY & SOL .... Annoying and Soliciting
APC... Actual Physical Control
APCV .... Actual Physical Control of a Vehicle
APIPOCC... Appropriating Property In Possession Of Common Carrier
APP. CT... Appellate Court
APPROP... Appropriating
APO .... Assaulting Police Officer
AR .... Anti-Racketeering
ARD .... Accelerated Rehabilitation Disposition
ARL... Antiriot Laws
ARMED WDW .... Armed With Dangerous Weapon
ARSON OF PERS PROP .... Arson of Personal Property
ASLT.. Assault
ASLT TO RA... Assault to Rob Armed
ASMB... Assembling
ASST.. Assisting
ASST ATT TO RAPE............................. Assisting in Attempt to Commit Rape
ASST PROST .... Assisting Prostitution
ATL .... Antitrust Law
ATPT.. Attempt
ATT .... Attempt or Attempted
ATT RA .... Attempted Robbery Armed
ATTEMPT .... Attempt to Steal, Commit, etc.
AUTO H & R .... Auto – Hit and Run
AUTO NO LIC....................................... Auto – No License
AVIN.. Altered Vehicle Identification Number
AWDW .... Assault with Deadly Weapon
AWDWIKISI .... Assault with a Deadly Weapon with Intent to Kill or Inflict Serious Injury
AWOL .... Absent Without Leave

B

B.. Breaking
B.. Battery (FBI definition)
B & E... Breaking and Entering
B of P .... Breach of Peace (FBI definition)
B/F .... Bond Forfeiture
BAIL JUMPG .... Bail Jumping
BATT.. Battery

BB .... Bank Burglary
BC .... Bad Check or Bogus Check
BF & E... Bank Fraud and Embezzlement
BI... Bodily Injury
BKMKG.. Bookmaking
BL .... Bank Larceny
BLKML .... Blackmail
BOND FORF....................................... Bond Forfeiture
BOP .... Breach of Peace
BORD... Bill of Review Denied
BORG .... Bill of Review Granted
BR .... Bank Robbery
BRBG... Bribing
BRBY .... Bribery
BRCSP... Buying, Receiving, Concealing Stolen Property
BTCP .... Probation Following Boot Camp Incarceration
BTG.. Beating
BNID .... Burglary Not In a Dwelling
BURG.. Burglary
BURN DEST INS PROP....................... Burning, Destroying, etc., Insured Property
BURN INT INJ INS .... Burning, Intent to Injure Insurer

C

C & F.. Stands for call and failed, which means voluntary dismissal by judge or court
C to D of M... Contributing to the Delinquency of a Minor
CAID .... Criminal Activity In Drugs
CAR B... Car Breaking
CAR PROWL....................................... Car Prowling
CC ABUSE/USE.................................. Credit Card Abuse
CCDW... Carrying Concealed Deadly Weapon
CCF.. Carrying Concealed Firearm
CCW .... Carry Concealed Weapon
CD.. Conditional Discharge
CDW .... Carrying Dangerous Weapon
CIT .... Citation Code (Georgia State)
CK .... (Check) can also mean Carnal Knowledge (FC: Female child)
CL .... Complied with Law
CMPT.. Contempt

CNSP	Conspiracy to Commit
CNTY CRT	County Court
COC	Contempt of Court
COMM IND ACT	Committing Indecent Act
COMN	Common (used with assault, cheat, drunk, etc.)
COMP FEL	Compounding a Felony
CONC EVID	Concealing Evidence
CONSP	Conspiracy
CONT DA	Controlled Dangerous Substance
CONV	Conversion
CPCS	Criminal Possession of a Controlled Substance
CPDD	Criminal Possession of Dangerous Drugs
CPSP	Criminal Possession of Stolen Property
CR B	Criminal – B (Not Felony)
CR to ANI	Cruelty to Animals
CR to CHDN	Cruelty to Children
CRIM CRLESS	Criminal Carelessness
CRLESS DR	Careless Driving
CRNL	Carnal
CRNL KNLDG	Carnal Knowledge (of FC – Female Child)
CRSP	Criminal Receiving Stolen Property
CRV	Conditional Release Violator
CSA	Controlled Substance Act
CSCS	Criminal Sale of Controlled Substances
CTFG or CTFT	Counterfeiting or Counterfeit
CW	Concealed Weapons
CW W/O PRMT OR LIC	Carrying Weapon Without Permit or License
CWIK	Cutting With Intent to Kill

D

D & D(C)	Drunk and Disorderly (Conduct)
D & S	Dangerous and Suspicious
DA	Drug Abuse
DAA W/O OP	Driving Away Auto Without Owner's Permission
DAMV	Destruction of Aircraft or Motor Vehicles
DAR	Driving After Revocation
DC	Disorderly Conduct
DCI	Driving Car Intoxicated
DCI (-D or -L)	Driving Car Intoxicated (-Drugs or -Liquor)

DCMW .... Drunk in Control of Motor Vehicle
DE .... Deferred
DEAL IN LOTT POL .... Dealing in Lottery Police
DECEPTIVE PRACTICE .... Writing Bad Checks
DEF BLDG.. Defacing Building
DEF BRAKES .... Defective Brakes
DEF GPVT BONDS .... Defacing Government Bonds
DEF OR DEST PERS PROP .... Defacing or Destroying Personal Property
DEF OR DEST PUB PROP.................... Defacing or Destroying Public Property
DEFR .... Defrauding
DELIN .... Delinquent
DEP.. Deportation
DEPOS IN US PO THRT....................... Depositing in U.S. Post Office Threat to Injure
                                                                           Person
                                                                           or Property of Addressee
DESER.. Desertion or Deserter
DESTR OF IP .... Destruction of Interstate Property
DGP .... Destruction of Government Property
DH.. Disorderly House
DIP... Drunk In Public
DIS... Disorderly
DISCH FIREARMS .... Discharging Firearms
DISM.. Charge Dismissed
DISP MTG PROP .... Disposing of Mortgaged Property
DISP STLN PROP.................................. Disposing of Stolen Property
DIST... Disturbance
DIST PEACE .... Disturbing the Peace
DISTIL.. Distilling
DISTR .... Distributing
DIV... Diverting
DL .... Drug Law
DMG PROP .... Damaging Property
DOF .... Desecration of Flag
DP.. Disorderly Person
DR W/O PRMT .... Driving Without Permit
DRK .... Drunk
DRUG/MOP SCH .... Drugs Manufactured or Possessed Near a School
DRW CHK W/O FDS .... Drawing Check Without Funds
DRW OR EXH FIREARMS.................... Drawing or Exhibiting Firearms
DSMD .... Dismissed

DSPLY VOID OP LIC .... Displaying Void Operator's License
DUI (L) .... Driving Under Influence (of Liquor)
DUS .... Driving Under Suspension
DV .... Domestic Violence
DW .... Dangerous Weapon
DWA .... Dangerous Weapon Act
DWAI .... Driving While Ability Impaired
DWD (-D or -L) .... Driving While Drunk (-Drugs or -Liquor)
DWI .... Driving While Impaired
DWLG .... Dwelling
DWLS .... Driving While License Suspended
DWLS/SR .... Driving While License Suspended/Sentence
                                           Reduced
DYN .... Dynamiting
DYN INH BLDG .... Dynamiting Inhabited Building

E

EAR .... Escape and Rescue
ECT .... Extortionate Credit Transactions
EFP .... Escaped Federal Prisoner
EGP .... Embezzlement of Government Property
EID .... Explosives and Incendiary Devices
EL .... Election Laws
ELIM .... Elimination
EMBZ .... Embezzlement or Embezzling
ENDANG .... Endangering
ENDANG L OR H OF CHILD .... Endangering the Life or Health of a Child
ENT (or E) .... Entering
ENTIC .... Enticing
ENTIC FEM U AGE .... Enticing Females Under Age
ENTIC INTO IMM PLACE .... Enticing Into Immoral Place
ESC .... Escaped
ESC CONV .... Escaped Convict
ESC FED CUST .... Escaping Federal Custody
ESC LAW FRAUD VIOLATION .... Employment Security Commission Law Fraud
                                           Violation (Welfare Fraud)
ESP .... Espionage
EV .... Evasion or Evading
EV TAX L .... Evasion of Tax Law
EVSDRP .... Eavesdropping

EXH.. Exhibiting
EXPLSV .... Explosives
EXPOS... Exposing
EXT .... Extortion

F

F1 – F6.. Felonies with F1 are the most serious offense type
FACL.. Facilitation Of
FAG.. Fraud Against Government
FAIL .... Failure
FAIL ANS SUM..................................... Failure to Answer Summons
FAIL ASST AFT CAUS WRK .... Failure to Assist After Causing Wreck
FAIL TO APP .... Failure to Appear
FAIL TO OBT LIC OR PRMT .... Failure to Obtain a License or Permit
FAIL TO PROV .... Failure to Provide
FAIL RPT ACC .... Failure to Report and Accident
FAIL RPT FEL .... Failure to Report a Felony
FAIL SRV LEG PROC .... Failure to Serve Legal Process
FAIL TO AID .... Failure to Stop and Render Aid
FALSE .... Pretenses Writing Insufficient Check
FCC.. False Claiming U.S. Citizenship
FCR.. Fines, Costs and Restitution
FEL RED... Felony Reduction
FERIC .... False Entries in Records of Interstate Carriers
FF... Fugitive File
FFA .... Federal Firearms Act
FFJ... Fugitive from Justice
FFST... Fail to File State Taxes
FHA.. Federal Housing Administration
FHIF .... Frequenting House of Ill Fame
FICT... Fictitious
FIREARMS A....................................... Firearms Act
FJDA.. Federal Juvenile Delinquency Act
FLS .... False
FLS ADV.. False Advertising
FLS CL... False Claims
FLS FIRE ALA .... False Fire Alarm
FLS POL ALA .... False Police Alarm
FMFR.. Failure to Maintain Financial Responsibility

FOA.. Fugitive Other Authorities
FORC ENT .... Forcible Entry
FORF .... Forfeiture, Forfeiting
FORG... Forged, Forgery
FORG & PASS .... Forging and Passing
FORG DR PRESC................................... Forging Doctor's Prescription
FORG US OBLI .... Forging U.S. Obligations
FORN... Fornication
FP .... False Pretenses
FR .... False Report
FRA.. Federal Reserve Act
FRD.. Fraud, Fraudulent
FTA/TP CST .... Failure to Appear to Pay Fine and Cost
FSRA .... Failure to Stop and Render Aid after a Collision
FUDE .... Fugitive Deserter
FUUSTC .... Forging and Uttering U.S. Treasury Check

G

GA.. Guilty in Absentia
GAMB .... Gambling
GL (A) .... Grand Larceny (Auto)
GLFR .... Grand Larceny from Retailer
GR BOD INJ .... Gross Bodily Injury
GRD THFT or GT(A)................................ Grand Theft (Auto)
GROSS CHT .... Gross Cheat
GROSS INJ .... Gross Injury

H

H of IF .... House of Ill Fame
H of PROST... House of Prostitution
HAB.. Habitual
HAB DRK.. Habitual Drunk
HARB CRIM... Harboring Criminals
HB .... Housebreaking
HLDP .... Holdup
HLDP DW .... Holdup with Deadly Weapon
HVSW .... Health Violation Solid Waste
HWY ROB.. Highway Robbery

I

ICC	Indirect Criminal Contempt
IGA	Interstate Gambling Activities
IGB	Illegal Gambling Business
ILL MFNG USE SALE emblems/Insignia	Illegal Manufacturing Use – Possession – Sale – Emblems - Insignia
ILLEG BUSN	Illegal Business
ILLEG COHAB	Illegal Cohabitation
ILLEG ENT US	Illegal Entry to U.S.
ILL PRAC MED	Illegal Practice of Medicine
ILLIC	Illicit
ILLIC DISTIL	Illicit Distilling
IMM	Immoral
IMM ENTNMT	Immoral Entertainment
IMP	Impersonating or Impersonation
IMP OFC	Impersonating an Officer
IMPR ST LIC	Improper State License
INCORR	Incorrigible or Incorrigibility
IND	Indecent
IND COND	Indecent Conduct
IND EXP	Indecent Exposure
IND LIB (MIN CHILD)	Indecent Liberties (With Minor Child)
INF	Infamous
INF CR AGST NAT	Infamous Crime Against Nature
INFL	Influence
INJCT	Injunction
INM DH	Inmate Disorderly House
INN	Innocent. Plea of not guilty, found innocent by the jury.
INST	Instructed verdict, found innocent of charge. (FBI definition is Instrument)
INSUF FDS or INSF	Insufficient Funds
INT	Intent
IOC	Interception of Communications
INT CS IN CO FAC	Introducing a Controlled Substance into a County Facility
INTCRSE WITH CHILD	Intercourse With Child
INTERF	Interfering
INTIM	Intimidation or Intimidating

INTIM GOVT WIT	Intimidating Government Witness
INTOX	Intoxication or Intoxicated
INV	Investigation
INVET VAG	Inveterate Vagrancy
INVOL MANSL	Involuntary Manslaughter
IPGP	Illegal Possession of Government Property
IPPL	Illegal Possession Prohibited Liquor
IRA	Internal Revenue Act
IRC	Internal Revenue Code
IRL	Internal Revenue Law
IRLL	Internal Revenue Liquor Law
ISS	Involuntary Servitude and Slavery
ISS FRD INST	Issuing Fraudulent Instruments
IT	Interstate Theft
ITAR	Interstate Transportation in Aid of Racketeering
ITF	Interstate Transportation of Fireworks
ITGD	Interstate Transportation of Gambling Devices
ITLT	Interstate Transportation of Lottery Tickets
ITOM	Interstate Transportation of Obscene Matter
ITPMG	Interstate Transportation of Prison-Made Goods
ITSA	Interstate Transportation of Stolen Aircraft
ITSC	Interstate Transportation of Stolen Cattle
ITSMV	Interstate Transportation of Stolen Motor Vehicle
ITSP (CT or MT)	Interstate Transportation of Stolen Property (Commercialized Theft or Major Theft)
ITWI	Interstate Transmission of Wagering Information
ITWP	Interstate Transportation of Wagering Paraphernalia
IWC	Issue Worthless Check
IWFC	Interference With Flight Crew

J

J SATISF	Judgment Satisfied
JCCP	Plea of not guilty, found guilty by the jury and sentenced by the jury.
JCJG	Plea of not guilty, found guilty by the jury and sentenced by the judge.
JD	Juvenile Delinquency
JDA	Juvenile Delinquency Act
JGSA	Judgment Set Aside

JL B	Jail Breaking
JN CLOSED	Judicial Number Closed
JOY RID	Joy Riding
JVGR	Finding for defendant to stand trial as an adult. Case transferred to grand jury.
JVJV	Juvenile case returned to juvenile court.
JVTR	Defendant found to be juvenile by the judge, case transferred to juvenile court.

K

KCSP	Knowingly Concealing Stolen Property
KFO	Killing Federal Officer
KHIF	Keeping House of Ill Fame
KID	Kidnapping
KPO	Killing Police Officer
KRA	Kickback Racket Act
KRSP	Knowingly Receiving Stolen Property

L

L & R	Larceny and Receiving
L AFT TRUST	Larceny After Trust
L and L	Lewd and Lascivious
L FR IS	Larceny From Interstate Shipment
LARC (or L)	Larceny
LASCV	Lascivious
LEWD & DISSOL	Lewd and Dissolute
LEWD & IND ACT	Lewd and Indecent Act
LI-S/R/D/AL/SUS OP/NEV APPL	License Suspended, Revoked, Denied; Applicant License Suspended, Never Applied
LIO	Lesser Inclusive Offense
LIQ	Liquor
LL	Liquor Law
LMFR	Larceny Merchandise From Retailer
LOIT	Loitering
LOTT	Lottery
LSA	Leaving the Scene of an Accident
LV ACC	Leaving the Scene of an Accident (FBI definition)

M

MAIN BAWDY H	Maintaining Bawdy House

MAIN DH.. Maintaining Disorderly House
MAIN LIQ NUIS .... Maintaining Liquor Nuisance
MAL.. Malicious
MANSL.. Manslaughter
MAT WIT.. Material Witness
MF .... Mail Fraud
MIP.. Minor in Possession
MISAP BY PUB OFC............................ Misappropriation by Public Officer
MISCOND.. Misconduct
MISD.. Misdemeanor Charge
MIST .... Mistrial
MKG FLS AFI .... Making False Affidavit
MOB ACTION .... Group Disruption
MOL .... Molesting
MUR.. Murder
MUTIL .... Mutilating
MVI.. Motor Vehicle Inspection
MVR... Mandatory Release Violator
MVR... Motor Vehicle Report

N

NACT .... No Action
NADG.. Non-Adjudication of Guilt (Agreed Plea)
NAFM.. No Alabama Fuel Marker
NAJG .... Non-Adjudication of Guilt (Open Plea)
NAOG .... Deferred Probation
NARA... Narcotics Addict Rehabilitation Act
NARC... Narcotics
NAT A .... Naturalization Act
NEG .... Neglect
NFA.. National Firearms Act
NFOG... No Finding of Guilt
NGRI.. Not Guilty by Reason of Insanity
NMVTA .... National Motor Vehicle Theft Act
NOL PRS .... Nolle Pros, Nolle Prosequi, or Nolle Prossed
NON SUP .... Nonsupport
NPCF BY MAGISTRATE........................ No probable cause found by Magistrate.
NRA (MD) .... National Resource Authority (i.e. fishing without a license, etc.)
NSP... National Stolen Property

NUIS .... Nuisance

NWNI .... Negotiating a Worthless Negotiable Instrument (bad check)

O

OAWI .... Operating Auto While Intoxicated

OBS LIT .... Obscene Literature

OBS PICT .... Obscene Pictures

OBTS FORMAT .... Offensive Base Tracking System (Florida computer system for law enforcement tracking of cases.)

OCC ROOM IMM PUR .... Occupying Room for Immoral Purposes

OCI... Obstruction of Criminal Investigations

OCO.. Obstruction of Court Orders

ODLA .... Driver License Amended

ODLD .... Driver License Dismissed

ODLG.. Driver License Granted

OGFP.. Obtaining Goods by False Pretense

OHIR... Operating House of Ill Repute

OMFP.. Obtaining Money by False Pretense

OMV PRMT SUSP.................................. Operating Motor Vehicle after Permit Suspended

OMV W/O (LIC PL or OC or PRMT) ...... Operating Motor Vehicle Without (License Plates or Owner's Consent or Permit)

OMVWI (-D or –L).................................. Operating Motor Vehicle While Intoxicated (-Drugs or -Liquor)

OOJ... Obstruction of Justice

OP LOT & SL MACH .... Operating Lottery and Slot Machine

OP STILL... Operating Still

Open Lewdness..................................... Lewd act observed by someone.

OPFP .... Obtaining Property Under False Pretenses

OPIUM .... Opium Resorts

ORD .... Ordinance

OUI... Operating Under the Influence of Liquor or Drugs

OVUI (-D or –L)..................................... Operating Vehicle Under Influence of (-Drugs or -Liquor)

OVUIL OR NARC .... Operating Vehicle Under Influence of Liquor or Narcotic

OVWD (-D or –L) .... Operating Vehicle While Drunk (-Drugs or -Liquor)

OWI... Operating While Intoxicated

P

P NC .... Plead No Contest

P/W INT DEL COC .... Possession with intent to deliver cocaine

PA .... Plea in Abeyance

PAND .... Pandering

PANH .... Panhandling

PASS BAD CHKS .... Passing Bad Checks

PASS CTFT CURR .... Passing Counterfeit Currency

PASS FORG PO MO .... Passing Forged Post Office Money Orders

PASS RAISED MO .... Passing Raised Money Orders

PASS WRTHLS CHKS .... Passing Worthless Checks

Pawnbrokers Act .... False reporting to a pawn broker

PBV .... Parole Violator

PCT .... Possession of Criminal Tools

PED .... Peddler or Peddling

PERJ .... Perjury

PERV .... Pervert or Perverted

PERV PRAC .... Perverted Practice

PFA .... Considered a Violation; Protection from Abuse

PGBC .... Agreed Plea of Guilty Before the Court

PGBJ .... Open Plea of Guilty Before a Jury

PGFR .... Agreed Plea of Guilty Before the Court. Felony
reduced to a misdemeanor

PGJG .... Open Plea of Guilty Before the Court

PIC .... Possession of Implement of Crime

PIE .... Presence in Illegal Establishment

PIMP .... Pimping

PIST L .... Pistol Law

PJ or PJC .... Prayer for Judgment

PL .... Petty Larceny

POIS .... Poisoning

POLY .... Polygamy

POS/CON F-WN/LQ/MXBV UNAUTH PR . Possession of a full container of wine, liquor or malt
beverage (beer) by an unauthorized person

POSS .... Possession

POSS BURG TOOLS .... Possession of Burglary Tools

POSS CONTR SUB .... Possession Controlled Substance

POSS CP CS – LT 28G .... Criminal possession of a controlled substance less
than (number of) grams

POSS DW .... Possession Dangerous Weapon

POSS SG .... Possession Stolen Goods

POSS STLN PROP .... Possession Stolen Property

POST L	Postal Laws
PP	Prepaid
PP	Pickpocket (FBI Definition)
PRCS	Probation Reduced and Case Set Aside
PRE-IND PROB	Accelerated rehabilitation program. Defendant is placed on probation. Defendant must complete class before charges will be expunged from the record.
PRE/OBS EXT FIRE	Preventing or Obstruction of Extinguishing Fire
PRES FLS CL	Presenting False Claim
PROB	Probation
PROC	Procuring
PROC FEM FOR H OF IF	Procuring Females For House of Ill Fame
PROC TO COMM ARSON	Procuring Person to Commit Arson
PROF	Profanity
PROST	Prostitution
PROWL	Prowling
PSC	Public Safety Violation Code
PT	Petty Theft
PTI	Pre-Trial Intervention
PUB INTOX	Public Intoxication
PUB NUIS	Public Nuisance
PUR/ATT F-WN/LQ/MXBV < 21	Purchase/Attempt to Purchase Fortified Wine/Liquor/Malt Liquor Beverage by Someone Under the Age of 21
PV	Parole Violator
PWOC	Passing Worthless Check

Q

QUAR	Quarantine

R

RA	Registration Act
RAPE MNR	Rape of Minor
RCA	Red Cross Act
REC	Receiving
REC & CONC	Receiving and Concealing
REC MON FR PROST	Receiving Money From Prostitute
REC PO MO	Receiving Post Office Money Orders
REAP	Reckless Endangering Another Person

RECDG WGRS....................................... Recording Wagers

RECK DR... Reckless Driving

REM OR CONC SPRTS......................... Removal or Concealment of Spirits Contrary to Law

REM IDENT ON GUN............................. Removing Identification on Gun

RENT LEWD BKS .... Renting Lewd Books

RESIST ARR .... Resisting Arrest

RESIST OFC .... Resisting an Officer

REST ARR W/O VIOL .... Resisting Arrest Without Violence

REVK... Revoked

RICO.. Racketeer Influenced and Corrupt Organization

RIF US MAILS .... Rifling U.S. Mails

RIOT .... Rioting

ROB (ARMED or UNARMED) .... Robbery (Armed or Unarmed)

RS OF W/O V .... Resisting Officer Without Violence

RSG... Receiving Stolen Goods

RSP.. Receiving Stolen Property

RSPMV .... Receiving Stolen Property – Motor Vehicle

RULE .... Probation Violation

RVRD... Probation Revoked and Sentence Reduced

RVSP .... Non-Adjudicated Probation Revoked and Sentenced to Straight Probation

S

SAB.. Sabotage

SAFECRK... Safecracking

SALE IND LIT .... Sale of Indecent Literature

SALE LIQ... Sale Liquor

SALE MTGD PROP................................. Sale Mortgaged Property

SALE NARC .... Sale Narcotics

SALE SEC W/O REG .... Sale Securities Without Being Registered

SED.. Sedition

SEDCT.. Seduction

SEDD 1,500... Securing and Executing a Document of at Least $1,500 but Less Than $20,000 by Deception or Fraud (Dallas County)

SELL SEC NO LIC................................... Selling Securities, No License

SELL UNREG REVLVR........................... Selling Unregistered Revolver

SES.. Suspend Entry Sentence

SEX A-V CH .... Sexual Assault of a Child, Anal and Vaginal

SFCAA.. State Firearms Control Assistance Act

SH	Shooting
SHPB	Shock Probation
SHPLFTG	Shoplifting
SKA	Switchblade Knife Act
SLAN	Slander or Slanderous
SLIP	Soliciting for Lewd and Immoral Purpose
SMUG	Smuggling
SNL	State Narcotic Law
SOD	Sodomy
SOL	Solicitation of Bribery (FBI Definition)
SOL	Stricken of Leave
SOL COMM SOD	Soliciting to Commit Sodomy
SOL FOR PROS	Solicitation for Prostitution
SOL IMM PURP	Soliciting for Immoral Purpose
SOL W/O LIC	Soliciting Without License
SOLC	Solicitation to Commit
SP	Suspicious Person
SPEED	Speeding
SSA	Selective Service Act
ST POIS A	State Poison Act
ST PROH	State Prohibition
ST WAGE L	State Wage Law
STAB	Stabbing
STAB WITH INT KILL	Stabbing With Intent to Kill
STAT RAPE	Statutory Rape
STEAL FR COMN CARRIER	Stealing from Common Carrier
STEAL SECR OR EMBZ MAIL	Stealing, Secreting or Embezzling Mail Matter
STET	Set Aside, Pending (non conviction)
STLN PROP	Stolen Property
STORE B	Store Breaking
STSN	Running a Stop Sign
SUBV ACTIV	Subversive Activity
SUN L	Sunday Law
SUP	Support
SUS IMP SENT	Suspended Imposition Sent. Non-Conviction.
SUSP	Suspicion
SW OVER $50	Swindling Over $50
SW UNDER $50	Swindling Under $50
SW W CHKS	Swindle With Checks

SWIT LIC PL	Switching License Plates
SWWC	Swindle With Worthless Checks

T

T	Theft
T BY BAIL	Theft By Bailee
T BY DECEP	Theft By Deception
T BY T	Theft By Taking
T OVER $50	Theft Over $50
T UNDER $50	Theft Under $50
T/O 200	Theft Over $200
TA	Tariff Act
TAMP	Tampering
TAMP GOV REC	Tampering with Government Records
TAWOP	Taking Auto Without Owner's Permission
TBC	Theft By Check
TBCI	Plea of not guilty, found innocent by the judge.
TBCT	Plea of not guilty, found guilty by the judge and sentenced by the judge.
TBD	Trial by Declaration
TDL	Texas Driver License
TFIS (-AH)	Theft from Interstate Shipment (-Armed Hijacking)
TGP	Theft of Government Property
THEFT 750 R AND C	Theft of $750 by Receiving And Concealing
THRT	Threat (FBI Definition)
THRT	Threat to Commit
THRT B OF P	Threatened Breach of Peace
THRT TO EXT	Threats to Extort
TOP	Theft of Property
TR RIDER	Train Rider
TRAF A	Traffic Act
TRAF ORD	Traffic Ordinance
TRAF SIG	Traffic Signals (Running Signal Light)
TRAN	Transfer to another County/District Court
TRANSP (LIQ or NARC)	Transporting (Liquor or Narcotics)
TRESP	Trespassing
TRU	Truancy
TWEA	Trading With the Enemy Act
TYPE OC	Original Capias (Warrant information)

U

U & P	Uttering and Publishing
U/U LIVESTOCK MV	Unlawful Use of a Livestock Motor Vehicle
UBAL	Unlawful Blood Alcohol Level
UCW	Unlawful Carrying of a Weapon
UDAA	Unlawful Driving Away Auto
UDFC	Utter Distribute Forged Checks
UFA	Uniform Firearms Act
UFAC	Unlawful Flight to Avoid Custody or Confinement
UFAP	Unlawful Flight to Avoid Prosecution
UFAT	Unlawful Flight to Avoid Testimony
UIBC	Unlawful Issuance of a Bank Check
UISC	Unreported Interstate Shipment of Cigarettes
UMTA	Using Mails To Defraud
UNA	Uniform Narcotics Act
UNL ASM	Unlawful Assembly
UNL DAA & ABNDN	Unlawfully Driving Away and Abandoning Auto
UNL ENT	Unlawful Entry
UNL MARR	Unlawful Marriage
UNL POSS FIREARMS	Unlawful Possession of Firearms
UNL POSS OR USE EXPLSV	Unlawful Possession or Use of Explosives (bombs, etc.)
UNL SALE OF SEC	Unlawful Sale of Securities
UNL USE W (OR UUW)	Unlawful Use of Weapon
UNLIC CHAUF	Unlicensed Chauffeur
UNREG STILL	Unregistered Still
UPRF	Unlawful Possession or Receipt of Firearms
UPUC	Unauthorized Publication or Use of Communications
USCC	U.S. Criminal Code or U.S. Criminal Court
USING MV W/O PRMS	Using Motor Vehicle Without Permission
USING PROF & AB LANG	Using Profane and Abusive Language
USTP	Unsatisfactory Termination of Probation
UTT	Uttering
UTT CHK	Uttering Check
UTT FORG INST	Uttering Forged Instrument
UTT FORG OBL	Uttering Forged Obligation

V

VAG	Vagrancy
VAGA	Vagabond
VAM	Veterans Administration Matters
VCSDDCA	Violation Controlled Substance Drug Device & Cosmetic
VEH	Vehicle
VEH NO LTS	Vehicle No Lights
VGCSA	Violation of Georgia's Controlled Substance Act
VIN	Vehicle Identification Number
VIO CITY ORD	Violating City Ordinance
VIO CSA	Violating Controlled Substance Act
VIO DAA	Violation Drug Abuse Act
VIO DDCA	Violation Dangerous Drugs and Control Act
VIO DYER A	Violation Dyer Act
VIO FED INJ	Violation Federal Injunction
VIO HNA	Violation Harrison Narcotic Act
VIO IMMI L	Violation Immigration Law
VIO NMVTA	Violation National Motor Vehicle Theft Act
VIO OF HL	Violation of Health Laws
VIO OF LL	Violation of Liquor Law
VIO ST GAME & FISH L	Violating State Game and Fish Law
VIO ST LL	Violation State Liquor Law
VIO TRAF REG	Violation Traffic Regulation
VIO UFA	Violation Uniform Firearms Act
VIRL (-L)	Violation of Internal Revenue Laws (-Liquor)
VOL MANSL	Voluntary Manslaughter
VOL MUR	Voluntary Murder
VOP	Violation of Probation
VT	Vehicle Taking or Vehicle Theft

W

W/S	With Specifications
WAND	Wandering
WC	Worthless Check
WC-OBT PROB	Worthless Check to Obtain Property
WIND PEEP	Window Peeping
WOUND	Wounding
WPPDA	Welfare and Pension Plans Disclosure Act

WPT .... Withdrawn Prior to Trial
WRONG LIC PL...................................... Wrong License Plates
WRTD .... Writ Denied
WRTG .... Writ Granted
WRTHLS INST .... Worthless Instrument
WSTA... White Slave Traffic Act

Quick-Find Index

Additional titles from
Facts on Demand Press

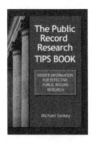

The Public Record Research Tips Book

The Public Record Research Tips Book provides "Insider Information" for searching for public records at thousands of government public record agencies and web pages. This resource provides the tips and practical knowledge to guide you to the right source and help you become an ultra-efficient searcher.

Michael Sankey • 1-889150-50-9 • 336 pages • $19.95

Business Background Investigations

Business Background Investigations provides the blueprint to perform proper due diligence and discover competitive intelligence when examining the backgrounds of businesses and the principals who run them. "Hetherington's methods" can be immediately integrated into an investigative operation – resulting in tremendous savings of time, effort, and money.

Cynthia Hetherington • 1-889150-49-5 • 288 pages • $21.95

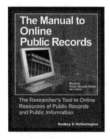

The Manual to Online Public Records

The Manual to Online Public Records teaches how to effectively search the Internet and professional online resources. It includes instruction for conducting research and how to evaluate online data for reliability and much more. More than a links list, this is valuable resource that will help the experienced researcher and the novice looking for insider tips when performing background investigations, locating people & assets, and performing legal research.

Sankey & Hetherington • 1-889150-53-3 • 360 pages • $21.95

The Safe Hiring Manual

The Safe Hiring Manual goes far beyond the typical hiring handbook. The Manual details how to exercise due diligence throughout the hiring process, significantly increasing an employer's chance of avoiding the financial and legal nightmares of even one bad hiring decision.

Lester S. Rosen, Esq. • 1-889150-44-4 • 512 pages • $24.95

Available at your favorite bookstore!

Facts on Demand Press • 1-800-929-3811 • www.brbpub.com

Annual Public Record Titles From
BRB Publications, Inc.

The Sourcebook to Public Record Information

Locate the Data You Won't Find With Google – or any other online search tool. *The Sourcebook to Public Record Information* in-depths details on over 20,000 government agencies that house public records. More than a directory, the agency profiles found in *The Sourcebook* include access procedures, record restrictions, online capabilities, all access methods with fees and turnaround times. Loaded with valuable record searching tips within its nearly 2,000 pages, this book weighs six pounds.

Print: 1-879792-89-3 • Updated Annually in January • 1,960 pages • $89.95

Online Version: *Public Record Research System Web* • Updated Weekly • $124 Annual subscription
The online version also includes the membership of the *Public Record Retriever Network* plus BRB's *National College & University Directory*.

Local Court & County Record Retrievers

Considered the "Who's Who" of the document retrieval industry, this online tool enables you to quickly and easily find the experienced, on-site, public records retriever you need. Search by state and county to determine the types of court or recorded records accessed daily by retriever. The tool also provides full vides profiles with detailed contact information, billing terms, turnaround times and additional information about more than 2,600 firms and individuals. Also provided are profiles of 600+ other Public Record Vendors and Screening Firm specialist.

Online Version: *Local Court & County Record Retriever's - Web* • Updated Weekly • $29 Annual Subscription

The MVR Book and The MVR Decoder Digest

Where would you go to investigate the driving restrictions and access procedures for all 50 states? What if you needed to decode a violation on an out-of-state MVR? For 19 years the *MVR Series* has provided the answers you need *in practical terms*. *The MVR Decoder Digest* translates the codes and abbreviations of violations and licensing categories that appear on motor vehicle records in all states. *The MVR Book* is the national reference that details privacy restrictions, access procedures, regulations and systems of all state held driver and vehicle records.

Print: *The MVR Book* • 1-879792-65-6 • Updated Annually in January • 336 pages • $23.95
The MVR Decoder Digest • 1-879792-66-4 • Updated Annually in January • 352 pages • $23.95

Online Version: *The MVR Book/Decoder Digest – Web* • Updated Periodically • $49 Annual Subscription

SSN Validator – Web *with Death Index*

BRB's *SSN Validator-Web* provides cost effective assurance of verifying identity and fighting fraud. Simply enter the 9-digit SSN and within seconds you will know if the number is valid. BRB's SSN Validator-Web also identifies the year and state of issue - a geographical clue to when and where the individual obtained the SSN. Added features include batch loading and a search of the SSA death index.

Online Version: *SSN Validator – Web* • Updated Monthly • $49 Annual Subscription

BRB Publications, Inc. • 800-929-3811 • www.brbpub.com

Meet the Authors

Derek Hinton has over 20 years experience in the field of employment screening and criminal records. He is a frequent writer, expert witness and speaker on the topics of commercial driver recruiting, screening, negligent hiring and the Fair Credit Reporting Act. His monthly column The Hire Road appears in several nationwide trucking magazines and has won two Gold Awards from the Truck Writers of North America Association for best article of the year. He is the CEO and Managing Partner of TIES, LLC (www.DOTJobHistory.com).

Mr. Hinton obtained his degree in journalism from the William Allen White School of Journalism at the University of Kansas.

Derek lives in Tulsa, Oklahoma and enjoys World War II history, college football and basketball and spending time with his beautiful wife and two children who have no arrests or convictions for felonies or misdemeanors between them.

To contact Derek, please email him at Derekh@DOTJobHistory.com

Larry Henry is a graduate of the University of Iowa College of Law. He began his legal career as a criminal defense attorney trying over 2,000 cases. Since entering a civil practice he has specialized in employment law. As part of his employment practice started over twenty-five years ago, he has and continues to represent screening companies across the United States.

His background in criminal, employment and Fair Credit Reporting Act laws provides him with the necessary experience to address background screening issues. Larry has served on the Board of Directors for the National Association of Professional Background Screeners and is a frequent speaker on FCRA issues.

Larry and his wife reside in Tulsa Oklahoma and they enjoy their time with their grandchildren.